LITERATURE AND THE DEVELOPMENT OF FEMINIST THEORY

Literature and the Development of Feminist Theory offers an insightful look at the development of feminist theory through a literary lens. Starting from the European Enlightenment, this book traces the literary careers of feminism's major thinkers in order to elucidate the connection of feminist theoretical production to literary work. In addition to considering such well-known authors as Mary Wollstonecraft, Charlotte Perkins Gilman, Simone de Beauvoir, and Hélène Cixous, this book reflects on the influence of postcolonialism, liberalism, and specific genres such as science fiction and modernist poetry. Written by leading scholars and focusing on the literary trajectories of feminism's noted contributors, *Literature and the Development of Feminist Theory* ultimately provides a new perspective on feminism's theoretical context, bringing into view the effects of literary form on feminist thought.

ROBIN TRUTH GOODMAN is Professor of English at Florida State University. Her previous books include *Gender Work: Feminism after Neoliberalism, Feminist Theory in Pursuit of the Public: Women and the "Re-Privatization" of Labor*, and *Policing Narratives and the State of Terror*. She has also contributed to such journals as *College Literature, Philosophy Today, Contemporary Literature, Symploke*, and *Conradiana*.

LITERATURE AND THE DEVELOPMENT OF FEMINIST THEORY

EDITED BY

ROBIN TRUTH GOODMAN

Florida State University

CAMBRIDGE
UNIVERSITY PRESS

CAMBRIDGE
UNIVERSITY PRESS

32 Avenue of the Americas, New York, NY 10013-2473, USA

Cambridge University Press is part of the University of Cambridge.

It furthers the University's mission by disseminating knowledge in the pursuit of education, learning, and research at the highest international levels of excellence.

www.cambridge.org
Information on this title: www.cambridge.org/9781107126084

First published 2015

Printed in the United States of America by Sheridan Books, Inc.

A catalog record for this publication is available from the British Library.

Library of Congress Cataloging in Publication Data
Literature and the development of feminist theory / [editor] Robin Goodman, Florida State University.
pages cm
Includes bibliographical references and index.
ISBN 978-1-107-12608-4 (hardback)
1. Feminism and literature. 2. Feminist literature – History and criticism.
3. Feminism in literature. I. Goodman, Robin Truth, 1966– editor.
PN56.F46L585 2015
809'.89287–dc23 2015018985

ISBN 978-1-107-12608-4 Hardback

Contents

Notes on Contributors

JUDITH A. ALLEN, educated at the University of Sydney and Macquarie University, joined Indiana University (Bloomington) in 1993 to found its Department of Gender Studies. Her scholarly work addresses histories of feminist theory and politics, the history of sex research, histories of interpersonal crimes, and of reproduction and sexualities. Author of *Sex and Secrets: Crimes Involving Australian Women since 1880* (Oxford University Press, 1990); *Rose Scott: Vision and Revision in Feminism, 1880–1925* (Oxford University Press, 1994); and *The Feminism of Charlotte Perkins Gilman: Histories/Sexualities/Progressivism* (University of Chicago Press, 2009), she co-edited *London Low Life: Street Culture, Social Reform and the Victorian Underworld* (Adam Matthew, 2010). Currently, she is Professor of History, Senior Research Fellow of The Kinsey Institute for Research in Sex, Gender & Reproduction, and Associate Editor of the *Journal of American History*, at Indiana University. She has two books in progress, *"Black Market in Misery": Criminal Abortion and British Sexual Cultures, 1780–1980* and *Alfred Kinsey, "Females" & the Feminine.*

MARLEEN S. BARR is known for her pioneering work in feminist science fiction and teaches English at the City University of New York. She has won the Science Fiction Research Association Pilgrim Award for lifetime achievement in science fiction criticism. Barr is the author of *Alien to Femininity: Speculative Fiction and Feminist Theory* (Greenwood Press, 1987); *Lost in Space: Probing Feminist Science Fiction and Beyond* (University of North Carolina Press, 1993); *Feminist Fabulation: Space/Postmodern Fiction* (University of Iowa Press, 1992); and *Genre Fission: A New Discourse Practice for Cultural Studies* (University of Iowa Press, 2000). Barr has edited many anthologies and co-edited the science fiction issue of PMLA. She is the author of the novels *Oy Pioneer!*

(University of Wisconsin Press, 2003) and *Oy Feminist Planets: A Fake Memoir* (NeoPoiesis Press, March 2015).

DOMINIQUE BOURQUE is Associate Professor of Women's Studies and of French Literature at the University of Ottawa (Canada). She has published *Écrire l'inter-dit: la subversion formelle dans l'œuvre de Monique Wittig* (L'Harmattan, 2006). Her interest for the self representations of marginalized social groups lead her to coedit, with C. Désy and F. Descarries, *Continuités et ruptures dans les représentations des femmes* (Cahiers de l'IREF, n° 5, 2013); with N. Hogikyan, *Femmes et exils: formes et figures* (Presses de l'Université Laval, 2010); and, with A. Kaouk, *The Lands Within Me, Expressions by Canadian Artists of Arab Origin* (Canadian Museum of Civilization, 2003). Her current research explores artists and authors' strategies to avoid social markers of sex, sexuality and "race."

MIRIAM COOKE is Braxton Craven Distinguished Professor of Arab Cultures at Duke University. Her writings have focused on gender, war, Islamic feminism, Syrian dissident cultural production, and tribal modernity in Arab Gulf countries. She is the author of several monographs and edited volumes including *War's Other Voices: Women on the Lebanese Civil War* (Cambridge University Press, 1996); *Women and the War Story* (California University Press – Berkeley, 1997); *Women Claim Islam* (Routledge, 2000); *Nazira Zeineddine: A Pioneer of Islamic Feminism* (Oxford OneWorld, 2010); and most recently *Tribal Modern: Branding New Nations in the Arab Gulf* (California University Press, 2014).

ROBIN TRUTH GOODMAN is professor of English at Florida State University. Her previous publications include: *Gender Work: Feminism after Neoliberalism* (Palgrave, 2013); *Feminist Theory in Pursuit of the Public: Women and the "Re-privatization" of Labor* (Palgrave, 2011); *Policing Narratives and the State of Terror* (SUNY Press, 2010); *World, Class, Women: Global Literature, Education, and Feminism* (Routledge, 2004); *Strange Love: Or How We Learn to Stop Worry and Love the Market* (co-written with Kenneth J. Saltman; Rowman & Littlefield, 2002); and *Infertilities: Exploring Fictions of Barren Bodies* (University of Minnesota Press, 2001).

JANE HIDDLESTON is Associate Professor of French at Exeter College, University of Oxford. She has published widely on francophone literatures, postcolonial theory and literary theory, including, for example, *Assia Djebar: Out of Algeria* (Liverpool University Press, 2006); *Poststructuralism and Postcoloniality: The Anxiety of Theory* (Liverpool University Press, 2010); and *Decolonising the Intellectual: Politics, Culture, and Humanism at the End of the French Empire* (Liverpool University Press, 2014). She is currently working on a project on francophone North African literature in French since 1980.

MARGARET HOMANS is professor of English and of Women's Gender, and Sexuality Studies at Yale University. She has published widely on feminist and queer theory and on British and U.S. women writers, starting with *Women Poets and Poetic Identity: Dorothy Wordsworth, Emily Brontë, and Emily Dickinson* (Princeton University Press, 1987). Her books also include *Bearing the Word: Language and Female Experience in Nineteenth-Century Women's Writing* (University of Chicago Press, 1989) and *Royal Representations: Queen Victoria and British Culture, 1837–1876* (University of Chicago Press, 1999). Her most recent book is *The Imprint of Another Life: Adoption Narratives and Human Possibility* (University of Michigan Press, 2015). She teaches courses on Virginia Woolf, feminist and queer fiction from Wollstonecraft to the present, and the intellectual history of feminist and queer theory.

JOY JAMES is F.C. Oakley 3rd C. Professor at Williams College. She is an advisory board member of CONNECT, a NYC nonprofit that works on issues of domestic/family violence and social justice. James is editor of anthologies on feminism and incarceration, and author of *Resisting State Violence* (University of Minnesota Press, 1996); *Transcending the Talented Tenth* (Routledge, 1996); and *Seeking the Beloved Community* (SUNY Press, 2014).

PEGGY KAMUF writes on literary theory and contemporary French thought, particularly that of Jacques Derrida. She has translated numerous texts by Derrida and several works by Hélène Cixous. Director of the Derrida Seminars Translation Project, she also co-edits the series publishing Derrida's teaching seminars in English. She is Marion Frances Chevalier Professor of French and Comparative Literature at the University of Southern California.

LINDA A. KINNAHAN is Professor of English and Hillman Distinguished Chair at Duquesne University in Pittsburgh. She is the editor of the forthcoming *Cambridge History of Twentieth Century Women's Poetry* (Cambridge University Press, 2016). Her publications include two books on twentieth-century poetry, *Poetics of the Feminine: Literary*

Tradition and Authority in William Carlos Williams, Mina Loy, Denise Levertov, and Kathleen Fraser (Cambridge University Press, 1994) and *Lyric Interventions: Feminist Experimental Poetry and Contemporary Social Discourse* (Iowa University Press, 2004). She has published widely on contemporary and modernist poetry in journals that include *Contemporary Women Writers*; *Contemporary Literature, Sagetrieb*; and *Poetry Review* (UK), and her essays have appeared in collections from Cambridge University Press, Iowa University Press, Blackwell, Edinborough University Press, Wesleyan University Press, and Oxford University Press.

LAURA KIRKLEY was a College Lecturer in French at The Queen's College Oxford and a Research Fellow at Trinity Hall Cambridge before joining Newcastle University as a Lecturer in Eighteenth-Century English Literature. Her research specialisms include eighteenth-century Anglophone and Francophone women writers, particularly Mary Wollstonecraft, and literary and cultural translation. She has recently edited a new edition of Isabell de Montoieu's *Caroline of Litchfield* (Pickering & Chatto, 2014).

SONJA E. KLOCKE is Assistant Professor of German at the University of Wisconsin–Madison. Her research interests focus on twentieth to twenty-first century German culture with a focus on postwar and contemporary German literature and film. This includes the legacy of the GDR and the Holocaust, women's writing, East German literature and film, contemporary writing on modern exile, migration and globalization, discourses on illness and the body, and gender theory. Most recently, she has published on Christa Wolf and her obituaries, and on transnational literature and post-GDR literature. Her monograph, *Inscription and Rebellion: Illness and the Symptomatic Body in East German Literature*, is forthcoming with Camden House in November 2015.

ANNA K. KUHN has published extensively on East German women's writing, especially Christa Wolf. Her study, *Christa Wolf's Utopian Vision: From Marxism to Feminism* (Cambridge University Press, 2009), was the first English-language monograph on the GDR's most prominent woman writer. She has also written on German-Jewish women writers and German minority writing, as well as on German drama and film. Her current research project addresses issues of memory and gender in German-American academic autobiographies.

LAKEY teaches Contemporary and Global Literature in the English Department at Florida State University. She is a member of the Delegate Assembly for the Modern Languages Association. She also serves on the Executive Board of the American Federation of Teachers AGEL, where she organizes with other activists to push back against the corporatization of higher education.

MARIA MARGARONI is Associate Professor in Literary Theory and Feminist Thought at the University of Cyprus. She has held Visiting Fellowships at the Institute for Advanced Studies in the Humanities (University of Edinburgh) and the Centre for Cultural Analysis, Theory and History (University of Leeds). Her publications include: *Julia Kristeva: Live Theory* (with John Lechte, Continuum, 2004); *Metaphoricity and the Politics of Mobility* (with Effie Yiannopoulou, Rodopi, 2006); *Intimate Transfers* (with Effie Yiannopoulou, special issue of the *European Journal of English Studies*, 2005); and *Violence and the Sacred*, special issue of *Philosophy Today*, 2012. A collection of essays co-edited with Apostolos Lampropoulos and Christos Hadjichristos is due to come out in 2015 (*Textual Layering: Contact, Historicity, Critique*; Lexington Books). She is currently finishing her monograph focusing on the thought of Julia Kristeva (forthcoming by SUNY Press).

ASHLEY KING SCHEU is Assistant Professor of French at Eckerd College in Saint Petersburg, FL. Her research interests include nineteenth- and twentieth-century French literature, French feminism, aesthetics, and the intersections between philosophy and literature. Professor Scheu's current research project is a study of Simone de Beauvoir's existentialist conception of philosophical literature. Previous publications include articles on Beauvoir in *Hypatia: A Journal of Feminist Philosophy* and in *Romance Quarterly*.

Acknowledgments

This book is dedicated, first and foremost, to all those in the past nearly 250 years and more who have made feminist thinking possible. Whether struggling for feminist rights and causes or building ideas and concepts that have given prominence to feminist ideals and agendas, such forbearers have created a language and a set of principles that frame essential debates in the quest for freedom for women everywhere.

Ray Ryan at Cambridge University Press has supported this book since its inception. I am grateful to him for his support and encouragement throughout the process, his inspiration, his patience, and his faith. I also wish to thank all those who assisted him at the Press.

Finally, I am enormously grateful to all the writers in this volume, whose diligence, expertise, commitment, and wisdom have made this book intellectually rigorous and inspiring. Additionally, a number of colleagues have lent important advice to the development of this project. Although of course it is impossible to name everyone, I wish to acknowledge the following for their insights and suggestions: Rachel Blau DuPlessis, Andrew Epstein, Barry J. Faulk, N. Katherine Hayles, Susan Manly, Toril Moi, Timothy Parrish, and Christian Weber.

CHAPTER I

Introduction

Robin Truth Goodman

Literature and the Development of Feminist Theory looks at the development of feminist theory through literature. It traces the literary careers of feminism's major thinkers in order to explore the connection of feminist theoretical production to literary work. It starts from the Enlightenment, analyzing how the literary was embedded within feminism's versions of the rational, in fact, how the literary was necessary for thinking like a feminist. Besides mainly considering particular authors who move from literature to theory and back, this volume also reflects on areas of literary study (like postcolonialism), genres (like science fiction and poetry), and central thematics (like liberalism, individualism, and work) in terms of how feminism constitutes itself and formulates its positions by thinking through the literary.

This book moves between contexts ranging from the United States to Africa, Europe, the Middle East, Latin America, and Asia, broaching fields from minority and ethnic studies to queer studies, area studies, philosophy, performance studies, pedagogy, sexuality studies, transnationalism, race studies, translation studies, and postcolonialism, examining genres from the novel to poetry, science fiction, theater, short stories, the essay, testimonial memoirs, travel memoirs, experimentalism, and romance. *Literature and the Development of Feminist Theory* will focus on the literary trajectories of feminism's noted contributors; it will offer a new perspective on feminism's theoretical histories, bringing into view an under-considered line of influence for feminism: the effects of literary form and content on the development of feminist thinking.

It is impossible to conceive of contemporary critical theory without referencing the feminist contributions that, at various moments, popularized it, deepened it, and politicized it. In fact, feminism has become so pervasive in graduate and undergraduate curricula as well as in scholarly research in the humanities and the social sciences that it is virtually impossible to avoid it in any academic context today. Yet, perhaps less

I

remarked: unlike any other theoretical enclave, feminist theory has had a particularly fervent relationship with the production of literary texts. Novels, poems, memoirs, and other fictive and non-fictive literary practices can be said to complete what is incomplete in theoretical critique and argument in feminism, and literary language and literary form can be said to inhabit and even influence the possibilities of feminist theory from inside its own design.

Feminist literary and theoretical writers have remarked on this combination in various ways. Virginia Woolf, most famously, explains, "[A]ll the literary training that a woman had in the early nineteenth century was training in the observation of character, in the analysis of emotion. Her sensibility had been educated for centuries by the influences of the common sitting-room" (*A Room of One's Own*, 70). Then again, Simone de Beauvoir speculates that "assuming the roles of housekeeper, wife and mother" ("Women and Creativity," 23) limits a woman's freedom rather than freeing up her powers of observation as Woolf claims, and the practice of the literary, in contrast, changes the limitations her situation imposes, allowing her to develop "the conditions most necessary for what we call genius to flourish" (23). Literature for Beauvoir is linked to freedom and, in particular, freedom from the worldly conditions that women absorbed in their social roles. Michèle Le Doeuff, meanwhile, notes that women can only gain entry into philosophy by acknowledging the incompleteness of traditional knowledge, that knowledge is always in debate, in dialog, and in context – an idea that resonates with the difference that literary language interjects within philosophical reasoning.

In *Playing in the Dark*, Toni Morrison argues that literature is a particularly fertile ground for recognizing difference. For Morrison, literature "prompts and makes possible [the] process of entering what one is estranged from" (4) and helps us see omissions, contradictions, and conflicts that register the presence of the excluded, the marginalized, the subordinated, and the non-hegemonic. Discourse and common sense are constructed to make these elisions and erasures seem normal, acceptable, even natural. Yet literary writers also have the ability "to imagine what is not the self, to familiarize the strange and mystify the familiar" (15). They can visualize identities that may not directly inhabit recognizable norms. Although Morrison is particularly interested in how the repression of race makes certain concepts of race visible within the American literary canon, she also sees that discourses with a willful and hysterical blindness to feminism affect the way women's issues are read into literature (14), and that nationalism takes shape in literature's mobilization of the limits to the national. Orienting nationalist rubrics like individualism, guilt and innocence, life and death, and gender often appear in response to a structuring absence that Morrison calls "a dark, abiding, signing African presence" (5) but that can equally – or differentially – be applied to other forms of what falls outside the dominant understanding. Such moments of unformed presence start to acknowledge alternative languages as instabilities and dynamisms that disturb accepted social realities. Literature is the place where such eruptions of incoherence open narratives up to noise and illogic, exhibiting the processes of social becoming that exist inside narrative forms. Narrative structures are constructed by plotting out the differences between what they hide and what they reveal.

As diverse as these reflections are, they share a sense of the literary as key to feminist critique. In other words, the literary within feminist subjectivity allows for the development of a feminist positioning, a feminist critique, outside of the reality that denies women the means and spaces of creativity. The literary frames feminist critique as the opening to a difference, a creative resistance. It de-solidifies the real, separating the claims of empiricism from the objects that it describes. For this – for the possibility of envisioning alternative social relations, outside of the dominant common sense – feminist theory *needs* literature, and feminist literature gives rise to feminist theory. Feminism blurs the difference between rational argument and literary form, as narrative and poetics invade critical articulations while theory itself breaks through from within, disrupting conventions and genres of the literary. The "apartness" or "distortions" of the literary show, first, feminist alienation from the world; second, how descriptions of the real disjoin from subjective experience; and third, how that alienation is necessary for the construction of a transformed imaginary.

At the peak of cultural theory's ascendance, many of the most referenced theories noted the border between fiction and philosophy to be problematic, dissolving, or untenable at best and incomprehensible at worst. Much poststructuralism conflated the literary as part of the philosophical, making literature but a continuation, an example, or a proof of philosophical argumentation without any identity of its own. Trends in historicist criticism tended toward dismissing the specifics of the literary as counterfactual. Meanwhile, popular culture critique dismissed the particularity of the literary as "disinterested," disembodied, ideological, and elite and promoted a type of analysis of all writing as equal to all other writing in its signifying or discursive role. These perspectives gave rise to fervent and exciting debates and new understandings of the cultural, the textual, the semiological, and their relationship, but at the expense of thinking about how literature as literature does what it does. *Literature and the Development of Feminist Theory* wants to address this issue, returning to the question of what literature is and what it does: how literature differentiates from the philosophical, the historical, and the contextual as well as how it feeds these other dimensions; what is specific about literature and why it persists; and why it is that literature as a theoretical discourse was particularly alive for feminism, that is, what feminism achieved by constructing itself in literary form.

This "return" to literature is important and vital. Cultural theory's evaluation of literature as equivalent to language use in general happened simultaneously (although not necessarily in conjunction) with a political attack on the humanities and an equally constructed promotion of education as exclusively preparation for the workforce, as well as a widespread acceptance that educational institutions, practitioners, and professionals were responsible for the economic downturn and the loss of global competitiveness, unresponsive to economic needs, and should be forced to justify their existence based on predictable outcomes and empirically measured accountabilities. Science, math, and engineering degrees, we have heard, create jobs, while humanities degrees cannot translate into social utility, wealth, or wealth-producing, marketable innovation.

It is not too outrageous to say that people with degrees do not create jobs, but economic policy, versatility, inspiration, investment, expansion, distribution, and activity do, and so the charges levied on the traditions of academic culture and in particular on the humanities are just targeting the humanities as a scapegoat for the failures of the captains and authors of economic change. The responses directed against such attacks have been many, from the obvious but accommodationist claim that creativity and knowledge of how narratives function are central to the new media economy, to the less obvious, Kantian claim that free and conceptual thinking – innovative thinking – cannot be codified, cataloged, or made obedient; it resists becoming an instrument of preconceived uses, systems, and methods or a data point that does nothing but repeat a preordained conclusion or ideology. It is not just an example that repeats some preordained understanding of the way things work. Literature, in particular, expresses dissatisfaction with the way things are in its insistence on imagining the way things might be different.

What gets lost in the erasure of literature's specificity is public memory: the tradition of thinking that literature allows. Literature provides a space for thinking about how the world might have been different and might be different still, or, as Theodor Adorno said, it "is the antithesis of that which is the case" ("Reconciliation under Duress," 159), the "negative knowledge of the actual world" (160). Literature in its specificity is in contrast to this instrumentalized thinking that has overtaken the academy; rather than chronicling the actual, it releases pure potential, even forgotten potential. Even within the limits of the twentieth century, the idea of literature in its specificity underlies essential social and political concepts. For all the criticism launched against Jürgen Habermas, for example, his insight that literature framed a way of speaking and living together – a structure for coming to agreement and critique that was autonomous from public regulations and state authority – is still worth considering. Literature, according to Habermas, "provided the training ground for a critical public reflection still preoccupied with itself – a process of self-clarification of private people focusing on the genuine experiences of their novel privateness ... [C]ritical debate ignited by works of literature and art was soon extended to include economic and political disputes, without any guarantee ... that such discussions would be inconsequential" (*The Structural Transformation of the Public Sphere*, 29–33).[1] Hannah Arendt, too, sees literature as necessary for politics because literature testifies to the presence of others, giving recognition to the "who" rather than the "what" that connects individual acts to social existence: "Compared with the reality which comes from being seen and heard, even the greatest forces of intimate life – the passions of the heart, the thoughts of the mind, the delights of the senses – lead an uncertain, shadowy kind of existence unless and until they are transformed, deprivatized and deindividualized, as it were, into a shape to fit them for public appearance. The most current of such transformations occurs in storytelling" (*The Human Condition*, 50). For Arendt, an action cannot be historically or politically significant unless it appears to be recognized before others, and literature is necessary for that process.

One might also note Mikhail Bakhtin's definition of novelistic discourse, where the literary word is in tension with itself, pulled in multiple directions, formative of the expressive dynamics of social conflict, unified in style and yet diversified in its sociopolitical purposes and individual origins, producing a dynamic of social intercourse: in his words, "polyphonic." Bakhtin understands literature as "a diversity of social speech types ... and a diversity of individual voices" stratified by "social dialectics, characteristic group behavior, professional jargons, generic languages, languages of generations and age groups, tendentious languages, languages of authorities, of various circles and of passing fashions, languages that serve the specific sociopolitical purposes of the day" (*The Dialogic Imagination*, 262), living in unresolvable struggle.[2] The insinuation that a particularly feminist shaping of politics and public life would rely on its continual literariness might have become emblematized, for example, when eighty-year-old feminist novelist Nawal El Saadawi appeared in a *Democracy Now!* interview, protesting in Tahrir Square in 2011 during the Arab Spring, having survived political incarceration at the hands of both the Sadat and Mubarak regimes.

These five examples – Adorno, Habermas, Arendt, Bakhtin, and El Saadawi (and there could be others) – raise the question for feminism of whether the insufficient attention to literature's specificity corresponds to a parallel demise of attention to feminism's politics. Does the neglect of a specifically literary feminism foreshadow and explain the humanities' defenselessness before the social forces that seek to instrumentalize all thought while refashioning thought itself as the repetitive production of quantifiable knowledge units and skills with no acknowledged connection to explicit philosophical or political judgments? Does the loss of a specifically literary concept correspond to social impoverishment, conformism, and dis-identification with politics? Is literature crucial to developing the ideas of social difference, consequential critique, dialog, conflict, autonomy, social interaction, emancipation, and opposition that feminism requires? Is it through its literary expression that feminism has developed its approaches to its formative political questions like: "What am I?" "What is experience?" "What is good?" "How do I relate?" "How do I live with others?" "How do I speak?" "How do things mean?" "How do I know?" "How do I belong?" "What form does power take?" "What is to be done?" and "What might the future look like?" Is the peripheralizing of the literary but another version of the loss of a critical vocabulary with which to address "the human" – with all its flaws and historical misuses – and the corresponding turn of the political away from considerations of "the human"? Does the persistence of a specifically feminist literary project allow the imagination of a type of "living together" that jars, distorts, challenges, exceeds, and innovates current unaccountable, disconnected, dystopic, even despotic social, political, and economic formations?

Feminist literature also is an integral component of the unapologetic cosmopolitanism of feminist thought. The "worlding" of women, their politics, their aesthetics, and their expression is not self-evident: feminism can be contentious, conflictual, even obnoxious when it tries to move its concepts between nations, classes, and contexts. It can display itself as the arm of power and, in its fervor, it can deny or usurp the cultural differences it hopes to explain and the particular lives it hopes to affect. However, the connection of feminism to literary practice demands that feminist ideas must make their way toward phenomena they were not necessarily constructed to experience or to note. Although formulated through reference to nationalities and language communities, the literary exists, in the words of Pascale Casanova, "as a worldwide reality," "having to abandon all the habits associated with specialized historical, linguistic and cultural research … to break with the national habits of thought that create the illusion of uniqueness and insularity" (*The World Republic of Letters*, 5) even as it adheres, in some sense, to those spaces, those meanings, and those customs. From literature, feminism adopts this posture toward the world. The literary calls out feminist ideas to travel and to translate; it reveals how ideas carry context from place to place; it shows how it is possible to re-narrate events and moments in a setting in which they did not originate, perhaps a discordant one, and develop meaning there. In their literary condition, feminist ideas are never really at home.

In fact, this volume itself is an example of feminism's cosmopolitanism. In light of feminism's inherent and unapologetic cosmopolitanism, the writers included in this volume hail from universities in multiple countries and from an even wider array of national origins, and write about authors who identify through various regional and national locales. In addition, it foregrounds the necessity of calling out inputs from a spectrum of disciplinary sites in order to ask questions of feminism, to consider its political momentum, and to work out its interpretive strategies. Approaches vary from assessing a particular author's life and career to analyzing a particular text to situating a genre or a theme within a feminist articulation or social movement. The essays participate in the feminist project of building an intergenerational and intercontextual field of influence, a type of lineage where a historical moment borrows, inserts, reflects on, cites, and manipulates the ideas that brought it into being.

Most readers of most thinkers addressed in this volume are mainly concerned with their theoretical contributions. In her introduction to *The Cambridge Companion to Feminist Theory*, Ellen Rooney comments that "literariness inhabits theory; that theory is, in fact, a genre of literature and not a metalanguage, that reading transacts an exchange between theoretical texts and literary works, rather than simply applying theory to an abject text the better to illustrate theory's profundity" (2). Nevertheless, this *Companion*, usefully organized according to the subfields through which feminist theory operates, focuses predominantly on texts and topics that sit squarely in the generic space of theory, the politics of texts and the politics of reading, the literary works serving mainly as marginal examples of theoretical argument. The relationship between literature and theory is not transparent and needs further interrogation. Is literature always but an example or an application, is it the signified to theory's mastery, the proof of theory's abstraction, and if not, as Rooney implies, than how else might it relate? Why does literature matter?

Cambridge's other feminist critical anthology, *A History of Feminist Literary Criticism*, illustrates critical thought as a conversation among literary critics about certain issues and thematics across time, privileging a backstory that develops into and deepens contemporary theoretical interests. The *History* clearly demonstrates that Second Wave theoretical concerns like the relationship between gender and textuality, between subjectivity and history, and the problem of representing "women" in writing about writing had moorings in pre-feminist criticism dating back to the medieval. As the editors explain in the general introduction, feminist criticism's "eventual self-conscious expression [in the Second Wave] was the culmination of centuries of women's writing, of women writing about women writing, and of women – and men – writing about women's minds, bodies, art and ideas" (Plain and Sellers, "Introduction," 2). Cambridge has also published *Companions* to particular authors who cross feminist theory with literature – for example, Simone de Beauvoir and Virginia Woolf. Although contextualizing these authors through their philosophical, aesthetic, and sociopolitical influences (in Simone de Beauvoir's case, with only one chapter devoted primarily to the novels that harvests them for their philosophical offerings), these volumes do not place the authors inside of a particularly feminist literary tradition or focus predominantly on the contributions to feminist thought made by specifically literary content.

Some of these concerns take up debates that have been framing feminist writings since the surge in interest in the Second Wave during the 1970s and 1980s but have recently changed direction, broadening the ways that the literary can be engaged. Most famously, Toril Moi in *Sexual/Textual Politics* read Virginia Woolf and Julia Kristeva as using some styles and techniques of fiction and poetic language – for example, their "use of mobile, pluralist viewpoints" (8); their call for " 'the spasmodic force' of the unconscious [to] disrupt their language" (11), creating a deferral of meaning – to dislodge, disrupt, and interrogate the totalizing humanist subject that grounded patriarchy. Moi saw feminist theorists like Elaine Showalter as falling into a "bourgeois realism" (4) that would separate aesthetics from politics and the real (and form from content) because it elided experience with knowledge, assuming experience to be transparent, accessible, predictable, and coherent. For Showalter, Moi suggested, feminism could only be located in the content of the representation, whereas the form – especially any form that distorted the clarity of the message – would be anti-feminist. Showalter was not the only critic at the time who wanted to pose literariness, at least modernist literariness, as counter to feminism. Sandra Gilbert and Susan Gubar also wrote that "sophisticated avant-garde strategies of linguistic experimentation need to be understood in terms of male anxiety about unprecedented female achievement in both the social sphere and the literary marketplace" (*No Man's Land*, 5). Meanwhile, Kate Millett famously posited a perfect equation between literary representation and women's psychologies under patriarchy, as though literature was the proof of "the interiorization of patriarchal ideology" (*Sexual Politics*, 54) that translated directly into the counterrevolutionary politics of sexual inequality, oppression, and subordination. What we can learn from Moi in her debate with (Showalter's) desire for the real in feminism is that what counts as "the literary" cannot be reduced to the content, the form, the objects of narrative, or the polemics alone, nor is it particularly sheltered in realism or guaranteed in any particular form or genre. This means that there is no easy equation between any part of the literary and its appearances, effects, and modes of connecting with the "extra-literary." "The literary tendency" for feminism has to have within its scope simultaneously many elements such as style, form, genre, tone, dramatic presentation, ideology critique, defamiliarization, point of view, excess, linguistic choice, narrative technique, interiority, detachment, innovation, conflict, interpretation, figuration, and an array of other meaningful, effective ingredients of literariness, or rather, as Moi herself says, "the possibility of transforming the symbolic order of orthodox society" (*Sexual/Textual Politics*, 11) using language, story, and imagination.

More recently, Moi has turned her critical energies against thinking that opposes the modernism defined through reflexivity, experimentation, and skepticism against an aesthetically naïve realism with its faith in empiricism and the stability of reference. Instead, for both literature and feminism, Moi has reframed the modern literary imagination as not opposed to realism and representation but rather to idealism and naturalism – that is, necessity subjected to determining natural laws, explainable by science. In fact, she says, realism can take many guises, some of which align with modernism and might be read as politically progressive or stylistically challenging. The solution to the problem of essentialism within humanist representation is, then, for Moi, no longer only recourse to the unconscious, negativity, linguistic fragmentation, or French poststructuralist theory – or rather, modernist techniques – but an espousal of ordinary language, or the meanings created by use in an everyday, phenomenal "encounter with the Other (society)" (*What Is a Woman?*, 79), or "lived experience" (*What Is a Woman?*, 63). The position of those critics she now labels "ideologues of Modernism" (*Henrik Ibsen and the Birth of Modernism*, 28), hating realism (as she might have been said to have done in *Sexual/Textual*), tend to reduce it to its one variant of "representation" or "reference" rather than to its capacities to question the inevitability of certain physical "laws" or moral imperatives based in a (naturalistic) faith in human perfectibility.

Moi's revisions of literary history challenge us to question how the literary responds to, inhabits, drives, or frames feminist practices and meanings within a much broader and more open-ended idea of what the literary might look like. Instead of privileging poststructuralist linguistic play or modernist representational breakages as the dominant or exclusive definitional structure of feminism's literary, Moi's recent analysis invites us to witness the effects on feminism of the many other historical appearances of the literary as well; it allows literary opposition to take other than modernist forms. In addition, whereas the earlier work assumes the hegemony of poststructuralist theory with its (modernist) modes of undermining reference, where the literary at its best could be conflated into the theoretical, the later work asks us always to be reconsidering the connections between the literary and the theoretical historically and redrawing their relationship, perhaps identifying the literary as, at times, working antagonistically toward theory's limits or, at others, standing in theory's needed defense or answering for theory's shortcomings. Within this broadened perspective, literature can have many types of appearances, taking on different meanings, definitions, functions, and forms at different historical junctures. *Literature and the Development of Feminist Theory* debates what form feminism might take through its various encounters with the literary. Whereas in her book *Literature after Feminism*, Rita Felski poses the question "How has feminism changed the ways we think about literature?" this volume raises the alternative question of "How has literature changed the ways we think about feminism?"

As with any project of this sort, this volume is incomplete. Many writers and ideas were left out because of space and other restrictions. In consultation with the press, I decided what were to be the broad areas of focus, and then each writer, according to her specialization and interests, shaped her own chapter and chose which texts and approaches would best suit her contribution, with some input from me. Still, there is plenty of work left to be done on this topic. Yet, all in all, *Literature and the Development of Feminist Theory* demonstrates that the theoretical history of feminist ideas is only half the story. Targeting experts and students in the field, *Literature and the Development of Feminist Theory* addresses the work of particular writers who bridge theory and literature but also concepts of theme, history, and genre that force an articulation of theoretical material in literary form.

WORKS CITED

Adorno, Theodor. "Reconciliation under Duress." In *Aesthetics and Politics: The Key Texts of the Classic Debate within German Marxism.* Trans. Ed. Ronald Taylor. London and New York: Verso, 1977, 151–76.

Arendt, Hannah. *The Human Condition.* Second Edition. Chicago and London: University of Chicago Press, 1958.

Bakhtin, Mikhail. *The Dialogic Imagination.* Ed. Michael Holquist. Trans. Caryl Emerson and Michael Holquist. Austin and London: University of Texas Press, 1981.

Beauvoir, Simone de. "Women and Creativity." In *French Feminist Thought: A Reader*, edited by Toril Moi. Oxford: Basil Blackwell, 1987, 17–32.

Casanova, Pascale. *The World Republic of Letters.* Trans. M. B. DeBevoise. Cambridge, MA and London: Harvard University Press, 2004.

El Saadawi, Nawal. "Leading Egyptian Feminist, Nawal El Saadawi: 'Women and Girls Are Beside Boys in the Streets.'" Interview with Amy Goodman. *Democracy Now!* January 31, 2011: http://www.democracynow.org/2011/1/31/women_protest_alongside_men_in_egyptian. Accessed December 23, 2014.

Felski, Rita. *Literature after Feminism.* Chicago and London: University of Chicago Press, 2003.

Gilbert, Sandra M. and Gubar, Susan. *No Man's Land: The Place of the Woman Writer in the Twentieth Century. Volume 2: Sexchanges.* New Haven, CT and London: Yale University Press, 1989.

Goodman, Robin Truth. "Feminism, Gender, and the Literary Commons." In *The Values of Literary Studies: Critical Institutions, Scholarly Agendas*, edited by Ronan McDonald. Cambridge: Cambridge University Press [forthcoming].

Feminist Theory in Pursuit of the Public: Women and the "Re-privatization" of Labor. New York: Palgrave, 2010.

Habermas, Jürgen. *The Structural Transformation of the Public Sphere: An Inquiry into a Category of Bourgeois Society.* Trans. Thomas Burger with Frederick Lawrence. Cambridge, MA: MIT Press, 1989.

Le Doeuff, Michèle. "Women and Philosophy." In *French Feminist Thought: A Reader*, edited by Toril Moi. Oxford: Basil Blackwell, 1987, 181–209.

Millett, Kate. *Sexual Politics: The Classic Analysis of the Interplay between Men, Women, & Culture.* New York: Simon & Schuster, 1969.

Moi, Toril. *Henrik Ibsen and the Birth of Modernism.* Oxford and New York:
   Oxford University Press, 2006.
   Sexual/Textual Politics: Feminist Literary Theory. London and New York:
   Routledge, 1985.
   What Is a Woman? Oxford and New York: Oxford University Press, 1999.
Morrison, Toni. *Playing in the Dark: Whiteness and the Literary Imagination.*
   Cambridge, MA and London: Harvard University Press, 1992.
Plain, Gill and Sellers, Susan. "Introduction." In *A History of Feminist Literary
   Criticism.* Cambridge: Cambridge University Press, 2007.
Rooney, Ellen. "Introduction." In *The Cambridge Companion to Feminist Literary
   Theory,* edited by Ellen Rooney. Cambridge: Cambridge University Press,
   2006.
Woolf, Virginia. *A Room of One's Own.* San Diego, New York, London: Harcourt
   Brace Jovanovich, 1929, 1957.

"Original Spirit": Literary Translations and Translational Literature in the Works of Mary Wollstonecraft

Laura Kirkley

From 1788, Mary Wollstonecraft was developing the feminist convictions that inform her *Vindication of the Rights of Woman* (1792) in a cosmopolitan literary and intellectual milieu. A prolific literary critic for the *Analytical Review*, which brought news of foreign literature to the British public, she often commented on the quality of English translations. She was well qualified to do so because she, too, was a translator of French and German texts. These translations gave Wollstonecraft insight into literary systems beyond her immediate sphere of influence and formed a crucial part of her literary apprenticeship.

Since the 1980s, the "cultural turn" in translation studies has invited scholars to understand translation as a creative practice.[1] Although exact equivalence in any process of linguistic transfer is impossible, translation need not represent loss or dilution of meaning. Instead, it can be understood as a (potentially critical) revision of meaning within a different ideological or cultural context. This definition allows for a broader metaphorical conception of "translation" as the transformative appropriation of source material. In her interventionist translation, *Elements of Morality for the Use of Young Children* (1790), Wollstonecraft reconstructs the German mother, Frau Herrmann, in Christian Gotthilf Salzmann's *Moralisches Elementarbuch* (1783), as Mrs Jones, an authoritative educator with feminist potential. Mrs Jones has much in common with Mrs Mason, Wollstonecraft's pedagogical alter ego in her conduct-book, *Original Stories from Real Life* (1788). This chapter argues that both characters are Wollstonecraftian alter egos who can, in turn, be regarded as feminist "translations" of the autofictional matriarchs dominating the works of Félicité de Genlis. At various stages of her career, Wollstonecraft translates, both literally and metaphorically, the figure of the mother-educator, who, in her final incarnation in *Maria, or The Wrongs of Woman* (1798) represents the most progressive stage in her revolutionary feminism.

Feminism and Creative Translation

Translation has often been figured as subservient to authorship and, as feminist translation theorists have pointed out, the metaphors were usually gendered. The feminized translator was cast in a reproductive role, one that demanded fidelity to the masculinized author, but could only ever bring forth a pale shadow of his creative original.[2] In light of this model, eighteenth-century women translators appeared to make a less controversial departure than women authors from their expected place as demure subordinates to men. Even so, some translated anonymously – including Wollstonecraft in her first translation, *Of the Importance of Religious Opinions* (1788) – and, although many did publish under their own names, in their prefaces they often adopted a conventional pose of humility vis-à-vis the author. It is clear, however, that in practice, many women did not consider translation an act of mere imitation. Some were keen to avoid the stigma of immodesty that accompanied female authorship, but translation nonetheless enabled them to engage critically with authoritative texts of the period.[3] Their interventionist strategies resulted in creative rewritings that invested their work with what Wollstonecraft calls the "spirit of an original."[4]

Scholars of feminism *avant la lettre* have dwelt on the determining power of discourses and literary forms preempted by men and the extent to which they inhibit the expression of nascent feminist thought. Feminist translation theory has focused, particularly, on the struggle for audibility between the historically muted – and feminized – translational voice and its historically dominant authorial counterpart, suggesting that a feminist translator might engage critically with patriarchal texts and significantly alter their ideological freight. For Barbara Godard, translation is a creative act of intervention, a form of rewriting: "The feminist translator, affirming her critical difference ... flaunts the signs of her manipulation of the text."[5] In practice, these signs can manifest themselves as excisions, interpolations, stylistic changes, and even thinly veiled textual self-constructions, all of which amount to a critical commentary on the ideological content of the source text.

Wollstonecraft was one of many women who were published authors in their own right, but also chose to translate.[6] Her English version of Jacques Necker's *De l'importance des opinions religieuses* (1788) was followed by *Elements of Morality* and *Young Grandison* (1790), an abridgement of an earlier translation from Maria de Cambon's *De kleine Grandison*. William Godwin also records that Wollstonecraft began a translation from a

French text, *The New Robinson,* and abridged Lavater's *Physiognomy.*[7] She regarded the translational process as an opportunity for intellectual exchanges with the authors of her source texts. The commercial success of *Elements* led to an exchange of letters with Salzmann, who subsequently published a German translation of the *Rights of Woman. Young Grandison, The New Robinson,* and *Elements* were all pedagogical works, which suggests that Wollstonecraft selected source texts from her sphere of expertise. An increasingly interventionist translator, she uses translation as a critical tool, a means of contributing to the international debate on education. In her Advertisements, she confesses to taking "Liberties" when she translates, at first attributing this strategy to a desire to "preserve the Spirit of the Original."[8] In later years, however, she seeks to give that "spirit of an original" to her translation, introducing "deviations" and "*material* alterations" into the language of her source texts.[9]

Despite the rhetoric of subservience surrounding translation, such interventionist strategies were common in the seventeenth and eighteenth centuries. Like their French counterparts, neoclassical translators such as Dryden and Denham often produced *belles infidèles* (beautiful but unfaithful translations), which tended to adapt source texts to local tastes and prevailing aesthetic values. Toward the end of the century, when Wollstonecraft was beginning to translate, interventionist strategies spoke to the growing enthusiasm among writers and literary critics of the period for literature that seemed spontaneously to express original thought. Edward Young, whose works Wollstonecraft admired, claims that, "*Originals* are, and ought to be, great Favourites," for they "extend the Republic of Letters, and add a new province to its dominion."[10] Alexander Fraser Tytler's *Essay on the Principles of Translation* (1791), a rare example of translation theory from the latter part of the century, also encourages translators to privilege originality over imitation.[11] Such inspired creativity was often regarded as the special province of male writers, but in her preface to *Elements,* Wollstonecraft's claims to give her text the "spirit of an original" establish just such a creative translational voice, which remains audible in the main text.

Elements of Feminism

The preface to *Elements* bears witness to Wollstonecraft's professional confidence. Instead of seeking anonymity, she signs her name at the end of the Advertisement, in which she also promotes her *Original Stories.* She observes that Salzmann's *Elementarbuch* contains a "well-digested system" and is written "on the same plan" as her own work, thereby aligning her pedagogical convictions and experience with those of the male educator.[12] Indeed, the two held a common belief that many of the world's evils might be eradicated by educational reform. Salzmann was a disciple of Johann Basedow's Philanthropinist educational movement, which, like Wollstonecraft, drew on the pedagogical theories of Jean-Jacques Rousseau, and in 1784, he founded the Salzmannschule in Schnepfenthal. Although the early Philanthropinists used Rousseau's construct of woman to restrict female education, Salzmann agreed with Wollstonecraft that the same pedagogical principles should be applied to male and female children, and in 1786, he converted this principle to practice by founding a girls' school. Despite this progressive move, however, he does not appear to have embraced the more controversial aspects of Wollstonecraft's feminism. In his paratext to the German version of her *Rights of Woman*, he rejects her call for female economic autonomy, asserting that women's biological makeup necessitates dependence on men.[13] Wollstonecraft does, however, often make the less inflammatory argument that improved education will better fit women to their wifely and maternal duties. Like many French revolutionaries and English reformers, she regards the home as a microcosm of the state, and the mother as a legislator-like figure whose duty lies in equipping future citizens with the moral strength to effect social change. Salzmann's paratext downplays the revolutionary potential underlying this vision of maternal virtue, but his work does strive to give cultural currency to the rational mother who raises virtuous citizens.

Where there is ideological parity in the views of Salzmann and Wollstonecraft, her translation often closely echoes the *Elementarbuch*. For example, few significant changes in meaning are made to the passages in which Salzmann extols the pleasures of motherhood. In her translational preface, Wollstonecraft defines herself as a judicious critic of the German text, and expresses admiration for its "very rational" pedagogical content: "the writer coincided with me in opinion respecting the method which ought to be pursued to form the heart and temper, or, in other words, to inculcate the first principles of morality."[14] By aligning her authorship and that of Salzmann, however, she also differentiates herself from the paradigm of the subservient translator. Although she has decided to "term" *Elements* "a translation," she does "not pretend to assert that it is a literal one."[15] On the contrary, she suppresses, interpolates, and reworks many aspects of her source text, both to domesticate it for her English readership, and to "give it the spirit of an original."[16]

This authoritative transformation of her source text brings feminist implications to Wollstonecraft's translational practice, partly because she puts her intellectual capacity on a par with that of the male author, and partly because she lays claim to the creative originality traditionally regarded as the province of men. Her feminist agenda is also clear, however, in the changes she makes to the text itself, not the least of which is the transformation of Frau Herrmann into Mrs Jones, a Wollstonecraftian mother-educator whose every word of advice or chastisement carries moral implications that transcend the domestic sphere.

This mother-educator wields power in a moral universe that differs subtly but significantly from that of the *Elementarbuch*. As Alessa Johns observes, whereas Salzmann's pedagogical strategy is geared to practical social improvements, Wollstonecraft frequently "raises the moral stakes in what would appear to be less than earthshaking events."[17] For instance, where Salzmann warns that overindulging in rich food will injure the health, Wollstonecraft connects immoderate eating with the sin of gluttony, depicted as a sickness of both mind and body.[18] Influenced by Barbara Taylor's analysis of the religious foundations of Wollstonecraft's feminism, Johns connects this aspect of the translational strategy with a "millenarian" cast to her writing.[19] For Wollstonecraft, moral development, in children and their parents, was part of a human march to perfection that would culminate in the revolutionary leveling of social injustices and an era of spiritual renewal. Galvanizing social change meant educating young people to resist, with the aid of reason, the corrupting effects of society; in Wollstonecraft's view, educators qualified to enlighten the younger generation were, unfortunately, few and far between as they, too, had been shaped by an unsatisfactory status quo.[20] In Mrs Jones, she creates an exemplary mother-educator who takes purposive control of her children's education. Her exchanges with her daughter, moreover, often have a feminist dimension lacking in Salzmann's text.

When little Mary (Luise in the *Elementarbuch*) is wearing her best clothes, she complains that she cannot join in the boys' boisterous games. Her corsetry leaves her breathless and her full skirt and accessories prove cumbersome. In Salzmann's text, the mother is sympathetic, but explains that, in polite society, convention dictates a formal dress code:

> *Ich weiß wohl, daß Poschen, lange Kleider, Schnürbrust und Frisur, Kindern sehr beschwerlich find, und daß du in denselben nicht so vergnügt und lustig sein kannst, als du wünschest. Deswegen habe ich dich zeither mit allen diesen Dingen verschonet. Aber heute – da du dich in einer so großen geputzen Gesellschaft zeigen wolltest, da konnte es nicht anders sein.*

> I know very well that children find false hips, long skirts, stays and dressed hair very cumbersome, and that you cannot be as cheerful and merry in them as you wish. I have therefore spared you all these things until now. But today – as you wanted to be seen in such grand and well-groomed company, it could not be otherwise.[21]

Wollstonecraft, who objected to separate, less energetic forms of play for female children, alters and extends Salzmann's paragraph, uniting the mother and daughter in a specifically feminine complaint. While Salzmann writes that children find such clothing uncomfortable, Wollstonecraft has the mother acknowledge her own discomfort:

> I know very well that a long train, stays with bones in them, and tangled hair, are very inconvenient, and that you cannot be as easy and gay as you wish. For that reason I have not till now teized [sic] you with such useless parts of dress.[22]

Wollstonecraft then takes the opportunity to expand the moral reach of the episode, echoing her claim in *Original Stories* that, "when internal goodness is reflected, every other kind of beauty, the shadow of it, withers away before it":[23]

> a good girl requires no ornaments; if she keeps her person clean, and puts her clothes on in an orderly manner, people will only look at her good humoured obliging face. But to-day you even wished to be dressed, and I had a mind to let you feel how much more comfortable you would have been in your muslin frock and pink sash.[24]

Fashionable society, which encourages women to value "ornaments," seems to promote the vanity that Wollstonecraft associates, in the *Rights of Woman*, with poorly educated women, culturally conditioned to exaggerate the so-called feminine charms of weakness and frivolity. Indeed, Mary is genuinely weakened by the discomfort of fashionable dress, and the implication is that Mrs Jones has subjected her to the experience so that she will prefer to avoid such gatherings in future. Crucially, Mary has not simply been taught a practical lesson; she has been encouraged to consider the moral implications of gendered norms in her society.

This subtly feminist passage is part of a broader attempt by Wollstonecraft to redress gender biases in her source text. For Johns, however, the millenarian dimension of her thought, while raising the moral status of the mother, actually functions to constrain her sphere of influence. She argues that, by exhorting her citizen-mothers to shine in their "natural" maternal role, Wollstonecraft makes the part they might play in any social or political change "removed and conceptual."[25] Citing Mrs

Mason as an example, she argues that, even though Wollstonecraft invites analogies between her mother-educators, the "unacknowledged legislators" of their microcosmic states, and legislators in the public sphere, the connections remain purely metaphorical so long as women are defined in terms of their domestic duties.[26] Even as she "rearranges" Salzmann's *Elementarbuch* "to put women at the center," Johns claims, "she unwittingly contributes to their ultimate marginalization."[27]

What Johns does not consider, however, is that Salzmann's *Elementarbuch* is not the only source text for *Elements of Morality*. Like Mrs Mason, Mrs Jones is also a "translation" of the mother-educators of Félicité de Genlis, a best-selling author in her native French and in English translation. Genlis's pedagogical works promote a model of female virtue attained, not by sincere scrutiny of the moral self, but by a practice of self-conscious performance. The habits of "virtue" thus inculcated are largely defined by gender norms that confine women to domesticity and economic dependence. Wollstonecraft translates, into her own works, the authority, near-omniscience, and autofictionality of Genlis's mother-educators, but in doing so, she also adapts them to her feminist agenda. The premise of Salzmann's source text, which focuses on the domestic life of a bourgeois family, defines Mrs Jones's narrow sphere of influence. If we read *Elements* in the context of Wollstonecraft's oeuvre as a whole, however, Mrs Jones can be aligned with a range of Wollstonecraftian alter-egos operating across different genres to challenge the disconnection, endorsed by Genlis, between a woman's inner self and her (gendered) social performances.

Original Spirits: Wollstonecraft's Mother-Educators

Genlis was the first woman in history to hold the prestigious position of *gouverneur* to the sons of her lover, the Duc d'Orléans. She educated them on a rural estate at Bellechasse alongside their twin sisters and her own children, and her pedagogical works frequently blur the boundaries between real-life experiences and fiction. One such work was *Adèle et Théodore*, an epistolary novel in which the Baronne d'Almane and her husband leave Paris for a rural life devoted to educating their children. The Baronne's letters, which focus primarily on the education of her daughter, the eponymous Adèle, often attribute Genlis's pedagogical works to her fictional counterpart. This technique highlights the connection between writer and alter ego, encouraging readers to regard *Adèle et Théodore* as a transparent account of Genlis's pedagogical practice and its impressive results.

Genlis maintained that a solid education would produce better wives and mothers, and therefore aimed to teach women reason and strength of mind. Despite her unconventional status as royal *gouverneur*, however, she was a traditionalist who never envisaged a role for women beyond the domestic sphere. The social order takes precedence over the individual and the wisdom of its patriarchal structure is taken for granted. The Baronne therefore raises Adèle to adopt the requisite "feminine" virtues to fulfill her future wifely and maternal duties. According to Genlis, virtues grow from habit; they are fictions rehearsed until they become a reality. The Baronne encourages Adèle to practice these virtues by warning her that she is under constant surveillance. When Adèle overindulges at a ball, her mother's rebuke not only makes her recognize her fault, but also reinforces her sense of ever-present maternal authority:

> Ceci doit vous apprendre deux choses: premièrement que la sobriété est une vertu aussi utile qu'elle est estimable; et secondement, que rien ne peut me distraire de vous, et que même, en ne paraissant pas vous regarder, je vous vois parfaitement.[28]

> This will teach you two things: First, that temperance is a virtue as useful as it is estimable; and secondly, that nothing can prevent my attention to you, and that, when I seem not to regard you, I see every thing you do.[29]

Her acute observational powers are the key to an authority that reaches sinister and at times tyrannical proportions, even after her pupils reach maturity. When Adèle is on the point of marriage, she claims that she cannot be separated from her mother and issues an ultimatum to her future husband, whereby he must agree to live in her parental home or to live apart from his wife. In short, the result of Adèle's education appears to be, not personal autonomy, but the transfer of worship from a male sovereign to his maternal counterpart.

In the *Rights of Woman*, Wollstonecraft expressed admiration for Genlis's pedagogy, but also identified in her works an "absurd manner of making parental authority supplant reason. For every where does she inculcate not only *blind* submission to parents; but to the opinion of the world."[30] Whereas Genlis encouraged obedience, Wollstonecraft's goal was to form individuals who, far from conforming to the status quo, would exercise their reason to recognize and resist injustice or tyranny. In the same year *Elements* was published, she wrote her *Vindication of the Rights of Men* (1790), which advocates political change designed to eradicate unjust social hierarchies, including the patriarchal tyranny she later identified in the *Rights of Woman*. While these convictions are not explicitly articulated in *Original Stories* or *Elements*, her subtle but significant changes to the mother-educators of her source texts reflect her feminist commitment to inculcating female independence of mind.

Wollstonecraft's first "translation" of Genlis's mother-educator takes the form of Mrs Mason, who assumes responsibility for the education of two girls named Mary and Caroline. Like the Baronne, Mrs Mason is transparently autofictional. Wollstonecraft published her first novel, *Mary, a Fiction* (1788), in the same year, and the reader is invited to draw parallels between the sentimental heroine and the impeccable Mrs Mason, perceiving in their creator the blueprint for both. They share a commitment to palliating suffering with charity and have similar (semi-autobiographical) backstories. Mrs Mason confesses to a "feeling heart" that has been "wounded by ingratitude," and laments a past filled with rejection and loss: "My fellow-creatures, whom I have fondly loved, have neglected me – I have heard their last sigh, and thrown my eyes round an empty world."[31] This melancholy is intensified in Mary and expressed in similar terms: "Too well have I loved my fellow creatures! I have been wounded by ingratitude."[32] The links between Wollstonecraft's different autofictional personae are crucial, not simply because they connect her writing practice with that of Genlis, but also because they invite an intertextual analysis of her mother-educators.

In common with the Baronne, Mrs Mason stages events that function as learning experiences. Her kinship with the authority figures of Genlis is clearest in the close watch she keeps over her charges. In order to eradicate their prejudices, we are told, "Mrs Mason never suffered them to be out of her sight,"[33] and Mary confesses to her sister that she cannot sleep because she is "afraid of Mrs Mason's eyes."[34] As the girls' behavior improves, she tells them: "You are now candidates for my friendship, and on your advancement in virtue my regard will in future depend."[35] Despite this emphatically conditional offer of affection, we are assured that Mary and Caroline grow to love and admire Mrs Mason, and in this way her authority over them becomes complete, for her judgments dictate their self-esteem: "She was never in a passion, but her quiet steady displeasure made them feel so little in their own eyes, they wished her to smile that they might be something; for all their consequence seemed to arise from her approbation."[36] In *Elements*, little Mary responds to praise from Mrs Jones with a similarly fervent desire for approval: "I will never be careless again that you may always look at me as you do now."[37] As Johns points out, Wollstonecraft's translation emphasizes "the mother's powerful gaze"; the German simply reads "ich will auch immer ordentlich seyn, liebe Mutter, daß Sie mir gut seyn können" ("and I want always to be so neat, dear Mother, so that you can be happy with me").[38]

Through these all-seeing mother-educators, Wollstonecraft constructs an authoritative textual persona capable of guiding those with underdeveloped reason. Despite her commitment to the principle of equality, this pedagogical interest in authority figures is also mirrored in her political texts. In her *Historical and Moral View of the French Revolution* (1794), she expresses a desire for strong leaders who can pilot the ship of state in the absence of a sufficiently rational populace. Yet at the same time, she claims – with a degree of wishful thinking – that the relatively enlightened 1790s have seen a widespread rejection of arbitrary power: no sensible person would subjugate a woman to a vicious husband, nor argue "that obedience to parents should go one jot beyond the deference due to reason, enforced by affection."[39] This latter statement returns primacy to the individual's freedom to exercise her own judgment in a text that elsewhere perceives flawed reasoning as a justification for subjugation to external authority. Mrs Mason and Mrs Jones embody just such an authority; but analogously, their pedagogical strategies also catalyze young women's progress to rational self-government.

At the end of the *Original Stories*, Mrs Mason announces that she has written a conduct-book to guide Mary and Caroline in her absence. Because the book appears to be the *Original Stories*, the episode blurs the boundary between her actual and fictional selves. Crucially, Mrs Mason relinquishes her authority at the end of her text, announcing her departure. Mary and Caroline are granted the freedom to use their own reason. An interpolated passage in *Elements*, in which Mrs Jones explains the instructional purpose of her actions to little Mary, recalls Mrs Mason's pedagogical strategy:

> All my commands have the same tendency, said her mother; I assist your weak mind, and I am endeavouring to make you wise and happy, when I deny you any present pleasure: for you are yet too young to know what is really good.[40]

For Johns, this dialog communicates the mother's "power to control her daughter's life in its minutest detail by denying pleasures";[41] but in her reference to Mary's "weak mind" Mrs Jones merely claims that her daughter's reason is not *yet* sufficiently developed. In other words, her authority will endure only as long as Mary is "too young" for self-government. Wollstonecraft brought similar pedagogical transparency to her posthumously published *Lessons* (1798), written for her daughter, Fanny Imlay, in which she seeks to explain the importance of maternal authority that diminishes with the child's growth in reason:

> When I was a child, my mamma chose the fruit for me, to prevent my making myself sick. I was just like you; I used to ask for what I saw, without knowing whether it was good or bad. Now I have lived a long time, I know what is good; I do not want any body to tell me.[42]

By recalling her previous, less educated self, the rational mother aligns her progress to self-government with that of her daughter. The implication is that the daughter will eventually qualify for the role of mother-educator. While there is little explicit suggestion in any of Wollstonecraft's pedagogical texts that her mother-educators might exert authority beyond the domestic sphere, through these personae she seeks consistently to inculcate independent thought and – crucially – to call attention to the social and political injustices analyzed elsewhere in her oeuvre.

In contrast to the Baronne, Mrs Mason does not aim to accommodate her charges to society. Instead, she teaches them to palliate suffering with charity. This benevolence is not simply a duty; it is also a comfort in a social order that is far from ideal. She relates stories "from real life" of virtuous characters who suffer terrible loss and hardship, often because of the greed and cruelty of their social superiors. "Crazy Robin" is driven mad by grief when the actions of an avaricious landlord unleash a chain of events that result in his wife and children dying, one by one, from overwork, starvation, and poverty-related diseases.[43] In a similar vein, Wollstonecraft alters chapter 3 of the *Elementarbuch*, which teaches children to manage fear, in order to bring a political dimension to a moral tale. In Salzmann's text, a soldier is so overcome by terror of imaginary foes that he runs straight into the path of the enemy. Wollstonecraft relocates the soldier to the plains of America, where his anxiety convinces him that he is being pursued by hostile Native Americans. Spurring on his horse to avoid the imaginary danger, he is thrown to the ground and breaks his leg. His rescuer turns out to be "one of those men whom we Europeans with white complexions call savages,"[44] a Native American whose tender care for the soldier suggests to children their common humanity with the indigenous peoples of America at a time of ruthless colonization. In both cases, Wollstonecraft encourages children to question social hierarchies and prejudices that Genlis and Salzmann uphold or overlook.

Although derived from Genlis and Salzmann, Wollstonecraft's mother-educators are invested with "original spirit" adapted to her feminist purpose. More importantly, they encourage a similarly independent spirit in the female children they educate, raising them to exercise their reason without reference to spurious authorities or social prejudices. The mother-educator takes her final, most explicitly feminist form in Wollstonecraft's unfinished novel, *Maria*. A rewriting of *Mary* with inter-texts that include Wollstonecraft's *Rights of Woman* and Rousseau's *Julie, ou La Nouvelle Héloïse* (1761), *Maria* also draws heavily on the novel of sensibility and the Gothic. As such, it can be understood as a translational novel, one that adapts existing source texts to Wollstonecraft's feminist agenda. In any such translational project, the feminist rewriter invariably risks being "spoken by" the language of her source texts. For many critics, Maria, who is in many respects a sentimental heroine, cannot be suffi-ciently dissociated from literary predecessors firmly embedded in demean-ing narratives of femininity. Read as a mother-educator, however, Maria evinces a similar commitment to rational independence of mind as her foremothers in *Original Stories* and *Elements*.

Confined to a lunatic asylum by her cruel and unfaithful husband, Maria decides to write her memoirs for the future benefit of her daugh-ter, from whom she has been separated. An obvious literary prece-dent for Maria's manuscript is Lady Sarah Pennington's conduct-book, *An Unfortunate Mother's Advice to Her Absent Daughters* (1761), written not only to give moral guidance but also to defend herself against her estranged husband's charges of adultery. Like Pennington, Maria claims that she was naïvely mistaken in her husband's character when she mar-ried him. For Wollstonecraft, this hard-won knowledge of the female con-dition equips Maria to give advice to her daughter. In other words, Maria is a pedagogical figure who, although not perfection incarnate, reflects on her past life "with the sentiments that experience, and more matured rea-son, would naturally suggest."[45]

Whereas Pennington and Genlis enjoined their daughters to respect social norms and codes of conduct, Maria regards conformity as a threat to her daughter's happiness. She expresses a conventional desire to "instruct her daughter, and shield her from the misery, the tyranny, her mother knew not how to avoid," but as her narrative develops, it becomes clear that happiness is not to be achieved by strict adherence to any arbitrary code of conduct.[46] In *Adèle et Théodore*, the Baronne personifies a code of conduct to which Adèle must learn to submit. By contrast, Maria tells her daughter that she intends "rather to exercise than influence [her] mind."[47] In refusing to exert authority over her daughter, however, she attempts to grant her the liberty to learn through experience: "Gain experience – ah! gain it – while experience is worth having, and acquire sufficient fortitude to pursue your own happiness; it includes your utility, by a direct path."[48] Maria advises her daughter to discover and pursue her individual path to happiness, although she acknowledges that living authentically in a patriarchal society will demand "fortitude," an uncompromising allegiance to the dictates of reason and conscience. In recommending rational – although not dispassionate – self-government, however, Wollstonecraft does not have her heroine privilege the individual at the expense of the collective; on the contrary, personal fulfilment is to include social "utility." Resistance to authority and fidelity to self are conceived, not as detrimental to the social order, but as instrumental in reforming it.

From her early translations to her final unfinished novel, Wollstonecraft's writing practice is translational. She draws on influential source texts but resists their putative authority, appropriating and transforming material in the service of her feminist agenda. Each of her works can also be said to rewrite – or translate – its predecessors, inviting initiated readers to draw intertextual connections. If we interpret Wollstonecraft's pedagogical alter egos as an intertextual collective, it becomes clear that they inculcate a healthy skepticism toward external authorities upheld by custom and prejudice. This resistance to authority has feminist implications. Whereas Genlis encourages conformity to a society that limits women's sphere of influence, Wollstonecraft's textual personae incite compassion for those suffering because of an unjust social system and promote the rational thought required to critique it. Mrs Mason uses the authority of the Genlisian mother-educator not to exact obedience, but to develop her charges' reliance on the internal monitors of reason and conscience. Mrs Jones emerges from Wollstonecraft's translation as a more subtly feminist figure than Salzmann's Frau Hermann and – crucially – she expects her daughter's independence to grow with her reason. Maria demonstrates resistance to patriarchal injustice, striving to live in tune with the internal promptings of her authentic self, and encouraging her daughter to do likewise. In short, Wollstonecraft's pedagogy promotes a critical engagement with existing authorities that is reflected in her writing practices. Dependent on dialogical relations with other writers and formed at the nexus of multiple source texts, her literary corpus is translational, born of a process of rewriting that invests each text with an original – and distinctly feminist – spirit.

WORKS CITED

Bassnett, Susan. "Introduction." In *Translation Studies*. London and New York: Routledge, 2014.

Genlis, Stéphanie-Félicité de. *Adelaide and Theodore, or Letters on Education* (1783), ed. Gillian Dow, trans. by Thomas Holcroft. London: Pickering & Chatto, 2007.

Adèle et Théodore, ou Lettres sur l'éducation, 2nd ed. Paris: Lambert, 1782.

Godard, Barbara. "Theorizing Feminist Discourse/Translation." In *Translation, History & Culture*, edited by Susan Bassnett and André Lefevere, 87–96. London and New York: Cassell, 1990.

Godwin, William. *Memoirs of the Author of A Vindication of the Rights of Woman in A Short Residence in Sweden and Memoirs of the Author of "The Rights of Woman,"* edited by Richard Holmes. London: Penguin, 1987.

Grieder, Josephine. *Translations of French Sentimental Prose Fiction in Late Eighteenth-century England: The History of a Literary Vogue*. Durham, NC: Duke University Press, 1975.

Hayes, Julie Candler. *Translation, Subjectivity & Culture in France and England, 1600–1800*. Stanford, CA: Stanford University Press, 2009.

Johns, Alessa. *Bluestocking Feminism and British-German Cultural Transfer, 1750–1837*. Ann Arbor: University of Michigan Press, 2014.

Salzmann, Christian Gotthilf. *Moralisches Elementarbuch* (1783). Dortmund: Harenberg, 1980.

Simon, Sherry. *Gender in Translation: Cultural Identity and the Politics of Transmission*. London and New York: Routledge, 1996.

Taylor, Barbara. *Mary Wollstonecraft and the Feminist Imagination*. Cambridge: Cambridge University Press, 2003.

Tytler, Alexander Fraser. *Essay on the Principles of Translation* (1791), ed. Jeffrey F. Huntsman. Amsterdam: John Benjamins B.V., 1978.

Wollstonecraft, Mary. *Rettung der Rechte des Weibes*, ed. Christian Gotthilf Salzmann, trans. by Georg Friedrich Christian Weissenborn, 2 vols. Schnepfenthal: Verlag der Erziehungsanhalt, 1793.

The Works of Mary Wollstonecraft, ed. Janet Todd and Marilyn Butler. London: Pickering & Chatto, 1989, 7 vols.

Young, Edward. *Conjectures on Original Composition* (1759). Leeds: The Scholar Press, 1966.

CHAPTER 3

Jane Eyre, Incidents in the Life of a Slave Girl, *and the Varieties of Nineteenth-century Feminism*

Margaret Homans

Fiction has long been a wild zone for feminism. Interrupting her own reasoned argument in *A Vindication of the Rights of Woman*, Mary Wollstonecraft expresses a "wild wish ... to see the distinction of sex confounded in society" (62). Fiction allows feminist visionaries to imagine what can't yet be argued for, and it can make radical ideas seem conceivable, palatable, and even normal by embodying them in credible characters and situations. Figurative language, too, in otherwise discursive prose can tell feminist stories. Wollstonecraft's sustained metaphor describing women as slaves and men as tyrants or kings, leading to the necessity for a "revolution in female manners," evokes the world-transforming violence of the French Revolution without proposing actual bloodshed, and when she wrote a novel to illustrate "the wrongs of woman," the heroine says: "marriage bastilled me." Through such figures, Wollstonecraft imagines a revolutionary future in which the prison walls of sex difference – the laws, economic practices, and social conventions that render women less than human – will have fallen.

That Charlotte Brontë's *Jane Eyre* has long been understood to represent feminism in fictional form has made it both beloved and excoriated. In 1855 Margaret Oliphant expressed disapproval by calling it "a wild declaration of the 'Rights of Woman' in a new aspect" (Allott, *The Brontës*, 312). The first history of the U.S. woman suffrage movement celebrated Brontë as "part of the great uprising of women [and] the complete revolution a thousand pens and voices herald at this hour" (Stanton, Anthony, and Gage, *History of Woman Suffrage*, 42). Anti-lynching activist Ida B. Wells "formed her ideals" in part from reading *Jane Eyre*, and M. Carey Thomas, later president of Bryn Mawr College, selected passages from *Jane Eyre* for her girlhood copybook (Sicherman, *Well-Read Lives*, 29, 116). In a New Woman novel's utopian procession of "pioneers down through the ages who had fought for Freedom, Justice, and Truth" the Brontë sisters can be seen marching (Flint, *The Woman Reader*, 313).

"It can be read ... as a fictional counterpart to Wollstonecraft's manifesto," explains a recent teaching guide to *Jane Eyre* (Diedrick, "*Jane Eyre*
and *A Vindication of the Rights of Woman*," 23), and Jane's desire for education, meaningful work, and equality in marriage anticipates in fictional
form the demands of the Anglo-American women's movement starting in
1848. Second-wave liberal feminists, too, found in it a model of their own
ideal: an independent heroine who claims her rights to self-determination
and to sexual self-expression. Looking back from the 1990s, it seemed
"the original feminist novel, in which female desire or the voice of femininity speaks out" (Azim, *The Colonial Rise of the Novel*, 88). It quickly
became part of the women's studies curriculum. Patricia Meyer Spacks's
1972 literature students wrote, "if we study how women express themselves and how they really feel, then that would be women's liberation,"
and they read *Jane Eyre* (Spacks, *The Female Imagination*, 1–2). The pioneering early 1970s books on women's fiction by Spacks, Ellen Moers, and
Elaine Showalter relied heavily on *Jane Eyre*, which also provided the central motif of Sandra Gilbert and Susan Gubar's 1979 *The Madwoman in
the Attic* and was one of two complete novels Gilbert and Gubar reprinted
in *The Norton Anthology of Literature by Women*. Even in the twenty-first
century *Jane Eyre* still has the power to define feminism for postfeminist
young women and to persuade them of the value of its goals (Varley and
Erdman, "Working for Judith Shakespeare").

Among other features that made the novel a beacon to some readers
and an outrage to others is its first-person narration, an unusual choice for
a novel in the 1840s that establishes the validity of the older Jane's voice
and keeps the narrative focused on the younger Jane's self-affirmations.
On the verge of yielding to Rochester's plea to run away with him, Jane
asks herself: "Who in the world cares for you? ... *I* care for myself. The
more solitary, the more friendless, the more unsustained I am, the more
I will respect myself" (270). Challenging the Victorian ideal of women's
selflessness, the novel put an important feminist idea into popular circulation by imagining what would later be called the subject of feminism. As
Nancy Armstrong argues, the novel invented what did not yet exist as a
social actuality.

The enormous popularity of the novel in Britain and the United States
gave it the power to nudge the reading public's thinking about gender.
But it nudged that thinking in several directions at once, and the kind of
feminism the novel is seen to represent has varied across time. This chapter will explore some of the contradictory feminist formations the novel
presents, tracing how it came to stand so affirmatively for second-wave

liberal feminism, the feminism of "I," and examining its less positive legacies by tracing its ambivalent reception by Harriet Jacobs's *Incidents in the Life of a Slave Girl*, a founding text for the feminisms of women of color of the past fifty years.

When *Jane Eyre* appeared in October 1847, reviewers found it "powerful" and "original," even if some incidents were melodramatic; "it is a book to make the pulses gallop, and the heart beat, and to fill the eyes with tears," displaying "great if undisciplined powers" (Allott, *The Brontës*, 68, 81). Positive and negative reviews emphasized the novel's innovative "anatomy of the mind" (Allott, *The Brontës*, 74), its unusually intimate portrayal of Jane's inner life. It became a best seller, going quickly into a second and then a third edition by January 1848. Within a year the American press was reporting "Jane Eyre fever," owing not only to its "freshness" and "power" but also to its "raciness" (Allott, *The Brontës*, 97, 99).

Its popularity led to debates about its morality, a topic that merged in some readers' minds with questions of economic and political revolution. An 1848 attack in the *Boston Daily Atlas* by "W." attributes *Jane Eyre*'s popularity to a "stealthy ... moral revolution" already going on in American society. In the novel, he complains, "woman is made the instrument to reward a life of crime"; a "true woman" would "shun" Rochester's "wickedness." Connecting the novel's revolutionary morals to the Burkean view of the French Revolution, "W." claims that the novel's "gilded pandering" to its characters' "impure" passions causes "injury to the public mind." France, he writes, "was literally poisoned by its authors, and its fair fields reeked with blood, poured out to satiate those who followed the wretched teachings which a corrupt taste demanded." By representing the revolutionaries as "authors," "W." equates *Jane Eyre* with the Reign of Terror and envisions Wollstonecraft's metaphoric "revolution in female manners" about to become a literal bloodletting.

Similarly, in probably the best-known review of *Jane Eyre*, Elizabeth Rigby acknowledges the novel's "genuine power" but, like "W.," finds the book injurious to public morals: the novel commits "that highest moral offence a novel writer can commit, that of making an unworthy character interesting in the eyes of the reader" (Allott, *The Brontës*, 107). She means Rochester, who is "coarse and brutal," but Jane too exhibits "gross vulgarity." Rigby castigates this "anti-Christian" novel, too, for its

> murmuring against the comforts of the rich and against the privations of the poor, which, as far as each individual is concerned, is a murmuring against God's appointment ... The tone of mind and thought which has overthrown authority and violated every code human and divine abroad,

and fostered Chartism and rebellion at home, is the same which has also written *Jane Eyre*. (Allott, *The Brontës*, 109–10)

Like "W.," Rigby identifies Jane and Rochester's dubious morals with the Reign of Terror and even with violent labor protests in industrialized England. The novel's unruliness is at once political and aesthetic: Jane's spirit is "unregenerate and undisciplined" and the writing "flows ungovernably" (Allott, *The Brontës*, 109–11). Eight years later, Margaret Oliphant disparaged the novel's "declaration of the Rights of Woman" and blamed on its "invasion" of literature a "revolution" to which, like "W." and Rigby, she attributes geopolitical scope. "Woman is the half of the world," and the novel suggests "talk of a balance of power which may be adjusted by taking a Crimea [in] a battle which must always be going forward" (Allott, *The Brontës*, 312–13). These responses to the novel's "power" see the novel's refusal to obey the rules of gendered behavior as having potentially global significance.

What in the novel were these readers responding to? Rigby particularly disliked the child Jane's talking back to her social superiors, as in the opening scene when she defends herself following an assault by her spoiled cousin John: "'Wicked and cruel boy!' I said. 'You are like a murderer – you are like a slave-driver – you are like the Roman emperors!'" Locked up in the "red-room" for punishment and told she lacks "equality" with her cousins, she recalls, "the mood of the revolted slave was still bracing me with its bitter vigour" (9–11). Moers comments: "From justice in the personal context there is, for Jane Eyre, no distance at all to justice in a social context wide enough to frighten" such a reviewer as Rigby (Moers, *Literary Women*, 26).

This linkage of personal to public injustice appears again in Jane's more mature reflections during her work as governess at lonely Thornfield Hall. Expressing what Rigby saw as "ungodly discontent," this passage was for Adrienne Rich in 1973 "Charlotte Brontë's feminist manifesto" (Rich, "*Jane Eyre*," 97). Beginning "anybody may blame me who likes," Jane claims her entitlement to a larger life, a need that only large-scale political change can meet:

> It is in vain to say human beings ought to be satisfied with tranquility: they must have action; and they will make it if they cannot find it. Millions are condemned to a stiller doom than mine, and millions are in silent revolt against their lot. Nobody knows how many rebellions besides political rebellions ferment in the masses of life which people earth. Women are supposed to be very calm generally: but women feel just as men feel; they need exercise for their faculties and a field for their efforts as much as their brothers do; they suffer from too rigid a restraint, too absolute a

stagnation, precisely as men would suffer; and it is narrow-minded in their more privileged fellow-creatures to say that they ought to confine themselves to making puddings and knitting stockings, to playing on the piano and embroidering bags. It is thoughtless to condemn them, or laugh at them, if they seek to do more or learn more than custom has pronounced necessary for their sex. (93)

In claiming that women are like men in the strength of their feelings and their need for education, meaningful work, and self-determination, Brontë echoes Wollstonecraft; and she does so as well in linking women's private frustrations with the broader public injustices suffered by "millions" and "masses" of downtrodden industrial workers poised for rebellion. Jane's yearning for personal and intellectual freedom not only speaks for all women; she equates their shared cause, in dignity and world historical significance, with the broadest movements for social and economic justice. The child who saw herself as a rebel slave has grown into a woman who embraces revolutionary causes.

But the novel's feminist politics pivots at this point. Immediately following this passage Jane meets Rochester, and the narrative sequence implies that their romance will resolve her "discontent" privately, disconnecting Jane from public political movements as Brontë "displaces class conflict onto sexual relations" (Armstrong, *Desire and Domestic Fiction*, 200).[1] When reviews such as "W.'s" castigated the novel's "morality," they focused on the romantic plot, objecting to Jane's "vulgar" expressions of desire and her failure to "shun" Rochester's "wickedness." Likewise Oliphant assigns the novel's "wild declaration of the Rights of Woman" to Jane's outspoken "love-making" (Allott, *The Brontës*, 312) when, provoked by Rochester's pretense of being engaged to the obnoxious Blanche, Jane violates the most basic of Victorian gender rules:

> "I tell you I must go!" I retorted, roused to something like passion. "Do you think I can stay to become nothing to you? Do you think I am an automaton? – a machine without feelings? ... Do you think, because I am poor, obscure, plain, and little, I am soulless and heartless? You think wrong! – I have as much soul as you, – and full as much heart! And if God had gifted me with some beauty and much wealth, I should have made it as hard for you to leave me, as it is now for me to leave you. I am not talking to you now through the medium of custom, conventionalities, nor even of mortal flesh – it is my spirit that addresses your spirit; just as if both had passed through the grave, and we stood at God's feet, equal, – as we are!" (215–16)

Jane justifies declaring her love by declaring at the same time her equality with Rochester. But is this declaration, which echoes her earlier claim that "women feel just as men feel," as "revolutionary" as Rigby, "W.," and Oliphant fear? She is not calling for equal work or pay or political representation, or for liberation for the "masses": only for her own spiritual equality with the man she loves. Jane's equality claims retreat behind closed doors, bent to the service of the novel's socially conformist goal, the happy marriage with which it concludes.

Integral to Jane's rebellious thoughts prior to meeting Rochester is her habit of pacing back and forth in the very attic where Rochester's wife, Bertha, imprisoned for sexual unchastity, similarly paces and foments rebellion. Linked to slave rebellions in the Caribbean where she comes from, Bertha is (Jane will later learn) the "mystery that broke out, now in fire, now in blood, at the deadest hours of the night" (179) and that will eventually burn down the prison-house where, like Wollstonecraft's Maria, she has been "immured." As she paces and thinks her revolutionary thoughts, Jane hears Bertha's laugh, as if she and Bertha were conspiring together against the patriarchal rule that confines and oppresses both of them. Momentarily allied with Bertha in the attic of Thornfield, Jane subsequently becomes Bertha's enemy: Bertha will want Jane dead, and Jane's happiness will depend on the death of Bertha.

Virtually all second-wave feminist readings observe that Bertha functions not as a political subject in her own right but as an "aspect" of Jane's psychology, the "dark double" and "alter ego" (Showalter, *A Literature of Their Own*, 121; Gilbert and Gubar, *The Madwoman in the Attic*, 168; Rich, "*Jane Eyre*," 97) who embodies Jane's anger and her unruly sexual passion. Thus psychologized, Bertha is Brontë's brilliant device for turning the girl who identified as a "rebel slave" into a middle-class subject by embodying her revolutionary impulses in an alien being. When they meet, Jane does not even recognize Bertha as human:

> What it was, whether beast or human being, one could not, at first sight, tell: it groveled, seemingly, on all fours; it snatched and growled like some strange wild animal; but it was covered with clothing; and a quantity of dark, grizzled hair, wild as a mane, hid its head and face.

When Grace reports that her charge is "snappish, but not 'rageous,'" "a fierce cry seemed to give the lie to her favorable report: the clothed hyena rose up, and stood tall on its hind feet" (250). With this description, Brontë not only displaces Jane's nonconforming impulses onto a monstrous being; she also identifies them with Mary Wollstonecraft.

Wollstonecraft's *Vindication* recommends women restrain their sexual desires, but after her early death from complications of childbirth, the memoir of her husband, William Godwin, revealed all too much about her shocking private life, including that she had previously had a child with a man to whom she wasn't married. Her reputation suffered so badly that all ideas and causes connected with her became taboo (Eberle, *Chasity and Transgression in Women's Writing*, 55–75). This disparagement reflects not only social shaming of a woman's sexual freedom but also the anti-Jacobin turn in England in the late 1790s: at the end of a 1795 letter about the Reign of Terror, published in 1798, Horace Walpole called her "a hyena in petticoats." Brontë has Jane advocate Wollstonecraft's feminist vision of freedom and equality, but by transferring this famous slur from Wollstonecraft to Bertha, she also disavows that vision for its dangerous connection to sexual promiscuity.

The novel instead defines equality within the confines of an upper-class marriage. Following their initial engagement, Jane insists on continuing to work for pay, to right "the balance of power" (Spacks, *The Female Imagination*, 79) between them. Resisting Rochester's patronizing effort to load her with expensive clothes and jewels, Jane invokes the idea of slavery, but instead of identifying with the injustice of chattel slavery as she did as a child, or with wage slavery as she did as a younger adult, Jane now invokes the harem only to distance herself from it: "I thought his smile was such as a sultan might, in a blissful and fond moment, bestow on a slave his gold and gems had enriched" (229). Half joking, Jane invites Rochester to make "slave-purchases" at the "bazaars of Stamboul," since she refuses to assume this incongruous role herself, and she promises "to go out as a missionary to preach liberty to them that are enslaved – your harem inmates among the rest" (229–30). Just as Jane drops her momentary alliance with Bertha, she shifts from feeling like a "rebel slave" to defining her free individuality in contrast to harem "slaves."[2] In pursuit of personal equality with Rochester, she writes to her wealthy uncle in Madeira, thinking "I could better endure to be kept by [Rochester] now" if she might later inherit wealth of her own (229). This letter leads to the revelation of Bertha's existence, which, however painfully, saves Jane from marrying as Rochester's economic inferior and from compromising her self-respect. Jane again exchanges collective revolution for individual advancement when she inherits her uncle's 20,000 pounds and plans to share it with her three newly discovered cousins. When the skeptical St. John challenges her plan, she responds: "You, penniless! Famous equality and fraternization!" As Susan Meyer argues, Jane converts the language of the French Revolution – liberté, egalité, fraternité – from a celebration of the dignity of all human beings to the sign under which she will divide her fortune among four members of her own social class (Meyer, *The Female Imagination*, 86–7). The equality she seeks and attains with Rochester is a kind of feminism, but "it is not a feminism which can preach or envision radical social change" (Moglen, *Charlotte Brontë*, 134).

Of all the political positions the novel takes up, the one that became its most enduring legacy arose from its creation and popularization of the desiring, strong-willed female subject – the subject of liberal feminism (Armstrong, *Desire and Domestic Fiction*, 198–9). Oliphant's criticism in 1855 focuses less on *Jane Eyre* itself than on the many "followers and imitators" writing novels about "dangerous" Jane-like heroines who reject comparison to "angel" or "lily" and turn love into a "battle" (Allott, *The Brontës*, 313, 312). "The influence of *Jane Eyre* on Victorian heroines was felt to have been revolutionary," writes Showalter, quoting an 1858 article calling for an end to "the daughters direct of Miss Jane Eyre" (Showalter, *A Literature of Their Own*, 122–3). Patsy Stoneman observes, too, in the 1850s and 1860s, a fad for the "crippled hero," a rash of utopian marriages, and increasingly explicit "recognition of physical desire," as the novel of sensation and the New Woman novel selectively exaggerated Jane's original traits (Stoneman 21, 24). It is not far from the sexual explicitness that shocked Oliphant and offended "W." – "He seemed to devour me with his flaming glance: physically, I felt, at the moment, powerless as stubble exposed to the draught and glow of a furnace" (271) – to the deliberate bigamy of 1860s sensation heroines. These novels seem remote from nineteenth-century feminist movements for suffrage and social and economic justice; as Cora Kaplan points out, the liberal feminist "emphasis on the unified female subject will unintentionally reproduce the ideological values of mass-market romance" (Kaplan, "Pandora's Box," 147–8). Yet *Jane Eyre* and its popular successors helped to establish as a credible human type the woman who makes claims for herself and her desires – the woman who says "I."

The equality Jane attains is confined to the private space of marriage, and her success and happiness come at a high cost: the sacrifice of Bertha. But what does Bertha's death mean? The "clothed hyena" may be merely a fantastical figure onto whom Jane's antisocial rage and desire are projected so Jane can consolidate the socially acceptable "I" of liberal feminism. But if you read her as Jean Rhys does in her novel *Wide Sargasso Sea*, as an exploited and abused wife driven mad by imprisonment and mistreatment; or if you read her as does Gayatri Spivak, for whom Jane's triumph epitomizes Britain's oppressive imperial power; then this "cult text of feminism" (Spivak, "Three Women's Texts," 244) defines feminism as the rise of the middle-class white woman at the expense of the colonial Other. For Spivak the story's meaning is clear: not only is "the 'native female' … excluded from any share in this emerging norm," but also "the 'subject-construction' of the female individualist" depends on that exclusion (244–5). Brontë inherits and shares Wollstonecraft's practice of defining the potential virtue and self-respect of British middle-class women against the degraded, merely sensual women of the "oriental" harem. The vilification and sacrifice of Bertha encapsulates liberal feminism's most troubling legacy.

In 1852, preparing to write about her life under slavery, Harriet Jacobs wrote to her friend Amy Post that the prospect brought "painful remembrances" and that it would be easier to write "if it was the life of a Heroine with no degradation associated with it" (Jacobs, *Incidents in the Life of a Slave Girl*, 232). This wish reflects the cultural power, in the early 1850s, of *Jane Eyre: An Autobiography*, the most popular heroine novel in circulation. Jacobs intends to write her story in the first person, a practice authorized not only by men's slave narratives (most visibly Frederick Douglass's 1845 *Narrative*) but also by Brontë's bold innovation. Yet Jacobs cannot make her life conform to Brontë's kind of "Heroine" because, as a slave who did not own her own body, she could not act on Jane's most fundamental claim: "*I* care for myself." Jacobs's "degradation" locates her instead with the slaves and concubines from whom Jane distances herself as she rises into prosperity and marital happiness. In an act of great courage, Jacobs claims a speaking "I" for the silenced Other of liberal feminism. Measuring her life against that of a "Heroine," she finds herself lacking, then makes a revolutionary claim: because "the condition of a slave confuses all principles of morality, and, in fact, renders the practice of them impossible … the slave woman ought not to be judged by the same standard as others" (55–6).

Jane Eyre has continuously played a role in the development of nineteenth- and twentieth-century feminisms. *Incidents in the Life of a Slave Girl Written by Herself*, by contrast, had a delayed effect on the creation and circulation of feminist ideas. Noticed in antislavery circles when it appeared in 1861, it soon faded from public view because its aim was to advocate for abolition. Memory of her authorship faded as well (like Brontë, Jacobs used a pseudonym), so that scholars returning to slave narratives in the wake of the civil rights movement dismissed it as a work of fiction. In 1981 Jean Fagan Yellin authenticated Jacobs's authorship and decoded the pseudonyms, enabling *Incidents* to be taken seriously as a slave narrative (Yellin, "*Written by Herself*," Introduction).

Two overlapping strands of black feminist scholarship on *Incidents* then emerged. One focuses on its differences from men's slave narratives. Because "Linda Brent" defines herself by her family ties, she is not free until her children are too, unlike her brother and uncle who escape alone, their stories matching Douglass's model. Her escape "is not the classic story of the triumph of the individual will; rather it is more a story of a triumphant self-in-relation" (V. Smith, "'Loopholes of Retreat,'" 216–17). The other strand asks how her use of white-authored fictional paradigms, drawn from the female-dominated sentimental novel and from gothic fiction, aids and/or disables Jacobs's efforts to tell her story. Starting with Jacobs, "black women had to confront the dominant domestic ideologies and literary conventions of womanhood which excluded them from the definition 'woman'" (Carby, *Reconstructing Womanhood*, 6); for Valerie Smith, nineteenth-century literary conventions of womanhood are like the grandmother's attic in which Linda hides for seven years: both a resource and a prison.

Both scholarly projects are "intersectional," and the founders of black feminist literary criticism in the 1980s trace back to Jacobs their understanding that the experiences of black women are distinct from those of black men and white women. Mary Helen Washington captures what distinguishes Jacobs's work from dominant literary paradigms:

> This question of a woman's shame over her sexuality is central to our understanding of Brent's narrative; for, unlike male slave narrators who wrote to show that they had the qualities valued and respected by other men – courage, mobility, rationality, and physical strength – Harriet Jacobs wrote to confess that she did not have the qualities valued in white women. (Washington, *Invented Lives*, 4)

Critiquing traditional accounts of African American literary history as exclusively male, both Washington's *Invented Lives* and Joanne Braxton's study of black women's autobiographies construct alternative traditions that start with Jacobs. The first extended readings in Hazel Carby's *Reconstructing Womanhood* and in Claudia Tate's study of "the black heroine's text" are of *Incidents*. Yellin argues that Jacobs influenced Frances Harper's 1892 novel *Iola Leroy*, and, through Harper "the writings of Zora Neale Hurston and other foremothers of black women writing today" (Yellin, Introduction, xxix).

Jacobs not only originates black women's literary traditions; she is also a founding figure of black feminism, who initiates an "assertive ... discourse of black womanhood" (Carby, *Reconstructing Womanhood*, 184).

That Jacobs demonstrated, "long before the rise of the women's movement," that "slavery ... is far more terrible for women" makes her a forerunner of Angela Davis, and, because the creation of black autobiography prior to emancipation was in itself a political act, her courageous role in creating that genre makes her an important figure in African American political history (Cudjoe, "Maya Angelou," 273, 277). Sociologist Patricia Hill Collins's widely read *Black Feminist Thought* credits Jacobs with having first articulated such recurrent themes in black feminism as the construction of black women as sexually degraded and of black mothers as self-sacrificing (Collins, *Black Feminist Thought*, 81).

Readings of *Incidents* that explore its use of sentimental or gothic literary models sometimes note its allusions to *Jane Eyre*. Because of Linda's seven years in the attic – where at best she can crawl, Bertha-like, on all fours, her body damaged by her cramped position, insect bites, and illness – some cite Gilbert and Gubar to describe her as a "madwoman in the attic" with a difference: she is sane and she controls the story (Yellin, Introduction, xxxi, xxxiv; Braxton, *Black Women Writing Autobiography*, 26; Winter, *Subjects of Slavery*, 92). Tate hears the echo of *Jane Eyre*'s most famous line ("Reader, I married him") when Jacobs concludes, "Reader, my story ends with freedom; not in the usual way, with marriage" (Tate, *Domestic Allegories of Political Desire*, 32). Given *Jane Eyre*'s popularity and Jacobs's wide reading, it is likely she had read the novel or at least knew the story.[3] But what do these allusions mean? Jacobs addresses the most celebrated "Heroine" novel of her day in order not only to use its resources but also to speak back, from the point of view of the dark woman on whose sacrifice Jane's liberation depends, to the white feminism it founded. Both a fallen woman and a heroic figure of freedom, Jacobs creates the subject of black feminism by both identifying with and revising Jane and Bertha, both the white subject and the black Other of middle-class Anglo-American feminism.

Among Jacobs's allusions to *Jane Eyre* is a scene in which she turns the colonial relationship between Jane and Bertha on its head. Linda is fifteen and legally defenseless against the "perfidious" master who daily harasses her. His wife is furious with jealousy, blaming Linda rather than her husband; she lacks "control over her passions" and her "temper" bursts into "fire" and "flame" (Jacobs, *Incidents in the Life of a Slave Girl*, 34). In *Jane Eyre*, shortly before the interrupted wedding, Bertha invades Jane's bedroom. A large, dark woman with "a savage face ... red eyes and [a] fearful blackened inflation of the lineaments," this "Vampyre" briefly dresses in Jane's wedding veil, then rips it up. Jane faints when her "fiery eye" and "lurid visage" "flame" over her (242). In *Incidents*, Linda describes a closely parallel scene:

> Sometimes I woke up, and found her bending over me.... If she startled me, on such occasions, she would glide stealthily away.... At last I began to be fearful for my life. It had been often threatened; and you can imagine, better than I can describe, what an unpleasant sensation it must produce to wake up in the dead of night and find a jealous woman bending over you. (34)

The black slave Linda takes the role of Jane and gives her white mistress the role of mad Bertha. Using yet critiquing Brontë's scene, Jacobs refutes a central tenet of Jane's white, middle-class feminism: it is not the white, upwardly mobile woman who is in danger here, but rather the disempowered black slave.

Under constant threat of rape, Linda enters into a sexual relationship with a white man with whom she has two children. Alternatingly describing this action as "deliberate calculation" and "a plunge into the abyss," Jacobs both accepts and resists the sexual standards of her audience, "ye happy women, whose purity has been sheltered from childhood" (53–4). "I tried hard to preserve my self-respect": echoing yet reversing Jane's "the more I will respect myself," spoken at the moment of refusing to become Rochester's mistress, Jacobs shows that the maintenance of Jane's self-respect depends not just on personal self-discipline but on race-based legal protections from which Linda is barred.

Jacobs insists on the public meanings of her private story, and while narrating her personal tale she also turns her attention to slavery's widespread injustices. Chapters on local incidents of racialized violence alternate with chapters about her "plunge." Connecting her individual struggle with broader public aims by claiming "Give me liberty, or give me death" as her "motto" (Jacobs, *Incidents in the Life of Slave Girl*, 99; see S. Smith, *Conceived by Liberty*, 136, 143), Jacobs does not simply privatize her liberty as Jane does when referencing "liberté, egalité, fraternité." She drills a tiny "loophole" in her attic's outer wall through which she can hear news of friends and community and sometimes hear and see her children, who both inspire her with the "will" to get free and "fetter" her efforts (85, 93). Her attic sightlines contrast to Jane's broader yet less enduring attic vision: while Jane will soon abandon her common cause with the "masses," Linda's focus on her children – her refusal to free herself without them – stands for her effort to end slavery for all. When Jacobs concludes, "Reader, my story ends with freedom; not in the usual way, with marriage," she challenges Brontë on the missed promise of Jane's solidarity with the "masses." Jane's happy ending exchanges the revolutionary fervor of the young woman for the settled comfort of the wife. Linda's struggle to attain freedom is arduous and incomplete: the Fugitive Slave Act of 1850 made her and her children vulnerable to recapture, and gallingly, in order to become legally free, she must accept her purchase by her employer, Mrs Bruce. While Jane retreats with Rochester to the deep solitude of Ferndean, Linda ends her story still lacking a home of her own to share with her children. So her focus remains on emancipation. After the conclusion of her personal story she added a closing "tribute" to John Brown's raid on Harper's Ferry that her editor Lydia Maria Child cut: it could have transformed the book into a call for violent insurrection (C. Smith, "Harriet Jacobs among the Militants"). While generations of readers have found in *Jane Eyre* a satisfyingly full representation of a woman's voice, Jacobs had to settle for the muting of hers.

Just as Wollstonecraft and Brontë bequeath to later feminisms not only their great calls for equality and human dignity but also the liability of their imperial racial assumptions, Jacobs's exposure of the white middle-class bias of "Heroine" novels such as *Jane Eyre* helped to enable powerful critiques of liberal feminism by feminists of color starting in the 1970s. Norma Alarcón, for example, observes that the paradigmatic "subject of Anglo-American feminism is an autonomous, self-making, self-determining subject," a "speaking subject" who is "blinded" to "her own class-biased ethnocentrism" (Alarcón, "The Theoretical Subject(s)," 357, 364). Given the dominance of this paradigm, "the freedom of women of color to posit themselves as multiple-voiced subjects is constantly in peril" (364). Like Jacobs struggling to make herself heard through literary conventions of "womanhood" that depended on her degradation and enslavement, "the multiple-voiced subjectivity" of women of color "is lived in resistance to competing" claims on "one's allegiance or self-identification" (366). Adapting Jane's speaking subjectivity and Bertha's point of view to "recreat[e] herself as the subject of her own discourse" (Yellin, *Women and Sisters*, 96), Jacobs imagines ahead of its time the "multiple-voiced subjectivity" that would become the hallmark of feminisms of color.

WORKS CITED

Alarcón, Norma. "The Theoretical Subject(s) of *This Bridge Called My Back* and Anglo-American Feminism." In *Making Face, Making Soul*, edited by Gloria Anzaldúa, 356–69. San Francisco, CA: Aunt Lute, 1990.

Allott, Miriam, ed. *The Brontës: The Critical Heritage*. London: Routledge, 1974.

Armstrong, Nancy. *Desire and Domestic Fiction: A Political History of the Novel*. New York: Oxford University Press, 1987.

Azim, Firdous. *The Colonial Rise of the Novel*. London: Routledge, 1993.

Barker, Juliet. *The Brontës: A Life in Letters*. New York: Overlook Press, 1998.

Braxton, Joanne M. *Black Women Writing Autobiography: A Tradition within a Tradition*. Philadelphia, PA: Temple University Press, 1989.

Brontë, Charlotte. *Jane Eyre*, 3rd critical edition, edited by Richard J. Dunn. New York: Norton, 2001.

Carby, Hazel V. *Reconstructing Womanhood: The Emergence of the Afro-American Woman Novelist*. New York: Oxford University Press, 1987.

Collins, Patricia Hill. *Black Feminist Thought*. Boston, MA: Unwin Hyman, 1990.

Cudjoe, Selwyn R. "Maya Angelou: The Autobiographical Statement Updated." In *Reading Black, Reading Feminist*, edited by Henry Louis Gates Jr., 212–26. New York: Penguin, 1990.

Diedrick, James. "*Jane Eyre* and *A Vindication of the Rights of Woman*." In *Approaches to Teaching Jane Eyre*, edited by Diane Hoeveler and Beth Lau, 22–8. New York: Modern Language Association of America, 1993.

Eberle, Roxanne. *Chastity and Transgression in Women's Writing, 1792–1897*. New York: Palgrave, 2002.

Flint, Kate. *The Woman Reader 1837–1914*. Oxford: Oxford University Press, 1993.

Gates, Henry Louis Jr. Preface and introduction to *The Bondswoman's Narrative*, by Hannah Crafts. New York: Grand Central, 2003.

Gilbert, Sandra M. and Susan Gubar. *The Madwoman in the Attic: The Woman Writer and the Nineteenth-century Literary Imagination*. New Haven, CT: Yale University Press, 1979.

Jacobs, Harriet. *Incidents in the Life of a Slave Girl Written by Herself*, edited by Jean Fagan Yellin. Cambridge, MA: Harvard University Press, 1987.

Kaplan, Cora. "Pandora's Box: Subjectivity, Class, and Sexuality in Socialist Feminist Criticism." In *Making a Difference: Feminist Literary Criticism*, edited by Gayle Green and Coppelia Kahn, 146–76. London: Methuen, 1985.

Meyer, Susan. *Imperialism at Home: Race and Victorian Women's Fiction*. Ithaca, NY: Cornell University Press, 1996.

Miller, Lucasta. *The Brontë Myth*. New York: Knopf, 2003.

Moers, Ellen. *Literary Women: The Great Writers*. New York: Doubleday, 1977.

Moglen, Helene. *Charlotte Brontë: The Self Conceived*. New York: Norton, 1976.

Rich, Adrienne. "*Jane Eyre*: The Temptations of a Motherless Woman." In *On Lies, Secrets and Silence: Selected Prose 1966–1978*. New York: Norton, 1979.

Showalter, Elaine. *A Literature of Their Own: British Women Novelists from Brontë to Lessing*. Princeton, NJ: Princeton University Press, 1977.

Sicherman, Barbara. *Well-Read Lives: How Books Inspired a Generation of American Women*. Chapel Hill: University of North Carolina Press, 2010.

Smith, Caleb. "Harriet Jacobs among the Militants: Transformations in Abolition's Public Sphere, 1859–61." *American Literature* 84 (2012): 743–68.

Smith, Stephanie. *Conceived by Liberty: Maternal Figures and Nineteenth-century American Literature*. Ithaca, NY: Cornell University Press, 1994.

Smith, Valerie. "'Loopholes of Retreat:' Architecture and Ideology in Harriet Jacobs's *Incidents in the Life of a Slave Girl*." In *Reading Black, Reading Feminist*, edited by Henry Louis Gates Jr., 212–26. New York: Penguin, 1990.

Spacks, Patricia Meyer. *The Female Imagination*. New York: Knopf, 1975.

Spivak, Gayatri Chakravorty. "Three Women's Texts and a Critique of Imperialism." *Critical Inquiry* 12 (1985): 243–61.

Stanton, Elizabeth Cady, Susan B. Anthony, and Matilda Joslyn Gage. *History of Woman Suffrage, Volume 1: 1848–1861*. New York: Fowler and Wells, 1881.

Stoneman, Patsy. *Bronte Transformations: The Cultural Dissemination of Jane Eyre and Wuthering Heights*. New York: Prentice Hall, 1995.

Tate, Claudia. *Domestic Allegories of Political Desire: The Black Heroine's Text at the Turn of the Century*. New York: Oxford University Press, 1992.

Varley, Jane and Aimee Broe Erdman. "Working for Judith Shakespeare: A Study in Feminism." *Midwest Quarterly* 45 (2003): 266–81.

"W.," *Boston Daily Atlas*, March 24, 1848, issue 228, column G.

Washington, Mary Helen. *Invented Lives: Narratives of Black Women, 1860–1960*. New York: Doubleday, 1987.

Winter, Kari. *Subjects of Slavery, Agents of Change: Women and Power in Gothic Novels and Slave Narratives, 1790–1865*. Athens: University of Georgia Press, 1992.

Wollstonecraft, Mary. 3rd critical edition, edited by Deidre Shauna Lynch, *A Vindication of the Rights of Woman*. New York: Norton, 2009.

Yellin, Jean Fagan. "*Written by Herself:* Harriet Jacobs's Slave Narrative." *American Literature* 53 (1981): 479–86.

Introduction to *Incidents in the Life of a Slave Girl Written by Herself*, by Harriet Jacobs. Cambridge, MA: Harvard University Press, 1987.

Women and Sisters: The Antislavery Feminist in American Culture. New Haven, CT: Yale University Press, 1989.

CHAPTER 4

Progressive Portraits: Literature in Feminisms of Charlotte Perkins Gilman and Olive Schreiner

Judith A. Allen

Introduction

Olive Schreiner (1855–1920) and Charlotte Perkins Gilman (1860–1935) are often paired as the greatest feminist theorists of the fin de siècle.[1] Their acclaimed nonfiction feminist theory – Gilman's *Women and Economics* (1898) and Schreiner's *Woman and Labour* (1911) – emblematized Progressive advocacy and reform, while their influence, Anglophone and beyond, forged discursive adjacency between them.[2] Yet both also used fiction to advance feminist transformation, not so far subject to equivalent comparison. This chapter characterizes Schreiner and Gilman's fiction – their sequence, characteristics, and preoccupations – in two portraits of transnational feminist literary engagements with Progressive-era reform. If Schreiner and Gilman's feminist *non*fiction converged, comparison of their fiction is more complicated.[3] "Portraiture" – in the sense of "the action or technique of portraying a person, event, in speech or writing; graphic verbal description" – can assist accounts of Schreiner and Gilman's fiction depicting women's subordination and advancing emancipatory strategies.[4]

Schreiner's fiction addressed genealogies and workings of female subordination. She used non-realist allegories to portray internalized psychosexual dimensions of male dominance. Gilman, preoccupied with Reform Darwinist theories of the rise of androcentric culture in ancient human history, used literary forms for both diagnosis and portrayal of an imagined better world, one ameliorating or dispatching present sexualized oppressions, via Progressive-era technology, administration, and arbitration. A brief narrative of their widely reported similarities clarifies the place of fiction within their careers as feminist public intellectuals. An examination of significant instances of their fiction permits portrayal of its contribution to their feminism. A final matter is evidence for depictions of influence between these oft compared theorists.

"Similar Cases" or a Phase Apart?

Published when their authors were aged thirty-eight and fifty-six, respectively, *Women and Economics* (1898) and *Woman and Labour* (1911) emerged from their authors' diverse oeuvres. The consonance of their simultaneous work, continents apart, without mutual contact is striking.[5] Principally Schreiner was a creative fiction writer. With chronic illnesses obstructing hopes for sponsored medical training in London, her college principal brother's allowance and royalties from her early best-selling novel, *The Story of an African Farm* (1883), provided for her. She wrote two other novels, *Undine*, completed by 1876, and *From Man to Man*, probably begun by the later 1870s, last revised in 1911.[6] She also published a novella, short stories, and allegories from the later 1880s to the 1890s, when she returned from England to South Africa.[7] Thereafter, nonfiction featured in writings on South Africa, race, war, pacifism, and "the woman question."[8]

By contrast, Gilman treated fiction instrumentally. Her output was vast, her "artistic" revisions few, dismissive of "art of art's sake."[9] Great writing left her awe-struck, positive it was not her calling. Nonfiction was Gilman's most representative genre: more than two-thirds of her 2,157 publications. Lacking financial support until her second marriage, at age forty – and even then the winter coal bill could tax the household's modest resources – Gilman wrote books, articles, stories, and poems, edited, and lectured for a living.[10]

Gilman and Schreiner inhabited trans-regional reform movements, of many inflections, in which they shared friends. As feminist theorists, their asymmetrical "sexual contracts" of marriage and prostitution (as Carole Pateman defined them) epitomized "the woman question" ailing *industrial* societies.[11] Women's oppression caused species retardation through women's economic dependence (Gilman) or "sex parasitism" (Schreiner). Androcentric cultures suppressed female labor and enshrined warfare, intemperance, and prostitution as male entitlements, while double sexual standards restricted women's erotic options and institutionalized sex divisions and inequalities.[12] Industrial sexual relations impaired individual and social motherhood as well as female solidarity.[13]

Their lives bore striking similarities. Both had failed breadwinner fathers in cultures prescribing female economic dependence. Their disciplinarian mothers' gender norms ill-accommodated the necessity of paid female work. Their relatives included reformer ministers, educators, and writers – in Gilman's Beecher clan, Lyman Beecher, Henry Ward Beecher, Harriet

Beecher Stowe, and Isabella Beecher Hooker.[14] Autodidacts because their
families denied daughters university education, both sought instruction
from male relatives and friends. Prescribed lists included Spencer, Darwin,
Mill, and other theorists. Ruminations on race, eugenics, ethnicity, and
male dominance became central. Both jettisoned Protestantism.[15]

Their upbringing in Rhode Island and South Africa respectively
entailed close female friendships and male suitors, but also recurring illnesses: Schreiner had asthma and angina; Gilman fought serious depression. In addition to miscarriages, each had one daughter – Schreiner's
dying after an hour, Gilman relinquishing custody to her remarrying
ex-husband to permit self-support. Both entered middle age with younger husbands, and as committed socialists living under capitalism. Both
embraced pacifism and vegetarianism.[16] Arguably, both opposed Jim Crow
and racism.[17] Both held as paramount the women's movement of their
time, evident in speech and writing skewering anti-suffrage misogyny.[18]
Their feminist work, though, was not "in sync."

Their 1870s and 1880s were a phase apart. Schreiner's tumultuous youth
followed her father's bankruptcy and family disaggregation. Her residency
with siblings, then governess work, could not conceal her homelessness.
Romantically linked with businessman Julius Gau, who opposed her continued paid employment, their engagement suddenly ended: Gau soon
married a wealthy widow – scholars speculate about seduction, pregnancy,
and abortion.[19]

Schreiner moved to London to establish a writing career. Her first
novel, *Undine*, which she completed at age twenty-one, narrated its heroine's early experiences, including seduction, abortion, and prostitution,
then her sacrifice and death.[20] She gave Havelock Ellis the manuscript,
instructing him to burn it.[21] Alternatively, her 1883 novel, *The Story of
an African Farm*, was never out of print. Thereafter she wrote her third,
arguably most feminist novel.[22] *From Man to Man* explored two sisters'
experiences of sexual contracts: (adulterous) marriage and prostitution. It
mirrored intellectual and political dimensions of "the woman question,"
as framed in 1880s Britain. The Men's and Women's Club debated prostitution, the age of consent, infidelity, the double sexual standard, and sex
equality.[23] A dismayed Schreiner raged at male erotic privilege. She and
Karl Marx's daughter, Eleanor, protested at public demonstrations against
sexual trafficking and male supremacist resistance to raising the age of
consent from thirteen to sixteen. She excoriated Ellis and editor William
J. Stead for obtuseness on the implications of condoned prostitution for

all heterosexual relations, including marriage.[24] Meanwhile, Schreiner's living alone in lodgings, unmarried, gave rise to petty gossip, one land-lady evicting Schreiner because of male visitors, inferring prostitution. Schreiner befriended prostitutes testifying about male sexuality and the lived impact of the notorious Contagious Diseases Acts. Police targeted her, while she was walking home after dinner, simply for being in the street.[25]

Another project delayed Schreiner's revisions to *From Man to Man*. She attempted an introduction to a centenary reissue of Mary Wollstonecraft's *A Vindication of the Rights of Woman*. Dissatisfied with the essential factual and scientific elements, with "too many ideas," she told Ellis that, despite resistance, her text kept turning into allegories; for "only poetry is truth ... other forms are parts of truth, but as soon as a representation has all parts, then it is poetry. As soon as there is the form and the spirit, the passion and the thought, then there is poetry, or the living reality."[26] Carol Burdett interprets Schreiner's anxiety as about writing style; her attempted "cre-ative break" into "scientific" nonfiction, admired by "woman question" guru Karl Pearson, failed.[27] Soon after she left England.

In contrast with Schreiner's 1880s, the young Gilman tried commercial art, flirted with both sexes, became a gymnast, and in 1884 succumbed unhappily to marriage to an improvident artist. Although she tried to write, pregnancy and depression soon followed. She began to study "the woman question" via readings from her local library and family woman suffragists. Distress at the loss of a local woman suffrage referendum in spring 1887 preceded her month's repair to the famous Dr. Silas Weir Mitchell's Philadelphia "rest cure."[28] In California, she worked for nation-alist and socialist women's movements while penning the later famous short story "The Yellow Wall-Paper" and tried same-sex romance in vain.[29] With divorce final in 1894, she mournfully relinquished custody of her daughter, then travelled nationally and internationally, her U.S. base Jane Addams' Chicago settlement movement. Summoned to Washington, DC, by Susan B Anthony to address Congress on woman suffrage in 1895, she there met sociologist Lester Frank Ward, and soon guest edited the *American Fabian*.[30] An 1897 reunion with cousin George Houghton Gilman, Wall Street attorney, led to courtship, the writing of *Women and Economics* by 1898, and remarriage in 1900.[31]

If Gilman launched a career across the 1890s, changes for Schreiner kept their phases apart. In late 1886, Schreiner's departure from England included an emotional tsunami involving Karl Pearson.[32] She wrote the allegories so central in her oeuvre, *Dreams* (1890) and *Dream Life and*

Real Life, A Little African Story (1893). In 1894, just as Gilman divorced, Schreiner married fellow English South African farmer-politician Samuel Cronwright (who took her surname), only to have a deceased newborn, then several miscarriages. Initially, this limited her feminist advocacies, as did the couple's focus on triangulated South African politics, making her "foremost critic of British imperialism, ethnocentrism, and racism" – prophesizing both negative outcomes of war and "the South African Union's racist legislation and constitution."[33] She also explored military sexual abuse of African women in an 1897 satire, *Trooper Peter Halket of Mashonaland*, despite house arrest for much of the Boer Wars. British soldiers burned down her home, according to her, destroying a "woman question" book manuscript. She reconstructed enough for a two-part 1899 *Cosmopolitan* article, which led critics later to compare Gilman and Schreiner.[34] The South African situation absorbed Schreiner's 1900s, while illnesses limited both her writing and living.

By contrast, the fin de siècle and beyond quickened Gilman's feminist advocacies. *Women and Economics* began her run of five nonfiction treatises.[35] From 1909 until 1916 her writing altered, with her monthly journal, *The Forerunner*. She wrote chapter-length monthly installments of serialized novels, short stories, poems, plays, brief allegories, book reviews, and short notices, as well as further nonfiction treatise chapters.[36] The result was seven novels: *What Diantha Did* (1910), *Moving the Mountain* (1911), *Mag-Marjorie* (1912), *The Crux* (1913), *Benigna Machiavelli* (1914), *Herland* (1915), and *With Her in Ourland* (1916), the bulk of Gilman's total fiction output.[37] Ironically, her period of largest fiction publishing began just as Schreiner's commenced more significant nonfiction.

From 1908 onward, British suffragette militancy, inspired both in their own national suffrage struggles. Schreiner's timely *Woman and Labour* (1911) soon became the Bible of the British women's movement. Her angina led her to Europe for treatment in 1913, when Gilman attended the International Woman Suffrage conference in Budapest. Both defended militants against lies and misogyny, denounced violent hecklers, and anxiously monitored imprisoned and hunger-striking friends.[38]

Of Mountains and Fictions

Yet Schreiner and Gilman's fiction diverged. "I wish you could go once to my old African world," Schreiner wrote to Karl Pearson, "to stand quite alone on a mountain in the still blazing sunshine ... the great unbroken plains stretching away as far as you can see, without a trace of the human creature." Then, she concluded, "You would know how the one God was invented."[39]

Mountains pervaded Schreiner's writing – a benign, spatial trope, an epistemic revelation, and, with her asthma, a breathable space. She adopted an Olympian frame in a claimed instructional mission: the impact of writing was greater than organizational political work.[40] On her vast fictional canvas, agency battled fates, cast in gendered and racialized terms. Here she featured exiled fallen women, abused live-in minority servants, biracial infants, miscarriages, stillborns, dead children, and a double sexual standard generating prostitutes and prostitution in its wake. Her retrospective and autobiographical fiction captured, for Edward Carpenter, her "ineradicable pessimism," grounded in unrealized maternity, political crisis, and marital estrangement.[41] With Undine's deception, abandonment, and self-sacrifice in her first novel, and Lyndall's romantic defeat, betrayal, and death in *The Story of an African Farm* (1883), critics cast Schreiner's fiction as stronger in diagnosis of sexual politics problems, or in the limits and "contradictions of available discourses of masculinity and femininity," than in depicting their "successful transformation." Her fiction proclaimed "the futility of a rebel's quest for self-realization within an arbitrary cosmos and within a colonial society riddled with race, class, and gender inequality."[42] If in her nonfiction Schreiner extolled work toward the "far, far future," Louise Green observes a vast gap between her programmatic vision and any attempted literary embodiments. Literary critic Cherry Clayton too portrays Schreiner's fiction as cluttered with mysteriously failed courtships, thwarted reproduction, betrayals of love and duties, and secret intimate lives with hidden traumas, intuited rather than narrated – mainly enacted against harsh, inhospitable farms/territories/borderlands. Even the imagined English countryside of "Greenwood" proved no kinder to her benighted heroines.[43]

Such assessments may underestimate the transgressive impact of her portraits of infidelity and betrayal. In *From Man to Man*, Rebekah's discovery of her husband Frank's affair with their Kaffir maid was electrifyingly suspenseful. One night, desiring to hold him, she found his bed empty. Brilliant moonlight illuminated him crossing the courtyard to the servants' quarters, to rap the shutter of a maid lately withdrawn and contemptuous toward Rebekah. Later, Rebekah chronicled his opportunistic adulteries in an excruciatingly bald letter. Instead of paying prostitutes, like his friends, he invested in dispatch of unwelcome offspring.[44] Rebekah's wearily and remorselessly detailed insights on seduction, prostitution, and adultery, by the last third of the novel, as Anne McClintock observes, ventriloquized Schreiner.[45]

Similarly, the political power of her allegories cannot be overestimated. This genre shadowed her Wollstonecraft project, revealing Schreiner's 1880s absorption in anthropological studies of patriarchy. Hence, her famous paragraphs on the origins of women's oppression:

> "Why does she lie here motionless with the sand piled round her?" And he answered, "Listen, I will tell you! Ages and ages long she has lain here, and the wind has blown over her. The oldest, oldest, oldest man living has never seen her move: the oldest, oldest book records that she lay here then, as she lies here now, with the sand about her. But listen! Older than the oldest book, older than the oldest recorded memory of man, on the Rocks of Language, on the hard-baked clay of Ancient Customs, now crumbling to decay, are found the marks of her footsteps! ..." And I said, "Why does she lie there now?" And he said, "I take it, ages ago the Age-of-dominion-of-muscular-force found her, and when she stooped low to give suck to her young, and her back was broad, he put his burden of subjection on to it, and tied it on with the broad band of Inevitable Necessity. Then she looked at the earth and the sky, and knew there was no hope for her; and she lay down on the sand with the burden she could not loosen. Ever since she has lain here. And the ages have come, and the ages have gone, but the band of Inevitable Necessity has not been cut."[46]

Her theme: the historicity of women's subordination, the use of reproduction and motherhood to immobilize them, but not necessarily. This inspired Gilman's further genealogical analysis of sex differentiation via Lester Ward's theories of gynocentric and androcentric cultures. She and her 1890s Californian friends sewed at night, reading Schreiner aloud.

> The air ships did make a difference. To look down on the flowing outspread miles beneath gave a sense of the unity and continuous beauty of our country, quite different from the streak views we used to get. An air ship is a moving mountain top. The cities were even more strikingly beautiful.
> – Charlotte Perkins Gilman, *Moving the Mountain* (1911), 191–2

Mountains also figured in Gilman's fiction. Epistemologically, height offered enlarged vision. She gleefully awaited civil aviation.[47] Her nonfiction undertook diagnosis and explanation. Fiction canvassed solutions. Even fixed mores – such as male demand for prostitution – could become unacceptable, she claimed, within thirty years.[48] Characterized as the "optimist reformer," unapologetically didactic, she called her poetry book (*In this Our World*) "a tool box. It was written to drive nails with."[49]

Paradoxically, Schreiner's focus was fiction. The novel her genre, she attempted only three, with just one published in her lifetime. By contrast, Gilman, who privileged nonfiction, produced vastly more, and more diverse, fiction than Schreiner's entire oeuvre. Gilman's fiction deployed dialog and arithmetic toward sexual/political confrontations. In *What Diantha Did* (1910), twenty-one-year-old Diantha Bell departed her failed breadwinner father's home to become a business entrepreneur, despite his angry appeal to filial obligations and financial debts to him. Her estimate of his costs to date was: $3,600.00. She offset it with hers, for labor, services, housekeeping, nursing, and home maintenance, at $4,147.00. Her father owed her an advance of $547.00. She quit New England for sunlit Orchardina, California, soon assembling investors, whose lives Bell revolutionized by reconfiguration of marketing, meal provision, cleaning, and childcare: higher-quality outcomes at a fraction of the cost.[50] Then Bell met demand for high-quality non-domestic catering, particularly from working and immigrant laborers without families. As well, employment with Bell freed girl servants from secret sexual exploitation, her mention of which angered a local women's club. The young stranger in employers' homes lacked neither "the freedom nor the privileges of a home," a peculiarly "defenseless position," which furnishes "a terrible percentage of the unfortunate."[51]

Gilman shared Schreiner's concern with prostitutes and prostitution. Her somber venereal diseases novel, *The Crux* (1911), coincided with nationwide inquiries. New Englander Vivian Lane lost contact with expelled ex-suitor Morton Elder. Re-encountering him in a Denver boarding house, she accepted his marriage proposal, despite disquiet at his coarse approach to women, with "an air of long usage." Her friend and co-resident, Dr. Bellair, was sterile from a syphilitic ex-husband. Jeanne, the cook, an ex-madam (who was "trying to have private life," but "private life won't quite have her"), had a son, crippled because of disease. Jeanne insisted that Dr. Bellair intervene because two of her prostitutes became infected after being with Elder. Meanwhile, Dr. Hale, a misogynist "clap doctor," treated Elder, but refused Dr. Bellair's urging that he inform Lane when she guessed Elder's condition. The period's compulsory notification controversy ended in Bellair telling Lane their engagement was off.[52]

Other stories highlighted hereditary birth defects, "pimping," and trafficking, while "Cleaning up Elita" (1916) squarely addressed men and demand.[53] With a visiting sociologist's lecture, town fathers arrested all prostitutes. Fine, said the visitor, but what will you do about your immoral men? Consternation greeted the visitor's large estimates of the number of townsmen, including husbands, keeping that number of women alive via demand. Clients vastly outnumbered any group of working women. Eliminating demand via various disincentives would be progress because, without demand, there would be no prostitution.[54]

Recruitment met another Gilman solution. In "Turned" (1911), Mr. Marroner returned home from a business trip to find Gerta, the servant he had secretly impregnated, and his wife gone. A year's search located them; his wife resumed her academic career and maiden name, sharing a home with Gerta and the baby. On their doorstep, the story's final words were: "What do you have to say to us?"[55] Such resolutions recur in Gilman's fictions, possibly inspired by others she and Schreiner admired, like Anglo-American Elizabeth Robins, in whose novel *The Convert* (1907) female solidarity ends the double standard, again, against a seducer with an abortion intimated. Gilman's novel *Mag-Marjorie* (1912), had Mag, the servant, abandoned by a doctor at her aunt's boarding house. Miss Yale, an older friend of the family, placed her in a Swiss medical school after baby Dorothy's birth, lovingly cared for until "Marjorie" (Mag) returned as working mother. Predictably transfixed with the now polished Marjorie, she dispatched the seducer with contempt to marry a fellow medical researcher.[56]

Although many critics see the utopian novel *Herland* as the key Gilman novel, arguably the most developed vision of the world she created was *Moving the Mountain*. Serialized in 1911, it was a Rip Van Winkle story. A traveler, injured in Tibet in 1910, waking from his coma in 1940, returned to Manhattan with his sister, a college president, who was agog at the transformation. His descriptions provided her detailed account of complete severance between domestic work, gender norms, and sexualities. Enhanced prestige and compensation attached to work such as cleaning, cooking, childcare, teaching, food inspection, and agricultural labor performed by men and women. Parasitic and exploitative professions subsided – advertising, tabloid journalism, prostitution, branches of law, and more. All adults had their own apartments; spouses had different surnames; no pollution remained; all could fly in the "moving mountains" – the airships.

"I Have So Long Reverenced Her?"

During long periods of itinerancy, Gilman always traveled with *Leaves of Grass* and *Dreams*. She keenly followed news of Schreiner's doings.[57] She explained to her daughter Katharine that Schreiner lost her

handwritten manuscript on "the woman question" due to wartime fire.[58]
With Schreiner's first 1899 "The Woman Question" article, Gilman
wrote urging her fiancé, George Houghton Gilman, to read it. Although
their approaches were consonant she called for no acknowledgment by
Schreiner. Instead, she described Schreiner's work here as "fine," praising
her great power as a writer. Then she added: "I don't see that she is saying
more than I do. But she says it splendidly and it 'carries' far and wide."[59]
Later, she added: "Do you see what an international force Olive Schreiner
Cronwright is becoming? Isn't it fine. It gives me great hope and high
ambition. 'O May I join that choir invisible ...'"[60]

Scholars rightly stress the transatlantic reach of these feminist and
reform discourses. Claims that Gilman was unknown to Schreiner may
need revision. In 1900, Gilman told Houghton of a friend of Schreiner's
writing her "that Olive Schreiner knows and admires my book – thinks it
the book. I am proud: I have so long and deeply reverenced her."[61]

The extent of Schreiner's "the woman question" manuscript by 1899 is
unclear. Her husband later told Ellis that he doubted it. With her previous unsuccessful nonfiction, it seemed unlikely.[62] Arguably though,
Cronwright's dismissal here underestimated the impact on his well-read
spouse of the "woman question" texts of the fin de siècle, perhaps including Gilman's. Inviting transatlantic work, theoretical writings on sex
oppression widely debated between 1890 and 1910, meant that *Woman
and Labour* had plenty of admirable predecessors and peers, so much so
that 1910s and interwar anti-feminists corralled them together in equally
transatlantic denunciations.[63]

War demoralized the maritally estranged Schreiner, her pacifism alienating intimates. Yet war also detained her in London until 1919.[64] A year
later she was dead. Like admirers worldwide, Gilman grieved, while
Schreiner's widower's aggressive appropriation of her letters and manuscripts, including extensive destruction, evoked widespread disgust.[65]
An incomplete letter to Gilman on a photo of Schreiner's re-burial on a
beloved mountain in 1921 deplored Cronwright's booted foot on her cof-
fin in the center, holding a baby: "The man is almost inconceivable. Yet
Olive Schreiner loved him. I think she was constantly mistaken in individuals, though rarely on human life."[66]

In 1930, Gilman received a surprising mention of Schreiner. Psychologist
and cultural critic Samuel D. Schmalhausen invited her to contribute a
chapter to an anthology, *Woman's Coming of Age*, because she was "the first
sociologist in America to discuss adequately women's parasitic psychology (under our social system, following the illuminating work of Olive

Schreiner)." No doubt her deep admiration for Schreiner tempered her response:

> My "Women and Economics" was published in 1898; Olive Schreiner's "Woman and Labor" after the Boer War. She was one of the greatest women of the age, far greater than I in literary power, but unless you refer to the suggestions in "The Story of An African Farm" and the far reaching vision of her "Dreams," my work on the economic dependence of women and its results antecedes hers.[67]

Yet, in a final tribute to one "so long reverenced," Gilman entitled her chapter in Schmalhausen's anthology "Parasitism and Civilized Vice."[68]

In 1932, Gilman gave a glimpse of her opinion of Schreiner's *Woman and Labour*. A friend of daughter Katharine held Gilman's work greater than Schreiner's. Gilman replied:

> If Miss Buchanan meant that my *W. & E.* was superior to Olive Schreiner's "Woman and Labor," I think she was right. But that was only on[e] reconstructed from a greater book on women O.S. had been years in writing & which the British soldiers destroyed. I think Olive Schreiner's "Dreams" are incomparably great. Such vast reach of thought with such perfect, beautiful, and exquisitely concentrated expression I know of nowhere else.[69]

Schreiner's knowledge of Gilman remains unclear, given gaps produced in the evidence. If the unnamed English friend in California's 1900 report is true, Schreiner did indeed know and admire Gilman's work. Constant illness made reading often all Schreiner could do. Possibly she read reviews of *Women and Economics*, or other profiles of Gilman, her correspondence documenting her familiarity with literary and cultural matters wherever she resided. Moreover, she knew of Gilman's Beecher clan, fictional characters for instance, casually mentioning grand-great uncle Rev. Henry Ward Beecher's last great sermon. Schreiner observed the limitations of whites, like herself and Harriet Beecher Stowe, writing about race, compared to the insights in W.E.B. Du Bois' works.[70] With press reports of Gilman's lecture tours, her poetry reprinted, her scandalous divorce probed, and her personality profiled, Schreiner was likely aware of Gilman's presence and advocacies, as debated across the latter 1890s, 1900s, and 1910s.[71] With Gilman's 1890s and 1910s international lecture tours, reviews of her books, and shared friends, it seems unlikely that Schreiner's two 1899 *Cosmopolitan* articles, "The Woman Question," and *Woman and Labour* (1911) were written with her being oblivious to Gilman's comparable work.

More plausibly, they operated as mutually intertwined influences on each other across two or more decades. Just as the young Gilman drew inspiration on her path as analyst of sexual relations from Schreiner's brilliant fiction – her 1883 novel and 1890s allegories – perhaps the middle-aged Schreiner drew inspiration from Gilman's nonfiction achievements, especially when contemplating the South African situation. Perhaps, also, Gilman's fictional table-turning solutions to instances of sex oppression influenced Schreiner.[72] In a Gilmanesque touch, Schreiner concluded this final revision of *From Man to Man* with Rebekah separated from her philandering husband, on her own farm, and his child of their Kaffir servant raised as sister to her several sons. Hence, Rebekah resembled many a Gilman older heroine. If confirmations are ruled out, resemblances certainly seem striking.

Conclusion

This chapter has compared Schreiner's and Gilman's different uses of fiction as contributions to feminist discourse. The comparison suggests the need to characterize core elements of feminism between 1880 and 1920 as considerably less bounded by "nation," and more convergent upon transculturally shared sexual politics concerns and activism, than revealed in one-nation studies.

That an English South African and a Connecticut Yankee could be hallmarks for Western feminist theorists is remarkable. It attests to the trans-regionalism of late Victorian and Edwardian or Progressive-era sexual conflicts and cultures, with the ready intelligibility of causes and campaigns across national borders. Striking was their intense concern with the interconnected domestic genesis of "seduction" and erotic deception or betrayal and sexual exploitation. The intricacies of the sexual double standard in morality and elsewhere, the routine problem of unwelcome pregnancies, with attendant appalling options, and the recruitment of women and girls to prostitution fired the imaginations of both.

Meanwhile, they both resisted the alleged ineradicability of male demand. Both dissected its modes of discursive legitimization and naturalization, powerfully demonstrating its costs for the majority of the population, women and their children. Through fiction they sought to make both men and women see, from above and in the largest framing possible, the vast cost to all of this particular form of male supremacism, and to imagine worlds free of it.

CHAPTER 5

Feminist Poetics: First-Wave Feminism, Theory, and Modernist Women Poets

Linda A. Kinnahan

The term *poetics* suggests an inherent, historical affiliation between poetry and theory, beginning with Aristotle's treatise on lyric poetry, epic poetry, and drama, in which "poetics" translates as "making." More broadly in contemporary usage, "poetics" denotes a theorizing of discursive forms and structures including but going beyond poetry (such as a visual poetics, or a poetics of war, etc.). Nonetheless, the concept of *poetics* carries the traces of poetry's distinguishing quality as a genre – its concentrated, intensified meditation on operations, structures, forms, and organizations of language. In the current field of poetry studies, the concept of poetics challenges a division between *theory* and *poetry* most acutely in arguing that the "formal features of poems" – the distinctive uses of poetic structures, language, figuration, spatial and linear arrangement, rhythm, and so forth – is "sedimented" by and through socio-historically engendered "debates, discourses, and relationships" (DuPlessis, *Genders, Races, and Religious Cultures in Modern American Poetry*, 13) that are "inscribed in poetic texture" (DuPlessis, *Genders, Races, and Religious Cultures in Modern American Poetry*, 30). In other words, while thematic and content-driven expressions within a poetic text can – and often do – register a conceptually discursive affiliation with theory, the poetic architecture and linguistic performance of a poem offer potent sites engaging theoretical investigation.

A *poetics of poetry* reveals and examines *how* meaning is made through the medium of language, its sociocultural operations, and its capacity to shape apprehensions of reality. Rather than merely serving as "an odd delivery system for ideas and themes," poetry's "conventions and textual mechanisms, its surfaces and layers" (DuPlessis, *Genders, Races, and Religious Cultures in Modern American Poetry*, 7) actively theorize. This theorizing function of poetry emerges, in part, from multiple formal strategies, including both the innovative (or "new") use of poetic materials and the revision or interrogation of traditional verse materials.

So what might we mean by a *feminist poetics*? Variously and across a long history, feminist poetic projects have done cultural work on many levels and through many layers, launching protests and social critiques; recording women's lives and breaking silences; expressing, multiplying, and exploding notions of identity; challenging gender and other normative codes; and seeking to re-signify, reexamine, and revise women's lives, bodies, experiences, and languages as they have been prescribed by male-centered worldviews. What we can now term *feminist poetics* has existed at least since Sappho, whose fragments of lyric expression powerfully express bodily desire and emotional passion with a woman-identified voice. In moving to the beginning of the twentieth century, however, the relationship between feminism and poetics enters a newly conscious moment ushered in by a sociopoliticized lexicon newly identified as "feminist." The popular use of the term *feministe* beginning in late nineteenth-century France and migrating as *feminist* to England and America by the first decade of the twentieth century signaled a shift from the "Woman Movement" – advocating equality with men within systems organized around and for men – to the "Feminist Movement," which introduced a more radical set of demands to dismantle economic, social, religious, and cultural institutions enforcing women's oppression and inferiority.[1] This historical moment comprising the sociopolitical phenomenon now known as first-wave feminism fostered heightened consciousness about gender as a social construction. As the "women's question" forcefully collided with modernity, "feminism" became a named and voiced concept urging a pronounced reconsideration of systems of power enforcing dominant gender ideologies.

The conjunctions of poetry, theory, and feminism arising in this First Wave of (Western) feminism play out in complex interactions between the formal, thematic, and topical dimensions of poetic texts. Not only in their content but importantly, for this chapter, in their formal, structural, and linguistic architectures, poems perform and activate feminist; poems also produce theory, often through interacting with ideas and new theories current to the moment. The writers to be discussed and the poetry they produced during the first three decades of the twentieth century exemplify how "social materials (both specific and general politics, attitudes, subjectivities, ideologies, discourses, debates) are activated and situated within the deepest texture of, the sharpest specificities of, the poetic text" (DuPlessis, *Genders, Races, and Religious Cultures in Modern American Poetry*, 12); their investigations of verse form, in particular, bring into being a poetics of theory, poetry, and feminism registered in the very materials and structures marking, while innovatively expanding, the genre of poetry and the "gender-laden complex of associations" operating across the "terrain of established poetic genres" (Keller and Miller, *Feminist Measures*, 11). Thus, the prose poem, the lyric, the sonnet, the catalog poem – all and more become modes of theoretical investigation through the apprehension and exploration of poetic form. Gertrude Stein's radical genre work with the prose poem and Mina Loy's experimental lyrics occasion a linguistic dismantling of gender conventions, breaking the structures of language to crack open decidedly phallocentric signifying systems. Lola Ridge adopts traditional forms to deconstruct their gender, race, and class ideologies, while African American women like Helene Johnson, Georgia Douglas Johnson, and others associated with the Harlem Renaissance deploy Western tradition's most heightened forms to theorize black female identity.

Gertrude Stein began writing *Tender Buttons* as she settled into Parisian life with her lifelong companion, Alice B. Toklas, hosted salons, collected modern art by Cézanne, Matisse, Picasso, and others, and discussed concepts of the "modern composition" with Picasso as he painted her portrait. Breaking and reassembling language structures, and often considered a Cubist experiment in language, *Tender Buttons* inherits and revises the prose poem form practiced by nineteenth-century French Symbolist poets like Mallarmé or Baudelaire. Organized within three sections entitled *Objects*, *Food*, and *Rooms*, the prose-poem pieces range in length from one sentence to multiple pages but most typically sit on the page as small titled blocks of several sentences. As prose-poems, they adopt the rhythmic, aural, and image-intensive qualities of poetry while foregoing the strictures of versification. A revolt against metric verse forms, the nineteenth-century prose poem asserted itself as poetry, adopting the semantic, figurative, and musical distinctions of poetry while confounding rigid genre boundaries to create a new, modern form. Stein further revises the form to reverse its typical male perspective – as the *flâneur* strolling through and observing urban streets, or the social rebel and deviant – to instead claim domestic space as her subject matter while transforming the heterosexualized and privatized assumptions of that feminized space. The text challenges the domestic's gendered associations with traditional models of womanhood in multiple ways, including a subversive expression of lesbian life and desire alongside a bisecting of the private with colliding, collaged discourses of public spaces and systems (such as economics), generated by and within a prose poetics of linguistic disruption, fragmentation, and radical parataxis.

Foregrounding the "individual word" through removing it from conventional grammatical or syntactical structures and habitual meanings, *Tender Buttons* plays with the linguistic sign precisely to unsettle the ideologies of gender informing patriarchal culture. Her interest in the word as sign resonates with linguistic theories developing at the time, suggesting the circulation of ideas most prominently explored by Ferdinand Saussure in lectures and writing at the time of Stein's initial move to Paris. Whether or not Stein was familiar with Saussure's particular theories, her training in psychology and medicine, along with the general atmosphere in Paris intellectual circles she encountered upon her move there in 1903, would have prepared her to question any account of language as a transparent medium conveying a singular truth. As she would state in a 1936 lecture, "words had lost their value in the Nineteenth Century, particularly towards the end, they had lost much of their variety, and I felt that I could not go on, that I had to recapture the value of the individual word" ("What Are Master-pieces," 84).

Stein's feminist work with language defies rules of logic and grammar and rearranges words from their customary functions, foregrounding the role of language in shaping perceptions of feminized spaces and hetero-feminized identity. The opening prose-poem, "A Carafe, That Is a Blind Glass," calls attention to systems of ordering as though to announce a textual "difference":

> A kind in glass and a cousin, a spectacle and nothing strange a single hurt color and an arrangement in a system to pointing. All this and not ordinary, not unordered in not resembling. The difference is spreading. (11)

The refusal to use language as a way of "resembling" the external world prompts commentary on linguistic systems, such as a "lamp is not the only sign of glass" (17), or the relation of word function and syntactical structure to meaning, as in "Vegetable": "What is cut. What is cut by it. What is cut by it in" (53).

Most often, though, the processes of breaking and reconstructing grammar produce wildly associational passages generated not by expected logic but by sound, repetition, and wordplay, such as in "A Box": "Out of kindness comes redness and out of rudeness comes rapid same question, out of an eye comes research, out of selection comes painful cattle" (13). Imagining language like the Cubist paintings she collected, which challenged mimesis through stressing the compositional act and the materiality of paint and canvas, the prose-poems break and reassemble the image of the referent. Stein's pieces often take on familiar titles ("An Umbrella"; "Roastbeef"; "A Table") that reference the domestic, while enacting an extreme defamiliarization. In reading language that breaks and reassembles the apparatus of the sentence and the function of grammatical structures, one experiences words as material and non-transparent. Their meaning-making capacity is multiplied through contextual relations between words, linguistically refusing the notion of the singular word as fixed in meaning or referent, insisting on context and linguistic relations that multiply and unsettle meaning.[2]

Revealing the word as sign, the text becomes a poetic site to play out Saussure's claim to an arbitrary relation between signifier (or phonic, graphic qualities) and signified (or mental concept stimulated by the signifier), while suggesting the role of language in constituting the world. Stein's feminist contribution insists on language's relation to gendered orderings. The words and topics circulating within *Tender Buttons* evoke explicitly feminine cultural associations of space, body, activity, and selfhood. Drawing on a domestic lexicon of sewing, cooking, housekeeping, and the like, the prose poems undo the customary connotations of such words, exploring how particularly gendered systems of language are regulated by social contexts or groups; indeed, such processes evoke Saussure's notion of *langue*, or the system of language controlled by the group, to reveal language's ideological constitution and enforcement of meaning. Alternatively, the aural and oral play stimulated by Stein's homonymic and pun-laden inscriptions is readily revealed through speaking the text rather than reading it silently. The oral speech act, termed *parole* by Saussure and attributed with individual agency rather than regulated by the group, is encouraged by Stein's language play, interrupting the written text to posit ruptures in patriarchal linguistic constructions of woman, femininity, and gender. In "A Long Dress," for example, the "current" of fashion is a "machinery" that "presents a long line and a necessary waist." Asking "What is this current," the piece evokes both "waist" and "waste," as *parole* (or the oral speech act) interferes with the written text to comment on the display of women's bodies as a primary mode of attaining cultural value in the position of womanhood – and therefore, a waste.

One might also think here of the analysis of "conspicuous consumption" that Thorstein Veblen developed, joining feminist voices at this time in critiquing the adorned display of women's bodies (through fashion, jewelry, etc.) as evidence of male pecuniary and consumer power. Charlotte

Perkins Gilman also viewed women's self-adornment as a taught mechanism for gaining a husband in the marriage market, leading to what she called the "oversexed woman," the woman objectified by and valued for her appearance. Emma Goldman's anarchist-socialist attacks on marriage, domestic labor, and the economics of housework also stand corollary to Stein's interrogation of the ideological construct of domestic space and female selfhood. Bringing a radically feminist approach to the economic analysis of capitalism buoying socialist activism in Europe and America, Goldman argued on the lecture circuit and in essays that the tyranny of patriarchal marriage hindered female sexual identity, collapsing the roles of wife and prostitute in sharing an economic function to serve men's needs. Goldman's economic view of marriage postulated the wife's body as "capital to be exploited and manipulated," thus causing the wife to "look on success as the size of her husband's income" (Drinnon, *Rebel in Paradise*, 149–50). The female wage earner, moreover, was placed in the position of economic prostitution within the capitalist system. Stein's poetic and linguistic attention to economies of value and waste in *Tender Buttons* echoes and performs perspectives akin to Goldman's discursive ideas on gender, economic exchange, and sexual commodification.

Mina Loy, a British subject who became an American citizen, and an early reader of Stein, responded to these ideas in poems appearing in American and European avant-garde little magazines also publishing Stein in the 1910s. Even before her first move to New York in 1916, Loy's reading of American feminism found it refreshingly less prudish than in Britain. Living in Florence in the early 1910s, Loy corresponded with good friends Mabel Dodge and Carl van Vechten, both conversant with strands of feminist thought active in Greenwich Village. Dodge took part in the feminist group Heterodoxy, which brought together women intellectuals, writers, and artists, including women entering the professions of law, medicine, and education, and met regularly in the Village to discuss ideas about women. The group included Gilman, whose 1898 *Women and Economics* promoted economic gender theories that also infuse her poetry, fiction, and journalistic writings through the 1910s.

The circuit of ideas coming from Loy's American friends and her European fellow artists, like Stein, informs Loy's early experiments in lyric form and subject matter in poems like "Parturition," "The Effectual Marriage," "Virgins Plus Curtains Minus Dots," and the long-poem sequence "Songs to Joannes." While the love lyric was considered the appropriate realm for women poets at the time, Loy torques poetic traditions of versification and diction in critiquing romantic ideology. Taking

on topics considered scandalous for poetry in general and for poetry
by a woman in particular, Loy introduces language and imagery with
graphic associations to bodily processes of childbirth – in "Parturition,"
the speaker is in labor and describes the "foam on the stretched muscles
of a mouth" and the "infinitesimal motion" of "Warmth" and "moisture"
against her thighs as the baby arrives (5, 6) – or lovemaking – in "Songs
to Joannes," the "mucous-membrane" and the "skin-sack" of genitals
introduce the long poem's challenge to the "erotic garbage" of culture's
promotion of fairy tale notions of romance that encourage women to be
dependent and needy (53). Poetry's customary attention to concrete, sensual detail is worked to a high pitch in such poems, conveying a visceral
apprehension of the female body and the sex function.[3]

Loy's language, revolutionary in its anti-poetic crossing of clinical, philosophical, mystical, scientific, and slang discourses, rides on lines abruptly
broken and collaged with rapidly juxtaposed images, or riddled with
white spaces that signify unspoken silences. In "The Effectual Marriage,"
a parody of the Italian Futurism art movement (and its infamous misogyny) and of her own relationship with Futurist Giovanni Papini, the
couple named Gina and Miovanni exist in a home divided by sexual ideologies privileging men as thinkers and makers of culture. Gina stays in
the kitchen, where "Pots and Pans   she cooked in them,"
and "he so kindly kept her." The white space hovers within the line, visu-
ally interrupting the naturalized equation of women and domestic work.
For Loy, the space around words contextualizes meaning, suggesting (and
showing) the incapacity of language to assume a full presence or stability
of meaning. The white spaces within her poetic texts promote a multiplicity of meaning while also conveying, in a graphic interruption of the
written text, the silences surrounding women's lives and their scripted narrative. Collaboration of visual and verbal techniques underlies the poem's
theorization about "Gina being a female," for she is "more than that":

> Being an incipience   a correlative
> an instigation of the reaction of man

Positioned as the "correlative" to man who mirrors his identity to him, the
"female" ranges in the Western cultural imagination from "the palpable to
the transcendent," from the body biologically tied to nature to the bodiless sign of the divine. She is also the

> Mollescent irritant of his fantasy
> Gina had her use   Being useful   (36)

The white space heightens our attention to the word "use" and its suggestions of economic exchange inform this process of sexual identity construction.

Indeed, in a less parodic vein, Loy theorized the construction of womanhood in her 1914 unpublished *Feminist Manifesto*, asserting that the "value of man is assessed entirely according to his use or interest to the community, the value of woman, depends entirely on chance, her success or in success in maneuvering a man into taking the life-long responsibility of her."[4] Marriage is one of the "trades" and presented as an "advantageous bargain" as a "thank offering for her virginity" (155). As in her poems, the visual page of the manifesto matters, experimenting here with typography, and individual words or clusters that break into the page with large fonts and bold type. The eye's tendency to scan these marked words on the page highlights the battle with language that Loy conducts, critiquing both the language of patriarchy and the language of a conservative feminism that is "**Inadequate**" in being willing to settle for "**Reform**" rather than "**Absolute Demolition**" (153). The "**Feminine**" is presently constituted as a choice between (in really big letters) "**Parasitism, & Prostitution – or Negation**," an "inadequate apprehension of **Life**" (154). Like the use of white space, the visual manipulation of typography participates in a poetics confronting the materiality of language, puncturing the assumed notion of language as a natural, transparent vehicle for truth and suggesting its role in actively constructing ideologies of gender.

Loy directly connects the power of cultural narratives to enforce, through a language of romance, the oppression of women and what Emma Goldman termed the "traffic in women," the exchange value of virginity in the marriage market. Goldman claimed that for a woman "it is merely a question of degree whether she sells herself to one man, in or out of marriage, or to many men" (20). Loy's "Virgins Plus Curtains Minus Dots" constructs virginity as an economic matter. The poem features virgins who "have been taught / Love is a god / White with soft wings" and are bolted in their homes by fathers controlling the marriage exchange, although "Nobody shouts / Virgins for sale." Marriage, in this market, is "expensive" but one-sided, for the women lack economic power or "coins / For buying a purchaser," while the economic motive is disguised as a moral virtue (22). The white spaces punctuating this poem evoke this unspoken reality.

For Loy's American contemporary Lola Ridge, women are forces for change but, if lacking feminist consciousness, can be the instrument of their own or other's oppression. Like Stein and Loy, Ridge regards language and its forms as shaping forces of gendered reality. Exploring this consciousness through the use of myriad poetic forms revisited throughout her publishing career (1918–35), Ridge embraces traditional and innovative poetics in conveying a distinctively feminist conceptualization of social justice. Her attention to the ideological work of poetic language, genres, and conventions often combines with figures of women as creative, powerful, or authoritative. The significance of women's voices and bodies emerges from Ridge's intellectual and activist combination of socialist and feminist thought, poetically staged in her first major work, *The Ghetto and Other Poems* (1918). As a socialist-feminist perspective on urban, industrial life, the long poem of the title, "The Ghetto," revises the traditional masculine epic form through adopting a nine-section structure evoking the maternal body's gestational time-sense, culminating in a generative "birthing" of a new vision of America's diversity and democratic resistance to capitalistic tyranny.

Set in the teeming, immigrant-filled streets of New York City's Lower East Side, "The Ghetto" presents images of women's bodies as factory workers, socialist comrades, Jewish matriarchs, and street vendors. The body is poetically theorized as a site of feminist history, especially in the generations of enduring Jewish women, and of future action, as in the factory worker Sadie and her female companions whose hours of labor combine with mindful study, revolutionary thought, and a commitment to a full life. This image of the working-class woman draws on the "industrial feminism" of this period. Galvanizing a working-class consciousness, industrial feminists combated prevailing economic theories equating value with consumer desire, arguing instead that economic systems should be organized around human need. Insisting on the necessity of living wages, good working conditions, education, safety, and better hours, industrial feminists joined with reform feminists and suffragists to promote reforms. Named such in 1915 "to describe working women's militancy over the previous six years," industrial feminism developed a political consciousness among working women and a "vision of change" for industrial capitalism (Orleck, *Common Sense and a Little Fire*, 54). This working-class feminist movement was particularly active and vocal between 1915 and 1921, when Ridge lived in Greenwich Village and hosted gatherings attended by poets that included Marianne Moore, Mina Loy, and social justice advocates Dorothy Day and Floyd Dell. Ridge was also living, working, and mingling with immigrant factory workers and activists in her own neighborhood.[5]

Ridge's feminist modernism is distinctive in pursuing *both* traditional and experimental forms, registering a consciousness of the work of form to promote or disrupt ideological social constructs. Throughout her oeuvre, Ridge's feminist convictions intersect with her formal experiments. She freely combined imagist free verse with metric forms (sonnet, fixed rhyme schemes, quatrain) and traditional genres (allegory, epic, meditation, lyric, song, catalog). "The Ghetto," shifting quickly between momentary images of the urban streets and inhabitants of the Lower East Side, demonstrates her early attraction to imagist and collage aesthetics that actively involve the reader in making connections between ideas. Moreover, the long poem revises the masculine epic to foreground female experience and adopt a female-centered gestational form.

The shorter lyric poems that make up the rest of the book's collection focus on forms of social and economic injustice from a decidedly leftist/feminist perspective, moving fluidly between traditional and free-verse forms. In some cases, the form itself is self-consciously parodic, as though identifying an oppressively ideological underpinning to the form. For example, "A Worn Rose" depicts a woman as a prostitute through a parody of the Renaissance poetic catalog, a litany of lines and images moving like a gaze upon and across a woman's body parts. The poem's insistent rhyme scheme employs end words like "buyer, fire"; "juice, use"; "lips, sips"; through this lexicon, the woman is a "spent form" serving others (97). The trope of the rose and the predictable poetic form are presented as worn out, paralleling a similarly exhausted form of gender construction. The insistently metrical form suggests an out-of-datedness that ironically underscores the regressive notions of women's service to men's pleasure, coupled with oppressive ideas of virtue.

Similarly, "The Woman with Jewels" uses the catalog form in a Veblian sense to critique the objectified display of women's bodies, particularly to signify wealth. "The woman with jewels sits in the café" with diamonds that "glitter on her bulbous fingers / and on her arms, great as thighs, / Diamonds gush from her ear-lobes over the goitrous throat" (83). Presented as a body of grotesque excess and display merging wealth and sexual availability (she is looking for companionship), the wealthy woman is equated with the prostitute, for "woman" is ultimately valued in the male-centered world as a commodity for display and exchange.

The psychological violence suggested in "Woman with Jewels" joins poems that portray more graphic and horrific violence. One of Ridge's most explicit renderings of violence follows the conventions of the lullaby, provoking a jarring dissonance between the feminized, maternal genre and the racial violence in the poem. Part of the poem's work, in distinction from a more discursive approach like the essay, is to *demonstrate* the sediment of cultural associations carried by habitual language structures (the lullaby's association with an idealized maternal) and to *interrupt* their power to conceal, oppress, or erase. "Lullaby" replicates the standard rhythm and form of the lullaby, rendered here in a racially inflected "mammy's" voice and dialect. Eight quatrains, with an abab rhyme scheme, follow the rhythm and diction of "Rock-a-Bye Baby," but depict events violently contrasted with the soothing song of sleep, the 1917 race riots in East St. Louis, Illinois, when white workers attacked black workers to drive 6,000 blacks from their homes and massacre 100–200 of the black population. The "lullaby" tells the story of a black baby thrown into the fire by a white woman. The gendered associations of the lullaby with a benevolent image of the "maternal" is made horrific as the white women – imagined as mothers – rock and sing the baby into the fire. Emphasizing the disjunction between the expectations of the poem's form and the poem's actual content, Ridge chillingly points to the racial dimensions of gendered identity and the construction of white womanhood as a form of racial violence.

The tension between idealized womanhood, racial identity, and the material lives of black women fueled discussions appearing in African American intellectual, artistic, and popular venues promoting the "New Negro" and ideas of racial uplift in the late 1910s and 1920s. The emergence of African American–controlled publications like *Crisis* and *Opportunity* magazines or the anthologies of black writing like Alain Locke's *The New Negro* or *Fire!* created venues for women artists, writers, and thinkers to voice their thinking about gender and race. Taken together, the literary and expository pieces by women and about women that appear in African American print culture during the Harlem Renaissance (roughly the late 1910s into the 1930s) constitutes a feminist theorization of race, gender, and class. Poetry's role in the emerging discourse of black womanhood was essential. Models of voice and embodied subjectivity, typically limited by and within discursive conventions of essays and articles, are made available through poetic expression, offering a more personal dimension that variously colludes and conflicts with more essayistic examinations of womanhood. Distinctively, the formal choices of many African American women poets remained relatively traditional, opting for metric or regular forms and preferring recognizable genres like the sonnet, dramatic monologue, or love lyric. In part, this choice reflects a larger impulse to present a cultivated image of African American personhood that challenged white-held prejudices, so that poetic form – even if seemingly traditional – carried a radical political force.[6]

Articles addressing socioeconomic concerns of black women proliferated. Marita O. Bonner, for example, writing in *The Crisis* in 1925, voices a keen awareness of racial constructions of womanhood, calling the "Anglo-Saxon intelligence" "warped and stunted," seeing womanhood only as "white": "Why do they see a colored woman only as a gross collection of desires, all uncontrolled ... ?"[7] Elsie Johnson McDougald, in "The Task of Negro Womanhood" (1925), identifies the black woman's body as a text carrying "traces of the race's history left in physical and mental outline" that result in great diversity of skin tones, a "colorful pageant of individuals," whose bodies "cannot be thought of in mass" or in monolithic stereotypes. The black woman is "racial sister" to other black women, but each maintains an individuality denied by white perspectives (103). McDougald registers the double consciousness of "Negro womanhood," a gender-specific consciousness "that what is left of chivalry is not directed toward her. She realizes that the ideals of beauty ... have excluded her almost entirely. Instead, the grotesque Aunt Jemimas of the street-car advertisements proclaim only an ability to serve" and produce a "sense of personal inferiority" (103, 104).

Poets took up this analysis of black womanhood. Helene Johnson's 1926 poem "Fiat Lux," appearing in *The Messenger*, underscores the sadistic violence of masculine whiteness defined through the oppression of the black female body. A woman prisoner who picks a flower in the prison yard is flogged by the white guard, "her humble back laid bare –/ soft skin, and darker than a dreamless night." Suggesting the oppressor's eroticization of domineering racial violence, the poem introduces romantic imagery, as "He tossed aside the burden of her hair," only to yoke this imagery to lines exposing the psychological and physical violence endured, as the guard states that flowers " 'ain't for niggers.' He began to flog." The body is "crucified" on "a cross of bigotry/ Because she was not white" (Mitchell, *Helene Johnson*, 29). Georgia Douglas Johnson, in her 1922 "The Octoroon," calls attention to histories of rape and possession of the black woman by the white male, figuring the body as violated and imprisoned by racial categories enforced by law and custom. Alluding to the "one-drop" ideology of white supremacy, the poem tropes on the "One drop of midnight" that "Marks her an alien from her kind, a shade amid its gleam," imagining the "stormy current of her blood" that beats "Against the man-wrought iron bars of her captivity" (154). Ambiguously leaving unresolved the question of "her kind" – the whites she most resembles or the "Negroes" deemed such by law? – the poem suggests an arbitrary construction of race (iron bars) enforcing whiteness.

Anne Spencer's poem "White Things," appearing in *The Crisis* in 1923, identifies whiteness with a "wand of power" that is "sired" by a horrific "hell" and requires the violent extinction of all that is not white. The "white things" "pyred a race of black, black men/ And burned them to ashes white," reveling in the perverse ability to transform blackness to whiteness and to be "'Man-maker, make white!'" by destroying blackness (228). Deploying the catalog form from a feminist perspective, Spencer's "Lady, Lady," in a 1925 *Survey Graphic*, views the aged body of a black washing woman, revealing economic oppression in its gaze upon body parts. The washer woman, who has "borne so long the yoke of men," has hands "Twisted, awry, like crumpled roots,/ Bleached poor white in a sudsy tub," the body signifying the hard domestic service and its ties to slave labor that continued to define work for black women well into the twentieth century. Nonetheless, the woman's "heart" holds the "tongues of flames the ancients knew," locating a power not extinguished (229).

The poem's construction of the racialized body as a confluence of history, power, and endurance counterpoints the era's dominant (white) repertoire of images of black womanhood. Black women combated stereotypes (as sexualized Jezebels or as subservient mammies) in essays analyzing economic and class systems as they intersect with race and gender. McDougald develops a class-based analysis identifying intra-racial gender conflicts between black women and black men that, she argues, confront working women at home (104). Identifying blatant discrimination in employment but noting the "growing economic independence of Negro working women," McDougald considers the impact of a self-directed womanhood on the black family structure, as independence encourages working-class women "to rebel against the domineering family attitude of the cruder working-class husband," whose "baffled and suppressed desires to determine their economic life are manifested in overbearing domination at home" (107). Marion Vera Cuthbert, in "Problems Facing Negro Young Women," a Depression-era essay in a 1936 *Opportunity*, also considers the woman worker's double shift, for "the Negro woman stands up under the terrific burden of child bearer, home maker, and toiler. For more than any other group of women in the country is she a toiler outside her home." On the job, "the Negro woman suffers from the double discrimination of sex and race," while at home she is expected to perform the majority of domestic tasks (117).

Indeed, the role of motherhood becomes a particularly vexed issue, putting allegiances to family, class, and race into conflict and often prompting the elevation of race interests above a priority on women. For McDougald, contemporary black mothers are "self-directed" rather than the "pitiable black mammy of slavery days" (105), although they must direct their efforts ultimately toward "enterprises of general race interest": "the Negro woman's feminist efforts are directed chiefly toward the realization of the equality of the races [with] the sex struggle assuming the subordinate place" (107). Alice Dunbar-Nelson's 1927 "Woman's Most Serious Problem," in *The Messenger*, addresses itself to the "young and intelligent women" of the emerging middle and upper classes to argue a relation of the "rise in the economic life of the Negro woman" and the "decline in the birth rate of the Negro" (115, 114, 114). Claiming that women in poverty are limiting offspring by "exercising birth control" (114), Dunbar-Nelson notes that "educated and intelligent classes are refusing to have children," particularly as more women move into professions. The "inevitable disruption of family life ... has discouraged the Negro woman from child-bearing," while the effects of the motherless home on children who are born leads to a "sharp rise in juvenile delinquency." For Dunbar-Nelson, motherhood is the site of racial progress, and the race cannot grow if birthrate declines or if the "training of human souls" cannot "begin at home in the old-fashioned family life" (115).

The conflict between work and motherhood inflects Anita Scott Coleman's 1929 poem, "Black Baby" (first printed in *Opportunity*), complicating Dunbar-Nelson's discourse of motherhood. The speaker understands her need to work as a material condition of her race and gender that mitigates against traditional notions of motherhood: "The baby I hold in my arms is a black baby. / I toil, and I cannot always cuddle him" (316). Coleman's poem points to the construction of maternal subjectivity as racialized and class-based. Similarly, Georgia Douglas Johnson recasts motherhood from an explicitly female and racialized perspective in "Motherhood," appearing in *The Crisis* in 1922. Refusing to give birth, the speaker begs

> Don't knock on my door, little child,
> I cannot let you in;
> You know not what a world this is.

The "world" consists of "monster men" and "cruelty and sin," steeling the potential mother against the possibility of birth. For black women, the poem suggests, the material fact of racial violence attenuates the feminist call for reproductive control and complicates "the maternal" by emphasizing sociohistorical intersections of gender, class, and race.

For poets and writers of the Harlem Renaissance, the need to offer new ideas as correctives to one-dimensional or negative notions of black womanhood complexly demanded attention to multiple sites of identity, producing a richly diverse set of voices during a moment of burgeoning racial consciousness in the twentieth century. Poetry's traditional emphasis on voice and interiority becomes, in this context, an expressive choice for imagining new forms of subjectivity, critiquing oppressive systems of power, and formulating intersections of gender, class, and race. Modernist poetry's revolutionary potential to join theory and praxis ranges richly across such diversely radical sites of feminist poetics.

WORKS CITED

Drinnon, Richard. *Rebel in Paradise: A Biography of Emma Goldman*. Chicago: University of Chicago Press, 1982.

DuPlessis, Rachel Blau. *Genders, Races, and Religious Cultures in Modern American Poetry, 1908–1934*. London and New York: Cambridge University Press, 2001.

Gilman, Charlotte Perkins Gilman. *Women and Economics: A Study of the Economic Relation between Men and Women as a Factor in Social Evolution*. New York: Dover, 1997.

Goldman, Emma. *The Traffic in Women and Other Essays on Feminism*. Albion, CA: Times Change Press, 1970.

Keller, Lynn and Cristanne Miller, eds. *Feminist Measures: Soundings in Poetry and Theory*. Ann Arbor: University of Michigan Press, 1994.

Loy, Mina. *The Lost Lunar Baedeker, Poems*. Ed. Roger Conover. New York: Farrar, Straus, and Giroux, 1996.

Madsen, Deborah L. *Feminist Theory and Literary Practice*. London: Pluto Press, 2000.

Mitchell, Verner D., ed. *Helene Johnson: Poet of the Harlem Renaissance*. Amherst: University of Massachusetts Press, 2000.

Orleck, Annelise. *Common Sense and a Little Fire: Women and Working-Class Politics in the United States, 1900–1965*. Chapel Hill: University of North Carolina Press, 1995.

Patton, Venetria and Maureen Honey, eds. *Double-Take: A Revisionist Harlem Renaissance Anthology*. New Brunswick, NJ: Rutgers University Press, 2001.

Ridge, Lola. *The Ghetto and Other Poems*. New York: B. W. Huebsch, 1918.

Stein, Gertrude. *Tender Buttons*. San Francisco: City Lights, 2014. Original publication in 1914 by Claire Maire.

   "What Are Masterpieces and Why There Are – So Few of Them." In *What Are Masterpieces*, edited by Gertrude Stein, 84–5. New York: Pitman Publishing Company, 1940.

Stott, Nancy F. *The Grounding of Modern Feminism*. New Haven, CT: Yale University Press, 1987.

CHAPTER 6

Woolf and Women's Work: Literary Invention in an Obscure Hat Factory

Robin Truth Goodman

If scholars studying Virginia Woolf agree on one thing, it is that *Night and Day* is a bad book. Alex Zwerdling, for example, asserts, "Woolf's *Night and Day* ... is often dismissed as a traditional novel with a predictable romantic plot (roughly, boy meets, loses, and gets girl)."[1] *Night and Day* is "trapped," cuttingly agrees Janis Paul, "in an antiquated Victorian form which could not encompass the new kind of 'reality' Woolf wanted to transmit, and its upper-class socioromantic entanglements seem a step backward from *The Voyage Out*."[2] Thirty years after the novel's publication, Woolf herself called the book "bad" and derivative – "I made myself copy from plaster casts" – attributing this badness to ill health, an attempt to prove her sanity.[3] Even upon the book's initial release, Katherine Mansfield disparaged it for its lifeless conventionality: "[i]t makes us feel old and chill: we had never thought to look upon its like again!"[4] Critics who want to defend the novel only do so by claiming it as preparing the way for Woolf's future, more serious, experimental, and modernist works where her real ambitions were realized: *Night and Day*, reads Ann-Marie Priest, "can be read as developing a kind of prototype of the alternative, and feminine (as opposed to patriarchal), modes of subjectivity that appear in Woolf's later work."[5] At best, it is "apprentice";[6] at worst, it is, as E. M. Forster spews sardonically, "a deliberate exercise in classism ... as traditional as *Emma*."[7]

There may good reasons for this rare critical harmony: besides the staid and over-familiar plotline and the unsurprising resolution in marriage, *Night and Day*, published before Hogarth Press was established as an outlet for modernist writing, is concerned with dialog rather than the form of monological streaming that came to be Woolf's trademark, with its challenge to the reification of social context, determining histories, objects, and essences. My intention here is not to "recover" the book, to somehow find a value in it that nearly 100 years of abundant Woolfian criticism has missed. Rather, I want to suggest that the nearly universal critical dismissal of *Night and Day* coincides with a neglect of a thematic configuration that is exclusive to this of all Woolf's fictional and much of her nonfictional published writings: that is, the theme of women's work.

Now, this allegation will seem preposterous to many readers of Woolf: What about, you will say, Mrs McNab – the pivot of the celebrated "Time Passes" section of *To the Lighthouse* – or Mrs Bast; or Crosby's importance in *The Years* along with Eleanor's charity visits; or Lily Briscoe, with her ruminations on the worth of her commitment to painting as a substitute for marriage; or Peggy Pargiter in *The Years*, who, remaining unmarried, studies to be a physician? What about, as Naomi Black has observed, the centrality of "the right to earn a living" in *Three Guineas* as Woolf responds to the 1919 passage of the Sex Disqualification (Removal) Act that prohibited the barring of women from public activities on the basis of sex?[8] Have I not considered, you may say, how modernist experimentations with their narrative inventions of the Unconscious were artistic responses, as Michael Tratner has noted, to syndicalist eruptions and working-class crowds in the wake of Sorel and Le Bon, bringing into textual form "changes in human relations ... that overcame the inscrutability of working-class women"?[9] Or Kate Flint's thesis about Woolf's response to the general strike, that "[t]he roots of Woolf's disquiet lie ... in an anxiety, even an uncontrollable physical repulsion which she could feel when confronted with the working classes *en masse*,"[10] or Fuhito Endo's related Kleinian interpretation that middle-class Britain's political anxieties in the context of the Labour Party's formation resulted from "a sense of apprehension about 'the masses'" when its class authority was on the decline.[11] What happened to Jane Marcus' notion that "the voices of charwomen, the cooks and maids, the violet sellers and the caretaker's children in *The Years* ... act as a chorus in all her novels"?[12] What about the ubiquitousness of female servants in all of Woolf's novels, as Alison Little reminds us, and how such women come to represent modernist tropes like the devaluing of the past or the autonomy of the individual or the breaking down of Victorian class differences?[13] It seems, let us conclude, that women's work and class were integral to Woolf's modernist experiments and that the criticism has been very diligent in asking that question.

However, *Night and Day* is the one place in Woolf's fiction where Woolf extensively envisions women's work neither as chiefly professional/artistic, leisurely/aristocratic nor as consigned to service but rather as absorbed into bureaucratic and industrial-like remunerative and productive schemes. *Night and Day* allows a particular glimpse, unidentifiable in the rest of the fictional oeuvre, where Woolf develops a substantial vision of particularly modern women's work. Alison Light's tale of women's service in relation to Woolf's life and work indicates that the First World War created a crisis in the market for domestic help, as working-class women migrated to factories, became shop assistants, office girls, or teachers, leaving the British middle and upper classes short of domestic service.[14] Whereas domestic service could be considered, says Light, a matter of British pride, the problem of women's modern labor would cause "considerable moral alarm,"[15] with anxious speculation on the decline of expressions of respect and submission, increased licentiousness, and loss of discipline. *Night and Day* explores the narrative moment of this rising class at a time when its tropes and formulas could still be invented. The novel's version of modern women's work is distinctly modernist: it suggests that at the time of the novel's writing, Woolf attached to modern women's work associations and narratives that we do not recognize as part of work's symbolic matrix. Linked to literature, women's work in *Night and Day* becomes in a sense theoretical: that is, not determined by the social history that brought it into being. I am using theory here in the way Theodor Adorno might formulate it, as "the concept of reason [that] necessarily contains matter alien to reason,"[16] a glimpse of something that is not yet. Because *Night and Day* develops modern women's work as an instance in the development of modern literature, the novel gives form to modern women's work as something yet unreadable.

As critics have remarked, *Night and Day* is predominantly in the model of a Shakespearian comedy[17]: two couples are set up at the start (Katharine Hilbery with William Rodney, and Ralph Denham with Mary Datchet) until they discover they are comically mismatched; all sorts of mishaps, digressions, romantic intrigue, and antics ensue, including a trip to the zoo and to Kew Gardens, many street walks and tea parties, until finally, everything is sorted out and balance is restored, partly through the interventions of Katharine's mother, recently returned from visiting Shakespeare's grave like a *deus ex machina*. This resolution is facilitated with the introduction of a fifth figure, Katharine's cousin Cassandra Otway, who enchants Rodney, freeing Denham to reconsider his options with Katharine. Therefore, Mary Datchet needs to be removed from the realigned quadrangle, like in a game of musical chairs. Although Avrom Fleishman proposes that Mary gets "left out in the cold,"[18] Susan Squier concludes that "[o]nly Mary Datchet is actually alone, working,"[19] and Eileen Sypher identifies Mary as a typical suffragist "represented as single women, women who have been left behind,"[20] Mary actually does re-partner: a sixth character is introduced. Mary is not the solitary woman of independent means who becomes the feminist icon of *A Room of One's Own*, living on an inheritance. Instead, "another love burnt in place of the old one."[21] In the aftermath of her attachment to Denham, Mary confesses that "Well, I'm afraid I like working,"[22] and "work is the only thing that saved me."[23] Mary works in a small, dingy office in Russell Square as an organizer on issues of suffrage[24] until, late in the novel, her work advances to cover a broader socialist political spectrum through "the Society for the Education of Democracy, upon Capital" for the purpose of educating labor. Against the "machinery," "blotting paper," "clock," "documents," and "statistical diagram" that tell of the aesthetic depravity of the office environment, Mary "seemed," Woolf expounds, "a compound of the autumn leaves and the winter sunshine; less poetically speaking, she showed both gentleness and strength, an indefinable promise of soft maternity blending with her evident fitness for honest labour."[25] Mary is eroticized by and for her work. Woolf sets up work as a figure in the spiral of romance, an object of rerouted desire that drives the novel's plot, resolving the conflictual odd number of dancers with the additional formation of a third couple. As a figure in a romance, work, for Woolf in *Night and Day*, is a character.

Now, calling work a character should set off bells in the minds of Woolf's readers who are familiar with her famous dictum: "that on or about December 1910 human character changed."[26] There has been plenty of scholarly speculation about what Woolf meant by that charge. Woolf is challenging the tradition of literature she calls "Edwardian" that shows no interest in what she calls character. Her challenge resides in an example: a Mrs Brown whom she observes on "the non-stop train" who (like Mary) did not inherit a means of independence, the previous paragraph infers, as she "had been left a little copyhold, not freehold, property at *Datchet*"[27] (my emphasis). "[T]ragic, heroic, yet with a dash of the flighty, and fantastic,"[28] complaining about the difficulty of finding reliable domestic servants, Mrs Brown, although now in her sixties, may have once been one of the "women in that factory"[29] that the Edwardian writers, about whom Woolf complains, were neglecting in their focus on the factory's exterior and social environment. As such, she "is human nature,"[30] and, Woolf concludes, as Mrs Brown disappears "into the vast blazing station," "I shall never know what became of her."[31] For Woolf, modern literature responds to the neglect of the literary tradition in understanding Mrs Brown's character. Similarly, Mary Datchet, either walking in a line with other workers or riding in a train or bus, is inscrutable, fading, like Mrs Brown, into the crowd of commuters, of shopkeepers and bank clerks.[32] As Mrs Brown's disappearance into the blazing station revolutionized literature, breaking character away from the imposing celebration of the "glories of the British Empire,"[33] Mary's thought, busily clicking through the repetition of her daily enterprise at "the center ganglion of a very fine network of nerves which fell over England," finally disappears into a "splendid blaze of revolutionary fireworks … 'What's the very latest thing in literature?' Mary asked."[34] Although most critics read Katharine as the principal protagonist, *Night and Day* is Mary's novel. Introducing modern work for women, Mary also, perhaps as Mrs Brown's younger self, simultaneously introduces character, that is, Woolf's incipient theory of modern literature within the novel.

You may retort, but much of Woolf's writing does fold women's work in with art as opposed to marriage. Look again, for example, at Lily Briscoe who, under Mrs Ramses' conventionalizing pressures encouraging her to engage with men, "remembered, all of a sudden as if she had found a treasure, that she too had her work. In a flash she saw her picture, and thought, Yes, I shall put the tree further in the middle."[35] And do not forget Woolf's famous threat to kill the "Angel in the House" by working for a living: "I made one pound ten and six by my first review; and I bought a Persian cat.... I must have a motor car. And it was thus that I became a novelist."[36] In contrast, in *Night and Day*, literature is captured in repetitions of its past – in inheritance – to which it must learn submission, while work and, ironically, mathematics, produces lines of escape and difference from that past. As the novel opens, Katharine Hilbery is assisting her mother in compiling a biography of her celebrated grandfather, the eminent English poet Richard Alardyce, where "a great part of her time was spent in imagination with the dead."[37] The Hilberys are having a tea party, and one of the invitees is Mr. Fortescue, a caricature of Henry James, who has "reached the middle of a very long sentence"[38] that never comes to an end; he is so eloquent and so witty, admits Mrs Hilbery, that she has grown tired and wants to turn out the lights. Hemmed in by walls exhibiting "the heads of three famous Victorian writers,"[39] in rooms giving off "memories of moods, of ideas … so that to attempt any different kind of work there is almost impossible,"[40] Katharine's attempts to read modern fiction to her parents are greeted with the pejorative "Please, Katharine, read us something *real.*"[41] The work on the literary biography goes nowhere, because sorting through the scraps of the fragmented past – photographs, old letters, memories of silver gulls and hyacinths, odds and ends – do not lead to a coherent narrative in the present: "And the clock was striking eleven and nothing done!"[42] Yet Katharine and her mother must return to the task daily, reviewing and reviewing the traces of the past, never moving forward. Unlike most of Woolf's heroines, Katharine herself claims never to read literature, and her misalliance with William Rodney is partly attributable to his pedantic lectures on the Elizabethan use of metaphor or his chronic citing of Shakespeare.

Woolf offers us Katharine and Mary as two alternative trajectories toward thinking of the modern as a break from such a deadening repetitive chore. In order to free herself from this submission to the past, Katharine secretly, rebelliously, and even shamefully practices mathematics at night, and her dream of pure numbers seems to intend to kill the angels of the past in ways that parallel the ideal of professional and artistic women's work that later became Woolf's feminist signature. Rather than principally linked to art, mathematics are linked to a type of indeterminate imagination that derives from Platonic forms ("the realities of the appearances which figured in our world,"[43] "the shadow of an idea"[44]), theory as opposed to art. "[I]n her mind," Katharine confesses, "mathematics were directly opposed to literature" and were "unwomanly," even "unseemly."[45] For Katharine, mathematics – an escape from the mundane daily demands of her work on the biography – were, alternatively, vigorous, lifelike, and enigmatic: "a sheet of paper lines of figures and symbols [that were] frequently and firmly written down,"[46] or the "sense of the impending future, vast, mysterious, infinitely stored with undeveloped shapes which each would unwrap for the other to behold."[47] Unlike literary tradition, numbers are, as Janis Paul remarks, "not ruled by social requirements ... beyond the physical and conventional world ... detached from society ... [and] marked by her complete emancipation from her present surroundings."[48] Although inscrutable and demanding endless scrutiny, such figures, coming to mind at moments of frustration, tear through objectivity with pure forms or ideals.

Katharine's interest in mathematics leads her, as well, to contemplate the stars. In their flames and brightness, numbers resemble the stars, also pure forms, which "bend over the earth with sympathy, and signal with immortal radiance."[49] Infinitely split and moving constantly, the starlight, like mathematics, is impersonal, ungrounded, devoid of particular human content or material bodies – "something that hasn't got to do with human beings"[50] – but, as in Woolf's later experiments in subjectivity, takes what is near and magnifies it, granting the small points of imaginative flights a randomness, a multivalence, and a significant point of focus. Like mathematics (and like what will later become the signposts of Woolfian modernist narrative), the stars allow multiple human consciousnesses to intersect, combining stages of history and dissolving "for ever and ever indefinitely across space."[51] Stars and mathematics open up, as Ann-Marie Priest expounds it, "Katharine's strange other realm [that] can be seen … as an attempt to re-create identity in ways that are not circumscribed by any existing models."[52] In fact, mathematics resembles what Erich Auerbach identified as unique and revolutionary in the sea change that Woolf introduced into narrative prose: "an insignificant exterior occurrence" – say, a number, a star, or later: a woman in a train, skywriting, a suicide, a brown stocking, a boat trip to a lighthouse – "releases ideas and chains of ideas which cut loose from the present of the exterior occurrence and range freely through the depths of time."[53] Mathematics allows consciousness to be "not tied to the present,"[54] to suggest something real that is not bound by the oppressive controls, the social determinants on the present but releases other possibilities, other sequences and stratifications for time, events, and material facts.

Like mathematics for Katherine, work for Mary defines her as character and, as such, work opens toward a literary imagining to be distinguished from the literary tradition's urge toward repetition and revision. The mathematics that Katharine craves parallels Mary's work in many ways, but not all. At a committee meeting of the suffrage movement, Mary, for example, like Katharine in her stargazing, "scandalously … was looking out the window, and thinking of the colour of the sky … she could not stop to consider what he [Ralph] had said, but he had somehow divested the proceedings of all reality."[55] Later on, she revises her office's card index, where she assesses the effects of the suffrage issue – "upon a large map of England dotted with little pins tufted with differently coloured plumes of hair according to their geographical position"[56] – as they move outward indefinitely, linking up moments of subjectivity as they pass across space like starlight. While engaged in repetitive tasks of reviewing newspaper clippings and leaflets, she finds that "something or other had happened to her brain – a change of focus so that near things were indistinct again"[57] as was true, too, in Katharine's gazing.

Daydreaming does not create a deviation from her work but is, rather, the very substance of it. It allows for a disengagement from social rules, from the way things are. She abstracts all the materials and tidbits of her daily work – the notecards and documents, the envelopes and bottles of ink – calling them a "machinery,"[58] even an "industry," as they, like Katharine's mathematical symbols, figures, and equations, "had all been shrouded, wrapped in some mist which gave them a unity and a general dignity and purpose independently of their separate significance."[59] In opposition to literary tradition, Mary's work, like mathematics, redefines things by separating them from their purpose and giving them a broader, ghostly significance and an inscrutable connection – even, possibly, a spiritual connection – beyond the factual; it teases out inscrutable subjective movement, beyond the present of things, without content: pure form, or pure theory.

Woolf's treatment of Mary's work as modernist deviates substantially from what we think about when we think about modern women's work. Mary expresses no sense of injustice, for instance, about her salary being lower than, say, Ralph's, who works in a law office, or about what must be the insecurity of a job dependent on paternalistic donations. Nor does she get mismanaged or exploited by her director, the only man in the office, who comes across as a vague and benevolent muddle of rambling commentary deferring to her advice and looking to her for guidance. Time for tea breaks, lunch, city walks, and friendly visits is amply provided. Mary recognizes that her assigned tasks are mundane if not rote, and questions their futility as well as the futility of the suffrage movement as a whole: "[w]ith a brain working and a body working," she laments, "one could keep step with the crowd and never be found out for the hollow machine, lacking the essential thing, that one was conscious of being."[60] At the same time, such tasks are not mind-deadening, as they free up her mind for fantasy, distraction, and reflection: "[s]he could hardly bring herself to remember her own private instrument of justice – the typewriter."[61] In short, Woolf imagines Mary's work much as she will later embellish professional or artistic work for women, in its independence. If Mary's work is just a structural placeholder to balance against Katharine's arithmetic as a means to express character, and if it has no – or very little – correspondence with how modern work regimes affect women, why call attention to it?

I contend that Mary's work has an important function that Katharine's mathematics is missing. That is, as Mary points out, "Katherine hasn't found herself yet. Life isn't altogether real to her yet,"[62] or as her cousin Henry Otway remarks, she is not yet "human."[63] Whereas Katharine's numbers skirt what Woolf wants to call human life, Mary recognizes in her work the reality that reason needs: "What is reason without Reality?"[64] Modern work has two characteristics that distinguish it from the unearthliness of numbers, according to *Night and Day*: 1) modern work can be sacrificial, luring one into a spiral of uselessness and repetition, of "infinite dreariness and sordidness,"[65] as Ralph warns his sister Joan who works to support the family: "We shall just turn round in the mill every day of our lives until we drop and die, worn out."[66] Like "Edwardian" or traditional literature, modern work, *Night and Day* admonishes, can lead to dependence rather than independence: gloomy, aimless, "bad for the soul,"[67] "harsh and lonely beyond endurance,"[68] compelling "the exercise of the lower gifts"[69] without poetry, restricting – as was the literary tradition – in the singularity of its perspective against "other points of view"[70]; and 2) encrusted with the material of life – precisely because of its dirtiness, its dependence – modern work, like modern literature (and theory), is the possibility of the future world expressed in its present form, the freeing of thought from things in the interest of thinking things again, but differently, in ways not yet thought. It is the matter of reason that is still alien to reason, an interruption of the present by a creative subjectivity yet to materialize and so as yet without content. As Mary works in the penultimate scene of the novel, Ralph and Katharine look at her lit window from the street below, seeing only her shadow as the form of an idea, inscrutable like the shadows in Plato's cave. Mary "is working out her plans far into the night – her plans for the good of a world that none of them were ever to know."[71]

The formulation of modern work as a release or a partial release from the social investment of meaning in things present might hit us as idealistic at best, and as classist, self-interested, and unaware at worst. Yet, Woolf also seems to be saying that work as we know it could be different because the worker herself "releases ideas and chains of ideas which cut loose from the present." If this is true, then work seems to be literary in a modern sense even as *Night and Day* opposes work to the literary tradition and its repetitiveness by aligning it with mathematics: that is, modern women's work is the narrative site where Woolf is developing her formative theory of modern literature. This would then suggest that work could be different – non-exploitative, cooperative, distracting, creative, visionary – because it has the same tendencies against inheritance as the modern in literature. *Night and Day* is not the only place we see Woolf taking this track on the subject of modern women's work. At the time she was writing *Night and Day*, Woolf was involved in the Women's Co-operative Guild (starting in 1913 and up until 1933[72]) for which she wrote two versions of the introduction to its published volume of letters, *Life as We Know It*, in 1930 and 1931. Woolf's attitude at the start of this essay is nothing short of heinous. After imparting a litany of the working women's complaints – low wages, long hours, lack of education, of sanitation, of rights to property ownership, divorce, and the vote (the letters were collected by 1918) – Woolf detaches her

class from any form of empathy toward these issues, even assessing that
her class would feel humiliated, enraged, and disillusioned by these
women's confessions of base desire and acquisitiveness: "our sympathy,"
notes Woolf (and if irony is intended, I cannot see it), "is largely fic-
titious," because, she continues, "it is much better to be a lady; ladies
desire Mozart and Einstein."[73] Woolf then disparages the guild members for deriding the ladies for being out of touch with their "reality"
(Woolf's scare quotes), and quips that if they do not like comfort and
are afraid that wealth will contaminate them, they are perfectly wel-
come to be foolish and keep their own such cherished "reality."

At this point, Woolf takes an interesting turn. Almost as though, like
in *Three Guineas*, she is in conversation with herself, she begins to read
the women's stories and finds they express "the strength of the human
instinct to escape from bondage," "the vitality of the human spirit,"
demonstrating that "the highest ideals of duty flourish in an obscure hat
factory."[74] Woolf then gives us a revised vision of the woman of independent means from her famous lectures: the guild furnished the working
women with "a room where they could sit down and think remote from
boiling saucepans and crying children ..., not merely a sitting-room
and a meeting place, but a workshop where, laying their heads together,
they could remodel their houses, could remodel their lives, could beat
out this reform and that."[75] This autonomous space for shared thinking
leads Woolf to evaluate whether the letters were literature, and she concludes that although they stand apart from literature, although they lack
"detachment and imaginative breadth ..., these pages have some qualities even as literature that the literate and instructed might envy."[76] Like
Mary Datchet, these working women are both immersed in the "real"
and detached through cooperative thinking, empathy, splitting and multiplying perspectives, and displacement from the immediate into an
autonomous social space, not prefigured and yet to be rationalized. In
the writings of the guild women, Woolf sees in this a literature, as in
modern literature, a literature not yet read that is outside of Shakespeare's
legacy, although related to it, and expressing a shared modern human
character in its blazing future splendor.

We know what happens next. The modern work that motors Mary's
desire in *Night and Day* splits, in the later work, between the artistic subjectivity of the professional woman in a room of her own and the woman
working in service – leaving absent or disparaged the subject of modern
work. "Before [I received my inheritance of 500 pounds]," Woolf writes in
A Room of One's Own,

I had made my living by cadging odd jobs from newspapers, by reporting a donkey show here or a wedding there; I had earned a few pounds by
addressing envelopes, reading to old ladies, making artificial flowers, teaching the alphabet to small children in kindergarten.... To begin with, always
to be doing work that one did not wish to do, and to do it like a slave, flat-
tering and fawning ...; and then the thought of that one gift which it was
death to hide – a small one but dear to the possessor – perishing and with
it myself, my soul – all this became like a rust eating away the bloom of the
spring, destroying the tree at its heart.[77]

Earning a living now obstructs detachment instead of conditioning it;
there is no thinking or imagination in the vicinity of the saucepans and
the workshop; "dirty work" is inimical to thought rather than releasing it;
professional and artistic life will be fatally contaminated by reality; work
itself cannot be creative but destroys creativity. In Woolf's next novel after
Night and Day, Jacob's Room – considered her first modernist novel, and
the first to be published by Hogarth Press – Jacob is not in his room on the
last two visits, just as Mary, too, is inaccessible for Katharine and Ralph's
final visits. The detached narrator, who has been told by Jacob's mother
that he (like Mary) is "hard at work after his delightful journey,"[78] finds
Jacob's room empty (unlike, we assume, Mary's room, where Katharine
and Ralph discern Mary's shadow): "Listless is the air in an empty room,
just swelling the curtain; the flowers in the jar shift. One fibre in the
wicker arm-chair creaks, though no one sits there."[79] Jacob is killed in the
war, replaced by writing, leaving behind only the emptiness of a character adrift, a pair of old shoes: "Nothing arranged," complains a friend.
"All his letters strewn about for any one to read. What did he expect?
Did he think he would come back?"[80] If *Night and Day* were translated
into the narrative thematic of *Jacob's Room*, Katharine and Ralph, rather
than gazing through her window from below, would have entered Mary's
room to find Mary's papers alone and unreadable, a form without content
like mathematics, rather than the shadow of her form planning a future
Reality for the present, a formal detachment not yet realized. In *Jacob's
Room*, Mary and her work have disappeared.

Woolf's move, after *Night and Day*, to separate modern literary subjectivity from modern work may have squelched a line of argument in
feminist theory's project. Did feminist theory lose an opportunity to
rethink work's possibilities in light of the literary innovations of modernism connected to it, to consider that modern women's work – even
as an irregular eruption, a source of anxiety or apprehension, a classist
repression – could also offer a form of understanding the organization

of social relations through cooperative and creative remodeling?[81] Is poststructuralist feminist theory unable to find embedded in its own source materials a logic of work that could counter the logic of instrumentalism? Woolf in *Night and Day* solicits work – as she will later solicit modern literature – to act on the reality of the world in order to bring out the forms of its future. In *Night and Day*, women's modern work is precisely what sets modern literature apart from the accumulations of past objects that grant a weighty, cumbersome value to the repetitions of the traditional. Like modern literature, for Woolf, work, in repeating its own forms – threatening banality, bureaucratization, and aesthetic depravity – finds its own material spiraling out of the restrictions established in these forms into something human that is not yet. The connection between modern work and modern literary practice – or character – reveals work's alienation as the possibility of breaking from historical determinants and social relations that seem drawn – like the conventional marriage plot – from older literary sensibilities that do not respond to current need. Because modern work, for Woolf in *Night and Day*, is literary, our imagination of our future relations with things inhabits what we do with things now, alienating work from the singular perspective of its present as nothing but the accumulated past. If Woolf and her followers had pushed forward this idea, feminist theory may have developed the thematic of work in conjunction with its dynamic of subjectivity, as what shatters old forms of reason with new creations of the real.

CHAPTER 7

Walking in a Man's World: Myth, Literature, and the Interpretation of Simone de Beauvoir's The Second Sex

Ashley King Scheu

Introduction: Problems of Translation and Interpretation

If an English-speaking student in an introduction to feminism class knows anything about Simone de Beauvoir's seminal work, *The Second Sex*, it is probably her famous line, "one is not born, but rather becomes, a woman." This line as we know it in English comes from the 1953 translation by H. M. Parshley, a translation that critics have often maligned for its cuts (near 15 percent of the original text), its inaccuracies, and its elimination of Beauvoir's philosophical voice.[1] In Constance Borde and Sheila Malovany-Chevallier's 2009 translation, the text is restored to its full length, the translators have corrected noted inaccuracies, and Beauvoir once again says *Dasein* instead of "the real nature of man."[2] Not incidentally, the famous line also changes. "One is not born, but rather becomes, woman," Borde and Malovany-Chevallier have Beauvoir say (293).

Although this tiny elimination of an indefinite article feels innocuous enough – particularly because, to an untrained Anglophone ear, it seems to follow Beauvoir's original grammatical structure more closely – the move from Parshley to Borde/Malovany-Chevallier has dramatic consequences for the philosophical meaning of Beauvoir's words. As Toril Moi pointed out in a scathing assessment of the translation in *The London Review of Books*, this small change alters the whole tenor of Beauvoir's philosophical voice:

> This error makes Beauvoir sound as if she were committed to a theory of women's difference. But Beauvoir's point isn't that a baby girl grows up to become woman; she becomes *a* woman, one among many, and in no way the incarnation of Woman, a concept Beauvoir discards as patriarchal "myth" in the first part of her book.

In other words, in Parshley's translation Beauvoir is talking about the individual woman we become. In Borde/Malovany-Chevallier, she is talking about the construct we become.

As is often the case, the stickiness of this problem of translation stems from a problem of interpretation, and this interpretative choice – between "a woman" on one hand and "woman" on the other – is what interests us in this contribution. Turning to the original French sentence on its own will not solve our interpretive problem. Grammatically speaking, whether Beauvoir had wanted to say "a woman" or simply "woman," she would have written "on ne naît pas femme, on le devient" because in French one does not use the indefinite article after "naître." Often instances in which the article is dropped do not indicate to a native speaker that there is some kind of strange or abstract, socially determined identity in question. A website called lanutrition.fr, for example, features an article entitled "le danger de naître homme" ("the danger of being born a man") that discusses men's health concerns. Given the context, it would be very strange indeed to attribute some kind of essentialist notion of man to the authors of this nutrition site. There is also the example of an 1872 sculpture entitled "La negresse" by Jean-Baptiste Carpeaux on which the artist has inscribed "Pourquoi! Naître esclave!" ("Why! Born a slave!"). Clearly this artist was not, in the late nineteenth century, making a claim about the social construction of race. If one wanted to make such a claim, however, one would say "on ne naît pas esclave."[3]

There is, simply put, an ambiguity in French that English cannot properly render, and Borde/Malovany-Chevallier had a difficult decision to make. In their article "Translating *The Second Sex*," they defend their choice not on grammatical but rather on interpretive grounds. They write:

> Here we understand Beauvoir as talking about *woman as a construct – not born but determined* – insisting that there is nothing essential to the second sex and that femininity is learned through socialization and is not "natural." (443, emphasis added)

As with many of Parshley's decisions, Borde and Malovany-Chevallier's interpretive gesture drew intense scrutiny from Beauvoir scholars. Although the 2009 translation of *The Second Sex* is new, it seems, the old controversy over its adequacies and inadequacies continues today, and the meaning Beauvoir's famous line implies is no exception. Strikingly, as far as I can tell, none of the Beauvoir scholars who have discussed the merits of the new translation have supported Borde/Malovany-Chevallier's truncation of Beauvoir's famous line.[4]

Such debates, however, do not fully explore the possibility that Beauvoir wanted to maintain the ambiguity between the interpretations implicit in the two translations. And yet, when French readers come upon that line in

The Second Sex, they could and probably would hear both. As this chapter will argue, a multivalent understanding of "on ne naît pas femme, on le devient" most accurately fits an analysis of what Beauvoir means when she talks about "the facts and the myths" of being a woman. In looking at the text as philosophical whole, the picture of how one becomes a woman in a world filled with patriarchal myths does not easily map onto the poststructuralist, externally determined "Woman" Borde and Malovany-Chevallier's translation suggests. And yet, something in *The Second Sex*'s descriptions of the myths of Woman led Borde/Malovany-Chevallier astray, causing them to eliminate that "a" and make Beauvoir's ordinary woman into a socially manufactured construct. Understanding what that "something" is will involve a closer look at myths as a type of literature and at the strange picture of intersubjective relations that literature provides in Beauvoir's aesthetic theory. Just as with any work of literature, patriarchal myths create a tension between the self and the other in which one can be first and foremost an individual woman but also – somewhere in the place where her lived experience opens out onto that of others – Woman.

Beauvoir's Literary Theory as a Theory of Intersubjectivity

In order to delve into the way myth acts as a literary work in *The Second Sex*, it will first be necessary to define a "literary work." Given the immensity of such a task – writers and theorist alike have written entire books on the subject – this chapter will take Beauvoir's aesthetic theory of literature as the basis for discerning if a story counts as literary. It will thus draw on the surprisingly rich body of work Beauvoir has created on the nature and purpose of art, theater, fiction, and literature. From articles in *Les Temps Modernes* such as "Literature and Metaphysics" to talks such as "What Can Literature Do?" and "My Experience as a Writer" to prefaces for others' novels, Beauvoir was a writer who constantly wrote about writing.

Until very recently, however, scholars interested in existentialist aesthetics have largely ignored Beauvoir's contributions to the field, and we are only beginning to uncover the meaning of Beauvoir's clear preoccupation with aesthetics in general and literature in particular.[5] One step in this direction is a collection of Beauvoir's works previously unavailable in English entitled *"The Useless Mouths" and Other Literary Writings*. Despite the emphasis on Beauvoir's play *The Useless Mouths* in the title, most of this volume gathers together Beauvoir's works of aesthetic theory and philosophical literary criticism. With each piece, scholars provide an introduction to Beauvoir's thought, opening the way for intellectual engagement with Beauvoir as an aesthetic theorist. Another important step comes through Toril Moi's recent work, including two articles: "What Can Literature Do? Simone de Beauvoir as a Literary Theorist" and "The Adventure of Reading: Literature and Philosophy, Cavell and Beauvoir." Whereas the former focuses on Beauvoir's understanding of literature as "the taste of another life," the latter looks at the ways literature has the power to absorb the reader, to draw her in. In both, Moi highlights what Beauvoir sees as the special status of literature.

Overall for Beauvoir, genre does not determine if a work counts as "literary." For example, in "What Can Literature Do?" Beauvoir brings up the example of "false literature" in which one takes a ready-made idea and dresses it up in a trendy story. Presumably certain novels would fall under this category of "false literature," but Beauvoir claims that novels, autobiographies, and essays could all count as real literature as long as they give their writer and/or reader a certain experience unique to the literary work. In a way, then, Beauvoir defines literature by doing a phenomenology of writing and reading; what counts is one's lived experience of the work (hence the title of her talk, "My Experience as a Writer").

The writer's lived experience of literature involves exploration and searching (*recherche*). If one already knows what one wants to say, Beauvoir argues, one should not write a literary work. The literary work that results from this investigation is thus open and ambiguous; it is, in Beauvoir's existentialist vernacular, an appeal to the freedom of the other in which I invite the other to create the meaning of the work with me.[6] In the case of fiction, this open appeal to the other comes, as Beauvoir writes in "The Novel and the Theater," through "creating an imaginary world, and making characters, whose story constitutes what is called the plot, enter into this world" (102).

The reader's lived experience of literature, on the other hand, involves entering into the world that the writer has created. To do so, the reader must step outside of herself or forget herself; she must walk in this world that is not her own. As Moi writes:

> For Beauvoir, then, a good novel had to have the power to absorb, to hold and bewitch, to transport the reader into its world, to make him or her not so much take the fiction for reality, as to experience the fiction as deeply as reality, while full well knowing that it is fiction. (Adventure, 134)

In "What Can Literature Do?" Beauvoir calls this experience getting "the taste of another life" (201).

On my reading, literature provides a strange blurring or openness at the edges of subjectivity that allows for communication in an intersubjective space similar to Heideggerian *mitsein*.[7] Even though that space is a part of our everyday lives, literature allows us to exploit it, to connect to each other in it authentically. Hence at the end of her preface to Violette Leduc's *La bâtarde*, Beauvoir invites the reader in as if she were opening the door to Leduc's home:

> [Leduc's] failure to connect with others has resulted in that privileged form of communication – a work of art. I hope I have convinced the reader to enter within: he will find within it even more, much more, than I have promised. (185)

In all of her writings on literature and aesthetics, Beauvoir is reaching for a way to describe this blurring and the space where it occurs without saying either that our separation from one another is absolute or that a separate subjectivity is not possible. The example Moi cited – literature as the taste of another life – is just one of those attempts. Beauvoir also uses the term *color* to speak of another's world shading my own, and twice in "What Can Literature Do?" she talks of a whirlwind of situated subjectivities turning around, enveloping, and opening out to each other. Beauvoir writes: "We are not monads. Each situation is open onto all the others and it is open onto the world, which is nothing other than the swirling of all these situations which envelop each other" (199).

One's experience of a literary text brings this open relationship between the individual and the world to the fore. In the phenomenological experience of reading, I feel myself as an "I" opening out onto or enveloping the outside world, which includes various situated "yous". There is, in Beauvoir's estimation, a certain amount of "confusion" between self and other going on when this opening/enveloping occurs, but the confusion is never complete. Beauvoir writes:

> Kafka, Balzac, and Robbe-Grillet invite me and convince me to settle down, at least for a moment, in the heart of another world. And that is the miracle of literature and what distinguishes it from information. A truth that is *other* becomes mine without ceasing to be an other. I abdicate my "I" in favor of he who is speaking, and yet I remain myself.
>
> This confusion is continually initiated and continually undone, and is the only form of communication capable of giving me the incommunicable – capable of giving me the taste of another life. I am thrown into a world that has its own values, its own colors. I do not annex it to myself; it remains separated from mine and yet it exists for me. And it exists for others who

are also separated from it and with whom I communicate, through books, in their deepest intimacy.

This is why Proust was right to think that literature is the privileged place of intersubjectivity. (201)

For Beauvoir, a theory of the literary work is a theory of intersubjectivity in which we are separate yet intertwined; it is nothing less than a theory that makes intersubjectivity possible.

Origins: Myth in *Memoirs of a Dutiful Daughter*

In all of her writings on aesthetics, Beauvoir speaks in positive terms about the liminal space created through the sharing of a literary world. When that liminal space becomes patriarchal myth, however, sharing suddenly becomes much less warm and fuzzy. And the sharing of a world is at stake when Beauvoir talks about myth in *The Second Sex*. In writing about the inspiration for her long existentialist study of women as Other, Beauvoir says that the realization of how masculine myths had affected her struck her like a thunderbolt:

> It was a revelation. This world was a masculine world, my childhood was nourished by myths concocted by men, and I hadn't reacted to them in the way I should have done if I had been a boy. I became so interested that I ... [began] to focus on women's condition in general. I went to do some reading at the Bibliothèque Nationale and studied myths of femininity. (Force 103)

In this passage, Beauvoir uses language that recalls the language of her aesthetic writings. Once again, Beauvoir felt that she was walking in another world – the world of men – and this world came primarily through the creation of myths.

The similarity in Beauvoir's language does not guarantee that Beauvoir would consider patriarchal myths literary. In order to count as literary narration, the myth would have to create the lived experience of writing and reading that Beauvoir describes in her aesthetic writings. Finding a text where Beauvoir describes her experience of these reifying myths does not prove difficult. As Beauvoir herself says, she grew up "nourished by myths concocted by men." There is no better place to look, therefore, than Beauvoir's account of her childhood, *Memoirs of a Dutiful Daughter*.

Myth, in fact, suffuses the pages of this first volume of Beauvoir's memoirs, and the young Beauvoir appears both as one who absorbs myths and (re)creates them. The myths she hears include mostly fairytales and biblical stories, and they influence the very way she views and understands the world.

Stories of wicked fairies, of Cinderella and her slipper, of the devil burning in hell – all of these stories filled Beauvoir's world, colored it, and split it evenly between Good and Evil. Although the young Simone had never seen them, she knew the Bad Guys were out there, doing Evil's bidding, and they stood in stark contrast in her mind to those she knew and loved. And yet this mythical world that layered onto her own remained abstract:

> Evil kept its distance. I only imagined its henchmen through mythical figures ... without having met them in the flesh, I reduced them to their pure essence; the Bad Guy sinned like fire burns, without an excuse, without a chance for appeal. (23)

In other words, just as in the reader's experience of a literary text, it added a different taste to her life while remaining other.

When Simone and her younger sister would play, they incorporated these myths into their world; they took up the well-known stories of martyrs and wicked stepmothers and manipulated them, recreating their stories as they pleased. The language Beauvoir uses to describe these childhood games evokes the bringing forth of another universe from the thin air of her rather bleak bourgeois home. "The games that I cherished most," she writes, "were those in which I embodied a character" (60). This embodiment of an imagined other allowed Beauvoir an escape from the mundane:

> Just when the silence, the shadows, the boredom of bourgeois buildings invaded the vestibule, I would unleash my fantasies; we would bring them into being [*les matérialisions*], enthusiastically supported with gestures and words, and sometimes, as we caught each other in our spell, we would succeed in taking flight away from this world, up to that moment when an imperious voice would call us back to reality. (61)

Play with the mythical narratives she had been given was truly a literary creation, worthy of any of her descriptions in her aesthetic writings.

Even in her acts of creation, however, the young Simone was acting within the confines of the stories she knew, sometimes with disturbing effect. The stories given to a young Simone, stories of Hans Christen Andersen, Perrault, and the Bible alike, presented ideal women as martyrs, as submissive creatures who glorified in the pain inflicted on them by more or less benevolent men. Hence, even though Beauvoir thought she was taking power into her own hands – "I flattered myself," she writes, "that I was ruling, alone, over my own life" – she was imagining the most abject role possible for herself. Beauvoir writes:

> Most real or imagined heroines – Saint Blandina, Joan of Arc on her pyre, Griselidis, Genevieve of Brabant – could attain glory and happiness in

this world or in the next only through painful trials inflicted upon them by males. (80)

As Christine Shojaei Kawan notes, these stories do not wholly subdue the rebellious forces within a young Simone. They often backfire, allowing Beauvoir to explore sexualized, masochistic fantasies that her milieu strictly forbade ("A Masochism Promising Supreme Conquests," 32). Hence this little girl, faced with myths of the Woman-martyr, finds her voice and her story. She is not subsumed within them. Instead, she defines her own world as a singular little girl in, through, with, and against those myths.

Myth as Literary Force in *The Second Sex*

This is the ambiguous picture of a woman living with myths of Woman that Beauvoir builds meticulously over the hundreds of pages in *The Second Sex*, and it is this ambiguity that Borde/Malovany-Chevallier have, with a strike of their proverbial pen, eliminated from the most emblematic line of Beauvoir's masterwork. After studying *Memoirs of a Dutiful Daughter*, Kawan sees a clear connection to Beauvoir's explicit discussions of myth in *The Second Sex*. In her article, she picks up passage after passage in which Beauvoir explores the effects of stories like *Blue Beard* and *The Little Mermaid*. And yet Beauvoir's description of myth in *The Second Sex* goes much deeper than that. Myth is not just stories we tell to children about supposedly idealized women. Myth is pervasive; it is in all stories we tell about Woman, and it infiltrates every social ideology, from novels destined for adults to psychology's understanding of women's minds to the story biologists tells about women's bodies.

Even in these supposedly objective fictions, there is an opening of Beauvoir's voice as a singular woman out onto the myths of Woman. Take, for example, her discussion of biology in the section entitled "The Given Facts of Biology."[8] In writing about how myths of the eternal feminine have infiltrated our stories about women's bodies, Beauvoir imagines a sexist other and has him speak in the midst of her text. She takes clear pleasure in the building of a literary image that absorbs the reader just as effectively as any nicely drawn characterization in a novel:

> The word female [*femelle*] evokes a whirl [*sarabande*] of images: an enormous round egg seizes and castrates the agile sperm; monstrous and stuffed, the queen termite reigns over the servile males; the preying mantis and the spider, gorged on love, crush and devour their partners; the dog in

heat runs through back alleys, leaving a trail of perverse smells in her wake; the monkey flaunts herself shamelessly and sneaks away, a hypocritical flirt. And the most splendid big cats – the tigress, the lioness, and the panther – lie down slavishly under the male's imperial embrace. (21)[9]

It is as if the sexist male, in attempting to justify his disdain for the female sex and his pretensions toward superiority, gets carried away in literary excess, creating image after image of women as devouring beasts or quivering prey. And in this instance, Beauvoir is using her imaginative literary powers to enter into a world of significations that is not her own. Clearly in this quote, Beauvoir the writer is taking on the perspective of the male sexist and delighting in building this obviously unscientific and literary image. The very length of this description and its abundantly rich detail attest to her pleasure in writing it.

Unsympathetic readers – and there are many of them – have found Beauvoir's pleasure too convincing. Beauvoir, they argue, is more than a writer caught up in the construction of a beautiful literary image; she is, at best, an outdated first-wave feminist who started us on the path but is not worth our time now; she is, at worst, a hypocrite, a woman hater dressed as a feminist, a masculinist, an outright sexist.[10]

Such uncharitable readings not only go against the grain of Beauvoir's explicit arguments, they miss the picture of intersubjectivity that Beauvoir is using her literary powers to create. Although she picks up staid images of women as cowering prey or rapacious whores, although she lingers there, drawing them out and seemingly taking aesthetic pleasure in their lurid lines, Beauvoir is, in the sheer force of her writing, also fighting against them. As these images pile on top of one another, as they whirl together under her deft pen, they begin to become ridiculous and incoherent. The reader jumps with Beauvoir from one myth to the other in rapid succession, and Beauvoir's ironic distance to these accumulated worlds comes through in her final assessment: "Inert, impatient, shrewd, stupid, cold, lewd, fierce, and humiliated, man projects onto woman all female animals at once" (21, translation modified).

Furthermore, Beauvoir believes these descriptions to be true, although not in the way her adversaries would have it. They are true as part of the sketching out of women's lived experience of their bodies or *corps vécu*.[11] For Beauvoir, we live our bodies not only with our personal subjective experience but also with the interpersonal layering of meanings that we take from and give to others. As part of women's overall situation, sexist readings of the female body become inescapable. For example, we have been living with ideologies that cast women who have sex as passive prey or rapacious whores, and thus as we have sex these ideologies color that experience. We may acquiesce to them or rebel against their injustice, but the fact is that they *are there*, and we cannot live our bodies without these ideologies either clamoring or whispering in the background.

Ironically, then, in order to tell the truth about a feminine *corps vécu*, Beauvoir must first explain women's experience of their bodies under patriarchy, and thus ironically she must enter into the sexist imaginary that colors their experience. Doing so requires exactly the kind of ethical reaching out toward another subjectivity that sexist oppression attempts to deny; it requires a literary imagining of the sexist's world.

Beauvoir's literary resistance to biological justifications of sexist oppression exposes the layer of meaning grafted onto the biological world. Beauvoir's project, however, is not merely descriptive; it is also creative. In response to sexist narratives of the female body, Beauvoir also creates her own, competing stories with her own meanings, and these literary creations contest scientists' masked literary tales. For example, Beauvoir writes new narratives about the spermatozoid and the ovum that counter the image of a passive female devouring a vigorous and rational male: "In truth, these are merely ramblings. Male and female gametes merge together in the egg; together they cancel each other out in their totality.... [I]n the act that merges them, their individuality disappears" (47). At first, Beauvoir's recourse to such a description seems contradictory. She has, after all, claimed that it is absurd to deduce anything about a woman's or a man's lived reality from the attributes of their sex cells. And yet, in rewriting the man's script to tell a narrative of union and equality rather than one of combat and male superiority, she demonstrates just how the same biological givens can create a plethora of meanings.

In Beauvoir's capable hands, the phenomenological approach becomes a powerful tool in dismantling sexist myths about women's bodies and hence in debunking biological determinism. She strips sexist significations away from the supposedly objective and universalizing narrative that men have made of women's bodies, and she exposes them as just so many stories that we have been told and that we have been telling ourselves. She then imagines alternate stories that compete with and displace the oppressive threads, stories that seem equally plausible and that contest any claims to universality or objectivity. In other words, her imaginative stories of women's bodies in *The Second Sex* ultimately expose old sexist stories as just so many fairytales, and she actively rewrites those fairytales from the inside out.

As with the young dutiful daughter, we will see a more seasoned Beauvoir fighting against the oppressive stories she uncovers while still fighting within the context of their narrative. Beauvoir's ironic distance to sexist myths certainly remains, and readers who see her as masculinist fail to take this into account. In the very excess of her literary zeal, in the sheer piling of one image on top of the other on top of the other, Beauvoir reveals the incoherencies and excess of the narrative about women's bodies. Writing through the voice of the character of the sexist, she picks up his language and imagery, an imagery that has been shared with her, thrust upon her, and through it all she remains a fiercely independent French intellectual woman, opposed to marriage, opposed to the submissive role offered to her, ironic, witty, and defiant.

Conclusion: The Literary Theory of Intersubjectivity at the Heart of *The Second Sex*

In researching this contribution, I sent out a Facebook message to my French-speaking friends asking about their interpretation of the line, "On ne naît pas femme, on le devient." Surprisingly, all of my American friends with a near native ability in French came down on the side of Borde/Malovany-Chevallier. Most of those who responded were French professors. Although none of them were Beauvoir experts, they had a more than passing familiarity with current feminist theory and with concepts of Woman as a discursively determined social construct, and they essentially mapped that understanding onto Beauvoir's words. This means that the new translation takes some of the strangeness out of what Beauvoir is saying for the current generation of students who have grown up steeped in the sex/gender divide and in postmodern notions of sex. In losing that distinction, Beauvoir's voice gets lost in the crowd of postmodern theorists who ascribe to a theory in which the words "subject" and "woman" have lost their ordinary meaning.

What Beauvoir has to say may have paved the way for such theories, but her nuanced understanding of how we could walk in the world of myth retains the sense that the word *woman* is not inherently oppressive and does not mean that one has become a social construct. The strangeness of what Beauvoir has to say may challenge our current feminist assumptions about what it means to say "woman" or "a woman," and Borde and Malovany-Chevallier have taken that strangeness away.

Beauvoir wanted to say "one is not born, but rather becomes, a woman" while also hinting that in becoming a woman, one risks giving oneself over to stories about what it is to be Woman. Beauvoir's understanding of myth as creating a literary grey space between two subjectivities turns out to be *the* theory of intersubjectivity underwriting all of *The Second Sex*. Like any literary story in Beauvoir's aesthetic theory, these myths of Woman infiltrate and captivate, they absorb and take over in a way that threatens the very integrity of a woman's subjectivity, but they never completely shape or displace the individual. In other words, if a woman does give herself over to the ready-made myths of Woman, she remains herself; she retains a subjectivity outside of the one society has thrust upon her, and she remains existentially free. In striking out this small, unassuming "a," all of this nuance to Beauvoir's phenomenological study of women goes along with it. Borde and Malovany-Chevallier thus create an incongruity between the shorthand that students use to talk about Beauvoir's philosophy and the philosophy itself. The coherence of Beauvoir's philosophical voice, it seems, rides on that indefinite article.

WORKS CITED

Bauer, Nancy. "Beauvoir's Heideggerian Ontology." In *The Philosophy of Simone de Beauvoir*, edited by Margaret A. Simons, 65–91. Bloomington: Indiana University Press, 2006.

Rev. of *The Second Sex*, trans. Constance Borde and Sheila Malovany-Chevallier. *Notre Dame Philosophical Reviews*, University of Notre Dame, August 14, 2011.

Beauvoir, Simone de. *Force of Circumstance*. Trans. Richard Howard. New York: Putnam, 1965. Print.

"Literature and Metaphysics." Trans. Veronique Zaytzeff and Frederick M. Morrison. *Simone de Beauvoir: Philosophical Writings*. Ed. Margaret A. Simons. Urbana: University of Illinois Press, 2004.

Memoirs of a Dutiful Daughter. Trans. James Kirkup. Cleveland, OH: World, 1959.

"My Experience as a Writer." Trans. J. Debbie Mann. In *Simone de Beauvoir*, edited by Simons and Timmermann, 282–301.

"The Novel and the Theater." Trans. Marybeth Timmermann. In *Simone de Beauvoir*, edited by Simons and Timmermann, 102–6.

"Preface to *La Bâtarde* by Violette Leduc." Trans. Marybeth Timmermann. In *Simone de Beauvoir*, edited by Simons and Timmermann, 174–87.

The Second Sex. Trans. Constance Borde and Sheila Malovany-Chevallier. London: Cape, 2009.

"What Can Literature Do?" Trans. Marybeth Timmermann. In *Simone de Beauvoir*, edited by Simons and Timmermann, 197–209.

Borde, Constance and Shiela Malovany-Chevallier. "Translating *The Second Sex.*" *Tulsa Studies in Women's Literature* 29(2) (2010): 437–45.

Card, Claudia, ed. *The Cambridge Companion to Simone de Beauvoir.* Cambridge: Cambridge University Press, 2003.

Carpeaux, Jean-Baptiste. *La negresse.* 1872. Cast terracotta. The Metropolitan Museum of Art, New York.

Daigle, Christine. "The Impact of the New Translation of *The Second Sex*: Rediscovering Beauvoir." *JSP* 27(3) (2013): 336–47.

Glazer, Sarah. "Lost in Translation." *New York Times.* August 22, 2004.

Gothlin, Eva. "Reading Simone de Beauvoir with Martin Heidegger." In Card, *The Cambridge Companion to Simone de Beauvoir*, 45–65.

Heinämaa, Sara. "The Body as Instrument and as Expression." In Card, *The Cambridge Companion to Simone de Beauvoir*, 66–86.

"Simone de Beauvoir's Phenomenology of Sexual Difference." *Hypatia* 14(4) (1999): 114–32.

Hekman, Susan J. *Gender and Knowledge: Elements of a Postmodern Feminism.* Boston: Northeastern University Press, 1990.

Kaelin, Eugene F. *An Existentialist Aesthetic: The Theories of Sartre and Merleau-Ponty.* Madison: University of Wisconsin Press, 1962.

Kawan, Christine Shojaei. "A Masochism Promising Supreme Conquests: Simone de Beauvoir's Reflections on Fairy Tales and Children's Literature." *Marvels & Tales* 16(1) (2002): 29–48.

Lloyd, Genevieve. *The Man of Reason: "Male" and "Female" in Western Philosophy.* Minneapolis: University of Minnesota Press, 1984.

Moi, Toril. The Adulteress Wife. Rev. of *The Second Sex*, trans. Constance Borde and Sheila Malovany-Chevallier. *London Review of Books* 32(3) (2010): n. pag.

"The Adventure of Reading: Literature and Philosophy, Cavell and Beauvoir." *Literature & Theology* 25(2) (2011): 125–40.

"What Can Literature Do? Simone de Beauvoir as a Literary Theorist." *PMLA* 124(1) (2009): 189–98.

"While We Wait: The English Translation of *The Second Sex.*" *Signs: Journal of Women and Culture in Society* 27(4) (2002): 1005–35.

Rodier, Kristin and Emily Anne Parker. Rev of *The Second Sex*, trans. Constance Borde and Sheila Malovany-Chevallier. *Symposium* 16(1) (2012): 300.

Scheu, Ashley King. "Living-with the Other's Pain: The Ethical Implications of Mitsein in Simone de Beauvoir's *Le Sang des autres.*" *Romance Quarterly* 59(4) (2012): 257–68.

"The Viability of the Philosophical Novel: The Case of Simone de Beauvoir's *She Came to Stay.*" *Hypatia* 27(4) (2012): 791–809.

Simons, Margaret A. "The Silencing of Simone de Beauvoir: Guess What's Missing from *The Second Sex.*" In *Beauvoir and The Second Sex: Feminism,*

Race, and the Origins of Existentialism, 61–71. Lanham, MD: Rowman &
Littlefield, 1999.

Simons, Margaret A. and Marybeth Timmermann, eds. *Simone de Beauvoir: "The
Useless Mouths" and Other Literary Writings*. Urbana: University of Illinois
Press, 2011.

Sommers, Christina Hoff. "Not Lost in Translation." Rev. of *The Second Sex*,
trans. Constance Borde and Sheila Malovany Chevallier. *Claremont Review
of Books* 10(4) (Fall 2010).

Souccar, Thierry. Le danger de naître homme. *LaNutrition.fr*. Axis Media, June
21, 2010.

CHAPTER 8

Decapitation Impossible: The Hundred Heads of Julia Kristeva

Maria Margaroni

Introduction: The Many-Headed Theorist

Speaking of J. K. ("Julia Kristeva," linguist, philosopher, and theorist of psychoanalysis), the psychoanalyst-narrator of *Thérèse mon amour*, the latest fictional installment of J. K. ("Julia Kristeva," the lesser known and much disparaged writer of fiction), comments: "Of Bulgarian origins, of French nationality, European citizen and an American by adoption? Journalist, psychoanalyst, semiotician, novelist, and what's to come? Mobiles, kaleidoscopes, in her too" (*Thérèse mon amour*, 482).[1] The comment is made in the context of the narrator's reflections on this hybrid species she calls "daddy's girls" (482), a species that includes (in addition to Julia Kristeva) artist Louise Bourgeois, philosopher Hannah Arendt, writer Colette, psychoanalyst Melanie Klein, and Saint Thérèse of Avila herself, the heroine of this profoundly dialogic and generically unconventional work. Daddy's girls, Sylvia Leclercq (the psychoanalyst-narrator) explains, are those girls who, "like Athena, were born out of Zeus' head" after he had swallowed (and hence impregnated himself with) their already pregnant mother, Metis, the goddess of craftiness and wisdom (481). Hybrid and restless creatures, these girls learn early enough the need to cross borders: "those of a language, a regime, a family, a father" (481). They are always "in quest of the father, while continuing to flee him" and "rediscover the profundity of the maternal by appropriating paternal ambition and healing the desire for power within man" (482). Daddy's girls are warrior girls who remain fully armed, as they were born.[2] They laugh in the face of the phallus and end up scorning fear itself (482–3). Incurable "runaway girls," daddy's girls never stop "escaping what precedes them in the direction of what exceeds them" and, like Thérèse, recreate themselves through re-founding laws, institutions, rituals, and communities (484). Because they retain the psychic plasticity of the adolescent (486, 490),

95

these girls "dare," as Kristeva puts it, "to say 'I' in lots of different ways" (*The Old Man and the Wolves*, 66).

And yet (Kristeva well knows), daddy's girls are never very popular. Preferring whisky or iced tea to mother's milk/ink, stubbornly holding on to their head and to an old-fashioned investigation of truth, both they and their writing are approached with suspicion, for the singularity of their style is not consistent with what is expected of the "feminine" and they refuse to follow uncritically a sanctified maternal tradition. In an interview with Alice Jardine and Anne Menke, Kristeva confesses: "I'm not at all one of those women who believes that when one is a woman, one must express oneself in a subterranean, elliptical, or rhythmic language. That can be one solution, but it's not the only one. We can simply change the objects of thought. The terrain of thought is not necessarily male, in my opinion, and women can do something right now by presenting new objects of thought" (Guberman, *Julia Kristeva: Interviews*, 124).

It is, therefore, far from surprising that Kristeva's ventures in literature were not particularly welcomed and embraced by feminist circles, as Hélène Cixous', for example, have been. In fact, the majority of female as well as male readers seem to experience the same discomfort in the face of her more creative work. Part of the disappointment confessed by a variety of readers seems to be caused by the fact that her fiction blatantly lacks the very poetic quality she herself has taught us to appreciate in the writings of the European avant-gardes. Michael Levenson, for instance, wonders: "Where is the shock to 'father's law'?" while Margaret Whitford admits to being unable to "respond to the book [*The Samurai*] as fiction" (Whitford, "Review of Julia Kristeva," 140). Commenting on Kristeva's *Possessions*, John Lechte, in his turn, writes: "If this novel itself could speak it would say that its author is the last one to be possessed, the last one to write in a delirium.... But there is certainly no violence *of* the text; it is not semiotic in this sense. It does not do violence to language, as Mallarmé was accused of doing.... The 'revolution in poetic language' has, one suspects, well and truly had its day" ("Fiction, Analysis, Possession, and Violence in Kristeva's Mirror of Writing," 130, 134–5, 137; emphasis in the original). As these quotations demonstrate, for these and other readers the problem with Kristeva's fictional works to date is that they are not sufficiently "literary"; they are too academic, too cerebral. In the midst of a terror-driven, mediatic universe of false, affect-bound selves, Kristeva, it appears, insists on remaining lucid, keeping *her* head firmly fixed on her authorial shoulders. Her fictional writing, then, can hardly be labeled "*écriture feminine*," a term defined and unpacked to a great extent with close reference to her early theoretical works (approached in connection with the works of other so-called French Feminists: namely, Luce Irigaray and Hélène Cixous).

As I have argued in a recent essay,[3] Kristeva's anti-avant-garde style in her fiction is not to be wondered at given that, as a number of feminist critics have rightly complained, "*écriture feminine*" in her theoretical writings has always been the son's rather than the daughter's affair. In other words, the "music in letters" that the readers of her fiction expect (Lechte, "Fiction, Analysis, Possession, and Violence in Kristeva's Mirror of Writing," 141) is the product of the incestuous game between phallic mother and the poet-son, which, by definition, keeps the daughter out. In this chapter I would like to approach Kristeva's fictional works as precisely the writing of the *other* woman left out from the mother-son idyll: the creative and disturbing output of the hybrid figure she describes repeatedly as a warrior-daughter, "daddy's girl." My task will be to demonstrate how this *writing in the feminine* (which is not to be confused with *écriture feminine*) develops from her first novel, *Les Samouraïs* (1990), to her fictional biography of Saint Thérèse of Avila (2008). As I will argue, this writing-in-the feminine reclaims the terrain of thought for the female intellectual who, as Kristeva insists in her interview with Jardine and Menke, needs to assume the important task of changing this terrain by introducing *new objects of thought*. Hence, I will contend, the proliferation and dramatization of multiple cerebral centers in her fiction, that is, privileged sites where detection, analysis, and scholarly speculation take place. In my reading, these (100 or so) heads spring up in the narratives to make up for the metaphorically or literally decapitated female bodies around which the plot turns. Kristeva's fiction, then, unfolds in the space of the playful ambiguity Max Ernst opens with his *Femmes 100* [Cent/Sans] *Têtes*.[4] As I will show, it consciously engages with "the 'capital' force" that, according to Cixous, "history keeps reserved for woman" (namely, the threat of decapitation, "Castration or Decapitation?" 42–3), sowing the seeds, at the same time, for the flowering of a new female species, a many-headed heroine whose distinct *style* as a speaking subject I would call "transphallic." Interestingly, this is the term Kristeva uses in *The Sense and Non-Sense of Revolt* to describe female psychic bisexuality, a disposition that involves "the conjunction" of a woman's "symbolic essence (phallic thinking subject) and her carnal essence (preoedipal sensuality, mother-daughter sensual duality, reduplication of female parents)" (104). In what follows, I will argue that part of the difficulty (and charm) of Kristeva's transphallic writing is that it paradoxically grows out of the exquisite cerebrality of irony (a position that privileges distance, critique, and dis-impassioning), while sustaining itself through the mundane bread and butter of what the analysts call "the transferential relationship" or, in Leclercq's translation, Thérèse's gift of "co-naissance": "the quest for oneself founded on the bond with the other" (Kristeva, *Thérèse, mon amour*, 36).

Decapitation: A Structural Necessity?

In a seminal 1981 essay ("Castration or Decapitation?") Cixous argues: "If man operates under the threat of castration, if masculinity is culturally ordered by the castration complex, it might be said that the backlash, the return on women of this castration anxiety is its displacement as decapitation, execution, of woman, as loss of her head" (43). For Cixous, this "capital" force that "history keeps reserved for woman" becomes synonymous with containing "feminine disorder, its laughter, its inability to take the drumbeats seriously" (43). It involves the displacement of women "outside the city," their condemnation to "complete silence," their reduction to "automatons" (43, 49): "They are decapitated, their tongues are cut off and what talks isn't heard because it's the body that talks, and man doesn't hear the body" (49).

Along similar lines, Kristeva exposes decapitation as the distinct fate of women in patriarchal societies. In *Visions capitales*, she writes: "One sees her head though not her being, which is her speaking body: one uses it, of course, but this is of no (visible) importance. In order to see this head, one cannot but hold a grudge against it, one cannot but wish to cut it off. But oh! Surprise, if one dares to commit the capital act, one finds neither the body nor the head. The executioner perceives that the feminine head has rejoined the being to which it always already belonged" (147).[5] What these reflections apropos Lewis Carroll's figure of the grinning Cheshire Cat suggest is that, historically, there has been a systematic attempt to keep women's heads separate from their being. Kristeva traces various manifestations of this attempt that, significantly, takes on the guise of an inevitability, a *necessity*. In *Visions capitales*, she connects the ancient cults of an acephalic-although-all-too-corporeal feminine (25) to artistic representations of decapitated or faceless women (26, 35–43, 133–7, 145–7), the now headless female statues from the past mutilated by "the guillotine of history" (18), the televised violations of female victims in recent civil wars (33), and the veiled heads of Iranian women (144). In her discussion of Louis Aragon in *The Sense and Non-Sense of Revolt*, Kristeva focuses on the surrealist fascination with a decapitated feminine: "the abysmal connotation of the feminine as the opposite of the representable, the visible, the phallic" (122), while her detective fiction is littered with the inert bodies of murdered female victims: that is, the decapitated body of Gloria in *Possessions*, the faceless corpses of the two women found drowned in *The Old Man and the Wolves* and *Murder in Byzantium*. My argument in this chapter is that the concept and experience of decapitation is one of the threads that can help us bring together not only Kristeva's theoretical concerns and her fictional oeuvre but, more important, her different experimentations in fiction from *Les Samouraïs* (written as a *roman à clef*) to her detective novels and the fictional biography of Thérèse.

"Decapitation" is, I argue, the structural, anthropological, historical *given*[6] that the female intellectual recharges and re-contextualizes as an object of thought. Although, as we have seen, Kristeva insists on the feminist stakes of rethinking the iconographies and structural logic of decapitation, her interest in this conceptual paradigm is informed by both her experience as an Eastern European intellectual who knows intimately the risks of thought in a totalitarian regime[7] and her human-centered agenda as a psychoanalyst. Decapitation, then, functions as a cluster-concept in Kristeva, which enables her to bring together a number of related concerns: a) the woman-theorist's concern with the "capital force" of patriarchal history which divorces women's existence in the symbolic from their sensory/bodily experience; b) the psychoanalyst's concern with the subjective as well as collective desire for/fascination with transgression (the Bataillean traversal of conscience) and the psychic risks of an acephalous existence;[8] finally, c) the Eastern European's pronounced concern over the close embrace between revolution (decapitation as the violence of the oppressed, "indispensable for the emergence of a new head, a new era"; *Visions capitales*, 102) and Terror, the threat of totalitarianism.

The significance of and interplay among these concerns may not be immediately visible in Kristeva's first novel, *Les Samouraïs*, which has invariably been approached as a house of mirrors reflecting back an aggrandized version of Kristeva the theorist and her intellectual circle. Far from narcissistic, I would contend, *Les Samouraïs*, is a profoundly pedagogical novel[9] that sets out to address a generation's anxieties about violence and transgression, desire, loss, and the traumas of an embodied, mortal existence. As the title suggests,[10] *Les Samouraïs* is also a warrior novel, aiming at teaching the children we all are about the art of war, or, in other words, the art of holding our head high against the fascination and risks of decapitation.

In its attempt to translate the voice and spirit of a generation ("we") into the register of the singular ("*Unes*"[11]), Kristeva's project in this first novel is, arguably, similar to that of Simone de Beauvoir in *The Mandarins*. Despite the much-discussed tensions between the two novels,[12] there is, I believe, a more congenial bond that unites these semi-autobiographical narratives. Indeed, both novels are concerned with the conditions of possibility and the nature of revolutionary experience; the ambiguous legacies of the French Revolution and the Enlightenment; the twentieth-century experiences of war and totalitarianism; the Cold War divisions as perceived in Western and Eastern Europe; the role of the public intellectual; the psychic challenges of a death-bound existence. Interestingly, in both novels the investigation of these issues takes the form of a meditation on this "oeuvre-in-black"[13] that the speaking human being is, divided by an intimate apprenticeship in violence, one threatening to erupt into a cult of death.

Rather than a settling of accounts between an existentialist and a post-structuralist Left,[14] then, *Les Samouraïs* develops, instead, out of questions, concerns, and dilemmas that Kristeva and Beauvoir share. Although, needless to say, Kristeva's take on these questions is not Beauvoir's, it clearly unfolds as a response to the disappointments, defeats, or belated realizations of Beauvoir's protagonists. In a discussion with Anne (his wife, a practicing psychoanalyst), Robert (the figure of the committed public intellectual in *The Mandarins*) argues: "Little disasters count, too.... I'm beginning to think a little like you – that the death or unhappiness of an individual can't be ignored" (268–9). *This* (i.e., the value of singular being in all its ordinariness and vulnerability) is, according to Kristeva, an important lesson to take up and pass on. She tells Bernard Sichère: "In the history of the West, left-wing thought seems to me linked to an ethical requirement that includes at the same time the dead ends of revolutionary movements and the Terror and the lessons to be learned from such dead ends" (Guberman, *Julia Kristeva: Interviews*, 174). From Kristeva's perspective as a committed intellectual, the ethical requirement that needs to frame and inform left-wing thought and revolutionary politics relates to the imperative not to ignore what Robert calls "little disasters" in the name of "the good of all." It also involves the necessity to recognize the limits and contingency of any hegemonic discourses, collective values, or revolutionary ideals. As I will go on to argue, Kristeva's fiction emerges as the terrain *par excellence* where this ethical requirement can be explored.

It is no wonder, in this light, that the figure of the guillotine, "this egalitarian institution of decapitation," appears to haunt Kristeva's fictional world (*Visions capitales*, 101), from the Paris of the May '68 revolutionaries[15] to the abject Santa Varvara of the detective novels[16] and the terror-riven globe Sylvia Leclercq inhabits.[17] In an attempt to make sense of the Paris youth uprisings she is witnessing, Joëlle Cabarus, a psychoanalyst like Beauvoir's Anne, performs a gesture that is to become typical of Kristeva's narrator-protagonists: that is, she turns her gaze to the past and ventures to reread history by activating a kind of transferential memory, a memory that enables her to affectively hook on to a female figure from the past. This helps the protagonist to evaluate the legacies of the past from the site of its impasses and to become a more attentive listener to the idiolects of history. In *Les Samouraïs*, Joëlle transfers herself back to the 1789 French Revolution and attempts to rethink its contemporary stakes through the eyes of Thérésa Cabarrus, the seductress-socialite who, in her adherence to personal interest and "the force of pleasant life" (181), opposed the revolutionary idealism of a Robespierre (176) and was, as a result, imprisoned as an "enemy of the people" during the reign of Terror. Joëlle reflects: "I have too many scruples to adhere without any reservation to such fierce pursuit of personal happiness, one which defies and belittles pure ideals, though it reveals at the same time their terrorist savagery" (*Les Samouraïs*, 181). According to Joëlle, it is this insight into the latent savagery of pure ideals that the young revolutionaries need to integrate into their future-oriented imaginaries if they are to avoid sobering up in a new age of Terror (190). In *Thérèse mon amour* Sylvia Leclercq confesses: "If the ultimate Kantian project of 'reuniting' morality and liberty interpellates me strongly, this is because the final metaphor of unity ... cannot be understood solely in the sense ... of solidarity, i.e. of fraternity. Reducing it to this sense results in cutting off the wings of the adventure and, in the process, cutting off a lot of heads as well" (65–6).

This is why in *Les Samouraïs* May '68 is approached as a potential completion of the French Revolution, one that might contribute to opening up the rights of Man to include the right to singularity and the concern for vulnerability (190): "(No) *more* politics: give way to solitude, to the minor pleasures and misfortunes of life" (244; my emphasis). One could argue, therefore, that the figure of "the Samurai" in the novel stands precisely for this ethical excess of revolutionary politics. However, if this figure counters that of "the Mandarins" in Beauvoir's narrative, this is not merely because, as Atack suggests, it foregrounds the "singularity of speech and of pleasure as opposed to the uniformity of a Message be that republican or militant" (242), but also because these warrior-figures emerge as both "courageous" *and* "ridiculous" – hence, fallible, vulnerable, open to critique and exposed to the risks of humiliation (Kristeva, *Les Samouraïs*, 355). On my reading, Kristeva's Samurai are certainly not the products of the "fulfillment of a powerful wish to *take the place of the hegemonic intellectuals*" (Atack, "The Silence of the Mandarins," 248), for what they discover (what they remind us) is that any hegemonic positioning is predicated on the forgetting of limits – the limits of pure ideals (which the seductress unwittingly exposes) as well as one's own limits as thinker and warrior. It is not that Beauvoir's characters are oblivious to such limits. On the contrary. This is the important realization that her intellectuals gradually make; a realization, however, they experience as a dead end or, at best, as the inevitability of compromise. By contrast, for Kristeva's Samurai the acknowledgment of limits becomes the very source of their strength: "the force comes," Hervé (one of the warrior-figures in the novel) tells his son, "if you are focused and if you have a sense of the limit. Learn your limits and those of others" (448).

Hervé's advice to his son is Kristeva's distinct response to "the blinding mirror of the guillotine" (178), a response that she reiterates in the fictional works following *Les Samouraïs*. In these works the desired sense of the limit develops through the protagonist-narrator's exposure to the ordinary singularity of a vulnerable other, "an X who exists just as he shows himself to you: irritating, thinkable, lovable" (Kristeva, *The Old Man and the Wolves*, 146). In *The Old Man and the Wolves*, this ordinary beloved X is the Old Man, a dying member of an endangered species, whose memory and value Stephanie Delacour, the female protagonist, will devote herself to protecting against the regime of Terror the wolves have established. In later novels, this "being that matters, no matter what" (Kristeva, *The Old Man and the Wolves*, 145) takes the form of a psychically or physically fragile youth: namely, Jerry, Stephanie's adopted son in *Possessions* and *Murder in Byzantium*, and Paul, Sylvia's autistic but musically gifted patient in *Thérèse mon amour*. Whether presented in terms of an allegorical confrontation or in the context of a more subtle juxtaposition of antithetical forces, the wounded intimacy of these characters serves to counter "a humanity possessed by the death drive" (Kristeva, *Visions capitales*, 11), flirting with the possibility of an acephalous and hence limitless existence.

Indeed, from the psychoanalyst's perspective, murder, Terror, and cruelty are all the product of a denial of limits – those posed by reason and moral conscience as well as the limits posed by the precariousness of our own human condition. It is in this light that we need to understand Joëlle's critical engagement with the figure of Scherner in *Les Samouraïs* (183–6) and his death-bound pursuit of pleasure.[18] Hence also Stephanie's concern over the increasing failure of the distinctly human response of *shame*, that is, the subject's ability to internalize the other's gaze as a limit to his/her desires and acts.[19] Not surprisingly, the serial killer in *Murder in Byzantium* signs his grotesque, morbid installations as "the infinite" – that is, the one who knows no limits (157), while in *Thérèse*, the boundless, uncritical love for an idealized absolute is approached as the source of political and religious Terror.

The task of the female intellectual, the father's warrior-daughter, in Kristeva's fiction is to reintroduce thought and the possibility of knowing as important subjective and communal defenses against the vertiginous experience of an acephalous existence. In contrast to Michel Foucault (the prototype for the figure of Scherner in *Les Samouraïs*), Kristeva refuses to understand the workings of knowledge solely within the matrix of a will-to-power. From her perspective as a psychoanalyst, knowledge can, *at the same time*, put limits to power and, more important, it can expose the limits of any desire for an existence beyond (*on the other side of*) power. One can argue, therefore, that what drives Kristeva's fiction from the 1990s to the present is a deep commitment to thought as the pursuit of a fundamental question that, according to Kristeva, defines the limits of the human: Where does "it" come from, this "desire of the human being to kill his/her fellow" (Kristeva, *Visions capitales*, 138)? If, in pursuit of this question, Kristeva feels the need to turn to the medium of fiction, this is because, as she admits, fiction enables her to approach the human desire to kill "from within" rather than "in a metalinguistic fashion."[20]

Clearly, then, for the female intellectual, the desire to know, far from being associated with a position of mastery and objectivity, is inextricable from the activation of a transferential process that blurs the boundaries between knower and known, self and other, subject and object. As we have seen, in Kristeva's fictional oeuvre this process may involve an identificatory or empathic connection across different historical periods and across generations. I have already discussed the significance of Joëlle's passionate (although not uncritical) transference onto Thérésa Cabarrus in *Les Samouraïs*. I have also traced a parallel transferential process that unfolds in *The Old Man and the Wolves*, one that enables Stephanie to transpose the Old Man's "obsessions," "his singing and ... suffering" into herself (170). In more recent works of fiction the subjective and communal possibilities opened through the protagonist's amorous investment in a figure from the past are explored further. *Murder in Byzantium* and *Thérèse mon amour* even come to adopt the intimate style of a love letter, unfolding (to a greater or lesser degree) as an amorous dialogue with this "other" across time, a singular being that, through language, exposes herself to us. In particular (after an opening typical of the detective genre), *Murder in Byzantium* develops gradually as a psychic journey back to eleventh-century Byzantium and to the seductive interiority of Anna Comnena, "the first female intellectual, perhaps even the first modern historian" (18). Anna Comnena's writings, read and reread in different contexts and by different characters, come to life and evolve as the site where the boundaries of the self dissolve. When confronted with Anna's story, Stephanie's skin becomes porous and she, as a result, can experience from within the troubled intimacy of one of the murderers, Sebastian, who is also an amorous reader of Anna. Using this female ancestor as her guide, Stephanie (the detective-journalist) translates Sebastian's psychic longing in terms that Rilsky (the police investigator) can understand, opening up the possibility for a crossing of pathways in an imaginary topos that distant others come to share.

Similarly, in *Thérèse mon amour*, St. Thérèse of Avila is not treated as the object of a biographical study but functions as a transferential site. To Sylvia, she is an affect-invested yet active and challenging interlocutor whose singularity the psychoanalyst lovingly reconstructs through a close reading of the Saint's own writings. Indeed, in its profound dialogic nature and its self-reflexive concern with writing as a process of *co-naissance* (i.e., a process of being born along with/through the other), *Thérèse mon amour* epitomizes a structure that, I argue, lies at the heart of Kristeva's fictional work to the present: namely, the analytic structure of transference/countertransference "in which the other person counts" (Kristeva, *New Maladies of the Soul*, 26). This structure, as I have suggested, enables Kristeva's female protagonists to activate the idiolects of official history in ways that address our contemporary concerns (e.g., the return of sacred violence and religious fundamentalism, foreignness and vulnerability, social and intimate cruelty).

Equally important, this structure of empathy and identification offers Kristeva's daddy's girls alternative positions from which their own intimate experiences of decapitation can take on the promise of renewal. It is from these transferential positions that the characters' desire to know is re-conceptualized and reactivated as a desire "to know oneself, and to transform oneself and grow" (Kristeva, *New Maladies of the Soul*, 43). More specifically, through their empathic journey across memory and across time, Joëlle, Stephanie, and Sylvia acquire the strength to confront key traumatic experiences in their lives (the death of a father or a mother, an abortion, the loss of a lover or a friend) and learn to keep a balance between their vulnerable, creaturely being and their head (i.e., their ability to reflect on their creaturely nature and claim a voice within the Symbolic). This, one might argue, is a quality that differentiates Kristeva's daddy's girls from an older generation of female characters, such as those Beauvoir depicts. In *The Mandarins*, for example, Beauvoir shows concern over the distinct dilemmas and impasses women face after the end of World War II. Her women characters, vulnerable but resilient, struggle to develop their own ways of surviving the traumas of war and their own personal deadlocks. Each of these women (Paula, Josette, Anne, Nadine) come to flirt with violence and self-destructiveness mainly because (in ignorance, self-defense, or fear) they remain distrustful of others. They are unable to travel across, beyond their own suffering, and connect with the pain of equally vulnerable others. Even Anne, the psychoanalyst, who is the most self-reliant female figure in the novel, comes very close to committing suicide at the end of a passionate love affair with an American writer. Anne is clearly troubled because of her inability to be response-able to a humanity in need: "What had I been hoping for?" she asks. "To see that familiar setting for a fleeting moment through Paula's eyes? To know from that setting the flavor of her days? No, the little monkey will never see with the eyes of man. And I will never slip into the skin of another" (Beauvoir, *The Mandarins*, 230).

By contrast, Kristeva's porous protagonists open themselves to the pain, the hatred, the psychic fragility, and the emptiness of both perpetrators and victims: "The void entered into me together with the smile of a father who sang with pain, and I am becoming that void," Stephanie confesses in *The Old Man and the Wolves* (170). Similarly, in *Possessions*, "Gloria's mutilated corpse seized hold of Stephanie, and the still invisible but mysteriously present scenes of carnage seemed to sully her and drag her down to the roots of degradation" (70). As these quotations suggest, the characters' porousness is achieved at a price, for their very identity is destabilized and their pursuit of knowledge endangered: "Gloria came to seem so near it was overwhelming. A bad sign for a detective. What about objectivity?" the narrator asks (127). Yet, according to Kristeva, it is precisely one's pretensions to objectivity that need to be sacrificed. In other words, what needs to be abandoned in this process of *co-(n)naissance* includes the detective/investigator's ability to remain neutral in the face of abject impulses, the psychoanalyst's insistence on "playing dead," or the author/ narrator's aspirations to detached omniscience. In her interview with Elisabeth Bélorgey, Kristeva discusses the need to compromise oneself. She tells Bélorgey: "One way to compromise yourself is to reveal yourself through a work of fiction that uncovers the different parts of the intimacy that allows you to understand other people, their pain, their perversity, and their desire to die, all of which resonate with your own" (Guberman, *Julia Kristeva: Interviews*, 251). It is their readiness to open up to (and echo from within) other characters' pain or hatred that renders Kristeva's daddy's girls the nodes of a multiplicity of connections within the novels, connections that, as we have seen, bring past and present together, but they also bridge the intra-fictional and extra-fictional worlds, serving as sites of identification and empathy for the readers.

At the end of *Visions capitales*, Kristeva asks: "What do they do, the man and the woman, once they know where *it* [ça] comes from?" Indeed, what do Kristeva's daddy's girls do once they have experienced the death drive from within and allowed it to destabilize their very existence? Kristeva continues: "They remember. They remain in transit. And they laugh *it* off" (153; my emphasis). As I will go on to argue, it is this liberating, defiant, sometimes insolent laughter that constitutes the distinct strength of Kristeva's warrior-daughters who may lose their bearings or their balance, although they never lose their head.

Decapitation Impossible: The Position of Irony

In the third part of *The Old Man and the Wolves*, Stephanie, still carrying the suffering and voice of the Old Man within her, remembers:

> So sometimes I would start to laugh. A diabolical counterpart to his angelism.... The Professor, like my father, would forgive me, though he was visibly upset. And then he would continue with his favorite song, in which the hero, about to be beheaded, asked to have his hair and his shirt washed so that he might be all clean and airy when he met his Maker. My nerves would now turn my giggles to hysteria: I felt like crying. And I used to slink out of the room, convinced once and for all that I was incapable of God. (152–3)

This is an important moment in the narrative that helps Stephanie accept and internalize the void left behind after the Old Man's death, a death that brings back the pain for the loss of her own father. At the same time, the memory of young insolent Stephanie enables the protagonist to adopt a distance from her filial position of mourning and from the two paternal figures in her life, the "men of sorrow"[21] who succumbed to the knowledge that "there was no longer a Berlin Wall between" "us" and "them," humans and the wolves, good and evil (177). Although seduced by the old men's faith in "God" (as the spiritual interval that keeps the death drive at bay (151)), Stephanie remains an atheist because she knows that the void of death, hatred, and crime is already within. Her stance, however, is not that of the nihilist, cynically embracing crime in the absence of God. If she laughs in the face of the old man's angelic faith (a faith that has proved' powerless against the wolves (174)), this is because, for her, "God" is a game of frames and limits that one needs to play well, both against those who take it seriously *and* against those who forbid it. This, according to Stephanie, is the stance of the artist for, as she puts it, "art is a game of God with God, which reveals only the gods – sublime but ephemeral forms" (173). This is also, as we shall see, the stance of daddy's girl who does not like giving in (*Possessions*, 209) and takes the challenge to survive in the "wilderness bequeathed to her by a dead father" (*The Old Man and the Wolves*, 175). It is no wonder, then, that Kristeva's warrior-daughters "avoid both murder and a good conscience" (*Possessions*, 106). Indeed, at the end of *The Old Man and the Wolves*, Stephanie admits that she is "a female wolf" – one, however, "who knows what's behind it all and is prepared to talk about it" (*The Old Man and the Wolves*, 183). It is this sense of complicity (inextricable from a sense of responsibility) that becomes the distinct signature of Kristeva's female protagonist. Cerebral and dispassionate, alert and playful, reflective and self-critical, stubborn in her quest for truth and always on the move, Kristeva's many-headed heroine emerges as a kind of paradox, an anomaly. In other words, she gives flesh and blood to that impossible creature of the imagination: the female ironist.[22]

In *Irony's Edge* Linda Hutcheon insists that irony "demonstrates an attitude and has an evaluative edge" (2). Similarly, in his own seminal study, *The Concept of Irony*, Søren Kierkegaard argues that irony needs to be approached "as a position" (253). Irony, then, is not simply a rhetorical figure but a subjective stance and a (self-)critical mode (Hutcheon, *Irony's Edge*, 30). It is the marker of the subject's singularity in relation to his/her contemporaries[23] and the index of his/her freedom with regard to actuality (Kierkegaard, *Concept of Irony*, 253). I believe it is in these terms that we need to appreciate Kristeva's sketching of a new type of female protagonist who is neither victimized by nor reconciled with the equally decapitating logic of a death-bound imaginary and an authoritarian Symbolic. One may, indeed, argue that it is the opening up of the possibility of irony as a viable position women can occupy that differentiates Kristeva's brand of feminist fiction from that of a previous generation. To go back to Beauvoir's *The Mandarins*, which in this analysis I have been treating as an important departure point for the novelist Kristeva, it is interesting to note that irony does not emerge as an empowering mode of female subjectivity. Nadine, Anne and Robert's rebellious daughter, is the one female character who comes close to this possibility. Yet Nadine's use of irony is more defensive than self-reflective and critical. As a result, it takes the form of scorn and unrestrained cynicism. According to Henri, her husband, irony is for her an excuse for remaining trapped in the past. It develops into an attitude of carelessness and suspicion, preventing the character from closely engaging with the present and those around her (Beauvoir, *The Mandarins*, 690, 721–4).

By contrast, "the touch of irony" that becomes the signature of Kristeva's detective-cum-journalist-cum-dedicated traveler-cum-psychoanalyst is an attitude that enables the protagonist to keep a critical distance from, while remaining engaged in, the world of actuality (*Murder in Byzantium*, 231). The influence of Kierkegaard on Kristeva's employment of irony cannot be missed here. For Kierkegaard, irony is the subjective mode of absolute negativity. The ironist is the singular individual par excellence who keeps him/herself apart from conventional views and "looks down on … plain and simple talk that everyone can promptly understand" (248). If s/he acknowledges the given, this acknowledgment is merely a "mask" that will permit the ironist to lead actuality "to its certain downfall" (264). The ironist is, then, a master of strategic distancing and double talk. As Hutcheon herself notes, irony operates on the threshold between the "said" and the "unsaid," the "heard" and the "unheard," the "seen" and the "unseen" (*Irony's Edge*, 9). This is why, she insists, "irony can only 'complexify'; it can never 'disambiguate'" (13).

This is precisely the stance of Kristeva's "dispassionate" female ironists (*Murder in Byzantium*, 74): "What I say is not what I think, my words describe an illusion that is the opposite of my sincere conviction, and I enjoy savoring this discrepancy, which I've made up on my own," Stephanie confesses to psychoanalyst Estelle Pankow, a knowing and inquisitive interlocutor (243). Similarly, Sylvia, Thérèse, and Joëlle take pride in their detachment, which takes the form of a "mild" (indeed a tender) irony[24] that, despite its "corrosive" effects, does not exclude "sympathy and affection."[25] Like the fox in La Fontaine's tale that Stephanie identifies with, Kristeva's protagonists know that "[t]he game of life is more complicated and really more mobile and playful," than "all the crows of Santa Varvara" are prepared to acknowledge (*Murder in Byzantium*, 244). Hence the conscious decision her daddy's girls make to think and act from the in-between position of the committed traveler, the stranger, the outsider: "I experienced Santa Varvara from within, but turned myself inside out like a glove in order to see and hear it as from a distance," Stephanie tells us (*The Old Man and the Wolves*, 141).

Yet, as Kierkegaard points out, although the "ironist ... is lighter than the world," s/he "still belongs to the world" (*Concept of Irony*, 152). In fact, as he explains in his discussion of irony after Fichte, "actuality (historical actuality) stands in a twofold relation" to the ironist: "partly as a gift that refuses to be rejected, partly as a task that wants to be fulfilled" (276). It is no wonder in this light that Kristeva follows Kierkegaard in associating irony not only with absolute negativity and critique but also with transformation and regeneration. Kierkegaard writes: The ironist "becomes intoxicated, so to speak, in the infinity of possibilities, and if he needs any consolation for everything that is destroyed, he can have recourse to the enormous reserve fund of possibility" (262). He goes so far as to insist: "Anyone who does not understand irony at all, who has no ear for its whispering, lacks ... the bath of regeneration and rejuvenation" (326). Along similar lines, Stephanie the ironist is convinced that "from this void new forms will be born" (*The Old Man and the Wolves*, 176) and does not hesitate to foreground the ironist's prophetic function for, as she tells Estelle, s/he "doesn't cease pointing at something to come without knowing exactly what, something still missing" (*Murder in Byzantium*, 243).[26]

It is this something, barely glimpsed in the present, that gives irony its critical edge, enhancing its potential to work as a "limiting power" not only with regard to what is taken as "given" but also with regard to the subject and its desire for absolute knowledge or power (Kierkegaard, *Concept of Irony*, 320). "Irony limits, finitizes, and circumscribes," Kierkegaard argues in his analysis of K. W. F. Solger (326). This is indeed the sense Stephanie gives to her distinctness as an ironist: "But that's enough for today – basta! That Audrey sure can be sentimental: no idea of going too far! In fact, my irony is precisely the opposite of Audrey's way: the presence of the finite within the infinite sentimental chatter that she so loves" (*Murder in Byzantium*, 232).

For the female ironist, then, irony becomes the mode of inhabiting a world she can always see through and remain critical toward. It is a conscious position of resistance from *within* inasmuch as the female ironist keeps her eyes fixed at "the underside of all the cards" while remaining a "complicit player" (Kristeva, *Murder in Byzantium*, 77–8). More important, irony in Kristeva's fiction emerges as a discursive site where a new form of community might be established. As Hutcheon rightly argues, irony is "a relational strategy in the sense that it operates not only between meanings (said, unsaid) but between people.... Ironic meaning comes into being as the consequence of a relationship, a dynamic performative bringing together of different meaning-makers" (58). This is certainly the basis of the bond formed between Stephanie and Estelle at the end of *Murder in Byzantium*: "Go there for the irony, Estelle, my vicious visitor," Stephanie prompts her (243). And it is this "rule of irony," demanding a sympathetic but "vicious" listener, that can account for the special friendship that develops between Stephanie and Rilsky, the police inspector (151, 243). Significantly, it is here, in this discursive space opened up by the double-entendre that Kristeva most engages her reader, inviting him/her to see and appreciate the female ironist's wink, although s/he needs to stay vigilant: "We understand each other, you and me," Stephanie nudges, addressing us (66).

As we have seen, Kristeva follows Kierkegaard in her employment of irony as a position of freedom, critique, and resistance, a position she consciously reclaims for the female subject. At the same time, however, Kristeva insists on reminding us that irony should not be conceptualized and used as a position of mastery for, as an attitude, it remains enabling only if the ironist acknowledges his/her limits. In her interview with Belorgey, Kristeva explains how in *Les Samouraïs* death, the characters' growing awareness of human mortality, "keeps the lightness of ... irony in check" (Guberman, *Julia Kristeva: Interviews*, 250). In *Murder in Byzantium*, Stephanie herself confesses: "The son of Gloria, my decapitated friend, who is now my son, my Jerry with his 'problems' ... is the only person I shelter from all irony" (233). This willing self-limitation that refuses to let irony turn into indifference or arrogance is what Kristeva defines in *The Sense and Non-Sense of Revolt* as the "traverse" of the phallic position "in the real presence of the child" (106), this vulnerable X who calls on the protagonist to reject "the comfort of knowledge" and venture "into care" (Guberman, *Julia Kristeva: Interviews*, 249), that is, into a life dedicated to alleviating suffering and misfortune.

In my analysis of what I have called Kristeva's *transphallic* fiction, my aim has been to trace this traversal in the female characters' assumption of the phallic position itself. This is why, I would conclude, for Kristeva's warrior-daughters, Cixous' question ("Castration or Decapitation?") poses only a false dilemma. Indeed, daddy's rebellious girls know that playing the game of the phallus demands that one is ready to lose it – again and again. Similarly, the threat of decapitation means nothing to the female ironist who, with a playful wink, can make her head disappear only to conjure it back anew in a multiplicity of positions, in the most unlikely guises, or as the most improbable, wondrous illusion: a headless, bodiless grin.

Conclusion

In this chapter I have departed from prevalent perceptions of Julia Kristeva's fictional oeuvre and its relation to her theoretical output. In contrast to critics who read her cerebral fictional style as a betrayal of her own theorization of avant-garde writing and of the expectations associated with *écriture féminine*, I have shown how her fiction grows out of a concern that is central in her theoretical writings, namely, her concern with the logic and iconographies of decapitation. As I have suggested, Kristeva invests this concern with feminist, psychoanalytic, political as well as ethical stakes, employing the paradigm of decapitation in an attempt to address questions that relate to a) the fate of women's embodied existence as thinking (phallic) subjects; b) the need to understand and mediate the human being's fascination with death; and c) the aporias and ethical lessons of revolutionary politics. If Kristeva turns to fiction as the terrain *par excellence* where such questions can productively be addressed, this is because, I have argued, the openness of narrative to the analytic process of transference/counter-transference enables us to understand the cult of death and the desire to kill from *within* and not simply in a metalinguistic/theoretical fashion. In addition, the fictional approach can throw into relief the value of every singular "X" in all his/her ordinariness and vulnerability, thus serving as a corrective lens through which an ethically sensitive revolutionary politics might be articulated. Finally, as we have seen, in Kristeva's hands the genre of fiction develops as the "promised land" where female psychic bisexuality can be activated, nourished, and socially appreciated (Kristeva, *The Sense and Non-Sense of Revolt*, 105).

This is why I have ventured to call Kristeva's writing-in-the-feminine "*trans*phallic" for, in contrast to more familiar practices of *écriture féminine*, it does not deny phallic positioning; nor does it attempt to erupt on the other side (indeed, on the *under*side) of the phallic. On the contrary, as my analysis of Kristeva's female ironists reveals, her fiction does not aspire to be "less phallic but more-than-phallic" (Kristeva, *The Sense and Non-Sense of Revolt*, 105), thus offering female readers a number of viable subject-positions from where both dispassionate critique *and* empathy, both knowledge *and* the assumption of responsibility are rendered possible. It is no wonder, in this light, that Kristeva's distinct response to the contemporary economies of decapitation comes from precisely these positions that are as empowering as they are life-affirming because they draw on the force of irony, a *tender* irony (as I have called it) that "refuses to surrender to the mere given" only to release faith in the promise of the given,[27] the love for life, and the gift of "co-naissance."

WORKS CITED

Atack, Margaret. "The Silence of The Mandarins: Writing the Intellectual and May 68 in *Les Samouraïs*." *Paragraph: The Journal of the Modern Critical Theory Group* 20(3) (1997): 240–57.

Cixous, Hélène. "Castration or Decapitation?" Trans. Annette Kuhn. *Signs: Journal of Women in Culture and Society* 7(1) (Autumn 1981): 41–55.

De Beauvoir, Simone. *The Mandarins*. Trans. Leonard M. Friedman. London: Harper Perennial, 2005.

Guberman, Ross Mitchell, ed. *Julia Kristeva: Interviews*. New York: Columbia University Press, 1996.

Hutcheon, Linda. *Irony's Edge: The Theory and Politics of Irony*. London and New York: Routledge, 1994.

Kierkegaard, Søren. *The Concept of Irony, with Continual Reference to Socrates*. Ed. and Trans. Howard V. Hong and Edna H. Hong. Princeton, NJ: Princeton University Press, 1989.

Kristeva, Julia. *Les Samouraïs*. Paris: Gallimard, 1990.

Murder in Byzantium. Trans. C. Jon Delogu. New York: Columbia University Press, 2006.

New Maladies of the Soul. New York: Columbia University Press, 1995.

The Old Man and the Wolves. Trans. Barbara Bray. New York: Columbia University Press, 1994.

Possessions. Trans. Barbara Bray. New York: Columbia University Press, 1998b.

The Sense and Non-Sense of Revolt: The Powers and Limits of Psychoanalysis, Vol. I. Trans. Jeanine Herman. New York: Columbia University Press, 2000.

Thérèse mon amour: Sainte Thérèse d'Avila. Paris: Fayard, 2008.

"Une(s) femme(s)." In Julia Kristeva, *Seule Une Femme*. Paris: Éditions de l'Aube, 2007. 114–28.

Visions capitales. Paris: Editions de la Réunion des musées nationaux, 1998a.

Lechte, John. "Fiction, Analysis, Possession, and Violence in Kristeva's Mirror of Writing." In *Kristeva's Fiction*, edited by Benigno Trigo, 125–41. Albany: State University of New York Press, 2013.

Levenson, Michael. "The Critic as Novelist." *The Wilson Quarterly* 18(1) (Winter 1994): 116–24. http://www.jstor.org/pss/40258822. Accessed December 29, 2010.

Margaroni, Maria. "The *Vital* Legacy of the Novel and Julia Kristeva's Fictional Revolt." In *Kristeva's Fiction*, edited by Benigno Trigo, 155–73. Albany: State University of New York Press, 2013.

Martinez, Roy. *Kierkegaard and the Art of Irony*. New York: Humanity Books, 2001.

Nikolchina, Miglena. *Lost Unicorns of the Velvet Revolutions: Heterotopias of the Seminar*. New York: Fordham University Press, 2013.

Whitford, Margaret. "Review of Julia Kristeva, *The Samurai: A Novel* and Luce Irigaray, *Sexes and Genealogies*." *Women's History Review* 4(1) (1994): 139–41.

CHAPTER 9

Shattering the Gender Walls: Monique Wittig's Contribution to Literature

Dominique Bourque

> The universalization of each point of view demands a particular attention to the formal elements that can be open to history, such as themes, subjects of narratives, as well as the global form of the work.
> Monique Wittig (*The Straight Mind and Other Essays*, 75)

In 1964, a French novel bearing a strange title, *L'Opoponax*, earned its author, Monique Wittig (1935–2003), the prestigious Prix Médicis. The writer published three more experimental novels (*Les Guérillères* in 1969, *Le Corps lesbien* in 1973, and *Virgile, non* in 1985), a fictive "dictionary" with Sande Zeig (*Brouillon pour un dictionnaire des amantes*, 1976), a play (*Le Voyage sans fin*, 1985), a collection of short stories (*Paris-la-Politique et autres histoires*, 1999), and articles on language and literature that also fed an essay on writing (*Le Chantier littéraire*, 2010). One of the author's unpublished short stories inspired the scenario of Zeig's film *The Girl* (2000).

In parallel, Wittig played a central role in the French women's liberation movement and in the development of materialist feminism, which in U.S. academic feminism has been largely sidelined in favor of the more psychoanalytically oriented forms that came to be known as "French feminism," an Anglo-Saxon invention (Delphy, "The Invention of French Feminism"; Moses, "Made in America"; Winter, "Mis(representations)"). Diane Crowder summarizes what distinguishes Wittig's perspective from the social constructivist approach in these terms:

> For a materialist like Wittig, gender is not at all a set of roles or expectations superimposed on biological sex. Rather, these roles and expectations follow logically and inevitably from material exploitation of the class "women" by the class "men." That exploitation, and the material benefits men derive from it, determines both sex and gender, the former being used (as black skin was used by slave owners) as a convenient "naturalizing" excuse for imposing the latter. ("Universalizing Materialist Lesbianism," 65)[1]

I want to acknowledge the institutional support of the Social Sciences and Humanities Research Council of Canada for its financial support, and to thank Julia Balén for her editorial comments.

Wittig's analysis of the "Straight Mind" and its "Category of Sex," as well as her elaboration of a lesbian materialist theory, both of which contextualize and develop this perspective, appeared in the French journal *Questions Féministes* (1977–80), and in the U.S. journal *Feminist Issues* (1980–92),[2] before they were published in *The Straight Mind and Other Essays* (1992).

Wittig understood literary and political activities as two different practices on the basis of their distinct usage of language. Literary writers, she contended, do not perceive language like general users do. For them words are not mere vehicles that convey meanings; they are material units composed of letters that strike the eye and sounds that vibrate in the ear. Because words possess physical and abstract dimensions, as well as etymological roots and a literary history, they are a particularly complex material to craft. But when writers successfully counteract words' petrification into clichés, they trigger their capacity to re*sign*ify and open up meaning. This reactivation of words is obtained by their defamiliarization, or reorganization in original sentences or structures.

As a consequence, literature does not only interpret "reality" as is the case for monological discourses (used in politics, sciences, discussions, etc.), it also contributes to creating it. According to Wittig: "meaning comes from the form, the worked words" (*The Straight Mind and Other Essays*, 72). Clearly for this author, the site of words' action in literature is less communication than perception. Furthermore: "For Wittig," notes Crowder, "words and works of fiction are material objects that can shape not only the mind but also the social and physical bodies of humans. Her fiction demonstrates how language maintains and perpetuates the physical exploitation of women and how it can change" ("Universalizing Materialist Lesbianism," 64).

Wittig inherited her materialist understanding of literature from writers referred to as the *Nouveaux Romanciers* (New Novelists). These writers were considered to belong to an "École du regard" (School of the Gaze) because of their focus on formal components and circumscribed elements. It could also have been called the School of Awareness, considering, for example, Nathalie Sarraute's minute attention to intonations, pauses, and rhythms to describe what she called "tropisms," "interior movements that precede and prepare our words and actions, at the limits of our consciousness."[3] What mattered to these formal writers was not *what* was said, by *whom* and *where* as is the case in Balzac's novels, but *how* and with *what effect*, thus positioning the readers as necessary participants of the book and, potentially, as writers.

The *Nouveau Roman* emerged in the aftermath of the Second World War at a time when human beings faced the extent of the horrors that humans were capable of inflicting on their fellow creatures. With modernism, artists had become increasingly "suspicious" toward the reliability of existing systems of representation to seize reality (Sarraute, *Tropismes*). Confronted with the vertiginous depth and complexities of both the world and the self, the *Nouveaux Romanciers* moved away from seemingly realistic stories (focusing on plot, characters with defined personalities, identifiable setting, etc.) and philosophical novels (*romans engagés*) to concentrate their attention on naked facts and perceptions. This led to the elaboration of a new realism formalized by anonymous "characters" instead of well-defined ones.

Wittig built her own fictions in this nexus of a material cognizance of the world (including its modes of representation) and a decentered perspective, except that in her fictions, the "anonymous" voices are specified. The voices are those of socially censored or disregarded characters. The introduction of their points of view, and not their identities, on the literary scene is consistent with the modernists' questioning of "objectivity" and interest in subjectivity as generating valuable, although conflicting, interpretations of the world. By shaping *perspectives* of young girls, feminist rebels, or lesbians, Wittig was thus not limiting the scope and the quality of literature, but rather adding colors, textures, and depths to its palette. As Julia Balén writes: "Wittig worked language the way a welder works metal – a brilliant mind burning white-hot bending language with a worker's materialist sensibility to make space for those it would erase" ("The Straight Mind at Work at the Heart of Queer Theory").

Interestingly, Wittig's first novel was published in 1964, just before the burst of the new social movements in France, when previously ignored or marginalized subjects started to gather to speak up and examine the structures behind their silencing. In the French language, the specific grammatical treatment of female locutors resulted in their animalization. Gender, by defining women by their sex rather than their humanity (Michard and Viollet, "Sex and Gender in Linguistics"), short-circuits their capacity to represent human beings not only in language but also in literature. Sarraute was well aware of this dehumanization: "I hardly ever think of gender when I write about my characters. I often prefer *he* to *she* because *he* is neutral but *she* is only female" (Guppy and Weiss, "Nathalie Sarraute, the Art of Fiction"). Wittig shared this awareness but expressed it in materialist terms:

> Gender is the linguistic index of the political opposition between the sexes. Gender is used here in the singular because indeed there are not two

genders. There is only one: the feminine, the "masculine" not being a gen-
der. For the masculine is not the masculine but the general. (*The Straight Mind and Other Essays*, 60)

In order to open up literature to all human perspectives, Wittig had to find "pathways and means of entrance into language" (*The Straight Mind and Other Essays*, 78). She focused her attention on "the only linguistic instances that designate the locutors in discourse" (78), which are personal pronouns. Although the specific manner with which she achieved their unlocking is fundamental in the recognition of her mastery of writing, it is not the main subject of the present text. On one hand, various scholars (Bourque, "Dire l'inter-dit"; Écarnot, *L'écriture de Monique Wittig*; Livia, *Pronoun Envy*; Zerilli, "A New Grammar of Difference") have successfully examined this question and, on the other, it is the extent and the coher-ence of Wittig's general treatment of perspective that can best help us understand her main contribution to literature.

Un-marking Gender

They must wear their yellow star, their constant smile, day and night.
Monique Wittig (*The Straight Mind and Other Essays*, 7)

Gender as we know it is not just a grammatical structure; it is also a trans-versal one affecting all dimensions of the "female" subject. In literature genres, themes, characters, and narration/perspective were all historically polarized along the sex line male/female: main or secondary, action or pas-sion, historical or personal, and so forth. To challenge the rootedness of genre in language and literature, Wittig had to re-carve these elements. The result is what she called a war machine:

> Any important literary work is like a Trojan Horse at the time it is pro-duced. Any work with a new form operates as a war machine, because its design and its goal is to pulverize the old forms and formal conventions. It is always produced in hostile territory. (*The Straight Mind and Other Essays*, 68–9)

On this view, language and literature are battle sites "where attempts at the constitution of the subject confront each other" (Wittig, *The Straight Mind and Other Essays*, 61).

Unlike Marxists, Wittig saw language "as a direct source of power" (Wittig, *The Straight Mind and Other Essays*, 73). She also saw the imprint of social relations in the different ways language handles male and female locutors. The fact that only the latter have to flash their sex when they speak or write in most European languages makes clear what defines them in Western societies. Because the value of those marked as women rests essentially in their bodies, they have to be quickly identifiable as such. This is exactly what Wittig contends that the mark of gender accomplishes:

> The result of the imposition of gender, acting as a denial at the very moment when one speaks, is to deprive women of the authority of speech, and to force them to make their entrance in a crablike way, particularizing themselves and apologizing profusely. The result is to deny them any claim to the abstract, philosophical, political discourses that give shape to the social body. Gender then must be destroyed. The possibility of its destruction is given through the very exercise of language. (*The Straight Mind and Other Essays*, 81)

Wittig's wrestling with the gender mark resulted in three main devices: avoiding it by resorting to the French neutral pronoun "on" (one), in *The Opoponax* (1964); giving it a "blow" by universalizing the third person "elles" (the plural of she), in *Les Guérillères* (1969); and taking it to the mat by shocking the authoritarian first person "je": "j/e" (I: /), in *The Lesbian Body* (1973). The first of these "Trojan horses" was able to introduce, within the walls of literature, young girls as full subjects. The second one did the same with feminist rebels, and the third one with lesbians. Of course, the carving of appropriate pronouns was only the beginning of the "war," not all of it, because language is, as previously mentioned, solely one of literature's aspects that bear the mark of gender. Nonetheless, working with perspectives rather than identities (with their inevitable relation to a norm) allowed the author to dethrone the "straight mind" from its pedestal and thus present it as one point of view among others.

Wittig's various literary angles of "attack" on the formal construction of the sex category, as well as on other socially asymmetrical categories, require new analytical tools. "Dé-marquage," "the action of undermining a marking" (Bourque, *Écrire l'inter-dit*), proves useful. Inspired by the French verb "se démarquer": "(sport) to lose or shake off one's marker; (fig) ... to dissociate oneself from,"[4] the hyphen between "dé" (un) and "marquage" (marking) highlights the word "marking," as in the sense of assessing, labeling, and branding.[5] It refers to the political phenomenon of marking social groups according to a random characteristic that can be a physical trait (sex, skin color, body size), a practice (sexual, political, religious), a social status (class, caste, "foreignness"), or an affiliation (to a family, a culture, a community).

The hyphen in "un-marking" carries another important signification. It indicates a degree of detachment from the "marking," ranging from a minimal one (its avoidance) to a complete one (its abolition). The function of un-marking is to undo the objectification of individuals or groups, so that they can regain their humanity and therefore their capacity to fully represent humankind, and not only the members of the identity they were reduced to (females, blacks, gays, etc.). Un-marking can be practiced in various ways in everyday life (where it will go unnoticed or be ridiculed), in politics (where it will be fought), or in arts (where it can appeal to people's consciences).

In the arts, the un-marking devices operate in four dimensions that concern the subject: linguistic, representational, dialogical, and conceptual. Wittig makes use of all of them (Bourque, "Un Cheval de Troie nommé dé-marquage"). To understand these devices in the French language, it is important to note that the grammatical gender has gained an important extension, in particular by means of the agreement of past participles and adjectives (qualifiers) in the case of female subjects (referents) and feminine nouns. As linguist Anna Livia outlines:

> The French gender system has spread its tentacles, as it were, from morphology, morphosyntax (showing which qualifiers belong with which nouns), and morphosemantics (providing some indication as to the gender of a referent) to cross clausal and sentential boundaries and exert a strong binding effect at the discourse level. (*Pronoun Envy*, 57)

Subsequently, its uprooting is bound to affect the structure of language as Wittig acknowledges:

> [A] modification as central as this cannot happen without a transformation of language as a whole.... Words, their disposition, their arrangement, their relation to each other, the whole nebula of their constellations shift, are displaced, engulfed or reoriented, put sideways. And when they reappear, the structural change in language makes them look different. They are hit in their meaning and also in their form. (*The Straight Mind and Other Essays*, 81–2)

Many scholars (Bourque, *Écrire l'inter-*dit; Chevalier, "Le Corps lesbian"; Écarnot, *L'écriture de Monique Wittig*) underline the originality of Wittig's writing at the various levels of the French language: onomastic, nominal, grammatical, and semantic, but none centered their attention on the deployment and repercussions of one word, by way of example, the title of the novel *L'Opoponax*.

"On est l'opoponax" ("One is the opoponax")

In French every noun possesses an arbitrary or fictive gender. As a consequence, every novice of this language must learn nouns' genders by heart. Because it is impossible to know the gender of all substantives in the dictionary, even francophone speakers will need to refer to a dictionary when confronted with an unfamiliar word. The word "opoponax" belongs to this category of specialized terms.

As a francophone reader, the first thing that struck me was its playful spelling: its three [o]s, two [p]s and very unusual ending [ax]. The repetition of the syllable [po] was evocative of a kids' riddle and reminded me of another fun word that entered my vocabulary as child: "hippopotame" (hippopotamus). When I look at this term now, I am more sensitive to its Greek roots *hippos*: horse, and *tamos*: river. In the case of the opoponax, the fact that I couldn't identify its roots drew my attention to the repetition of the syllable [po] and its bouncy rhythm.

Such an intriguing-looking and -sounding word arouses curiosity. Will Wittig unsettle us like Lewis Carroll did with *Alice's Adventures in Wonderland*, or make us travel in a different historical time and space? If the title rings a Greek bell to most Westerners, only those who know this language or have etymological knowledge of it can see in "opoponax," or "opopanax," the roots *opos*: "juice," and *panax*: "all healing." And only those who learned or checked it up know it refers to an acacia tree, a plant belonging to the parsley family, a fragrant gum resin or the extracted perfume of this resin.

Surprisingly, when we finally come across the word "opoponax" two-thirds of the way through the novel, the word is given none of these definitions. These referents are all alluded to, though, with the exception of "acacia," which is explicitly mentioned. This word shares with "opoponax" the playful rhythmic repetition of a vowel and two consonants. Instead of the aforementioned definitions, Catherine Legrand, the protagonist, whose apprenticeship we have been following since her first day in school and who is by this point in the novel around twelve years old, describes it in this manner:

> On ne peut pas *le* décrire parce qu'*il* n'a jamais la même forme. Règne, ni animal, ni vegetal, ni minéral, autrement dit indéterminé. Humeur, instable, il n'est pas recommandé de frequenter l'opoponax[6] (179–80) (One can't describe it because it never has the same form. Kingdom, neither animal nor vegetable nor mineral, in other words indeterminate. Humor, variable, it is not advisable to frequent the opoponax).

The pronouns "le" and "il" inform us that Catherine Legrand refers to the opoponax in the "masculine" form, in accordance with the gender it is given in the dictionary. However, because this "gender" and the neutral forms are the same, the masculine gender *is* neutral and represents the general as opposed to the particular. Coupled with the use of the indeterminate (in gender as well as in number) pronoun "on," this play on the indeterminacy of the kingdom of the opoponax renders gender categories null. Moreover, the pronoun runs like an obsessive repetition throughout the novel, at times representing one person, at others, many. "On" and the "opoponax" thus partake this trait of changing form all the time, of not fitting in a fixed classification or category.

Unable to describe or draw the opoponax, Catherine Legrand ends up concentrating on its manifestations. They all turn out to be annoying, mysterious moments like when it is impossible to close the top of one's desk: "it doesn't do any good to look[,] one doesn't see anything, or to force it, the top won't go any further. It's the opoponax" (162); or when a leaking faucet makes sleep impossible. "One gets up and turns the tap. Good. It's stopped. But then it begins all over again.... This is the work of the opoponax. And it's also [the opoponax] when one feels something run over one's face when one is lying in bed" (162–3), as if something Catherine Legrand could not see or grab was interfering with the normal course of life, but what?

The first occurrence of the substantive in the novel is immediately preceded by a high rate of appearance of the pronoun "on" (twenty-four times on the previous page). It coincides with Catherine Legrand's obsessive interest for a bold and independent classmate, Valerie Borge,[7] who tells funny stories, knows how to shoot, and loves to walk in the convent's forbidden "allée des acacias" (*acacia* path) (176, 177, 200, 260, 276), a very sensuous part of the convent park where the nuns grow flowers, fruits, and vegetables. It is located on a pre-Christian site, as a Gallo-Roman statue of an impressive woman attests (177).

Soon after Catherine Legrand has appropriated the word "opoponax" to name what she could perceive but not seize, she starts using it in anonymous notes she sends to Valerie Borge to capture her attention. She opens and ends her strange and sometimes threatening messages with the same sentence: "Je suis l'opoponax" (230, 240, 242) ("I am the opoponax"). This is a device that recalls Lewis Carroll's habit of starting his letters to his favorite young readers with his signature and ending them with his greeting. But where the structure of Carroll's epistle is reversed, Catherine Legrand's is circular. Her letters have thus no beginning or end; they are movement, flow. Moreover, by defining the "I" as the opoponax, the protagonist turns it into an indeterminate pronoun like "one."

The appropriation of a word to name an invisible, or perhaps invisibilized, reality (emotion, state, sensation, etc.) is a daring gesture on the part of Catherine Legrand. Similarly to Cervantes' Don Quixote, she stands up for what she seems to be alone in perceiving: the opoponax. Writing to Valerie Borge is a way to alert her of its/her presence, because what she feels in/for her is real although nowhere acknowledged in her textbooks. Such boldness on her part stems from their reading and memorizing epic poems (119, 156–7), some of them referring to powerful women warriors ("Guibourc et les dames d'Orange"). At this point of the story, though, both girls have turned their attention to lyrical poetry (Duffy, "Jean Duffy Rereads *L'Opoponax* by Monique Wittig") and its expression of intense feelings.

After Catherine Legrand has sent her third note and a discussion on the real identity of the opoponax has taken place among the classmates (247–9), Valerie Borge responds that she wants to correspond with the opoponax and that she will pretend she is the opoponax to stop the "which" (one of us) hunt (249). Soon afterward, the girls hold hands for the first time. This moment coincides with the last occurrence of the word: "On dit qu'on *est* l'opoponax" ("One says one is the opoponax") (255). This is an ambiguous enunciation. It could mean that Catherine Legrand is revealing to Valerie Borge she is the one behind the opoponax, or it could also mean that both girls declare they are the opoponax. In any case, because of "one's" plasticity, the statement is not exclusive: anyone can be the opoponax; furthermore, the opoponax can be anyone.

If one possible interpretation of the opoponax is an active and passionate love (a blending of what is conventionally referred to as the masculine and the feminine, or the epic and the lyric), then the sex/gender of the lovers would be irrelevant. This indeterminate emotion would obviously include the "love that dare not speak its name" (Douglas, "Two Loves"). Because "pagan" love is not discussed in Catholic schools, the girls have to decipher its allusions in their Greek and Latin textbooks (Virgil, Tibullus) and in Baudelaire's poem "L'invitation au voyage" (254, 268, 270, 276, 281) from his *Flowers of Evil* anthology, where references to beauty, love, death, "rare flowers," and amber fragrance[8] recall Sappho's lyrical verses. Known as Homer's equal, Sappho is celebrated for her capacity to capture emotions in their material manifestations, like the physical changes the sight of the beloved one generates (speechlessness, sweat, shivers). The subjectivity Sappho successfully renders, through the expression of desire or any other emotion (jealousy, anger, joy), is "beyond difference, beyond categories such as male/female, masculine/feminine" (DeJean, *Fictions of Sappho*, 21).

On the linguistic level, Wittig's choice of a title rooted in the ancient Greek culture positions readers as newcomers about to enter an enigmatic world. In this poetic universe, punctuated by the French "on," the noun "opoponax" makes sense graphically and phonetically before becoming an attribute and the cryptonym of the main character. Its unfamiliarity allows it to escape the fictive gender French ascribes to substantives and subtly announces the emergence of an ungendered perspective of human beings.

Because of its elusiveness, the opoponax can only be represented through its manifestations and changing moods. This recalls the *Nouveau Roman*'s "character" whose intriguing perceptions or reactions, which Sarraute named "tropisms," are left to the reader's interpretation. The circular definition – "one is the opoponax" – blends the indeterminacy of the pronoun with the mobility of whatever interpretation we give the opoponax: "childhood" (Duras, "Une oeuvre éclatante"), "desire" (Stampanoni, "Un nom pour tout le monde," 1985: 93), "a threatening force" (Ostrovsky, *A Constant Journey*, 18), lesbianism[9] (Écarnot, *L'écriture de Monique Wittig*, 35), "Catherine Legrand" (Auclerc, "'On dit qu'on est l'opoponax,'" 263).

Structurally, the word deploys its effects in a transversal fashion. Its playful spelling, alluding to the number zero and geometrical figures, operates in accordance to the apprenticeship of the protagonist, from the title throughout the novel. Once instructed on her immediate surroundings (geology, biology, geography), Catherine Legrand is taught medieval literature and ancient languages. These subjects expose her to different ways of seeing the world. The opoponax is located at the crossing of two sets of poetic quotes, the first one belonging to epic forms (*The Odyssey, Song of William, Aliscans*), historically reserved for male authors and associated with "masculinity," and the second belonging to lyrical forms (Tibullus's *Elegies*, Maurice Scève's *Délie*, Louise Labé, Baudelaire's *Flowers of Evil*, etc.) traditionally practiced by "homo/bisexuals," dandies and women, or any writers considering the individual perspective, as opposed to the "collective" or authorized one, worthy of representing the general. The merging around the word "opoponax" of learning and creating, action and passion, society and person, on both the narrative and intertextual levels, makes it a powerful axis for a novel that works toward the universalization and the deepening of the *bildungsroman* and the *kunstleroman*, two genres traditionally concerned with the social success of white heterosexual male characters.

Finally, the conceptual dimension of the word revolves around the notion of meaning. What is knowledge? Officially what we learn in institutions, informally what life teaches us. When learned and lived knowledge do not converge, chances are there will be no (accessible) name for the non-normative experience, as if it were an illusion. Catherine Legrand never denies the sanctioned meaning of the word "opoponax" in the novel, but the material qualities of the term itself echoed what she could not find a name for: the mysterious and charged perception that resisted simple categories, classifications, kingdoms, genres, and genders. The word "opoponax," like the neologism "guérillères" or the odd expression "corps lesbian" ("lesbian body") in Wittig's other novels, calls for a reconceptualization of our representational tools. It acts as an open sesame to enter the unknown, a world that would not reduce female humans, for example, to their bodies and what they can procure and produce, love to heterosexuality, and lesbianism to sex. For Wittig, underlines Crowder, "it is not desire of sexual practice that defines a lesbian, but a political, social, economic, and symbolic action of refusing the myriad institutions that comprise heterosexuality" ("Universalizing Materialist Lesbianism," 71).

Shattering the Gender Walls

> Humanity must find a new name for itself and a new syntax that would do without gender, the linguistic index of political oppositions.
>
> (Wittig, 1992)

There has been a variety of readings of *The Opoponax*: "the revelator of 'little girls' potential to challenge and transcend women's socialization" (Wenzel, "Le discours radical de Monique Wittig," 52), a "combat against all literary conformity" (Ostrovsky, *A Constant Journey*, 3), a feminist *bildungsroman* "employing the stylistic patterns of the *Nouveau Roman*" (Davis, *Coming out Fighting*, 1), "the universalization of the particular" (Hewitt, *Autobiographical Tightropes*, 136), "a landmark not just in fiction about childhood but in fiction more generally" (Duffy, "Jean Duffy Rereads *L'Opoponax* by Monique Wittig," 169). These various interpretations clearly demonstrate the polysemic quality of this oeuvre.

But the most striking accomplishment of Wittig in *L'Opoponax*, as in her other novels, is her shaping of an autonomous subjectivity as opposed to a "relative" one, to use Beauvoir's terminology in *The Second Sex*. She achieved this by un-marking gender on the four levels that formalize the narrative subject: language, representation, dialogism, and conceptualization. Although the angle of vision displayed in *The Opoponax* is that of a girl from a modest social status in a Catholic environment, it is not Catherine Legrand's "identity" (gender, class, culture, sexuality, etc.) that unfolds from chapter to chapter, but her perceptions of the world as she acquires more skills (in reading and writing) and becomes more knowledgeable, more experienced, and in short more equipped to distinguish reality's hidden side.

This capacity to think critically is passed on to the adult protagonists of the next novels, where it translates into actions that counter what Wittig has called in her essays the heterosexual regime. She describes this regime as based on "sexage" (sexlavement), a concept Colette Guillaumin elaborated to account for the reduction of women to their bodies (hetero/sexism) as well as their appropriation and exploitation (enslavement) ("Pratique du pouvoir et idée de Nature," 21). Wittig herself proceeds by using new narrative voices, themes, textual references, and composition.

In *Les Guérillères* the author crafts the original points of view of feminist warriors and storytellers confronted with patriarchal institutions and discourses across the world, as well as the task of replacing them. With *Le Corps lesbien*, Wittig carves the perspectives of literary lesbian lovers obliged to tear each other apart and create (word by word) one another in order to gain a body (of texts) of their own. Finally, for *Virgile, non*, she fashions the viewpoint of an antiheroic writer disarrayed by the sight of women's exploitation and wounds. Named "Wittig," this writer is instructed by her materialist lesbian guide to find words to describe a paradise that could stand as an alternative to this inferno where violence perpetrated against women is trivialized.

These are some of the models Wittig's work offers for challenging oppression in language and literature in general, for blowing to smithereens the invisible bell jars that display human females like merchandise accessible twenty-four hours a day, every day.

WORKS CITED

Auclerc, Benoît. "'On dit qu'on est l'opoponax': Invention lexicale, innommé, nomination." In *Lire Monique Wittig aujourd'hui*, edited by Benoît Auclerc and Yannick Chevalier, 257–79. Lyon: Presses universitaires de Lyon, 2012.

Balén, Julia. "The Straight Mind at Work at the Heart of Queer Theory: Excavating Wittig's Radical Lesbian Materialism from Misappropriation."

TRIVIA: Voices of Feminism (Summer 2014). http://www.triviavoices
.com/the-straight-mind-at-work-at-the-heart-of-queer-theory.html#
.VKoQRabvjOo.

Bourque, Dominique. "Dire l'inter-dit: La subversion dialogique chez Monique Wittig." In *Parce que les lesbiennes ne sont pas des femmes*, edited by Marie-Hélène Bourcier and Suzette Robichon, 111–35. Paris: Éditions gaies et lesbiennes, 2002.

——. *Écrire l'inter-dit. La subversion formelle dans l'oeuvre de Monique Wittig*. Paris: L'Harmattan, 2006.

——. "Un Cheval de Troie nommé dé-marquage: la neutralisation des catégories de sexe dans l'oeuvre de Monique Wittig." In *Lire Monique Wittig aujourd'hui*, edited by Benoît Auclerc and Yannick Chevalier, 67–87. Lyon: Presses universitaires de Lyon, 2012.

Chevalier, Yannick. "Le Corps lesbien: Syntaxe corporelle et prédicat lesbian." In *Lire Monique Wittig aujourd'hui*, edited by Benoît Auclerc and Yannick Chevalier, 233–54. Lyon: Presses universitaires de Lyon, 2012.

Crowder, Diane Griffin. "Universalizing Materialist Lesbianism." In *On Monique Wittig: Theorectical, Political, and Literary Essays*, edited by Namascar Shaktini, 63–86. Urbana and Chicago: University of Illinois Press, 2005.

Davis, Jamie. "Coming out Fighting: The Warrior Girls of Monique Wittig's *L'Opoponax*." In *Crisolenguas: A Multilingual Electronic Journal*, Universidad de Puerto Rico 1(2) (December 2008): 1–10.

DeJean, Joan. *Fictions of Sappho 1546–1937*. Chicago: University of Chicago Press, 1989.

Delphy, Christine. "The Invention of French Feminism: An Essential Move." *Yale French Studies* 87 (1995): 190–221.

Douglas, Lord Alfred. "Two Loves." *The Chameleon* 1(1) (December 1984): 27–8.

Duffy, Jean. "Jean Duffy Rereads *L'Opoponax* by Monique Wittig." *(Re)lire Revue critique de fixxion française contemporaine. Critical Review of Contemporary French Fiction*, 2012, 157–73: http://www.revue-critique-de-fixxion-francaise-contemporaine.org/rcffc/article/view/fx08.16/835. Accessed November 27, 2014.

Duras, Marguerite. "Une oeuvre éclatante." *France Observateur* 757 (November 5, 1964): 18–19.

Écarnot, Catherine. *L'écriture de Monique Wittig: À la couleur de Sappho*. Paris: L'Harmattan, 2002.

Guillaumin Collette. "Pratique du pouvoir et idée de Nature (1) L'appropriation des femmes." *Questions Féministes* 2 (February 1978): 5–30.

Hewitt, Leah D. *Autobiographical Tightropes: Simone de Beauvoir, Nathalie Sarraute, Marguerite Duras, Monique Wittig, and Maryse Condé*. Lincoln and London: University of Nebraska Press, 1990.

Le Robert & Collins. Glasgow, UK, Don Mills, Canada and Paris, France: Collins Publishers, and S.N.L. Dictionnaire Le Robert, 1983.

Livia, Anna. *Pronoun Envy: Literary Uses of Linguistic Gender*. New York: Oxford University Press, 2001.

Michard, Claire and Catherine Viollet. "Sex and Gender in Linguistics: Fifteen Years of Research in the United States and Germany." *Feminist Issues* (1991): 53–88.

Moses, Claire. "Made in America: 'French Feminism' in the Academy." *Feminist Studies* 24(2) (Summer, 1998): 241–74.

Ostrovsky, Erika. *A Constant Journey: The Fiction of Monique Wittig*. Carbondale and Edwardsville: Southern Illinois University Press, 1991.

Sarraute, Nathalie. *Tropismes*. Paris: Minuit, 1956.

Shusha, Guppy and Jason Weiss. "Nathalie Sarraute, The Art of Fiction" (interview). *The Paris Review* 115 (Spring 1990): http://www.theparisreview .org/interviews/2341/the-art-of-fiction-no-115-nathalie-sarraute. Accessed December 5, 2014.

Stampanoni, Susanna. "Un nom pour tout le monde: *l'Opoponax* de Monique Wittig." *Vlasta. Spécial Monique Wittig* 4 (June 1985): 43–52.

Wenzel, Hélène V. "Le discours radical de Monique Wittig." *Vlasta. Spécial Monique Wittig* 4 (June 1985): 43–52.

Winter, Bronwyn. "(Mis)representations: What Feminism Isn't." *Women's Studies International Forum* 20(2) (1997): 211–24.

Wittig, Monique. *L'Opoponax*. Paris: Minuit, 1964.

   The Opoponax. New York: Simon and Schuster, Inc., 1966.

   The Straight Mind and Other Essays. Boston, MA: Beacon Press, 1992.

Zerilli, Linda M. G. "A New Grammar of Difference: Monique Wittig's Poetic Revolution." In *On Monique Wittig: Theoretical, Political, and Literary essays*, edited by Namascar Shaktini, 87–114. Urbana and Chicago: Illinois University Press, 2005.

CHAPTER 10

Hélène Cixous: Writing for Her Life

Peggy Kamuf

If I were deprived of writing, I would die.

Hélène Cixous

Surprise! Translated right away into American, my Medusa departed. And what a journey! Without end, without age. And, so to speak, without me. For a performative of independence, it certainly is that. The Medusa went much faster, farther, stronger than my texts of fiction and later my theater. Frankly, I was annoyed.[1]

This is Hélène Cixous writing a few years ago on the occasion of the republication in French of the two texts that, for many years and even still today, were very often the only ones by which she was known outside France. "I became," she writes, "the author of 'The Laugh of the Medusa,' in the universe, that is, its father, or its servant! Wherever I look, wherever I go, she is there: from Japan to Turkey, from Iran to Guatemala, from Argentina to Malaysia, from Lebanon to Korea." Anthologized and reprinted countless times in English and other languages, "The Laugh of the Medusa" had never reappeared in France and in French after its initial publication in 1975 in an issue of the journal *L'Arc* devoted to Simone de Beauvoir (whom Cixous never mentions there). A similar fate had overtaken "Sorties," which had made its first sortie the same year in the form of Cixous's contribution to the joint work with Cathérine Clément that was baptized *La Jeune née*, translated as *The Newly Born Woman*. Thirty-five years later, then, in 2010, Cixous resolved to set aside her exasperation with these uppity offspring and let them appear once again in their original French costume, the one that several generations of English-language readers had had to strip away in the process of solidifying the American-born idea of "French feminist theory" while confirming Cixous as one of its principal exponents.[2]

To this new edition, Cixous gives the title *The Laugh of the Medusa, and Other Ironies.* Irony should no doubt be understood here less in the sense of the discursive trope, whereby one says deliberately the contrary of what one means, and more in the sense of the irony of fate, what the Oxford English Dictionary describes as "A state of affairs or an event that seems deliberately contrary to what was or might be expected; an outcome cruelly, humorously, or strangely at odds with assumptions or expectations." This irony is the trick played on Medusa's inventor, the one who stole away this target for men's legendary hatred and violence so as to let her fly on the wings of uncensored feminine tongues. "She played a damnable trick on me: I who thought I had invented her, freed her from the myth, here she's gone and caught me in her snares" (ibid.). Having been freed by "The Laugh of the Medusa," this title character goes and turns her liberator into a servant. The trap is laid by, among other transfer protocols, translation. As a writer whose pen flies on the wings of amphiboly – the multiplicity of possible word senses when these are aligned in a syntax – Cixous writes, like her mentor James Joyce, untranslatable texts. One has always to think *Finnegans Wake* when reading Cixous, to the despairing delight of her translators. And like Joyce, although she writes primarily in one language, there are many others crossing and cross-fertilizing with it: German, English, Spanish, Yiddish, Russian, Portuguese, Latin, and so forth. She writes in tongues, you could say, but above all it is her principal idiom of French that is detonated by all the little bombs of her sentences. "The Laugh of the Medusa" is a manifesto *for* this kind of writing, which is pluralizing feminine writing. As such it is doing what it calls for, its performative call is also a performance of response to the call.

Although amphiboly is but one resource of this pluralization, it is perhaps the most recalcitrant when faced with translation. This is because it often relies on homonymic possibilities that rarely carry over from one language idiom to another. To take just the example that Cixous herself singles out in her text for this new edition, the French lexicon of *voler* (v.) and *vol* (sb.), no simple English equivalents let one read the indecision between the two possible senses of flying/stealing or flight/theft.

> But all the same it bothers me sometimes to see that *Vol*, which is so dear to me and especially because of the homonymy it enjoys in French, is but a half-*vol* in English, where the indecision is extinguished in translation. It's as if my Medusa flew with just one wing [*ne volait que d'une aile*], she who has so many. In translation they will have stolen from us one *vol* [*on nous aura volé un vol*]. (30)[3]

This remark about an extinguished homonymy contains in fact an even more forbidding obstacle to translation, the homophonic echo between *aile* and *elle*, "wing" and the pronoun "she." The irony is that *elle* who has so many *ailes/elles*, who is thus essentially feminine plural, has been snared by the other language into a singular meaning.

This one-winged, crippled figure is created by translation's unavoidable snares especially when they are abetted by assumptions that writing in any language is the indifferent means to its end in meaning. As Jacques Derrida began to show in the 1960s, these are among the oldest and most intractable assumptions of philosophy in the West. Cixous encountered Derrida's thought about writing as the repressed of philosophy when she herself was beginning to write seriously. Her first work of fiction, *The First Name of God*, was published in 1967 and a year later appeared her hefty state doctoral thesis, *The Exile of James Joyce*.[4] In the same years, Derrida published *Voice and Phenomenon*, *Of Grammatology*, and "Plato's Pharmacy," the key texts in his deconstruction of the speech/writing opposition.[5] Cixous was among the first to take up deconstructive thought for the leverage it provided against patriarchal, phallocentric, or, as Derrida has also called them, phallogocentric structures. "Sorties" begins with a kind of poetic, shorthand recapitulation of these oppositional structures before suggesting that they are all finally related to the couple man/woman:

> Speech/writing
>
> High/Low
>
> Through dual, hierarchical oppositions. Superior/Inferior. Myths, legends, books. Philosophical systems. Everywhere (where) ordering intervenes, where a law organizes what is thinkable by oppositions (dual, irreconcilable; or sublatable, dialectical). And all these pairs of oppositions are *couples*. Does that mean something? Is the fact that logocentrism subjects thought – all concepts, codes and values – to a binary system, related to "the" couple, man/woman?[6]

The text's first footnote signals unequivocally this alliance with Derrida's thought,[7] which Cixous has reaffirmed countless times since, throughout her oeuvre. Thus, what she famously named *écriture féminine* in 1975 also echoes the Derridean preoccupation with writing, not only in its tenets and themes but also in its pluralizing, disseminating practice, which she aligns with the feminine. In Cixous's book, Derrida is, like Jean Genet, one of those men-writers "who aren't afraid of femininity" ("Laugh," 885).[8]

Perhaps, then, the greatest irony of "the Medusa effect" was to turn a fluid writing into the stone tablets of a manifesto that was an anomaly, even a hapax, in Cixous's literary output. As she writes in *The Laugh of the Medusa, and Other Ironies*, it happened only once that she cried out like this "in literature":

Enough!

I cried out.

One cries out once.

I had already written a lot [in 1975]. Texts that were free, beyond, auda-
cious, dateless. It still happens that I cry out, but not in literature. One
cries out only once in literature. I cried out. Come on. One good time.
I reset the clocks [*J'ai fait date*]. One time. Did I calculate it? No. It was
time. An emergency. A dislocation. The cry that gushes forth at the articulation of times. One must cry it out in writing [*le crier par écrit*]. Print the
laughter. (*Laugh*, 27–8)

And even as she yields to the necessity of reissuing these one-time texts in
their original form, she protests, "I am not an *author of manifestos*. Do you
hear me? I write. I am someone quiet, withdrawn" (*Laugh*, 30).[9]

Cixous has published forty-eight novels or fictions to date (2015), and
more than thirty other major works including literary essays, plays, long
interviews, and collaborations with other artists. That is more than one
book for every year of her life (she was born in 1937) but compressed into
the lifetime of the author who was newly born fewer than fifty years ago,
in 1967. Many of her initial writings appeared under the designation of
novels, no doubt at the insistence of publishers who needed to soothe
readers' suspicions about this very unconventional prose.[10] The concession
to generic convention conventionalized her first "novel," *Dedans*, enough
to win a prestigious French literary prize in 1969. In 1975, however, the
same year as "The Laugh of the Medusa" and "Sorties," the designation
"novel" was dropped as Cixous began publishing with the feminist press
Éditions des femmes. From thereon out, she will refer to these books as
"fictions," but the books themselves appear without any generic marker.[11]
From here on, Cixous's oeuvre makes its own mark as feminine writing.

Recall that, for Cixous, the concept of writing has been deconstructed
and displaced by the more generalizable, even universalizable idea of what
Derrida calls (after Freud and Emmanuel Levinas) the "trace." Writing, in
the restricted or so-called literal sense, is but one kind of trace, which is to
say, one kind of repeatable mark that remains readable in the absence of
any origin or originator. In its most expanded sense, however, trace names
the movement of *differance* (both differing and deferring) that allows for
any structuring repetition of the same, including but not limited to the
structures of a language. The idea of the trace emerges from Derrida's
thinking of life as an auto-affection that has to pass by way of another,
that cannot repeat itself as self-same without repeating the difference of

the other. Life, then, as also its other, as the death-in-life that Derrida terms living on.

It is to this idea of trace (or writing) as the life of living-on that Cixous brings the prodigious proof of her oeuvre, a life's work. It is prodigious not just by its vast accumulation but first of all because it plies so compulsively the differential space between life and work, living and writing, until no space can seem to remain between them, so saturated is it with threads tying the two together. One place where this difference almost dissolves altogether is the dream, a common feature in Cixous's fiction. She has always acknowledged her extraordinary capacity to dream and to remember her dreams. And she has often described how they accompany her in writing and in life as the space of poetic transformation: life←–dream→writing. In 2003, she even collected a number of her transcribed dreams in a volume, *Dream I Tell You*.[12] A few years later, *Hyperdream* (2006) takes the power of dreaming to the next level, the power to let the dead live again in a hyperdream reality.[13] And in 2009, Cixous rediscovers a literary precedent for such hyperdreaming, the 1891 novel *Peter Ibbetson* by George du Maurier in which lovers, separated cruelly in life (she's married and he's in prison), meet every night in their dreams and live out a long dream life together.[14]

Dreams punctuate all Cixous's fictions, or rather they permeate them. Sometimes they are clearly signaled as such, but at other times one merely senses that language has shifted into a dream gear as it were. Here is a fragment from the dream (or dreams) Cixous situates in *So Close* just before she arrives in Algeria and returns to the land of her birth for the first time in thirty-five years:

> *I do not find my truth, someone tells me it is in the back of the room to the right, I cross the room, I see the landscape from afar, the sea raises its waves, it's sumptuous, the way the city raises its buildings like waves, I scan the vastness, my head turned toward the beauty behind the window, if only I could sit down, contemplate, but there is no room all is full, not a table, not a chair, where is my truth? it's probably that way says the café waiter, further on, to the right, I plunge into a dark corridor feeling my way, the moment I lean on the wall a shower is set off, I'm soaked, so that's how it is with my Algerrancy, for nights on end I am almost there, I start over, I am not discouraged by the hotelkeeper I circulate for a long time wet without ever finding my room again . . .*[15]

Even if the italics didn't signal it, it is hard to mistake the rhythm of dreaming in these lines. It is the rhythm of first this and then that and then that. What is missing from such syntax are the logical conjunctions that connect and order sheer sequence into a pattern of meaning: not only this *then* that, but that *because of* this. But dream logic is other, and it comes from that other called the unconscious. This other logic is what Cixous's writing taps into. In the extract just cited, the jerky action of the dreamer who careens like a pool ball across a room, then scans a vast landscape before rolling into a wall and getting soaked, has that hallmark of dream action that is the absence of its apparent reason in the eyes of whoever is no longer dreaming. For of course, this dreamer has awakened from her dream when she recalls it and writes it down; therefore, she cannot recount it without beginning to transform it poetically while translating the trace of the dream into the written trace of language and narration. And yet these lines convey the rawness of the dream caught before any conscious censor or interpreter has taken it over for inspection.[16] Only in the last lines of the extract does one sense the intervention of the censor/interpreter. The one writing this book about what will have been her "Algerrancy," the errancy with which she turns around the return to Algeria, seizes upon the dream's power to say "how it is with my Algerrancy, for nights on end I am almost there, I start over, I am not discouraged … " before plunging back into the dream logic that knows no reason: " … by the hotelkeeper I circulate for a long time wet without ever finding my room again."

There are many other "Algerrancy" dreams scattered through the book, in fact permeating all its pages. For finally there is no telling dreaming from writing or, within the narrative, dreaming from waking life. Indeed, very early on the narrator concedes that she had long thought the ideal would be to go to Algeria "as in a dream": "To go there as in a dream, that would be the ideal I used to say to myself. To go there as *a dream*, I dreamt" (*So Close*, 12). Each step taken toward the decision to go there actually, in waking reality, is described in a dreamlike way but also sifted through dreams as they come in the night. What is so momentous about this decision, we understand, is that the writer fears that Algeria today and in the daylight of the present will destroy the Algeria of her dreams, her childhood, the memory of her father, everything that has irrigated her life and her writing since.

And yet, once there, she begins to accumulate experiences in which the present repeats, recovers, or retains the past as she had never yet dreamt it could. The past comes alive again in these encounters, not yet as hyperdream – although there are several of these recounted in *So Close* – but as if desire were managing everything from somewhere offstage. When, for example, she revisits the site in Algiers where her family's home stood, she finds that no trace remains, but then a shopkeeper claims to remember her father's large, lush garden, and invites them onto the roof of the ugly building that now stands where the garden was, whereupon the writer gazes on the city landscape of her childhood. Even though she knows she is awake, it is as if she were dreaming because the past is so improbably accommodated in the present: "My dream has a lot of imagination. I didn't expect such a faithful metamorphosis" (*So Close*, 109). When a rooster crows and her host assures her it is a white rooster just like the one that still crows in her memory of childhood, the narrator reflects: "So I'm dreaming. So I'm not dreaming: it's indeed a dream that is happening in reality" (110). Another dream seems to happen in reality when, in Oran, she is persuaded to enter her first childhood home which, unlike the site in Algiers, is still standing although it is much deteriorated. Her fear is at its most acute of losing the light shed on her life, her dreams, and her writing by this intimate setting of her past as she remembers it. The entryway and stairs to the house are crumbling, friends have to urge her forward, and then, as in a dream, she comes upon the Benaouf family, a father, mother, grandmother, and two small children, which mirrors exactly the writer's own family when she lived there. Once again, it's as if she had dreamed what she calls both a translation and a transposition of "Cixous" by "Benaouf." The past has not been destroyed but inherited, passed down, retraced. As she exits the house, however, "the anaesthesia wears off and I find myself again Rue Philippe I wake up while rapidly losing the taste of the dream of transposition" (*So Close*, 140).

What is patent throughout Cixous's work is that writing, like dreaming, is allied with life even as it seeks to preserve traces of the dead and the past. The traces of her father, who died of tuberculosis at age thirty-nine, are kept the most compulsively close, to be rearranged in writing where new patterns can be found. Cixous has often asserted that her father's death determined her as a writer.[17] In *Or, The Letters from My Father*, she even copies down his writing as she relates the momentous experience of reading for the first time unearthed letters from her youthful father to the one who would become her mother.[18] The next year, in 1998, she published *Osnabrück*, which takes its title from her mother's birthplace in Germany. This text marked a turn in Cixous's work toward her mother, Eve Cixous (née Klein).[19] Even though she bears the name of the mother of all humanity (according at least to some), this Eve is never simply confused with "the" mother or "the" woman. Writing under the influence of Eve, as she has done more and more insistently during the past fifteen years, Cixous lovingly traces the features of the woman to whom she owes life: her speech, in its singular rhythms and forcefulness, her resolute practicality, her stories, and then the depredations of her body as she approaches and surpasses the century mark. Each year another book, for Cixous writes with the regularity of the seasons, according to a rhythm that orders her life around two uninterrupted summer months when she retreats to her "writing house" in southwest France. The most recent book to date, *Homère est morte* (2014), traces the last months of Eve's life, which ebbed away in her daughter's home in Paris, an agony that is unsparingly recounted. The title, which defies simple translation, announces the death of the ur-Poet, Homer, who is also Mère and thus the mother of literature.[20]

This kind of superimposition, which lines the figure of her mother up with the fount of poetry and literature, alerts one clearly enough that, even as Eve's being in the world is put into language with great care for singular details and even though the writer-narrator shares the author's first person, this is something other than what we think of as "autobiography." It has rather the character of what should be called *writing for her life*. Hélène Cixous writes for her life. What does that mean?

"To write *for* your life" can mean a number of different things at once:

1) to write so as to save or to keep your life, to keep living, or to keep life alive. In this sense, *for* can signal an exchange or an equivalence in some economy or other, for example, in the marketplace economy where writing can earn you a living, but also in the singular economy of the living organism that must write in order to live, like the one who affirms, "If I were deprived of writing, I would die."[21]

2) to write *in favor of* life, to be on the side of life, to be "for life." In *H.C. for Life*, his magnificent tribute to Cixous and her work, Derrida meditates at length on the senses of the phrase "for life" as he has learned to understand them from her and from her work. The principal thread he follows is the sense of her being on the side of life, *du côté de la vie*, an affirmation that gives her work its power or what he analyzes very powerfully as its performative *puissance*;[22]

3) to write *in the place* of life, to stand in for it and in its stead. With this sense, one approaches the naïve idea of autobiography, that is, a writing that represents faithfully the life the author has lived. Because Cixous's work makes constant reference to the persons, events, and places that fill her life, this representational or referential sense can never be simply dismissed, but it is always undergoing transformation by the text and into the text. Every page of her work could illustrate

this transformation but here, for example and chosen more or less at random, is the beginning of a page from *Osnabrück*:

> MUTTER, KANN ICH TRENNEN, when I was little that's what I used to say to Omi as soon as I had finished stitching a square of fabric, *may I unstitch it* this comes back to me in the morning, I didn't sew very well, no sooner stitched than unstitched, says my mother while chopping onions we were standing in the kitchen where we have never sat down in our lives, and now as soon as I get up I see myself going into Omi's bedroom in Osnabrück every morning. *Trennen*, that means to undo, unstitch. Rip out the thread.
>
> –It means to separate, I was thinking.
>
> Mother may I separate? Can I?
>
> You permit me, do you permit me mother separation?[23]

A sentence, a question, would seem to be exactly rendered as it was spoken in life: *Mutter kann ich trennen?* This is Eve speaking and she is speaking of her own mother, Omi, and a question that floats up from her childhood. The writer, HC, records the sentence again on this page along with the translation and circumstances of its utterance, first in her mother's own past and then as repeated many years later in a kitchen where onions are being chopped. This represented scene is thus overwritten, overdetermined already in the very words recalled and respoken. For who is speaking to whom or for whom? A daughter to her mother or a mother to her daughter, the one who reutters and translates the words silently as an impossible question back to her mother the daughter? Mother may I, can I separate? What is the referent of the question? A piece of stitched cloth or lives and voices so stitched together as to be inseparable? And is the question asking permission – may I? – or is it inquiring about the very possibility of separating the inseparable – can I? Cixous sews so seamlessly between her, her mother, and her mother's mother that there is no pulling them apart from the text, which simply is that stitching;

4) the phrase "for life" can also mean a kind of promise, the promise to continue, repeat, or remember for life.

This list could continue, but the point is: the assertion "Cixous is writing for her life" engages all of these senses at once. And because her texts effectively enjoin readers, at almost every turn of phrase, to let go of single, proper meaning, they make constant sorties against what she called, in 1975, "The Empire of the Proper."[24] Such a divestment of the proper and of proper property, however, complicates at the very least what is in play in the possessive attribution of *her* life.[25]

To pursue this complication a little further, we can turn to a very recent book, *Chapitre Los* (2013). It bears on its cover a kind of super-title or genre designation: *Abstracts et Brèves Chroniques du Temps*. An epigraph reminds us that the phrase is a quotation from *Hamlet*, Act 2, scene 2.[26] With this plural designation, Cixous perhaps foresees or hopes that there will be chapters to follow this one. Indeed, the title *Chapitre Los* is preceded by a roman numeral I, which seems to indicate the opening of a series. In the few pages of presentation that she wrote upon publication of the book, Cixous explains: "This book is a chapter of *The-Book-I-do-not-write*. It is the first one to have presented itself but, in the end it will not be chapter one, I am almost sure of that, there will not be, among the chapters, one chapter that is more first than another."[27] Italicized and hyphenated, *The-Book-I-do-not-write* has become over many years Cixous's shorthand for the book of her *My Life*, as Henri Beyle (whose *nom de plume* was Stendhal) called it when he resolved to write autobiographically and yet still pseudonymically his *Vie de Henry Brulard*. "Stendhal had to change into a Henry Brulard in order to write his *My Life* by gathering pieces of the life of Henri Beyle." For Cixous, the Book-I-do-not-write is the book of which she has been dreaming for thirty years: "It is the master, the double, the prophet, almost the messiah of all the books I write at its call. This book precedes me and sums me up. It gathers all my lives and all my volumes. It haunts and guides me" (ibid.). It is thus once again a momentous event when she can affirm that *Chapitre Los* is a chapter of this book, the "first to have presented itself."

How this happened, how it presented itself is the story of *Chapitre Los*. The story begins "the night I am preparing myself for Maman's death," her mother having just so firmly announced that death is near that she, the narrator, is reluctantly persuaded to believe it.[28] The narrator awakes the next day, May 15, to find, first, that her mother is still alive – wondering what's wrong with her daughter and asking "Was ist los?" – and, next, to hear the radio announce the death of the great writer and her long-lost friend Carlos. Preparing to grieve for the nearest one, her mother, she had forgotten to prepare for this other distant one's sudden absence from among the living.

But then, the next day, an extraordinary thing happens: Carlos comes back, revivified, given an *other* life:

> Carlos lost: Carlos returned. It is the strange theorem of resistances to states of nothingness. Nothing of what has ceased ceases being other-wise.... I could fill six pages with *clear* memories. These are not the faded

> and mummified images commonly called memories, but moments of life
> begun again, as in the theater where lives are replayed every day with
> vigor, flesh, voice, life that is in no way different from true life. (*Chapitre
> Los*, 23)

What astounds the narrator is the rapidity of the transformation from
"true life" to this other life, the speed with which Carlos returns to live
again for and in view of this book. She even wonders if she should feel
guilty for having yielded to such a rapid conversion of energy between the
two poles of life and literature, the interval in which "the wound makes a
work [*la lésion fait oeuvre*]" and where "[o]ne energy is transformed into
another energy. We just have to find within ourselves the passive force
of the transfer: to accept the transfiguration" (*Chapitre Los*, 24). What is
called here, oxymoronically, a "passive force" is key to the dynamic of this
wound-made-work, this writing that accepts the transfiguration of one
life into another, what she also describes as the annihilated particles of
Carlos – the very cells of his body – transformed right away into the radia-
tions of fiction. Whatever guilt this transfiguration has stirred up is dis-
pelled when the narrator realizes that the cause is "the nature of the very
particles of Carlos. Los. All his being was always attached to transforming
his own sources of energy into an extraordinarily diversified human material. So many characters were launched into worldwide memory by his
acts of imagination" (*Chapitre Los*, 25).[29]

The book that results from this rapid transfiguration, *Chapitre Los*, is
described in the folio as having presented itself:

> all at once, "one fine day," entirely written, floating just in front of my
> study window, clearly constituted, like a dream brought to term by the
> head of the dream. I quickly recopied it, without taking my eyes off it,
> while scrupulously preserving its indications, rhythms, moments of silence.
> I found it. Just as you see it.

It would be a mistake to read these statements as only figurative or having
only a figurative value and meaning. Because Cixous insists that she found
it "[j]ust as you see it," there is no figurative escape from the counterintu-
itive implication that this first chapter of *My Life*, signed Hélène Cixous,
is a copy made from an original "entirely written" by another or others.
Yet, and still counterintuitively, she is not for all that proclaiming plagia-
rism or a fraudulent signature. And if this sounds like a riddle, then recall
once again that for Cixous the concept of writing has been entirely deconstructed, which means that the touchstone of *literality* itself, of that which
is to be taken *à la lettre* as one says in French, has become detached from

itself and set adrift among the endless sorts of traces of which writing, in the *literally* literal sense, is but one. Copying what is "entirely written" thus becomes an act of the passive force that accepts the transfiguration of the traces of "true life" for the other life that is no different. Because it presented itself thus, *Chapitre Los* achieves the dream of *The-Book-I-Do-Not-Write*, which is to receive it as (if) written by the other.

To receive the other's trace in and as oneself, to affirm "I is another" with the poet Rimbaud (one of her heroes), this passive ability or passive force is how Cixous in 1975 spoke of femininity:

> But I am speaking here of femininity as keeping alive the other that is confided to her, that visits her, that she can love as other. The loving to be other, another, without that necessarily entailing the abasement of the same, herself. ("Sorties," 86; trans. mod.)

Writing is feminine in this sense when it keeps the other alive by transforming its traces poetically. *Chapitre Los* makes manifest that in the transformation or transfiguration, life "in no way different from true life" lives on – writing. Whatever one wants to call writing. Cixous, who maintains "If I were deprived of writing, I would die," calls it living on with the living and the dead, with all their traces.

Subversive Creatures from behind the Iron Curtain: Irmtraud Morgner's The Life and Adventures of Trobadora Beatrice as Chronicled by Her Minstrel Laura

Sonja E. Klocke

In the 1970s, the socialist German Democratic Republic (GDR, also known as East Germany, 1949–90) saw two noteworthy developments: a rise in fantastic fiction, and the spread of a distinctly socialist version of feminist thought that was enunciated primarily in literature.[1] In the absence of a critical media scene, GDR fiction participated in – and often initiated – the public discourse on essential topics. Accordingly, literature was crucial in critiquing patriarchal structures, and in developing and spreading feminist ideas – without ever using the term "feminism," which was considered a "problem" of capitalist countries, and negatively connoted in the GDR.[2] Contradicting West German feminism, which emphasized the fight for gender equality, GDR ideology positioned class as the primary essence and gender as a secondary attribute. Accordingly, authors like Irmtraud Morgner believed that women's emancipation happens as part of the general liberation of humankind from capitalist means of production and class-related dominance; a liberation that can only be achieved as a joint effort of both women and men. Today, literary texts such as Morgner's *Trobadora Beatrice* present an illuminating source of knowledge about the position of women and the discourses surrounding feminist issues in the GDR. This chapter therefore highlights how Morgner's novel, in lieu of feminist theory that could not be published in the socialist country, disseminates and advocates GDR-specific feminist thought, and simultaneously criticizes notions of feminism emanating from capitalist countries.

One of the most talented and controversial female authors in East Germany and prominent for her style reminiscent of Magic Realism, Morgner has lately obtained revived interest.[3] Thwarting socialist realism, a literary trend prescribed by the GDR government and aimed at elevating the reality of life under socialism, the fantastic mode allowed authors to escape censorship and to express doubts about the Occidental model of civilization. Among female writers criticism extended to women's prescribed social roles in socialist society, roles that despite progress regarding women's constitutional rights were still influenced by bourgeois norms. While women in GDR society were expected to shoulder the double burden of waged work and the bulk of household responsibilities and childrearing, their position was regarded as evidence of the damaging effects the remnants of bourgeois society had for individuals of both sexes. "GDR feminism" – a term applied retrospectively because it could not have existed in the GDR where the notion of feminism was either negated or presented as the *bête noire* unique to capitalist societies – differed significantly from its West German counterpart: in the East, emancipation from gender inequalities was considered complementing liberation from class oppression. Still, while GDR writers' compassion was with the oppressed of both sexes, women authors' primary concerns were often the multifarious constraints obstructing women's self-realization within the specific social and cultural conditions determining women's realities under socialism.

A committed socialist striving to improve quotidian life in the GDR particularly for women and for members of the working class, Morgner deliberately stages her fantastic world as a version of realism. While her prose relates to everyday life under socialism, she also opens up possibilities of imagining an even better socialist world.[4] Based on tangible events of the present, she envisions a future in which the prerogatives of subjects historically privileged because of their gender and class affiliations as well as the institutional structures and norms buttressing them will be overcome. Morgner integrated a plethora of fantastic elements into *Trobadora Beatrice*. Particularly striking are the female characters with supernatural bodies that allow them to surpass the laws of time, space, and plausibility in order to imagine a new reality for the GDR in which women can relate as subjects of history equal to men.[5] These characters force readers to question socially accepted and fossilized norms by highlighting the arbitrary social construction of gender, and by undermining power hierarchies and social relations based on specific gender and class positions. Following a compendious introduction of the plot line, I illustrate the significance of the innovative narrative form Morgner calls the "operative montage novel" (TB, 175) for implementing the project of envisioning new female positionalities along the lines of GDR-specific feminist thought. This study then turns to select fantastic characters and gods who inhabit *Trobadora Beatrice*. My analysis reveals how Morgner employs both the form of the "operative montage novel" and fantastic characters to propel ideas that can be described as "GDR feminism"; a feminism that, unlike the West German feminism she opposes, does not aim at redefining the gender binary with reversed signs but at dissolving all binary relations that can be considered responsible for suppressing individuals based on class and/or gender affiliation.

Trobadora Beatrice

The main plot centers on the eponymous *Trobadora Beatrice*, a medieval noblewoman and the only female troubadour. Discontented with the misogyny in twelfth-century France, she requested from Persephone 810 years of slumber in hopes of finding women's equality realized when she awakes. Beatrice's sister-in-law, the beautiful Melusine who was granted prolonged life by the goddesses in return for her work for the restoration of matriarchy, provides the rebellious Sleeping Beauty with up-to-date information about political developments. When Beatrice awakes in 1968, she is disillusioned by the patriarchal structures and the ongoing violence against women. In Paris, she meets a GDR journalist who praises his home country as a "land of miracles" (TB, 3) that has realized gender equality. The *trobadora* decides to move to the GDR, where her pragmatic friend Laura, a socialist, specialist in German literature, engine driver, and single mother, informs Beatrice about the discrepancy between the GDR government's claims and the actual situation of women.[6] Despite the GDR constitution's promise of gender equality, working mothers in particular do not possess a subject position that allows them to fully exercise political, social, and cultural power. Because of the double burden of professional life and childrearing, they suffer from reduced possibilities for creative work and societal engagement. Men still dominate the public sphere, and their supremacy is linked with war, violence, and rationality. Incited by Laura's idea to save the world from hunger, wars, patriarchy, and capitalism, Beatrice starts her "quest" in medieval tradition to find a unicorn whose dried brain, once added to the drinking water, will turn everyone into peaceful communists (TB, 174). Her travel reports, which reveal capitalist countries as hopelessly corrupted and "reactionary" (TB, 173), justify the women's fight for gender equality and the abolition of classes. Moreover, they highlight the superiority of the socialist GDR, which is – while not the perfect state yet – repeatedly portrayed as the best of all existing countries. Only in the GDR do efforts to overcome the bourgeois traditions that programmatically exclude those who do not or cannot aspire to the hegemonic norm yield fruit, and point to an even better future under socialism.

The Operative Montage Novel as a Feminist Mode of Writing

With the words, "[o]f course this country is a land of miracles," Morgner introduces both the GDR and *Trobadora Beatrice* (TB, 3), and prepares us for a capacious novel full of rhetorical and theoretical flamboyance. From a multitude of perspectives, the novel's thirteen books and interwoven seven intermezzi reflect on power, gender, desire, and disillusionment. They conjure up mythical traditions, legends, fairy tales, dreams, songs and poems, adventure stories, news reports, letters, telegrams, scientific reports, legal documents, interviews, speeches, and more – only to reveal and mock the underlying literary conventions. Particularly witty are parodies of typical GDR genres such as brigade diaries, Beatrice's self-critique, and a satire on the "novel of arrival," a genre that developed after the building of the Berlin Wall (1961) to support and praise young citizens' "arrival" in GDR reality. Sometimes contradicting each other, these items belonging to various genres unfold in creative non-order to support Beatrice's attempt to rewrite history by including formerly unheard voices.[7] The multitude of narrative perspectives and genres systematically constructs and destroys established notions of privilege and hierarchy, and challenges the constraints inflicted by patriarchal logos. Proclaimed "the novel form of the future" (TB, 175), the *Trobadora Beatrice*'s montage and its polyvocality formally reflect Morgner's ideological intention and accentuate her refusal to take on the speaking position of a supposedly universal subject.

In the 1970s, both its innovative form and fascinating content accounted for the popularity of *Trobadora Beatrice* on both sides of the Iron Curtain, particularly among readers interested in questions of gender equality. Not surprisingly, the novel triggered diverging interpretations in the East and in the West. Following official GDR politics that insisted that gender inequality was emblematic for capitalist countries and abolished in the GDR, most East German critics – and Morgner herself – denied feminist positions in *Trobadora Beatrice* and scorned the term "feminist" as apolitical. Their rejection of West German readings that emphasized the emancipatory aspects of the novel highlights how in the GDR, notions of feminism and feminist ideas had to be carefully incorporated in fiction that balances concerns for gender equality with an engagement for the working class.[8] In the United States, the novel triggered criticism among some feminist scholars who criticized the alleged lack of female agency, the remaining within the heterosexual paradigm, and the privileging of class over gender.[9] Reluctant to acknowledge that Morgner intended to propel ideas of gender equality in a socialist society in which the notion of feminism was either negated or negatively connoted as distinctive for capitalist societies, these critics overlooked the innovative ways the Marxist author wished to spread ideas that were at heart feminist in her prose. Other American scholars immediately praised *Trobadora Beatrice* as the *Dr. Faustus* for feminists.[10] They laid the foundation for the interpretations that have become dominant in the past few decades and that recognize *Trobadora Beatrice* as "a key feminist text in the GDR."[11]

Based on this understanding, I consider it crucial to appreciate Morgner's agenda to utilize her "operative montage novel" to voice progressive thoughts on gender equality that were meant to boost the realization of women's rights that were granted in the GDR constitution. Deconstructing conventional modes of narrating for the purpose of negating a presumably universal, effectively male subject position, Morgner led the way for feminist concerns in the GDR while she deliberately contested Western feminism.[12] She used the montage novel to thematize gender relations and women's demands for a public voice and a place in historiography, without losing sight of other problems GDR society and the world were facing. In order to popularize feminist thought in the GDR, Morgner had to carefully wrap her ideas that were feminist at heart within the complex web of the montage novel. *Trobadora Beatrice* had to combine questions of gender equality with global issues such as the Vietnam War, the Cuban Missile Crisis, ecological concerns, and feeding the Third World. In the GDR context, the novel advocated for a GDR-style feminist agenda by disrupting literary conventions to allow for rewriting history and for imagining a better future for everyone – independent of gender, class, or ethnic affiliation.

Challenging Hegemonic Historiography: The *Trobadora Beatrice's* Project

Beatrice explains her 808 years of sleep and her clearly defined political agenda to Laura: "I have exited history because I wanted to enter history. To appropriate nature. First of all, my own. Tackle the making of humanity head-on" (TB, 115). In other words, the *trobadora* claims a space in historiography and in literary history. During a visit to Diocletian's palace in Split in the former Yugoslavia, she illustrates her twofold mission: on one hand, to excavate the traces of women's engagement in historical processes by working through the multiple layers of historical knowledge so that their influence becomes visible and on the other, to write women's experiences into history (TB, 198–203). Beatrice aspires to destroy the patriarchal images in historical myths that shape the collective memory of a misogynist history – a truly feminist agenda that reveals how dominant legends are interlaced with their alleged logos. Obscuring the boundaries between historical facts and the imaginary by charging the empty spaces in the historical Beatrice de Dia's vita with feminist thoughts of the resurrected, fictional *Trobadora Beatrice*, Morgner allows her literary character to enter history without being trapped in the logos that initially excluded her. She reveals historical knowledge previously deemed "universal" epistemic knowledge as part of the culturally fluctuating modes of producing, categorizing, and hierarchizing information. Thus, women are excluded from hegemonic historiography because the acquisition of historical knowledge and the evaluation of what is "worthy" of being included are socially created. The underlying constructed norms bar women and members of certain classes. Beatrice contests prevailing models of gender and sex conformity and limitations based on class affiliation as well as hegemonic notions of acquiring knowledge that lead to an exclusive historiography.

Speaking from the position of a noble woman with firsthand historical knowledge reaching back to the Middle Ages, the *trobadora* assumes the privilege of speaking univocally for women of all classes to enable them to enter history. The montage novel undercuts Beatrice's goal of presenting a universal female subject position through its idiosyncratic polyvocality and heterogeneity. In individual stories called "Bitterfeld Fruits," for example, Morgner has her *trobadora* collect accounts of lives of people in the workforce, particularly of representatives of the working class that was celebrated in the GDR. At a time when in West Germany, women had only just become contractually capable (1969), still depended on their husbands' consent to be able to earn a living (until 1977), and were rather invisible in the workforce, Morgner's depiction of women in the GDR supports the notion of socialism as progressive and superior. Stressing individuals' belonging to the working class and portraying both sexes in socialist production, the *Trobadora Beatrice* adheres to the ideological requirement for ranking class before gender. At the same time, the "Bitterfeld Fruits" reflect and also defy GDR cultural policies known as the "Bitterfeld Way," named after the first writers' congress in Bitterfeld (1959), which formulated the goal to incorporate the world of production in the creative arts.

Echoing this objective, the "First Bitterfeld Fruit: The Legend of Comrade Martha in Testimonials" (TB, 363–72) presents the legend of railroad worker and mother Martha Lehmann, who is constructed as a highly valorized comrade. An analysis of this exemplary story reveals how the "Bitterfeld Fruits" contribute to the *trobadora's* project of rewriting history by giving members of the working class, in particular female communists, a voice. The "First Bitterfeld Fruit" includes Martha's writings, consisting of messages she included on her monthly rent payments. Still, the twofold filter that censors her voice indicates the artificial design of this account and reflects on the constructiveness of history and knowledge. Aspiring to depict his mother as a loyal socialist, Martha's son Walter in the "First Bitterfeld Fruit" compiled her notes and comments from contemporary witnesses for a literary contest before Beatrice selected the parts she would utilize for her own agenda. In the *trobadora's* fictional portrayal, Martha is a model working-class woman and staunch socialist, who grieved her son Rudi's death on the battlefield, but happily contributes to rebuilding Germany after World War II. She marvels at her recollections of the socialist marches she has attended since 1900, and freely donates money for poor people in the context of the GDR's "international solidarity."

Beatrice comments on the educational and propagandistic function of this "Bitterfeld Fruit," namely to create a legendary history for working-class women (TB, 364). The female railroad worker Martha Lehmann emerges as a perfect medium for the *trobadora's* agenda of promoting women's entry into historiography because Martha allows for balancing gender and class issues. Revealing the railroad worker's legend as constructed, the *trobadora* accentuates and sustains the idea that propaganda is a legitimate, necessary, and potent tool for advancing the position of women in socialist society.[13] This reasoning also justifies her posthumous representation of Martha, which entails that the *trobadora* adopts a political speaking position for the woman who cannot tell her story any longer and artistically depicts the perfect socialist as an ideal ambassador of the new working-class elite. Beatrice's creative work replaces hegemonic historiography, starring those who exercise power, with an innovative history that embraces those previously excluded because of their class and gender. This "First Bitterfeld Fruit" makes the hitherto invisible Martha visible, and reveals that historiography is not fixed, but can be reshaped along the lines of a specific ideology with the support of legends. Such propaganda is positively connoted as long as it aims at ideological improvement, that is, it serves women's liberation as part of humankind's release from class oppression.

Similarly, *Trobadora Beatrice* renders surveillance by the notorious GDR intelligence agency, the Stasi, rather propitiously when it supports socialism. The novel presents a fictional writer named Irmtraud Morgner and the character I.M. – not only an acronym for the author, but in the GDR also for *inoffizieller Mitarbeiter*, unofficial Stasi collaborator. The resulting narrative ambiguity replicates the commonplace insecurity in the GDR regarding who was engaged in surveillance activities, and hints at Morgner's own rather hazy relationship with the Stasi.[14] In *Trobadora Beatrice*, Laura's activities – she discloses her ideological training and her engagement in Beatrice's socialist reeducation, and some of her notes are reminiscent of Stasi reports – suggest that she spied on her friend.[15] Because the narrative does not challenge Beatrice's successful reeducation, surveillance appears as an ordinary fact of life, and indispensable for securing the socialist agenda. Because socialism allegedly presents the most progressive system, indoctrination along the party line and Stasi observation are equally justified as they serve to achieve the goals of class and gender equality.

Tacitly identified as the most sophisticated ideology, communism exclusively claims the means to save the world and particularly the female sex from the destructive traits of capitalism: war, violence, suppression of women, and hunger. During her "quest," which takes her to capitalist countries, Beatrice identifies the need to tackle class before gender issues in order to free both women and men from capitalist means of production. Explicitly opposing what she considers "emancipatory faddishness," she explains,

> a woman of character today can only be a socialist ... In ... capitalist countries, she first has to enter politics.... Moral relations can only be revolutionized after the revolutionizing of economic relations. One cannot take the second step before the first. In the GDR the first step has long since been taken. Now we are working on the second one, selah. (TB, 402)

Trobadora Beatrice presents the capitalist West as precarious, especially for women and the working class. In contrast, the GDR – while not yet the paradise the *trobadora* envisioned upon her arrival – is depicted as the best of all present worlds. Here, surveillance and propaganda support the country's path toward a marvelous future. Praising the socialist state for having taken the first step in liberating humankind, namely having altered economic relations and abolished class differences, Beatrice can announce the GDR's next step aimed at achieving freedom for everyone independent of their sex. Incidentally, the *trobadora* addresses the remaining gender inequalities in the GDR, and thus propagates their abolition. In her project of rewriting historiography and finally entering history as a woman, the spread of socialism, the abolition of the bourgeois class system, and the advancement of women's position in society are inextricably linked.

Patriarchy, Matriarchy, and the "Third Order" of the Future

Claims to agency not exclusively based on sex also fuel the battle between various supernatural forces in *Trobadora Beatrice*, forces that represent three specific groups in the German reality of the 1970s. The patriarchal divine order led by the omnipotent "Mr. Lord God" equally dominates the proponents of restoring matriarchy, the goddesses Demeter and Persephone, and the "third order" or "opposition," which is "neither patriarchal nor matriarchal but human" (TB, 16). Placed in heaven and partially linked with state institutions in the GDR as well as hegemonic power structures in capitalist countries, "Mr. Lord God" and the subordinated male gods act in the background. They are associated with evil and violence, and significantly curb Demeter and Persephone's power. The male gods sequester the goddesses to a cubic bunker, and grant them only a small quota for approved miracles to be distributed to collaborators like Melusine. By detaining the goddesses and denying them any means of control over their coworkers, "Mr. Lord God" invigorates their desire for revenge.

Frustrated with their confinement and the limitations to their magic, Demeter and Persephone subscribe to a feminism that intends to redefine the gender binary with inverted signs. They echo the aspirations of the West German feminist movement – in other words, of women subjected to patriarchal rule in capitalist countries. In an ironic scene portraying the goddesses, the narrative distances its call for further improvements regarding gender equality in the GDR from West German feminist thought. Spoofing the goddesses in a depiction with an angel who salutes by sharply raising her right arm, the narrative connects the realm of the gods, including the goddesses who represent the caricatured West German feminists, to German fascism (TB, 16). *Trobadora Beatrice* thus follows official GDR ideology, which considers capitalism a version of fascism and West Germany the legal successor of Nazi Germany. The novel identifies the power structures underlying both capitalism and fascism as the prompter for a radical feminism – represented by Demeter and Persephone in Morgner's fictional world – that spreads in capitalist countries. In the GDR, where the constitution grants women equal rights, such Western-style feminism seems out of place, as Beatrice's behavior exemplifies: confronted with female suppression in capitalist France during her "quest," the *trobadora* empathizes with terrorism and realizes that "her sympathies now belonged to the vindictive movement that was planning retaliation" – despite her better knowledge and logic (TB, 56). As soon as she reenters the GDR, however, Beatrice resumes her sympathy with the "Persephonic opposition," also called the "third order" – a group that strives for the eradication of gender inequality together with class differences and can be considered as representing "GDR feminism."

Beatrice's fluctuating sympathies, with West German but also "GDR feminism" depending on the social environment she moves in, accentuate the link between the goddesses, radical West German feminism, and capitalism on one hand, and the "third order" that strives to achieve equality among all humans in a socialist system on the other. Despite their subjection to "Mr. Lord God's" goodwill, this oppositional "third order" is clearly non-confrontational. It resides as a round table reminiscent of the King Arthur legends in a fantastic realm "between Caerleon on Usk and the future" (TB, 16), and points to the future and the GDR as the only place where evil associated with the supremacy of any sex can be overcome. This secret opposition aims to defeat the universalist paradigm at the core of the existing social order imposed by the male gods as well as the detained goddesses' reactionary efforts. Resembling "GDR feminism," the illegally operating "third order" consists of women and men – usually Marxists and labor leaders – who strive to abolish any remaining gender inequalities and class differences in the GDR. The group thus signifies a space beyond the patriarchy/matriarchy binary in the realm of fantasy. Unlike West German feminism, represented by the goddesses who aim to reinstate matriarchy and thus suppress men as a result of redefining the gender binary with reversed signs, the "third order" intends to permeate binaries such as male/female, real/imaginary, legal/illegal, and past/future.

The opposition's efforts to challenge established boundaries are reflected in Melusine's hybrid body that combines the beautiful human upper body with the lower part of a dragon. This physical constitution benefits her illegal activities because it allows her to overcome time and space and to fly without being detected by military radar screens.

Relying on modified laws of nature, Melusine's body corresponds to the novel's claim to influence the future by means of the marvelous, only possible in the GDR, the "land of miracles" (TB, 3). *Trobadora Beatrice* thus resembles Judith Butler's notion of fantasy not as opposite to reality but rather marking reality's limits:

> The critical promise of fantasy, when and where it exists, is to challenge the contingent limits of what will and will not be called reality. Fantasy is what allows us to imagine ourselves and others otherwise; it establishes the possible in excess of the real; it points elsewhere, and when it is embodied, it brings the elsewhere home. (Butler, *Undoing Gender*, 29)

Fantasy's subversive potential lies in imagining a feasible tomorrow – precisely the mission of the "third order." Instead of striving to reverse prevailing binaries in order to triumph over men in a backward-looking matriarchy favored by the goddesses, the "third order" focuses on dissolving remaining dichotomies and on transgressing universally accepted laws in the effort to improve the future for all of humanity. Portraying the activities of this oppositional group's members, who – like Melusine – represent the embodied transgressions of existing norms, *Trobadora Beatrice* sustains an alternative reality based on a different set of laws. Simultaneously, the terminology typical of GDR bureaucracy, for example, the "[d]amn official channels" that regulate the "third order's" magic (TB, 419), playfully links the divine sphere with GDR reality and reveals life devoid of hegemonic dichotomies and hierarchical structures as an ideal yet to be realized. Still, the novel offers a glimpse of a utopian ideal inspired by Ernst Bloch's principle of hope, and points to a future that can be implemented in a land based on the principles of the miraculous – the GDR. Evoking Bloch's "concrete utopia," in which hope constitutes the essential principle in a process aimed at realizing a better future for humankind, Morgner challenges the patriarchal structures lingering in the GDR, and simultaneously imagines the fulfillment of the ideal of a truly egalitarian society.[16]

The "third order's" present modus operandi, which depends on collaboration with the divine world whose prerogative to power is never challenged, accentuates the fact that resistance is only possible within power. Allegedly merely wanting to relieve "Mr. Lord God" of "half of the celestial burden," the "third order" realistically balances the desire for unreserved gender equality and viable implementations in order to carefully enforce political developments (TB, 373). In these negotiations, Melusine, the most feminine mythical figure who officially serves the goddesses on whom she depends for consent for her magic, emerges as a strategically operating politician focused on improving the living conditions for women without alienating men.[17] Prohibited from employing magic for political purposes, Melusine engages in seemingly private, yet effectively political acts that snub patriarchal power structures and the private/public divide characteristic of traditional gendered systems. Accordingly, the fairy fosters the love relationship between Laura and Benno by arranging for the unconscious man to appear on his future wife's balcony in a "celestial vehicle" for inspections (TB, 192, 264–7, 276–8, 282–5). The outwardly private meetings acquire political significance because Melusine effectively initiates an exemplary marriage, characterized as socialist and achieving the ideal of gender equality (TB, 352). Benno emerges as model and utopian vision of a future non-phallocratic man who shares ideas on childrearing and gender roles with Laura. In all her political acts, Melusine's reliance on magic and divine miracles for the objectives of the oppositional "third order" exposes how the aspired-to order of the future challenges the rationality of current modes of constructing and exercising power.

Conclusion

"GDR feminism," clearly distinct from its counterpart in capitalist countries, emphasizes the ideological requirement for ranking liberation from class oppression and capitalist means of production before gender inequality. While this bias led some feminist scholars in the United States to reject *Trobadora Beatrice* as insufficiently feminist, the novel is nowadays appreciated as one of the most significant texts articulating and advancing feminist thought as it developed in a socialist society in the GDR. Concerned with the limitations thwarting women's desire for self-realization, Morgner imagines a fantastic sphere that is linked with women's quotidian life experiences in the GDR and inhabited by characters challenging patriarchal structures and the hegemonic binary oppositions that negatively affect women's lives. Living and writing in a society that considered the term "feminism" an invective, the author carefully and creatively fashioned a means of propelling feminist thought through creatures such as Melusine and her collaborators in the "third order." They develop strategies that destabilize authoritarian structures based on distinctive gender and class positions, and contest universal understandings of "reason" – without alienating men, or aiming to replace patriarchal by matriarchal structures. Unlike the goddesses Demeter and Persephone, in the novel associated with West German feminists, the members of the "third order" promote the spread of communism, which they identify as a prerequisite for women's emancipation. They blur the borders between historical facts and the imagination to establish a new historiography that deducts the authoritative status of "historical truth" by revealing its patriarchal construction. The montage novel Morgner introduces buttresses her political and ultimately feminist message: corresponding with the "third order's" ideals, the numerous texts belonging to a wide range of genres stand on equal footing, quasi "sisterly" and "brotherly." The voices we hear support the notion of a new history devoid of privilege.

Despite limitations emanating from the symbolic "Mr. Lord God" who represents GDR state institutions still partially following bourgeois norms and the power structures governing capitalist countries, characters such as Laura, Beatrice, and Melusine challenge the authorities objectifying them and subjugating them in both the public and private spheres. They defy the conventions that exclude them from history, politics, and the sciences, and contest the legitimacy of both the objects of historical knowledge and the underlying epistemic processes. Particularly the female characters supported by magic can attain subject positions traditionally denied to them by virtue of their gender. They utilize utopian images that point to a more viable future, and ultimately regain agency.

WORKS CITED

Bammer, Angelika. *Partial Visions: Feminism and Utopianism in the 1970s.* New York: Routledge, 1991.

Bloch, Ernst. *The Principle of Hope.* Trans. Neville Plaice, Stephen Plaice, and Paul Knight. Cambridge, MA: MIT Press, 1986.

Butler, Judith. *Undoing Gender.* New York and London: Routledge, 2004.

Dahlke, Birgit. "Leben und Abenteuer der Trobadora Beatriz nach Zeugnissen ihrer Spielfrau Laura. Roman in dreizehn Büchern und sieben Intermezzos (1974)." In *Meisterwerke. Deutschsprachige Autorinnen im 20. Jahrhundert,* edited by Claudia Benthien and Inge Stephan, 278–96. Cologne: Böhlau, 2005.

Damm, Sigrid. "Irmtraud Morger: Leben und Abenteuer der Trobadora Beatriz nach Zeugnissen ihrer Spielfrau Laura." *Weimarer Beiträge* 9 (1975): 138–48.

Detken, Anke. "Weibliche Geschichte und Erinnern: Irmtraud Morgners *Leben und Abenteuer der Trobadora Beatriz nach Zeugnissen ihrer Spielfrau Laura.*" In *Geschichte(n) – erzählen. Konstruktionen von Vergangenheit in literarischen Werken deutschsprachiger Autorinnen seit dem 18. Jahrhundert,* edited by Marianne Henn, 125–44. Göttingen: Wallstein Verlag, 2005.

Emmerich, Wolfgang. *Kleine Literaturgeschichte der DDR. Erweiterte Neuausgabe.* Berlin: Aufbau Taschenbuch Verlag, 2000 (1996).

Gerhardt, Marlis. "Geschichtsklitterung als weibliches Prinzip." In *Irmtraud Morgner. Texte, Daten, Bilder,* edited by Marlis Gerhardt, 93–9. Frankfurt a.M.: Luchterhand, 1990.

Herminghouse, Patricia. "Taking Back the Myth and Magic: The 'Heroic Testament' of Irmtraud Morgner." *German Life and Letters* 57(1) (2004): 58–68.

"Die Frau und das Phantastische in der neueren DDR-Literatur. Der Fall Irmtraud Morgner." In *Die Frau als Heldin und Autorin. Neue kritische Ansätze zur deutschen Literatur*, edited by Wolfgang Paulsen, 248–66. Bern: Francke Verlag, 1979.

Hilzinger, Sonja. *Als ganzer Mensch zu leben. Emanzipatorische Tendenzen in der neueren Frauenliteratur der DDR*. Frankfurt a. M.: Peter Lang, 1985.

Huffzky, Karin. "Produktivkraft Sexualität souverän nutzen. Ein Gespräch mit der DDR-Schriftstellerin Irmtraud Morgner." *Frankfurter Rundschau*, August 16, 1975.

Kaufmann, Eva. *Aussichtsreiche Randfiguren. Aufsätze*. Neubrandenburg: Federchen Verlag, 2000.

"'Der Hölle die Zunge rausstrecken...' Der Weg der Erzählerin Irmtraud Morgner." *Weimarer Beiträge* 9 (1984): 1515–32.

Landa, Jutta. "Feminismus und Systemkritik im mittelalterlichen Kostüm. Irmtraud Morgners 'Trobadora' Roman." In *Medieval German Voices in the 20th Century: The Paradigmatic Function of Medieval German Studies for German Studies*, edited by Albrecht Classen, 199–210. Amsterdam: Rodopi, 2000.

Lange, Inge. *Ausgewählte Reden und Aufsätze*. Berlin: Dietz Verlag, 1987.

Lemmens, Harrie. "Frauenstaat. Interview mit Irmtraud Morgner." *Konkret* 10 (1984): 54–61.

Lewis, Alison. *Subverting Patriarchy: Feminism and Fantasy in the Works of Irmtraud Morgner*. Oxford and Washington, DC: Berg, 1995.

Linklater, Beth. V. *"Und immer zügelloser wird die Lust." Constructions of Sexuality in East German Literatures. With Special Reference to Irmtraud Morgner and Gabriele Stötzer-Kachold*. Bern: Peter Lang, 1998.

Martens, Lorna. *The Promised Land? Feminist Writing in the German Democratic Republic*. Albany: State University of New York Press, 2001.

Martin, Biddy. "Socialist Patriarchy and the Limits of Reform: A Reading of Irmtraud Morgner's *Life and Adventures of Trobadora Beatriz as Chronicled by her Minstrel Laura*." *Studies in Twentieth Century Literature* 5(1) (1980): 59–74.

Marven, Lyn. "The Trobadora's Legacy. Two Generations of GDR Women Writers." In *Women's Writing in Western Europe: Gender, Generation, and Legacy*, edited by Adalgisa Giorgio and Julia Waters, 54–68. Newcastle: Cambridge Scholars Publishing, 2007.

Morgner, Irmtraud. *The Life and Adventures of Trobadora Beatrice as Chronicled by Her Minstrel Laura: A Novel in Thirteen Books and Seven Intermezzos*. Trans. Jeanette Clausen. Introduction Jeanette Clausen and Silke von der Emde. Lincoln: University of Nebraska Press, 2000.

Nordmann, Ingeborg. "Die halbierte Geschichtsfähigkeit der Frau: Zu Irmtraud Morgners Roman *Leben und Abenteuer der Trobadora Beatriz nach Zeugnissen ihrer Spielfrau Laura*." *Amsterdamer Beiträge zur Neueren Germanistik* 11–12 (1981): 419–62.

Rytz, Juliane. "Pandora auf dem Brocken. Irmtraud Morgners Versuch einer feministischen Mythenkorrektur im Roman *Amanda*." In *Pandora. Zur mythischen Genealogie der Frau/Pandore et la généalogie mythique de la femme*, edited by Heinz-Peter Preußer et al., 251–68. Heidelberg: Universitätsverlag Winter, 2012.

Soproni, Zsuzsa. "Raum und Identität in Irmtraud Morgners Roman *Leben und Abenteuer der Trobadora Beatriz nach Zeugnissen ihrer Spielfrau Laura*." In *Gelebte Milieus und virtuelle Räume. Der Raum in der Literatur- und Kulturwissenschaft*, edited by Peter Lökös, Zsuzsa Bognar, and Kalar Berzeviczy, 147–57. Berlin: Frank & Timme, 2009.

von der Emde, Silke. *Entering History: Feminist Dialogues in Irmtraud Morgner's Prose*. Bern: Peter Lang, 2004.

Westgate, Geoffrey. *Strategies under Surveillance: Reading Irmtraud Morgner as a GDR Writer*. Amsterdam and New York: Rodopi, 2002.

Wildner, Siegrun. "'Odysseys and the Silent Sirent': Irmtraud Morgner's Feminist Subversion of Greek Myths through Utopian *Umfunktionierung*." *Seminar* 40(4) (2004): 368–85.

———. *Experimentum Mundi: Utopie als ästhetisches Prinzip. Zur Funktion utopischer Entwürfe in Irmtraud Morgners Romanwerk*. St. Ingbert: Röhrig Universitätsverlag, 2000.

Wölfel, Ute. *Rede-Welten. Zur Erzählung von Geschlecht und Sozialismus in der Prosa Irmtraud Morgners*. Trier: Wissenschaftlicher Buchverlag Trier, 2007.

CHAPTER 12

Christa Wolf: Literature as an Aesthetics of Resistance

Anna K. Kuhn

The role of literature in Eastern Bloc countries like the German Democratic Republic (GDR) differed fundamentally from that in the West.[1] Its official function was to propagate and strengthen socialist values and to help develop the communist state. In the face of censorship and in the absence of an open public sphere, however, imaginative literature often became a space of resistance, an arena in which social contradictions and volatile political and social issues could be addressed. Writers like Christa Wolf (1929–2011) became adept at addressing politically and culturally taboo issues by displacing them into the distant past,[2] employing seemingly apolitical genres such as science fiction or fantasy[3] and developing complex writing styles[4] – strategies that enabled them to circumvent the censors. Wolf's writing praxis was designed to develop critical and emancipatory consciousness and to further both the writer's and the reader's self-understanding and self-actualization[5] – goals that deviated widely from socialist realism's orthodox function of advancing the Marxist telos. Increasingly, this brought her into conflict with the SED (Sozialistische Einheitspartei Deutschland), the Socialist Unity Party. As East Germany's most acclaimed woman writer, Wolf had enormous stature as a public intellectual. The GDR prided itself on being a *Literaturgesellschaft*, a society comprised of readers of literature, and Wolf became a household name: her readings attracted large audiences and sparked heated debates. Although she initially wrote about and for a GDR audience, Wolf's works of the 1970s and 1980s addressed such issues as the psychic and social costs of patriarchal gender socialization; the roots of alienation and human self-destructiveness; the dangers of militarism, war, and nuclear proliferation; and the Chernobyl nuclear disaster. This broader perspective gained her a wide readership in the West as well, particularly among women.

Like other GDR women writers, Christa Wolf categorically rejected the term "feminism," which was viewed as a movement born of and applicable solely to Western capitalist societies. In keeping with Marxist doctrine that the "woman question" would be resolved once women had been integrated into the sphere of production and socialism had been fully achieved, GDR women were guaranteed economic and legal parity. They began to realize, however, that this parity had not freed them from the patriarchal attitudes and structures that still prevailed in the GDR. The 1970s saw the development of a historically grounded feminist critique of social relations in the GDR, a critique that called for the emancipation of both men and women from patriarchal power structures. Christa Wolf's was among the most articulate voices of this critique. Although there was no feminist movement in the GDR, Wolf's rejection of feminist separatism[6] makes clear that she was familiar with some issues central to women's movements in the West. We know from her *Cassandra* project that in the 1980s she familiarized herself selectively with feminist theoretical writings in the context of her work on the transition from a matriarchal to a patriarchal society.[7] With the exception of Luce Irigaray's and arguably Virginia Woolf's, these were not texts being discussed in Western feminist debates of the time. Indeed, it is highly unlikely that Wolf was conversant with issues at the forefront of second-wave feminist discussions. It is therefore all the more remarkable that her writings would address, indeed, often anticipate, some of the leading Western feminist debates of the 1970s and 1980s, including the gender ramifications of object relations theory, the radical feminist critique of patriarchal gender relations, feminine/feminist aesthetics, the epistemic advantage of marginality, standpoint epistemologies, and the feminist critique of science. Feminist in both form and content, Christa Wolf's writings embody literature *as* feminist theory and praxis.

As a committed socialist, Wolf is heavily indebted to Enlightenment thought, specifically to two Kantian principles: faith in the power of reason to emancipate humankind from its self-incurred minority, as elucidated in his essay "What Is Enlightenment?", and the categorical imperative[8] that enjoins us never, under any circumstances, to use people as a means to an end. Crucial for Wolf's understanding of the function of literature and the development of her aesthetics are the wording of Kant's definition of enlightenment, his subsequent elucidation of "Unmündigkeit" (minority) as "self-incurred ... when its cause lies not in lack of reason but in lack of resolution and courage to use it without direction of another," and his call "*Sapere aude!* Have courage to use your own reason!" (85).

Wolf's vision of a human socialism, in turn, is informed by the early Marx's concept of non-alienated social relations that resonates with Kant's principles:

Assume *man* to be *man* and his relationship to the world to be a human one: then you can exchange love only for love, trust for trust, etc. If you want to enjoy art, you must be an artistically cultivated person; if you want to exercise influence over other people, you must be a person with a stimulating and encouraging effect on other people. Every one of your relations to man and to nature must be a *specific expression*, corresponding to the object of your will, of your *real individual* life. (*Economic & Philosophic Manuscripts of 1844*, 169)

Wolf's writing is dedicated to overcoming alienation by helping create the subjects of history needed to actualize Marx's emancipatory vision of a society comprised of individuals with fully developed personalities who respect and treat all other human beings as subjects. The discrepancy between her understanding of socialism and the repressive Marxist-Leninism that prevailed in the East German state made her ever more critical of the GDR's "actually existing socialism," a pragmatic term Erich Hoeneker coined in 1971 that signaled East Germany's turn from its idealistic beginnings to an acceptance of the economic and political exigencies of the status quo. As she became increasingly disillusioned with East German socialism, Wolf developed a feminist lens[9] through which to criticize social relations both in the GDR and in the West. Despite her criticism of the GDR, she remained steadfast in her conviction that socialism, with its belief in human perfectibility, had the potential to develop a humane society. She devoted her life and writing to help realize that end. As Helen Fehervary and Sara Lennox have noted, Wolf's writings were not an alternative to Marxism, but a means of its renewal ("Introduction to Christa Wolf's 'Self-Experiment,'" 109).

Wolf's formulaic 1961 debut work *Moscow Novella* and her controversial novel about the division of Germany, *Divided Heaven* (1963), which emerged directly out of the Party's *Bitterfelder Weg* initiative – commanding writers to enter factories and write about production – complied to varying degrees with prescribed socialist realist norms. Her 1965 novel, *The Quest for Christa T.*, a work of mourning in which the first-person narrator struggles to come to terms with the premature death of her friend, marked a radical break with those norms and became a cause célèbre. In the GDR, efforts to delay and limit its publication backfired; extant copies were passed hand to hand and Wolf's readings were packed as audiences grappled with such existential issues posed by the text as "Was ist dieses Zu-Sich-Kommen des Menschen"? ("What does this coming to oneself mean?"). In terms of content, *Christa T.* flew in the face of prevailing GDR aesthetic norms. In lieu of a positive, robust hero working to further the goals of the socialist state, Wolf presents us with a non-conformist, pensive, sickly woman who rejects the ethos of the pragmatic *Hopp-hopp Menschen* (the up-and-doing-people) valorized by the Party, who strives for self-actualization and for the full development of her personality. Unwilling to accommodate herself to the mechanistic society that characterized the GDR of the 1950s and 1960s, she suffers from her inability to contribute productively to the development of socialism to which she is morally committed, retreats into the private sphere, and ultimately succumbs to leukemia. In the somewhat hyperbolic words of West German literary critic Marcel Reich-Ranicki: "Christa T. dies of leukemia, but her real sickness is the GDR."

Christa T. sounds the theme of "the difficulty of saying 'I.'" GDR critics regarded this subject as an affront to socialism's insistence on the subordination of the individual to the communal and resoundingly rejected as solipsistic Wolf's articulation of the difficulty of speaking in the first-person singular. Feminist interpretations of *Christa T.* in the Federal Republic and the United States, where it was widely read and positively reviewed, stressed the gender specificity of the text; the problematic nature of saying "I" was read in the context of phallogocentrism (Love, "Christa Wolf and Feminism") and as an indication of women's subjugation in patriarchal society (Clausen, "The Difficulty of Saying 'I'"). Although Wolf would have rejected these readings at the time, by 1977, when she wrote "Berührung" ("Touching"), she would come to acknowledge the patriarchal structures in her society that silenced women's voices.

If the content of *Christa T.* was unconventional, the form of Wolf's novel was truly revolutionary and became the hallmark of her new, unique way of writing. What distinguishes Wolf's oeuvre from *Christa T.* on is the interjection of authorial subjectivity, a phenomenon she called "subjective authenticity,"[10] into the literary text. Melding author and narrator and employing such modernist writing strategies as contradiction, ambiguity, montage, reflections on the act of writing, and textual lacunae, Wolf explodes socialist realist expectations by abandoning a linear, mimetic narrative. Addressing Christa T., herself, and the reader, *Christa T.*'s narrator/author employs a dialogic voice and creates a self-reflective, multi-temporal, multivalent, open-ended text – one that calls on the reader to actively engage in its constitution. Marilyn Sibley Fries claims that the international recognition Wolf's oeuvre has garnered lies less in its "dissident" content than in its form: in the "'modern' sophistication of her style" and in "the undeniable moral impulse of her works [that] aims at the 'very inmost part [of the reader of prose]' to call that reader's thinking and life into question and stimulate self reflection" (30).

In "Reading and Writing" (1968), an essay written shortly after the completion of *Christa T.*, Wolf elucidates her new aesthetic. Rejecting socialist realist claims to objectivity and its insistence on narration as the mimesis of empirical reality, Wolf argues that the writer constitutes the subjective dimension of the literary text, imbuing it with *Zeitgenossenschaft* ("contemporaneity," 37). The writer's task is not simply to mirror reality, but "to invent something faithful to the truth, based on her own experience" (33). In its insistence that authorial experience produces knowledge that leads to authenticity and truth in writing, her new aesthetic rests on the feminist notion of situated knowledge and anticipates feminist standpoint epistemologies[11] that reject the concept of objectivity and absolute truth. In claiming that she can write only about topics that affect her, that the process of writing allows her to work through issues with which she is grappling, she acknowledges the autobiographical basis of her work. Writing for Wolf is not a process in which she asserts mastery over her subject matter, but rather a dialectical process, a mutual exchange between the writer and the subject of her narration, a point she will elucidate in her work on Cassandra. Following Brecht, she invokes the concept of "epic prose" to describe her new writing praxis. Like Brecht's epic theater, Wolf's aesthetic of subjective authenticity is designed to make readers conscious of contradictions in their society, encourage them to use reason to make those contradictions productive, to become *mündig* in the Kantian sense, and to work for social change. Epic prose, for Wolf, has a utopian dimension: "it can expand the limits of what we know about ourselves." It helps humankind to become conscious subjects. "It is revolutionary and realistic; it seduces and encourages us to do the impossible" (48).

In her 1966 "Interview with Myself," Wolf discusses the process of writing *Christa T.* and explains that she had originally thought she was writing a biography of her deceased friend, but later noticed that "[s]uddenly it was *myself* I was facing" (16). In recreating her friend and reassessing her own life in light of Christa T.'s uncompromising commitment to her principles and herself, Wolf creates an intersubjective relationship between the narrator and Christa T. Myra Love persuasively argues that in remembering her friend in this way, by creating a mutual relationship between narrator/author and Christa T., Wolf treats Christa T. not as an object of narration, but as a subject. In doing so, Love concludes, Wolf has successfully broken the patriarchal connection, which is built on objectification and domination.

In Christa T. Wolf has created a figure that embodies those characteristics necessary, in her view, for the actualization of her vision of socialism: imagination and conscience. Imagination, described in "Reading and Writing" as the play with the possibilities open to us (31), works against mental stasis and the reification of social structures, keeping alive the possibility of alternative futures, while conscience addresses the ethical dimensions of Wolf's vision of socialist society. Christa T. follows Kant's moral principles, treating everyone with whom she interacts as an equal subject. But she is also concerned with the interconnectedness of human community, a concern that "broadens the parameters of Kant's moral code, which is justice-oriented and based on the primacy of duty, to include a moral consciousness based on responsibility and care" (Kuhn, *Christa Wolf's Utopian Vision*, 86).

The representation of Christa T.'s ethics adumbrates the understanding of mature female morality developed in Carol Gilligan's *In a Different Voice*, a work published seventeen years after *Christa T.* Gilligan found that in situations of moral conflict involving self and others, the criteria for moral decisions differed by gender. Decisions made by the male subjects in Gilligan's study were grounded primarily in a morality of rights, predicated on a sense of equity, while those of the women manifested a morality of responsibility centered on connection and tended to be based on specific context and need. Gilligan drew on work by feminist object relations theorists like Nancy Chodorow to argue that men's more rigid ego boundaries and an identity predicated on a sense of otherness informed a morality that tended toward trans-contextual absolutes and defined justice in terms of separate but equal rights. Female identity, based on connection to and sustained attachment to the mother, led to a sense of identity that stressed intimate relationships, a sense of care, and an ethics based in relationship and the inclusion of diversity.

In her 1973 science fiction short story "Self-Experiment" and the essay "Touching" (1978), Wolf articulates a radical feminist epistemological understanding of gender difference. In her 1973 "Conversation with Hans Kaufmann," Wolf noted that "Self-Experiment" was meant to provoke such questions as: "Is the goal of emancipation, is it even desirable, to have women 'become like men,' able to do the same things, acquiring and protecting the same rights, when men themselves are so in need of emancipation?" (*GW* 4, 430). In "Self-Experiment," a successful male-identified woman scientist undergoes a drug-induced sex change that transforms her into the male Anders.[12] Her sexual transformation is immediate. During the thirty-day psychological masculinization process, s/he becomes aware that the price of masculinity is emotional atrophy, that the secret of male invulnerability is indifference, and that the secret of the hyper-rational, workaholic professor, whom she loves, is that he is an emotionally disengaged voyeur who experiences life as though he were at the movies and is therefore unable to love. S/he breaks off the experiment and reverts to being a woman. Wolf thus rejects as pernicious the Cartesian epistemology that informs the male perception of the world, with its dichotomous opposition of self and empirical reality, believing that it leads to objectification, fragmentation, alienation, and ultimately the inability to love. She concludes her narrative on a hopeful note; the female scientist declares: "Now my experiment lies ahead. Which incidentally can also lead to fantastic inventions – to the creation of the person one can love" (131).

The female narrator's negative experiences in the hierarchal, male-dominated, achievement-oriented, sterile world of the scientific laboratory make clear that Wolf has distanced herself from the orthodox Marxist view, where equity in the world of production leads to women's emancipation and from the GDR's valorization of science and technology as the forces of social renewal. Anders' experiences as a transsexual demonstrate that masculinity, far from leading to emancipation, leads to alienation. Wolf sees women, who have not suffered the debilitating of effects of patriarchal masculine socialization, as offering the possibility of a renewal of social relations that could lead to emancipation for both genders. In her move from a feminism based on gender equality to one predicated on difference, Wolf anticipates the Western radical feminist debates of the 1980s.

Wolf wrote "Touching" as the introduction to Maxie Wander's *Guten Morgen du Schöne* (*Good Morning, You Beauty*), an anthology of nineteen protocols with GDR women ranging in age from sixteen to seventy-four. Harking back to the theme of saying "I," Wolf credits Wander with giving voice to women who would otherwise have remained speechless. In acknowledging that marginalized groups, including women, are silenced in patriarchal societies, she echoes Western feminist critics of *Christa T.*

Commenting on the recurrent themes sounded – a lack of intimacy, conformity to narrowly defined gender roles in the private sphere, patronizing attitudes and invisibility in a hierarchal workplace, and stress arising out of women's double burden – Wolf calls attention to the discrepancy between the theory and praxis of gender equality in the GDR: "Economically and legally we are equal to men … and now we experience to what degree the history of a class society, the patriarchy, has deformed its objects and how much time it will take until men and women become subjects of history" (*GW* 8, 122). *Guten Morgen* makes clear that socialist changes in the mode of production have not overcome alienation; wage parity and equality before the law have not eliminated patriarchal attitudes and structures in East German society. However it is precisely because GDR women enjoy legal and economic parity with men, Wolf argues, that they – unlike women in Western capitalist countries, who are still fighting for the most basic needs – can recognize that equality does not equal emancipation. The coming into being of conscious subjects, essential for emancipation, cannot be accomplished by entry into the existing hierarchal structures of a masculinized society based on competition and the pressure to achieve. Heartened by the women's demand "to live as complete human beings," Wolf calls on GDR women to work with men to achieve emancipation for all: "How can we women be 'liberated,' as long as all human beings are not?" (129). In doing so, she assumes a stance that is closer to that of U.S. third-wave women of color feminists like bell hooks and Gloria Anzaldúa, who recognize that their men are also oppressed by virtue of their race, than it is to second-wave white feminists who focus on male privilege and domination. She also explicitly rejects the idea that women constitute a "class" and thus repudiates both Marxist and second-wave feminist thought that fails to take into account differences among women. In framing difference not only in terms of women's difference from men, but also as difference *among* women, Wolf's comments are in concert with U.S. third-wave feminists, who advocate an intersectional analysis of positionality.

The "unreserved subjectivity" the women display in their interactions with one another stands in contrast to the alienation and isolation that they encounter in their work lives and the lack of emotional intimacy, the sense of not being known, they so often experience in the domestic sphere. Taken together, Wolf argues, the conversations in *Guten Morgen* adumbrate a community based in "sisterliness," whose characteristics are "empathy, self-respect, trust, and friendliness." Drawing on Ernst Bloch's heterodox Marxist notion of concrete utopia,[13] understood as historical moments that keep alive hope for the realization of a truly human socialist order, Wolf claims that "the spirit ... at work in *Guten Morgen* is the spirit of real existing utopia, without which reality becomes unlivable for humans" (115). In invoking Bloch's concrete utopia, Wolf makes clear that the sisterly qualities these women embody hold out the possibility for social renewal, for overcoming alienation.

Wolf also raises the issue of female authorship in "Touching." Speaking of the obstacles confronting women in the period around the French

Revolution who were trying to "fight their way into the literary arena" she raises issues of gender and genre. Noting that women "often expressed themselves in diaries, letters, poems and travelogues, the most personal and subjective literary forms" (121), she argues that these genres afforded them a greater spontaneity and sociability than did the novel or drama. Like Virginia Woolf, Wolf points to the material and economic conditions that impede women's writing. But in her view an even greater impediment is their lack of "the minimum of self confidence needed to undertake this venture" (122). In *No Place on Earth*, her story about German Romantic writers Heinrich von Kleist and Karoline von Günderrode and in her essays on Günderrode and other women Romantic writers, Wolf addresses issues gender and authorship in greater detail.

Wolf's deliberations on gender and writing culminate in *Conditions of a Narrative*, the essays that accompany her narrative *Cassandra*, in which she delivers a resounding critique of the male Western literary and aesthetic tradition. In 1982 Wolf was invited to hold the prestigious Lectures on Poetics at Frankfurt University. She prefaced her lectures with the claim that she had no poetics and then went on to deliver a powerful feminist anti-poetics. She rejects the traditional definition of "poetics" as "theory of the art of poetry, which at an advanced stage – Aristotle, Horace – takes on a systematic form." In her view, prescriptive normative poetic forms objectify: they are based on mastery over, not a mutual exchange with, the writer's material. Thus "there is and there can be no poetics which prevents the living experience of countless perceiving subjects from being killed and buried in art objects" (*CON*, 142). Wolf casts her Frankfurt poetics lectures, which explain how she came to rewrite the story of the Trojan War from the perspective of the losers, that is, from the vantage point of the marginalized figure Cassandra, in those genres she had coded as female: travelogue, diary, and letter. Her retelling connects the fall of Troy with the rise of patriarchy and faults the classical literary tradition for its exclusion of women and its glorification of war and the heroic.

Using the metaphor of weaving, quintessential women's work, she presents "the aesthetic structure" that informs her writing as a "fabric" composed of multiple threads with tangled motifs. Far from being a closed structure, "[t]here are wefts which stand out like foreign bodies, repetitions, material that has not been worked out to it conclusions." One cannot, she claims, extract a single "skein" without damaging the whole fabric (*CON*, 141–2). She faults the Homeric epic for extracting "the blood-red thread from the fabric of human life ... the narrative of the struggle and victory of the heroes, or their doom" (*CON*, 296–7).

Wolf's final comments on female authorship are an amalgam of Enlightenment, Marxist, and feminist thought. Her valorization of human autonomy is based on Kant's concept of *Mündigkeit*; her discussion of objectification is a feminist inflection of Marx's concept of alienation; and her understanding of women's difference is of a piece with feminist standpoint epistemologies that argue that women's socialization leads to different perceptions of the world. In Wolf's view, "women's writing" comes into being when women give voice to the historically grounded different reality they experience. When women, "unqualified members of the subculture," "objects of objects, second-degree objects, frequently the objects of men who are themselves objects," no longer strive to "integrate themselves into the prevailing delusional systems" but instead "writing and living, ... aim at autonomy" (*CON*, 259).

Although Wolf was familiar with Luce Irigaray's *This Sex Which Is Not One*, she does not enter the discussion of feminine aesthetics from the vantage point of Lacan and Derrida, as do the French feminists of *écriture féminine*. Instead, in line with feminist standpoint theorists, she argues from an historical materialist perspective, claiming that women's socialization and lived experiences in patriarchal culture have led to a specifically female epistemology. Her reflections on women's writing hark back to her comments about the function of literature in "Reading and Writing." In light of the exigencies of our modern world, "the only alternative left is the narrow path of reason, of growing up, of human awareness, the conscious step out of prehistory into history. What is left is the decision to become an adult" (RW, 48). Given Wolf's debt to Idealist philosophy, it is not surprising that she framed her discussion of female authorship in terms of the coming to consciousness of autonomous female subjectivity.

Wolf began work on her *Cassandra* project in 1980, during a resurgence of Cold War animosities, when the two superpowers contemplated waging a "limited nuclear war" in Europe. In keeping with her notion of "contemporaneity," Wolf's temporally most distant text contains reflections on technology, militarism, war, and the "delusional thinking" that has brought humankind to the brink of self-annihilation. Drawing on Horkheimer and Adorno's *Dialectic of Enlightenment*, she articulates her lament for the failed project of Enlightenment and develops a critique of the perversion of Kant's emancipatory notion of reason into one-sided, male, instrumental rationality. She goes on to connect Western civilization's dualistic thinking, its valorization of the rational with the concomitant denigration and atrophy of the non-rational and its exclusion of women, to the profound alienation pervading contemporary society. Confronted with the possible annihilation of her continent, she is horrified by the "delusional thinking" of those in power: by the "grotesque calculation" that nuclear proliferation on "both sides creates a 'balance of terror' that reduces the danger of war; that in the long run it even offers a minimum of security" (*CON*, 229). Wolf's reflections about what has brought humankind to the brink of annihilation are inextricably connected to her ongoing critique of science and technology. In the early 1960s, the GDR, along with other Soviet satellite nations, invested heavily in the "scientific technological revolution." Building on Marx's statement in *The German Ideology* that the development of industry, commerce, and agriculture was necessary for human liberation, the SED equated science and technology with progress and extoled them as essential for the development of communism. Wolf was skeptical of scientific ideology based on a presumption of a value-free objectivity, its insistence on emotional detachment, its claim to universal truth, and especially its disregard for moral questions regarding the technological ends of scientific inquiry.

She had satirized this position in "New Memoirs of a Tomcat," linked it to the inability to love in "Self-Experiment," and lamented the psychically deadening effects of utilitarianism brought on by the Industrial Revolution in her work on the Romantics. Wolf's feminist critique of science culminates in her *Cassandra* project and in *Accident*, written in the wake of the Chernobyl nuclear meltdown. Her critique of science and technology parallels those formulated by feminist standpoint epistemologists Nancy Hartsock, Sandra Harding, and Hilary Rose, among others.[14]

The proliferation of nuclear arms in NATO and Warsaw Pact nations in the 1980s triggered peace protests in both Eastern and Western Europe, as well as in the United States. At a 1981 Berlin meeting of European writers and scientists, Wolf spoke out against the perverse notion of nuclear war in Europe: "A civilization which is capable of planning its own demise so precisely and which, through incredible sacrifices, creates the means to do so, ... is 'sick,' probably mentally ill, perhaps mortally ill" (*GW* 8, 220).

Wolf's position was consonant with that of feminist peace activists in the United States In 1980 and 1981, for example, in response to the U.S.–Soviet nuclear escalation, the Women's Pentagon Action, using weaving as a metaphor of women's resistance, wove the door to the Pentagon shut with brightly colored yarns. Their 1980 "Unity Statement" is similar to Wolf's in tone and sentiment:

> We have come here to mourn and rage and defy the Pentagon because it is the workplace of the imperial power, which threatens us all.... [T]he

colonels and generals who are planning our annihilation walk calmly in and out the doors of its five sides.... They have proclaimed Directive 59, which asks for "small nuclear wars, prolonged but limited." ... The Soviet Union works hard to keep up with the United States' initiatives. We can destroy each other's cities, towns, schools and children many times over.... We are in the hands of men, whose power and wealth have separated them from the reality of daily life and from the imagination. We are right to be afraid. (*Women's Lives*, 531)

In Wolf's acceptance speech for the Georg Büchner literary prize, she credits the nineteenth-century Büchner with an untimely, modern sensibility in recognizing that "progress, just then being cranked up in grand style, had the makings of a new myth" and that "the passion the new era found in itself was in itself was rooted in the passion for destruction" (BP, 6). Connecting Büchner's time with her own, Wolf states: "Sober to the marrow, we stand aghast before the dreams made real by instrumental thinking that still calls itself reason, although it has long since lost its enlightened impulse toward emancipation, and has entered the Industrial Age as barefaced utilitarian mania" (BP, 4). She lauds Büchner for attempting what she considers an essential function of literature: "to render the blind spot of this culture visible" (7), an undertaking that informs her writing as well. She concludes with the passionate plea: "today literature must be peace research" (10).

Reaffirming her faith in the redemptive power of literature to change human consciousness, she calls on it to confront the "map of death" being drawn by the nuclear staffs through its descriptions of places and people:

> all the localities and landscapes, human relations that literature described so accurately ..., painfully, critically, devotedly, fearfully and happily, ironically, rebelliously, and lovingly should be erased from the map of death and be considered rescued.... Perhaps a General Staff may really find it harder to target a city that was described intimately and accurately than to target one that no one knows. (11)

Wolf hopes that literature's ability to infuse objective reality with subjective experience will allow it to be "applied to the preservation of human affairs" (11).

Intended as a contribution to peace research, Wolf's *Cassandra* project traces the origins of alienation and human (self-)destructiveness back to the cradle of Western civilization. *Cassandra* can be read as an anti-*bildungsroman* in which the heroine, rather than being integrated into her society, is desocialized and achieves autonomy. Cassandra's coming into self-consciousness is presented as a painful process of separation from the familial and hierarchal power structures of the palace. By no longer identifying with those in power, she gains the epistemic privilege of the marginalized and can extricate herself from the delusional thinking of the powerful. The price of her autonomy is death, a fate she chooses freely. Killed by the victorious Greeks, she goes to her death "more alive than ever before." Through her resistance, Cassandra becomes a subject of history, and serves as a model of the coming into being of autonomous female subjectivity.

Calling her *Cassandra* narrative a roman à clef, Wolf situates her story at the historical transition from a matriarchal to a patriarchal society and offers striking parallels between Cassandra's doomed Troy and Wolf's Europe. Prime among these are a pervasive war mentality, the ascendancy of dualistic thinking, and the creation of *Feindbilder* (images of the enemy). Political expediency leads to the marginalization and objectification of women. Rewriting the history of the Trojan War from the perspective of the losers, Wolf argues that the Trojans were vanquished not only because of the Greeks' military superiority but because they had abandoned their egalitarian principles and adopted the patriarchal values of their enemy. In emulating the Greeks' ruthless aggression in battle and their instrumental credo that the ends justify the means, they compromised their moral integrity.

The themes of instrumental rationality and the exclusion of women also inform *Accident: A Day's News* (1987). The 1986 Chernobyl reactor meltdown confirmed Wolf's worst fears about nuclear catastrophe. Written shortly after the disaster, *Accident* continues Wolf's critique of science and technology as it probes the causes of human destructiveness. Throughout Wolf juxtaposes the reactions of the narrator/author with those of the scientists reporting on the event. Responding to the physicists' use of abstract scientific language incomprehensible to a layperson, she questions the value of knowing that there are "'fifteen millirems of fallout per hour.'" While the scientists speak in terms of measurable, quantifiable data, the narrator seeks to understand the danger in human terms: "How long would I, how long would a child of one, how long would an embryo in the womb have to be exposed to it in order to be harmed" (*A*, 41). In the name of scientific progress, the scientists' reports minimize the human cost of nuclear energy: "Now we hear that every new technology requires sacrifices at first" (42). Wolf recalls the victims of such technological progress when she alludes to the fishermen killed by the fallout from the U.S. H-bomb tests in the Pacific in 1954.[15]

Wolf's deliberations on the relationship between masculinist science, men's inability to love, and human destructiveness culminate in the narrator's discussion of the "star warriors," researchers at the Lawrence Livermore Laboratories working on the Strategic Defense Initiative (SDI). Their objective: "to construct the nuclear-powered X-ray laser at the core of that fantasy of an America rendered totally secure through the relocation of future nuclear battles to outer space" (*A*, 63). Her description of these one-dimensional, hermetically sealed off *homines technici*, monomaniacally focused on a technical problem, whose only relationship is to their computer, "to which they are bound, shackled, as only ever a slave to his galley" (62–3), leads her to conclude that it's "not the phantom 'security' – no: [it's] the maelstrom of death, the fabrication of the void, which herds some of the best brains in America" (64).

Wolf's conclusions are of a piece with those of sociologist Hilary Rose who asserts that "the attitude dominant within science and technology must be transformed, for their telos is nuclear annihilation" (Rose, "Hand, Brain, and Heart," 265). Patriarchy's sexual division of labor, Rose maintains, its disregard for the caring labor associated with women, has brought scientific inquiry to its current impasse. "Women's work is of a particular kind ..., it always involves personal service. Perhaps to make the nature of this caring, intimate, emotionally demanding labor clear, we should use the ideologically loaded term 'love.' For without love, without close interpersonal relationships, human beings ... cannot survive" (275). She concludes that "a theoretical recognition of caring labor ... is necessary for any adequate materialist analysis of science and is a crucial precondition for an alternative epistemology and method that will help us construct a new science and a new technology" (275). Rose, like Wolf, calls for a synthesis of hand, brain, and heart to derail society from its current destructive trajectory.

Accident is Wolf's most dystopian narrative. Only the figure of Peter Hagelstein, one of the star warriors, who is profiled in a journal article the narrator reads,[16] offers readers a glimmer of hope. Comparing Hagelstein's story with that of Faust, the narrator claims that, unlike Goethe's hero, this nuclear age Faust is driven by a quest for knowledge not for its own sake, but as a means to an end. His ambition to win the Nobel Prize leads Hagelstein to compromise his principles. His goal was to invent an x-ray laser for peaceful purposes. At Livermore he allows himself to be persuaded to work on his invention for military uses instead. Motivated by personal ambition and pragmatism, Hagelstein has perverted the liberating concept of reason as a thirst for knowledge in the service of community into instrumental rationality. Enter Hagelstein's lover, Josephine Stein, Gretchen to his Faust, who becomes a voice of conscience and a catalyst for change. When Hagelstein, in violation of his ethics, produces a blueprint that will help develop the x-ray laser to be used for Star Wars, Stein protests and eventually leaves him. This modern Gretchen is no longer a passive victim, but a moral agent of resistance. Several months later the narrator, upon learning that Hagelstein has abandoned the SDI and left Livermore, rejoices: "Somebody made it. Nothing is final. I'll have to reconsider the destinies and decisions of modern Faust" (93).

Christa Wolf claimed that writing was for her a form of therapy, a process of working through issues that affected her, a means of gaining self-knowledge. Writing afforded her the possibility of confronting the contradictions and blind spots in herself, in GDR society, and in the world at large. It allowed her to violate taboos and become a voice of resistance. She was driven by a passionate belief in the ability of human beings to change and attributes to literature the power to help readers become subjects of history. Guided by a moral vision of a humane society, her oeuvre and her life bear witness to her confrontation with the forces that impeded the realization of that vision. As late as November 1989, when the Eastern Bloc began to crumble, Wolf encouraged GDR citizens to stay in the country and finally actualize her dream of socialism with a human face. Although her hopes were disappointed, her writing doubtless helped change the consciousness of GDR readers and helped to bring about the "peaceful revolution" that precipitated the fall of the Wall. Thus it fulfilled the revolutionary goal Wolf had set for epic prose in "Reading and Writing": to entice and encourage us to achieve the impossible. Christa Wolf's writings are as relevant today as ever. We can all benefit from her understanding of literature as an aesthetics of resistance that can serve as a bulwark against alienation and can offer its readers the possibility of self-actualization and autonomy.

WORKS CITED

Clausen, Jeanette Clausen. "The Difficulty of Saying 'I' as Theme and Narrative Technique in the Works of Christa Wolf." In *Gestaltet und gestaltend. Frauen in der deutschen Literatur*, edited by Marianne Burkhard, 319–31. Amsterdam: Rodopi, 1980 *Amsterdamer Beiträge zur neueren Germanistik* 10.

Fehervary, Helen and Sara Lennox. "Introduction to Christa Wolf's 'Self-Experiment': Appendix to a Report." Trans. Jeannette Clausen. *New German Critique* 13 (Winter 1978): 109–12.

Fries, Marilyn Sibley. "Locating Christa Wolf: An Introduction." In *Responses to Christa Wolf: Critical Essays*, edited by Marilyn Sibley Fries, 11–54. Detroit, MI: Wayne State University Press, 1989.

Gilligan, Carol. *In a Different Voice*. Cambridge, MA: Harvard University Press, 1983.

Hartsock, Nancy. "The Feminist Standpoint: Developing the Ground for a Specifically Feminist Historical Materialism. In *Feminist Standpoint Theory Reader*, edited by Sandra Harding, 35–53. New York/London: Routledge, 2004.

Kant. Immanuel. "What Is Enlightenment." *Foundations of the Metaphysics of Morals*. Trans. Lewis White Beck. Indianapolis/New York: Liberal Arts Press, 1950, 85–92.

Kuhn, Anna K. *Christa Wolf's Utopian Vision: From Marxism to Feminism*. Cambridge/New York: Cambridge University Press, 2008.

Love, Myra. "Christa Wolf and Feminism: Breaking the Patriarchal Connection." *New German Critique* 16 (Winter 1979): 31–53.

Marx, Karl. *The Economic & Philosophic Manuscripts of 1844*. Trans. Martin Milligan. Ed. Dirk J. Struck. New York. International Publishers, 1964.

Reich-Ranicki, Marcel. "Christa Wolfs unruhige Elegie." *Die Zeit* (May 25, 1969).

Rose, Hilary. "Hand, Brain and Heart. A Feminist Epistemology for the Natural Sciences." In *Sex and Scientific Inquiry*, edited by Sandra Harding and Jean F. O'Barr, 265–82. Chicago/London: University of Chicago Press, 1987.

Rossbacher, Brigitte. *Illusions of Progress. Christa Wolf and the Critique of Science in GDR Women's Literature*. New York: Peter Lang, 2000.

Wolf, Christa. *Accident: A Day's News*. Trans. Heike Schwarzbaur and Rick Takvorian. New York: Farrar Straus Giroux, 2002.

"Berliner Begegnung." In *Gesammelte Werke* 8, edited by Sonja Hilzinger, 220–5. München: Luchterhand. 2000.

"Berührung." *Gesammelte Werke* 8, edited by Sonja Hilzinger, 115–29. München: Luchterhand, 2000.

Cassandra. A Novel and Four Essays. Trans. Jan Van Heurck, New York: Farrar, Straus, Giroux, 1984.

"Interview With Myself. Trans. Jan van Heurck. In *The Author's Dimension: Selected Essays*, edited by Alexander Stephan, 16–19. New York: Farrar, Straus, Giroux, 1993.

The Quest for Christa T. Trans. Christopher Middleton. New York: Farrar. Straus, Giroux, 1972.

"Reading and Writing." Trans. Jan van Heurck. In *The Author's Dimension: Selected Essays*, edited by Alexander Stephan, 20–48. New York: Farrar, Straus, Giroux, 1993.

"Self-Experiment: Appendix to a Report." Trans. Jeanette Clausen. *New German Critique* 13 (Winter 1978): 113–31.

"'Shall I Garnish a Metaphor with an Almond Blossom?': Büchner Prize Acceptance Speech." Trans. Henry Schmidt. *New German Critique* 23 (Spring/Summer 1981): 3–11.

"Subjektive Authentizität: Gespräch mit Hans Kaufmann. *Gesammelte Werke* 4, edited by Sonja Hilzinger, 401–37. München: Luchterhand, 1999.

Women's Pentagon Action. "Unity Statement." In *Women's Lives* 5th edition, edited by Gwyn Kirk and Margo Okazawa-Rey, 531. Boston, MA: McGraw Hill, 2010.

CHAPTER 13

Naked Came the Female Extraterrestrial Stranger: Applying Linda M. Scott's Fresh Lipstick to Sue Lange's The Textile Planet

Marleen S. Barr

I will focus on the "dressing while female" problem by reading a feminist science fiction novel in terms of feminist fashion theory. Integrating feminist science fiction within feminist theory is still an emerging form of feminist writing. Via a specific discussion of feminism and fashion, this chapter contributes to the emergence of feminist theory, which includes feminist science fiction. More specifically, I will enable Sue Lange's *The Textile Planet* closely to encounter Linda M. Scott's *Fresh Lipstick: Redressing Fashion and Feminism*. This reading brings feminist science fiction into the feminist discourse fray pertaining to fashion and feminism. This chapter's first section, "Establishing First Contact with the Textile Planet," introduces Lange's protagonist Marla Gershe and the worlds she inhabits. The second section, "Stranger in a Strange Land," describes Marla's quest to find a Goldilocks planet of her own that will enable her to transcend the "dressing while female" problem. To suggest that feminist discourse should be open to science fiction and fashion, the third section, "Redressing Reality-Centered Feminist Discourse," brings Scott's feminist fashion theory to bear upon Lange's feminist science fiction.

Literature and the Development of Feminist Theory is concerned with feminist theory and its literary roots. I conclude by positioning Marla as being emblematic of this purpose. Marla is a literary feminist science fiction protagonist. Feminist science fiction parameters enable her eventually to emerge as a feminist theorist who can author an entire planet's society. *The Textile Planet* is a wonderful feminist science fiction adventure story about how a woman successfully balances love and work. Because Lange emphasizes clothing, in an essay collection about feminist theory and its relationship to literature it is interesting to read her novel in terms of Scott's arguments against the belief that American women have to eschew fashion in order to achieve liberation and equality.

Establishing First Contact with the Textile Planet

Marla is desperately seeking a Goldilocks planet that is just right for her (astrobiologists define the Goldilocks zone as "the habitable zone around a star" "Goldilocks Principle"). Upon arrival, clothing would not undermine her efforts to find love and work in terms of power parity with men. Marla, a native of a planet devoted to manufacturing clothing, manages weavers employed at "the Mill." She does not initially reside on one of her universe's multitudinous economically specialized planets. These specialties include, for example, "transport from the leather planet ... [and] fragrances from exotic spice planets (126). Immediately after Marla participates in an insurrection aimed at improving the weavers' lives, "a policeman shot her through the mid-section with one of those new-fangled xanthan guns. This simple act changed her life forever" (2). The technologically sophisticated xanthan guns signal that the weavers do not inhabit a green, medieval, castle-sodden fantasy world. The Textile Planet's workers include the still science fictional "mannequins, a mob of gibbering, jabbering, primping robots in the style of Rosie, the Jetsons' maid" (19). Marla is surrounded by many other American cultural accoutrements: "Scarlett O'Hara" (131), "*The Planet of the Apes*" (160), "Charleton Heston," (172), and "Ralph Kramden" (180), for example. The Textile Planet is a world dedicated to laser beam–focused specialized American capitalism.

Marla participates in a frenetic interplanetary *bildungsroman* in which she searches for a means to avoid being what exaggerated capitalism wishes her to be: a mannequin, a robot cog in the manufacturing wheel, what Kurt Vonnegut called a "meat machine." As Marla's friend Charney explains: "management has been trying since the beginning of time to produce humans that are like machines ... Machines are ten times more economical than any living thing as far as producing work.... They do as they are told" (182). It is necessary for Marla to break out of the circumscribed constructed confines of her world in order to learn to develop both her female and human identity. She has difficulty fitting into the Textile Planet's world; readers initially have difficulty discerning the characteristics of that world. (Readers, for example, must reach page fifty-eight to be informed that the means to travel "[o]ff-planet" via an interplanetary transportation system is as routine as real airplane flights.) Marla and readers are as confused as women who stereotypically stand in front of their closets trying to discern what to wear. Marla decides to come out of the closet, the enclosed limited damaging personal and professional psychological work identity space that comprises her life on the Textile Planet.

Marla, a woman in her early thirties who has never ventured beyond her neighborhood, abruptly boards the train to Gatown, the location of the interplanetary airport (128–9). Her successful off-planet venture is as unlikely as an indigent person taking public transportation to Kennedy Airport and accessing, say, a South African Airlines flight. As the following conversation shows, Marla's escape from the planet of the aping mimicking textile capitalists involves ambiguity in regard to attire:

> "Where are the flats?" [Marla asks a maintenance worker].
> "Shoes?"
> "No, it's someplace outside."
> "Oh, the Flats. Of course, no luggage." ...
> "A faded sign on the side of the building states, 'Gatown Flats, Inc.'" ...

The place smelled faintly of heated mink oil, suggesting a shoe factory or tack shop. Just as she was losing the bit of resolve she'd mustered to crawl through the window, the lights came up, revealing a naked room with cracked wallboards.... The conversation's emphasis upon clothing continues:

> "There you are." A man in a white shirt, black tie, tidy crew cut, and unstylishly short black pants ... rushed in from the doorway. "You're going to be late if you don't hurry." (142–4, 149)

"The flats" are not shoes. They are, rather, a decaying clothing factory, an economically nonviable location resembling the Cape Town Flats. Like Alice venturing down the rabbit hole, Marla enters a "naked room." A complexly attired man, Marla's fantastic white rabbit informing her that she will be late, miraculously hands her a ticket to a technologically marvelous escape machine. Readers know the details of the man's attire; not so for Marla who travels to another planet without luggage. The "naked room" functions as her transit lounge portal to eventual viable living room – her final destination planet (called XKJ10) located far away at the boundary separating charted and uncharted outer space. Marla's eventual ability to own XKJ10 enables her to inhabit a space devoid of negative representation in regard to women and clothes.

Marla will always wear the necklace that includes the precious stateroom key she manages to secure on the "bubble jet" she boards at Gatown. This newly decorative key might refer to understanding that Marla's relationship to feminine adornment – clothes – is a key to reading *The Textile Planet*. Lange's novel, no frivolous science fiction chick lit about fashion, concerns clothing's adverse representational impact on women. Marla changes planets as often as women change clothes:

> Marla was not happy. As much as she hated XKJ10, she had nowhere else to go. Everyplace she'd gone, everything she'd tried in the last two years of her life had been worse than before. For most people change means an improvement, but not Marla. Change always proved worse. The [mental] hospital [on the Textile Planet] was worse than the Mill. The ride to Walloon [an interplanetary way station] was worse than the hospital. The ride to Ansonia [a Wild West planet] was worse than the ride to Walloon. (375–6)

Engaging with *The Textile Planet* involves closely encountering the multitudinous occurrences that constitute Marla's circumstances on numerous planets. Analogous details regarding what she wears are strikingly never forthcoming, however. Lange eventually does get around to revealing that Marla is "thirty-two" (279). And Lange does not rush to drop this appearance bomb: a man named Trest is "a Throwback. Had black hair and white skin. Not paper white, just not brown like everybody else" (338). All the people who live in Marla's universe have brown skin. Lange, to enable Marla to escape the consequences of dressing while female, at first simply refuses to describe her clothes. Change – of planets, not clothes – will ultimately improve Marla's life.

Before readers learn exactly how and why Marla lives happily ever after, they engage in a reading process that is analogous to changing clothes – to continually transforming style, to the caprice of fashion. Just as readers become accustomed to the Textile Planet, it is time to take off to Walloon, before venturing to pioneer planet Ansonia, and leaving to head for XKJ10. Further tumult ensues when Marla leaves XKJ10 and returns to the Textile Planet to rescue her friend named Saddle. Hence, readers are saddled with a return trip from XKJ10 back to the Textile Planet – and another trip from the Textile Planet back to XKJ10. They are as dizzy as a Baby Boom generation mother confronted with her twenty-first-century teenage daughter wearing 1960s-era bell bottoms. No structural narrative flaw, Marla's incessant change of planets purposely reflects the deleterious impact of saddling women with the need for repetitive fashion change. Although *The Textile Planet* is not about fashion and the protagonist's clothes are mentioned as briefly as possible – reading this novel resembles continually changing clothes.

Marla is the Lady of XKJ10; she controls, develops, and operates XKJ10's lucrative new hotel. If she chooses, she can be seen naked in her hotel's public areas – or anywhere she wishes on XKJ10. She can science

fictionally go where no woman has gone before – to a planet where
women can escape the deleterious consequences of dressing while female.[1]

Stranger in a Strange Land

The Textile Planet presents readers with continuous "cognitive
estrangement" (Darko Suvin's term). Readers are never at home on the
planets Marla frequents. "Mini, midi, mod, or full-length": (324); Textile
Planet, or Ansonia, or XKJ10? This protagonist who is treated as an experimental animal by "BAC Enterprises" (the corporation that controls the
Textile Planet – (3)) functions as a fashion blank page who searches for
self-realization. When Marla arrives on Ansonia, she is attached to no
one: "[S]he had no intention of ever getting so comfortable here that it
became her home" (227). Lange includes only one reference to Marla's
family (228). Meko, Marla's employer on Ansonia, describes her lack of
human connection: "You don't have children. You never had a lasting
relationship. You've not seen your parents in ten years" (313). Unattached
to any person or culture – as well as culture's emphasis on women's
clothing – Marla lights out to the territories. Rejecting civilization, she
is a female Huck Finn who ventures beyond civilization to planet XKJ10.
This protagonist who "lost all capacity for human intimacy" (286) enacts
an extreme and feminist version of Leslie Fiedler's *Love and Death in the
American Novel.* Fiedler famously observed that American literature is
characterized by white men, accompanied by a male companions of color,
who cannot achieve mature love relationships. Marla is a brown woman
accompanied by no one; she enjoys her most attached relationship with
her backpack.[2]

Meko describes Marla's psychology of alienation in terms of clothing
and nakedness: "your whole psychology was laid bare. I saw you naked
even as you came to work fully clothed ... You are alone because you are
searching" (310). At the end of her search, Marla finds the end of civilization. When she crash lands her solo spaceship version of Huck and Jim's
raft into desert planet XKJ10, she at first finds no love and seemingly inevitable death. "So she'd gone to a place at the absolute end of the Universe
and it was unlivable. So where to now?" (344). Lange's protagonist, a person familiar with Scarlett O'Hara, seems to echo Scarlett asking where
should she go and what should she do. The answer Marla receives: frankly,
my dear, the entire universe doesn't give a damn. Faced with this attitude,
upon arrival on XKJ10 it is perfectly reasonable for her to decide to jetti-
son her clothes: "Next day she rose realizing her clothes were superfluous

at this point. Even if she came across some living thing, far from being human, it wouldn't know a titty from a dicky and what was the point of modesty? The clothes were hot and despite the dry climate managed to develop moisture stains under the pits that required washing she could ill afford" (343). XKJ10, a planet located at the end of the known universe, is where women must go to escape patriarchal clothing imperatives.

Beauty myths do not exist on XKJ10. Not so for Ansonia. Marla's fellow office workers on that planet discuss a beauty myth called "The Peacock Syndrome" (246):

> In our culture, women are expected to be beautiful. We are judged by current standards of comeliness.... Males ... must attract, woo, and compete.... Well women are not programmed to be competitive.... We developed culture. Culture dictates rules of behavior.... So how come female humans are the pretty ones? ... We discovered death and with it the desire to overcome it. Males especially. (265–7)

"The Peacock Syndrome" beauty myth involves love and death. *The Textile Planet* is feminist metafiction – what I call feminist fabulation[3] – a fiction about patriarchal beauty myth fictions. Lange, in terms of feminist science fiction, rewrites beauty myths in general and Fiedler's conception of love and death in the American novel in particular.

XKJ10 provides Marla with the greatest singles' event in the universe. Lying prostrate in the sand and nearly dead from thirst, using her last ounce of strength, she looks up and sees her perfect match: "Marla stared at a naked human foot planted in front of her face.... She ... stared up at the grizzled man with the three foot long beard and piercing eyes.... Like her he was unclothed, except for the beard" (352). Naked came the stranger. And so ends the need for clothing – the need for the Textile Planet's entire enterprise, the need for all the clothing restrictions patriarchy assigns to women. Marla does not have to use clothes to attract her naked soulmate named Sol. Further, Marla and Sol are not alone. Sentient technologically sophisticated garrulous ants inhabit XKJ10. Gender is irrelevant in relation to Lange's ants. "It wasn't clear if the ants had gender or not" (374).

After discovering that XKJ10 is located at a bonanza point, the gateway to the discovery of the relationship between matter and antimatter, clothing and shopping finally matter to Marla. This woman who spent her entire life fleeing from a corporation alone becomes an entrepreneur involved in a relationship. As the owner of XKJ10, Marla becomes a capitalist incarnate: "We got a way to make a living now. We'll set up shop, get the importers in on a regular basis. We can start a hotel for miners, a store for their supplies. We'll sell them shirts at top-gauge prices" (391). As Marla begins her "fourth great incarnation ... [s]hopping became a daily activity" (410). *The Textile Planet* is about when Marla changed.

Marla is an insurrectionist against capitalism who becomes the CEO of her own planet. The conclusion of *The Textile Planet* describes Marla's "first day of business" (478). She is no longer a homeless, impoverished, lonely refugee fleeing from corporate oppression. She finds herself – and the means to own and preside over her own private civilization. She rewrites *Love and Death* from a female point of view; her eventual male lover saves her life. She dresses for success and love according to her own terms.

It is not unusual to associate science fiction with fashion.[4] Clothing designer Suzanne Rae, for example, explains that a science fiction novel inspires her:

> The S14 collection, inspired by the book *2150 AD* by Thea Alexander, is about a humanitarian utopia, about clothing that inspires us to be open-minded, accepting, knowledgeable, responsible, and loving.... The Collection has a futuristic feel as well as this down to earth vibe. (One on One)

Rae equates her creative process as a fashion designer with Alexander's *2150 AD*; I equate Marla's creative efforts to design her future with Linda Scott's *Fresh Lipstick*.

Redressing Reality-Centered Feminist Discourse

Scott agrees with Lange's premise that fashion and feminism do not have to be from different planets. *Fresh Lipstick* argues that fashion and feminism are not antithetical, that using makeup is not analogous to putting on lipstick to please a male chauvinist pig. To correct the fact that "American feminism takes a dim view of beauty," Scott proposes that "established feminist theorists ... need to experience a change in consciousness with regard to the politics of personal appearance" (1). When Lange startlingly pays minimal attention to Marla's appearance and clothing, she contributes to this change. I say "startlingly" because a Textile Planet denizen who is devoid of appearance and fashion markers is as aberrant as an illiterate English Department Planet citizen. Marla is science fiction's very positive invisible woman. The near silence pertaining to her sartorial choices acts as a protective force field that protects her from the discrimination Ralph Ellison's invisible man endures. Marla, then, is a model for the change in consciousness Scott advocates. Because this protagonist's clothes and appearance are nearly invisible, no one – including feminists – can find fault with her self-presentation.

"No one can dress in a way that signifies nothing" (Scott, *Fresh Lipstick*, 12). Marla, as I have argued, most certainly can. When she is at first alone in planet XKJ10, her attire – and lack of attire – signifies nothing; no one is present to view her. On XKJ10, women's relationship to fashion and beauty – and feminism's negative view of this relationship – signify nothing. Science fiction enables Marla to exist outside of classification systems. "Presenting oneself in a way that expresses availability and desire is the way humans ... get the love they need" (Scott, *Fresh Lipstick*, 234). When Marla is initially alone on XKJ10, no matter how she presents herself – no matter how beautiful she is or what elaborate costume she wears – it seems impossible for her to find love on a planet that at first appears to be devoid of other people. Marla is not one of "us" in terms of this generational female power struggle. Her outsider status is extreme to the extent that she cannot experience the body image self-hate that plagues so many women.

Mirrors are initially nonexistent on XKJ10. Sand is pervasive. The planet has conditions that enable readers to picture "a woman as she would be found 'in nature,' without 'man-made' intervention" (Scott, *Fresh Lipstick*, 11). Because no one can initially see Marla and she cannot see herself, she is outside "the marker of the gender system at work"; her appearance and dress cannot be "policed" (Scott, *Fresh Lipstick*, 217). She lacks tools to foster beauty. Yes, "[t]o imagine a material life without any elements of cognitive significance, spiritual sustenance, or social convention is difficult to do" (Scott, *Fresh Lipstick*, 213). Science fiction enables Lange to make it possible for Marla (albeit temporarily) to live without these elements. Lange uses science fiction to nullify all discrimination relating to fashion and beauty.

Science fiction is relevant to feminists' fears about fashion. Scott refers to science fiction when describing 1950s-era anxieties; she mentions a science fiction film, witches, space aliens, and mad scientists: "During the 1950s, fears about brainwashing and mass control were at a high pitch and the fashion sciences of the mind, Freudian psychoanalysis and Skinnerian behaviorism, gave way to popular anxieties. Films, plays, and books, ranging from *The Crucible* to *The Invasion of the Body Snatchers*, also focused public consciousness on the ways in which witches, communists, space aliens, mad scientists, and even unconscious desires could steal into ordinary Americans' lives unnoticed and destroy them from within" (Scott, *Fresh Lipstick*, 223). Like *The Textile Planet*, *Fresh Lipstick* situates fashion and beauty in terms of science fiction. Invading humans' lives and destroying humans from within are science fiction tropes. Both Lange and Scott address the question of whether women's fashion and beauty obsessions destroy women from within.

Lange uses "space aliens" – feminist science fiction – to echo Scott's discourse about women and fashion. In relation to this discourse, Scott blurs the distinction between the real and the unreal, truth and falsehood. According to the science fiction tenets Lange includes in her all-powerful power fantasy for women, Marla can create her own cultural categories; she can world create. XKJ10 is the most austere, scary, and confusing vacuum imaginable; Marla fills the vacuum with something: clothes garnered by dint of shopping with her female friend Saddle. "Shopping" takes on new meaning in light of Marla's fantastic circumstances. This extraterrestrial who was devoid of friends travels to another planet – the Textile Planet, a place where Marla is endangered – finally to reach out and assist Saddle, a female comrade. Marla's interplanetary "shopping" foray is an act of extreme female solidarity and bonding, not a mundane pathway to further exploitation. "Extreme" aptly describes Marla's decision to leave her newfound comfort zone on XKJ10 in order to undertake a journey through outer space to a potentially dangerous planet.

I have been stating that Marla's nudity is positive in relation to women because it allows women to escape from judgment about their clothes. But the "natural" – the absence of the accoutrements of fashion – is not *always* positive in relation to women. As a brown woman, Marla seems to draw on the history of her people when she decides to become an entrepreneur on steroids. Slave owners who withheld "grooming tools also dehumanized black women in order that they could be traded as commodities and owned as property – masters often groomed their slaves for market using the same tools they used on animals. Thus these women were 'natural' as a direct consequence of their utter powerlessness and chattel status" (Scott, *Fresh Lipstick*, 17). Marla, who derives positive consequences from nudity, also retreats from the natural as a direct consequence of her science fictional fantastic powerfulness. Her decision indicates that *The Textile Planet* is a Horatio Alger science fiction story that demands to be read in terms of fashion and feminism. Marla, who initially has nothing – including bootstraps – pulls herself up anyway. She rises from being an intruder in the XKJ10 dust to becoming the planet's capitalist tycoon. Owning XKJ10 enables Marla to have the privileges of American aristocrats Scott describes: "As large landowners, they lived off their rents ... as well as from investments. They were the only Americans of the preindustrial period who might be said to be economically self-sufficient, having their own shops, laundries, foundries, and the like on their estates" (*Fresh Lipstick*, 26). (Scott does not mention finding fault with the fact that these aristocrats lived off of other people's labor; she treats the situation matter of factly.) As a large landowner who owns a planet, Marla will forever be economically self-sufficient. Science fiction's anything-is-possible scenario enables her to achieve self-sufficiency in a potentially non-exploitative manner. (For example, on *Star Trek*'s starship *Enterprise*, food instantaneously appears within a machine. The *Enterprise* is devoid of exploited food service workers.) "XKJ10" is a one-size-fits-all clothing size that is custom tailored to fit Marla's beyond-all-reality strictures and economic good fortune.

She is Rockefeller, Carnegie, Mellon, Morgan, Frick – and every fantastically rich male entrepreneur in American history – combined and recast in the guise of one woman. "The young single woman who could earn her own money didn't have to mind her superiors anymore" (Scott, *Fresh Lipstick*, 171). Marla can wear what she wants. She literally controls "global capitalism" (Scott, *Fresh Lipstick*, 326). It is important to remember that for Marla "global" does not mean planet Earth. She acquires wealth and possessions under the auspices of controlling an entire planet, no mere room of her own. It is possible for her to create an entire something new under a different sun economic system that does not function at the expense of others. She can create a system that eradicates domination and impoverishment. She can, for example, enable all the inhabitants of XKJ10 to own the planet equally. Science fiction often functions in terms of sequels (especially trilogies). Lange could follow *The Textile Planet* with a subsequent novel that explains how Marla institutes a new feminist economic system on XKJ10. Hence, when I talk about the CEO and the entrepreneur, I am discussing egalitarian feminist agency rather than corporate positions. Lange's feminist science fiction text makes it possible to understand this model of agency outside of the global corporatism that exists on Earth.

How is Marla's particular science fictional CEO agency congruent with feminist agency? How can she run an entire planet, be an owner, without exploiting people? To answer this question, I again refer to *Star Trek*'s starship *Enterprise*. Captain Kirk leads a complex community without exploiting any of his crew members. Science fiction makes this egalitarian situation possible. For example, if the crew wishes to travel from the starship to the surface of a planet, they merely "beam down." Exploited laborers are not involved in transporting people. Similarly, Marla, in her future, could conceivably "beam down" building materials to XKJ10 and use non-sentient robots to construct things. Science fiction enables Marla to avoid exploiting *people*.

Marla can also be understood in relation to the real and imaginary women Scott describes when discussing American fashion history. Elizabeth Arden and Arden's friend the prominent lesbian Elisabeth Marbury have a separatist approach to land use. Arden and Marbury purchased two large Maine estates. When Marbury died, Arden combined the estates and "opened her now world-famous spa, Maine Chance. The idea was to create a monument to Marbury by celebrating the beauty of women. No men were allowed" (Scott, *Fresh Lipstick*, 141). "New Girl" Marla, in contrast, develops her planet in a manner that at once takes advantage of its economic potential and enables it to serve as a comfortable post-separatist home for her and Sol. Marla is a poor immigrant who makes good. She shares the situation of fashion industry moguls "[l]ike [Charles] Revson, [Estée] Lauder, [Lawrence M.] Gelb, [Gerald] Gidwitz and [Louis] Stein all [who] were poor Jews who had immigrated themselves or were the children of immigrants – thus none of them ... can be said to have been part of the existing power structure" (Scott, *Fresh Lipstick*, 198). If this is the case, the Textile Planet's Jews are brown.

The fact that Marla, a management-level employee, emanates from the Textile Planet supports Scott's notion that "[c]haracterizing the beauty and fashion industry as a patriarchy has therefore never been accurate or fair" (Scott, *Fresh Lipstick*, 3). Scott describes the business of the Textile Planet when she states that "[t]extile mills ... produced an explosion of prosperity that had profound effects on both labor and consumption ... At every level of this broad scale economic change, women were implicated: as laborers and consumers, but also as designers, writers, editors, artists and manufacturers" (*Fresh Lipstick*, 3). Marla's participation in the fashion industry involves managing a textile mill. Because she works with other women – and her main enemy, the BAC Enterprises agent, is a woman – the Textile Planet, like Scott's description of the fashion industry, is not a patriarchy devoid of female participation.

When Marla pulls herself up by her bootstraps, she does so in accordance with the tenets of a particular Jewish woman: Helen Gurley Brown. Scott reports that Brown "exhorted her readers to 'do your own work. Don't live off of anybody else, don't be a parasite, make your own money, use your talent, live up to your potential ... You have to do it yourself, so you might as well get started'" (*Fresh Lipstick*, 246). *The Textile Planet* is a feminist science fiction version of *Sex and the Single Girl*. Marla, following Brown's advice, ends up with her own money – and her own man.

Marla is certainly unrealistic. Lange's purposefully fantastic premise, however, is not false in relation to women's real quest for attaining economic independence, balancing love and work, and satisfying aesthetic sensibilities in terms of fashion. Feminist science fiction should not be a forbidden territory for feminist theorists who are not science fiction scholars. Anti-science fiction prejudice can be understood in conjunction with what Scott calls "antibeauty prejudice": "At the base of the antibeauty prejudice is a compulsion to enforce homogeneity. Put differently, what we are dealing with here is the *intolerance of difference*. Feminist criticism glosses over this issue by insisting on our sameness" (*Fresh Lipstick*, 9). Feminist science fiction is feminist discourse with an unrealistic difference, a difference that should not be subjected to "intolerance." Feminist science fiction imbues feminist discourse with heterogeneity. Feminists who demand realism dismiss feminist science fiction. Creative endeavors should not be labelled as being "damaging."

As Suzanne Rae illustrates, feminist science fiction can inspire the creating of sustainable feminist fashion. And feminist beauty criticism can in itself be at one with feminist science fiction. Naomi Wolf, for example, created a feminist utopian vision that is as liberating as Joanna Russ's "Whileaway." "In *The Beauty Myth*, Naomi Wolf wrote of a utopian vision, in which 'young girls could find a thousand wild and tantalizing visions of possible futures'" (Scott, *Fresh Lipstick*, 278; Wolf, *The Beauty Myth*, 2). The unreal acts as a catalyst for imagining possible feminist futures that can become real. Insisting on realism is narrow minded: "By insisting on realism as the first and last principle of picturing, we ignore the range of purposes for which images are employed as well as the broad spectrum that picturing takes" (Scott, *Fresh Lipstick*, 93). Feminist insight can be garnered via picturing a feminist utopian denizen dressed in, say, a shiny silver spacesuit. Ditto for picturing Marla, attired in simple garments, standing as the sole owner of an entrepreneurial gold mine planet. No real human will ever be as powerful as Marla; this goal is unreal. But closely encountering her makes women feel more powerful – and potentially gives them the power to make room for better futures of their own.

Marla, a science fiction protagonist, signifies that the feminist sensibilities of women who imbue culture with consumer goods will matter in the future. Marla is the manager of the interplanetary marketplace. She is the CEO and Federal Reserve Board head of XKJ10. Feminist science fiction writers are best suited to propel readers to imagine women's ability to manage the future global marketplace.

"I am simply suggesting that true feminists consider the possibility of a view from *elsewhere*" (Scott, *Fresh Lipstick*, 330). Feminist science fiction – power fantasies for women – can enhance real women's power to be in the position to dress for success according to woman-centered priorities.

The *elsewhere* Marla inhabits is a literary fiction that enables her to function as a feminist theorist. The undeveloped social and structural terrain constituting planet XKJ10 is, for Marla, what Isak Dinesen called a "blank page." Marla has the ability to fill this page with a feminist theory text and turn this text into social praxis. Feminist science fiction gives Marla the power to theorize new feminist definitions for "corporation" and "clothing" and to – in a manner that echoes *Star Trek*'s Captain Picard issuing an order – make them "sew." I hope that Sue Lange will write a sequel to *The Textile Planet* that describes the social fabric of Marla's brave new feminist world – and her fresh feminist approach to lipstick.

WORKS CITED

Alexander, Thea. *2150. A.D.* New York: Warner Books, 1976.

Brown, Helen Gurley. *Sex and the Single Girl.* New York: Random House, 1962.

Dinesen, Isak. "The Blank Page." *The Last Tales.* London: University of Chicago Press, 1955.

Ellison, Ralph. *Invisible Man.* New York: Random House, 1952.

Fiedler, Leslie A. *Love and Death in the American Novel.* New York: Criterion Books, 1960.

"Goldilocks Principle." *Wikipedia.* http://en.wikipedia.org/wiki/Goldilocks_principle.

Heinlein, Robert A. *Stranger in a Strange Land.* New York: Putnam's, 1961.

Hillard, Scott. "10 Weirdest Inventions Predicted in Sci-fi Novels." August 10, 2013, http://listverse.com/2013/08/10/10-weirdest-inventions-predicted-in-sci-fi-novels.

Lange, Sue. *The Textile Planet.* Book View Café, 2010, http://bookviewcafe.com/bookstore/book/the-textile-planet.

Medine, Leandra. *The Man Repeller.* http://www.manrepeller.com.

"One-on-One Interview with Suzanne Rae." *Socially Superlative.* January 21, 2014, http://sociallysuperlative.com/2014/01/21/one-on-one-with-suzanne-rae.

Russ, Joanna. "When It Changed." In *Again, Dangerous Visions*, edited by Harlan Ellison, 229–41. New York: Doubleday, 1972.

Scott, Linda M. *Fresh Lipstick: Redressing Fashion and Feminism.* New York: Palgrave MacMillan, 2005.

Wolf, Naomi. *The Beauty Myth.* New York: William Morrow, 1990.

CHAPTER 14

Captive Maternal Love: Octavia Butler and Sci-Fi Family Values

Joy James

Introduction

Through fiction, Octavia Butler (1947–2006) influences the political landscapes of literature, critical race, and feminist theories.[1] Her writings discussed here are low-tech. Prevalent in science fiction (SF) film and literature, human/robotic inventions are largely absent in Butler's work. Most present in her oeuvre is what is most missing in American SF: the dispossessed black female protagonist as "captive maternal." The raison d'être for the captive maternal is her own survival and the flourishing of her family and community. The captive maternal is identified by four qualities: nontransferable agency; combative peer relations, usually with privileged males; a radical vision for life without trauma; and the desire and capacity to "love" through familial and communal ties that cross boundaries and sustain freedom. As spectrum, the captive maternal displaces narratives of agency dominated by masculinized master races. Butler offers this embattled maternal as the primary agent responsible for stability and sanctuary despite dystopia, slavery, exile, war, and racial-sexual violence. This protagonist, in speculative fiction that parallels and opposes neo-slavery, reflects the subordinate cultures of all worlds. Captivity created the black matrix, yet the matrix reproduces resistance detrimental to the conditions from which it emerged. Butler's work cannot default into whiteness because of the constant specter of racism. Given its legacy in the half-a-millennium histories of black captivity in the Western world, the apocalypse the captive maternal resists is familiar. Yet bleak portraits of female life – human or nonhuman proxy – are offset by maternal abilities to transmit culture, intimacy, and honor, all that deflect macro and micro aggressions. The black female protagonist provides "mirrors" – where the marginalized see themselves in narratives; "windows" – where the normative look inside worlds that overlap their own; and "sliding glass doors" that permit passage.[2]

Initially, one assumes that Butler's contributions are based in her introduction of SF black heroines as healers, cleansers if not saviors, and creators of civilizations. Yet her "black women" resonate within emancipated transracial and transgender and transhuman protagonists, with virtues and vices, that overwhelm traditional or stereotypical categories; and complicate texts without fixed gender and racial identities.

"Captive Maternal Love" explores select writings by Butler: *Kindred* (1979), *Wild Seed* (1980), *Mind of My Mind* (1977), and "Speech Sounds" (1984). These works fashion the world(s) in ways Western thought had denied as possible: as a place where black (female) agency, even when guised in alien forms, wields an indomitable will and political strength to politically procreate whatever undermines captivity. Butler's captive maternal possesses a "black matrix"[3] capable of undoing the world and building new realities; from the "matrix" or breeding female animal and the "mater" or mother, the combined contributions or exploitations of reproductive and productive labor under captivity establish the conditions for revolution.

Butler recounts how once, as the only woman and person of color on a science fiction (SF) conference panel, she asked her co-panelists why no black characters or protagonists existed in their works. One author responded that blacks were not needed because aliens were present. During another interview, she observed that typical SF depicts the future as more or less of the same: it repeats variables in conventionally known and lived experience to different degrees. Standard SF, for all of its imaginative promises, provides variations on predictable experiences. Thus, the marginalization or erasure of blacks (especially black women) and their "nonhuman" status as interchangeable with aliens is SF futurism's old past in the tiring present. Butler's writings provide a vision to destabilize both convention and the forced exile of the black maternal from the future. Her writing unmakes the political worlds reinforced by popular SF literature and film.

The upheavals in the late 1970s to the mid-1980s that followed the cataclysmic battles for the future fought in the 1960s are reflected in twentieth- and twenty-first-century SF. The popularization of SF through U.S. film began during an era that saw the de-radicalization or commercialization of the black and feminist liberation movements. Butler synthesizes two seemingly divergent trends in late twentieth-century U.S. progressivism: feminist ideologies centered on white women's economic and political parity with authoritative white privileged males; and black feminist or "womanist" critiques of structural white supremacy and capitalism/ imperialism as antithetical to black women and their families. Unwanted domesticity, reproductive rights, pay inequity, access to careers and positions at the highest levels, all fueled the politics of the former group.

Inequities in education, employment, and safety, racial denigration, and sterilization abuse alongside reproductive rights shaped the politics of the second. Maternal "captivity" in the suburbs differed substantively from the violence of racially fashioned "plantation" domesticity[4] and poverty against black life and families. Traditional feminist goals of female leadership in government and in corporate and military structures would not liberate everyone.

Butler's feminism and fiction are antithetical to convention. Her protagonists exist to free themselves in worlds where violence and terror are expressions of the enslavement of black life (now the metaphor for captivity). This violence and terror are not more, or less, of the same human tragedies. This is not a variation of the white norm. For collective terror in white sovereign life arises as the result of invasion or war. Without whiteness as existential property and the material benefits it accrues, black collective life, particularly female life, experiences terror and violence as typified in domestic life not through foreign invasions (to which black life is also vulnerable).[5] In conventional SF, the human faces the aggressor as alien/robot/android engineered by humans or the hostile indigenous as "discovered" by humans; these are the foils by which the human heroically defines and saves himself (and his moral compass) through others. That normative protagonist is subject not object; his humanity is a birthright, and his ability to be noble as a race traitor who opposes colonization and enslavement (through sentiment of acts of violence) is also part of that birthright. This SF does not need the captive maternal; it has taken her biography and replaced her in her own autobiography with an understudy as substitute who only gestures toward the possibilities of degradation and rebellion under enslavement that constitute her black matrix.

Although to date, none of Butler's writings have been adapted to film, she has rewritten the script for a mass readership that brings her lens to visual texts; that ken indicts wars of captivity by also implicating the heroic protagonists – something largely unthinkable until Octavia Butler herself appeared in SF as a protagonist. If the absence in cinema is supposed to be reality, can the black female agent be considered the embodiment of the real?

Absence in the Cinematic Norm: Butler's Maternal Protagonist

Cinema democratized, commercialized, and disseminated SF. We read movies in simultaneous, mass gatherings tracking flickering screens. Yet SF films, as visual texts, veil the captive maternal and the productive value of her black matrix, promoting a global literacy in futurisms where black

female protagonists are chimera. The master-slave, antislavery, decolonization narratives are lifted from the diaries of captive maternals with a focus
on abuses of rights and productive labor but not on reproductive labor.
Butler's queries, rephrased here as "Why aren't there any blacks/black
women?" and "Why is SF so 'normal'?," are answered with another question: "Can two captivities, in which the heroic liberator is implicated in
the violence against the captive, coexist at the same place in the same time
and still be found entertaining?" The master race narrative poses as both
captor and captive. A SF version of "blue-eyed soul," the master-slave narrative, replaces the fear of fertile blackness with race anxiety over aliens,
androids supplant race fear of fertile blackness, and the agency of suffering and resistance to slavery, also represented by the master race, is far
flung from a half millennium of black histories, even if it makes for a
good cover.

(Euro)Futurism failed to depict the terrors of captivity shaped by race,
reality, and materiality. So *Afro*futurism had to be created. Afrofuturism
channels factual horror into the imaginative future with the specificity of black history: enslaved production, raped reproduction, bodily
theft for nation building under law (U.S. Constitution's Three-Fifths
Compromise); decriminalization of rape, incest, domestic battery, forced
pregnancy, and murder under slavery; criminalization of sexuality in freedom; decriminalization of homicide in convict prison work camps after
emancipation and legalization of slavery (Thirteenth Amendment) –
these, and more, formed the black matrix in worlds neither mirrored nor
windowed in traditional SF. Hence, no sliding glass door. The conventional world of misogyny/racism/poverty inadequately theorizes violence
that implicates its elites. Butler's words allow the births of other species,
protagonists who cannot be usurped by alien, android, minor character,
love interest (*Star Trek*), or black male lead (*Star Wars*).[6]

Off screen, the absent protagonist as black captive maternal reads visual
texts in which characters struggle with the central themes of her life: violent interruption of intimacy and connectedness amid slavery, colonization, and genocide.[7] A brief survey of SF Hollywood illustrates the world
altered by Butler.

In 1979's *Alien*, Sigourney Weaver's Ellen Ripley brought a new action
heroine to horror SF. The 1986 sequel, *Aliens*, with its uber violence and
militarist themes taken from U.S. marines and the war in Vietnam, transforms the white, single, female lead into a maternal figure providing protective care for an orphaned, petite, white child, Carrie Henn's Rebecca
"Newt" Jorden. The carnage of the movie concludes with an exo-suited

Ripley, having destroyed the Queen's eggs, battling the Alien Queen mother aboard the returning spacecraft with militarized and masculinized technology that can destroy her exoskeleton. Violent warfare is fought on the colony or in space as Ripley ensures that aliens do not enter Earth to use human bodies as incubators for their eggs. Her life prior to space exploration on an imperial mission, which the military-industrial complex planned unknown to her, was unfulfilling but not traumatic. Terror occurs through foreign wars, not domestic violence or domestic captivity. Ripley as a sovereign white woman is free after she destroys the Alien Queen because she was never a captive to her race, although she faced gender discrimination. As maternal protector, she spoke the mater's language. That makes a world of difference. Black female terror (which is both individual and caste-fashioned) is tied to trauma from everyday life as well as vulnerablility to foreign warfare. It does not possess the master's speech.

In the 1982 classic noir fiction (as *Aliens* became classic horror SF), film *Blade Runner*, not the colony but Earth is dystopia. *Blade Runner*'s traditional hetero male hero, bounty hunter Deckard, played by Harrison Ford, kills android "replicants" seeking freedom. Deckard lives on "the knife's edge between humanity and inhumanity" as do four renegade replicants, including Rutger Hauer's Roy Baty and Darryl Hannah's Pris. As murderous fugitive rebels, replicants seek a cure to their four-year programmed lifespan, or incept date, and freedom.

Assimilated and passing as human, Sean Young's Rachael saves Deckard by using his gun to kill a male replicant avenging the hunter's brutal slaying of his female lover. Hired to execute the off-world renegades seeking their father-creator's key to life, Deckard fails to kill a single male but manages to grotesquely "retire" two female replicants (who serviced humans as exotic dancers or sex workers). Recovering from the fight that she had settled in his favor, he rapes or initiates rough sex with Rachael – trapping her in his apartment, pinning her to a wall, instructing her to repeat "I want you" until she is capable of embracing a man authorized to kill her – the human and replicant fall in love. During the final film battle, when Roy Baty's incept date occurs, having grieved over the bloodied body of his lover Pris, he saves her killer. Perhaps this act of grace toward the master is the slave's only power over death. Deckard flees with Rachael to the outer colonies from police who will hunt and destroy her, and from democracy's dystopia. Miscegenation's maroons avoid captivity. They have no maternal or nurturing ties to progeny and communities to make them vulnerable. Deckard is a master human; Rachael is a superior replicant. Despite her unknown incept date, their union has a future. Engineers defy, sometimes with impunity, laws they authorize and enforce. Although criminalized and "queered" (whether same sex[8] or hetero), master-slave sex/rape can be controlled and consumed with impunity by the master (e.g., Rufus's relation to Alice in *Kindred*[9] or Thomas Jefferson's relationship with Sally Hemmings). The captive maternal breaks law and prohibition with lethal consequences; hence her eventual triumph is presented as uncertain.

Two years after *Blade Runner*, Sean Young played another female sexual partner nurturing a heroic male protagonist. In the 1984 film *Dune*, based on Frank Herbert's 1965 *Dune*, winner of the 1966 Hugo (the prestigious SF literary award for which Butler's "Speech Sounds" would be honored in 1984), Young's character Chani, the fierce, indigenous Fremen leader resisting colonization, teaches survival and war skills to – and awakens the heart of – royal Paul Atreides (played by Kyle McLaughlin). The exiled young Atreides regains the colonial throne to the desert planet Arrakis (Dune), and the life-enhancing "Spice." The film's willful, powerful, political colonial women – for example, eugenicist Bene Gesserit's order, whose members include Paul's mother, Lady Jessica (played by Francesca Annis), as well as the Fremen – all come under the rule of the young Atreides. Female agency remains, willingly or unwillingly, the enabler of elite men, and it remains nonblack. Through Chani and Paul, Fremen merge with the House of Atreides. The women of Dune birth and bury children, but they are not hunted as slaves; they are members of the households of rulers. They inherit economies, political connections, royal bloodlines, religious-political orders, and lands. They are not disposed; the Dune women are sovereigns. Butler's black female protagonists, however, are the dispossessed who battle all for resources to achieve some measure of safety and sovereignty. As disposable women they are attached to black men who lack resources, and tend to rage over their loss, and inabilities to wield power in the existing order. Butler reserves extraordinary and transformative powers for her female protagonists.

Two decades following *Dune*, a black male lead appeared in a major SF film. Evoking Isaac Asimov's 1950 short story *I, Robot*, in the 2004 *I, Robot*, Will Smith's Detective Del Spooner rescues humanity from a feminized renegade robot who honors the directive of preventing harm to humankind by eradicating humans given their destructiveness. To the degree that the black film star has transracial appeal, the absence of key black characters or signifiers of a racial order, the only black persona *as black* fades. A masculinized robot and a compassionate white woman humanize Del Spooner; the absence of a black female protagonist endures, which also proved true of televised SF. In 2004, the 1978 television series *Battlestar Galactica* was reassigned gender roles (controversial for some) so that a white woman, Katee Sackhoff, became Starbuck and an East Asian, Grace Park, played Boomer (originally played by African American Herbert Jefferson).[10] In the series, a straggle of human survivors, under the presidency of Laura Roslin played by Mary McDonnell, seek a planet after the destruction of their home planets by humanoid Cylons, former slaves of humans. In the series remake, a heterosexual female battles alien invaders, drinks, smokes, and loves "like a man." Her Cylon enemies are good and bad, and predominately led by white women; Park (as a double agent, Cylon 6) is an exception. The female captives and combatants, human or humanoid, have maternal instincts, kill, die, and rebirth violently. They are masculinized as warriors and mostly, but not always, mate with men. They live and function as soldiers for their respective armies. With the minor roles of one Latina fighter pilot, one black woman love interest (who suicides), and a black woman healer who all die (no black male appears in the series as a regular character), there is the noticeable absence of black female protagonists in a military drama, in which humans flee and fight Cylons seeking human annihilation and security. Survivors of both races find sanctuary when they colonize new Earth. Cylon 6's half-human daughter will be Earth's new biracial "Eve," and the humans' cycle of life, war, death, and resurrection begins again.

In James Cameron's 2009 film *Avatar*, black women appear in anime. Afra-Latina (Dominican and of Haitian descent) Zoe Saldana's Na'vi leader Neytiri, aided by her mother, Mo'at, played by African American C. C. H. Pounder, changes a bitter, paraplegic white man with a Na'vi avatar into a liberator of a living planet. (Saldana and Pounder play one of the few black mother-daughter roles in popular SF film.) Using his Westernized training and Na'vi re-socialization, he becomes capable of organizing diverse indigenous nations to defeat an imperial military. The black woman here is blue, and hence she has transracial appeal although her features and hair and those of her mother are clearly African. She is Africanized not as human but as alien; blacks and aliens now are blended, with the alien made even more exotic. When she chastises Sam Worthington's Jake Sully, whom she rescues as he stumbles about the jungle in his avatar Na'vi guise, she scolds him for acting dangerously like a baby. She becomes his protector and enabler, making him into a liberator through tutelage, love, and sex. Her transformative powers are derived from Gaia, Pandora's "earth mother" god, and from her own Na'vi mother who survives when her Na'vi father and former betrothed are killed in battle with the imperialists. The deaths of those "blue men" conveniently clear the path for Jake's succession.

Jake, the white man inside the Na'vi body, could have become Neytiri's theoretical avatar, if she had been willing or able to control him, that is, if the white male authors had permitted this. Instead, she chooses to love him. She cradles him and gives him oxygen after the final battle, and later anxiously leans over him during the permanent transference of his consciousness into his Na'vi body. She personifies the maternal liberator who is focused on Jake, not Na'vi children. She gives birth to a white man-child, the only one who has the power to vanquish other white men's militarism, technology, and greed. Jake is more powerful than Neytiri; he unseats her ancestral lineage and usurps every indigenous as rightful heir to political power. Neytiri's babies will not be plantation babies. Like all of the other women discussed here, she has a powerful male to protect her (this is not true for Dana in *Kindred*, Ayananwu in *Wild Seed*, Mary in *Mind of My Mind*, or Rye in "Speech Sounds"); patriarchy is portrayed as functional for some females. Beneficiaries of "alien love," Jake, Paul, and Deckard possess a (hetero) sexualized maternal who has empowered them. These male protagonists do not want as life partner a captive maternal: a poor, prostituted, raped, enslaved potential revolutionary whose rebellion might turn against their household.

There always appears to be an exception to the norm. In 1995, *Strange Days* was that anomaly for which Kathryn Bigelow became the first woman to receive a Saturn Award for Best Director; Angela Bassett received a Saturn Award for Best Actress. (James Cameron co-wrote and co-produced the film.) In the film, Ralph Fiennes's Lenny Nero is protected by a bodyguard, Bassett's Lornette "Mace" Mason, who is friend to Lenny, a dishonored former LAPD cop selling illicit SQUID ("used emotions" of other lives in addictive virtual reality devices). Unrequited love allows Mace, a former waitress and black single mom, to repeatedly risk her life to bring safety and moral consciousness to Lenny on the eve of the new millennium. In 1999 Los Angeles, L. A. is the dystopia-in-waiting that appears in *Blade Runner*. Mace met and was mentored by Lenny when he was a honest cop, so there is reciprocity in the relationship. As he investigates a string of murders committed by corrupt LAPD members and woos his former criminal white lover, Faith Justice (played by Juliette Lewis), the fabric of justice, social order, and romantic love disintegrate. The murderous LAPD cops involved in the illicit trade have tried to kill Lenny and Mace, and successfully kill others as the clock counts down to the New Year. In the streets, the partying multiracial witnesses a brutal

Rodney King–style beating of Mace by rogue cops who command the citizenry to stand back. As she is about to be executed, the citizen rabble violates the law and intervenes, and the corrupt police suicide or are arrested as the honest police chief establishes order following the urban rebellion. The people prevail and they are multiracial and black. Lenny's obsession with the white, cyberpunk femme fatale singer, which had eclipsed the protective love of the black mother, ends. The antihero, a flawed and ineffective liberator, is changed by the closest approximation of the captive maternal. She, like other stereotypical black women, is masculinized as a sidekick. Hers is the big (shot)gun. She is renamed "Mace" and so masculinized and weaponized that she nurtures Lenny more than her preteen son; the new name positions Mace close to but outside the black matrix. The mirrors and windows are present, but the sliding door seems stuck.

In the 2000 SF horror *Supernova*,[11] Angela Bassett plays medical officer Dr. Kaela Evers – a tortured domestic survivor who has lost her ability to give birth – who partners with James Spader's pilot Nick Vanzant. Aboard their deep space medical ship, Evers originally disdains Vanzant as a recovered addict (her abusive ex-partner was a drug addict), but bonds with him as they fight her former batterer who has been transformed by ninth-dimensional matter and is rescued by the crew from a mining colony. The only human survivors, the couple kills the supernatural predator (who was rebuffed when he sought reunification with Kaela and so attempts to kill her also). They riskily climb into the only dimensional stabilizing pod, designed for one, to return to Earth. The ship robot announces that they have arrived safely with intermingled DNA – each has one blue and one brown eye – and that Kaela is pregnant with a girl. The sliding glass door has enabled them to have half a century of an earth family before the approaching supernova either elevates life or extinguishes it. As advanced as these two roles for black women in SF may be considering the prevailing norm, the characters are formed and validated by their ability to protect and serve the white male protagonist who in turn offer them love.

Protagonist as Captive Maternal

Kindred, Mind of My Mind, Wild Seed, and "Speech Sounds" all center on the challenges of constructing family where none should exist, of love and kinship despite dispossession. The transcendent values and aspirations of family, as an ideal, constitute intimacy and protection from a hostile world.

In *Kindred*, Dana, a literary person, lives in San Francisco in an interracial marriage. Her white husband is progressive and loving, yet she is estranged from her family and has no black female friends in the 1970s Bay Area. Likewise, she will have no peers when she begins to time travel, a power outside of her conscious control, back into the antebellum South to rescue a white male ancestor. The good white man, her husband, Kevin, and the bad, her ancestor Rufus, are cared for by her; but it is her ancestor whom she meets as a boy who requires her constant maternal protection. Dana is held captive by the fact that he must stay alive to create a family tree that allows her existence. The most important people – white men – in her life consume her but provide no protection from violence. Her husband lacks the power; her ancestor the desire. When Dana's husband, Kevin, grabs her as she is transported back to rescue Rufus, he inadvertently travels back with her, and finds that he, as a white man, can offer her limited protection from trauma and terror in the antebellum South; he leaves to work in the Underground Railroad.

Dana's attempts to bring late twentieth-century antiracist sensibilities into the antebellum South fail miserably. The structure, slavery, does not permit its own undoing through love; it cannot be humanized. It is opportunistic. Dana is too as she struggles to stay alive and to keep Rufus alive as well. She will fail with Alice, but that was not her primary function. Dana learns the maternal arts of cooking and healing on the antebellum plantation. She is traumatized by violence against herself and other black slaves and the depravity of the slave masters and mistresses. Yet, while weeping at the brutal whipping of a slave, she realizes that the children witnessing the horror are perhaps better emotionally equipped than she to handle the terrors of captivity; that is, they face the terrors in the reality of their unfolding, not in the emotional or imaginative desire that they will diminish or disappear.

Dana does not resist Rufus's request that she serve as the middleman between Alice and him, her enslaved maternal ancestor. This act of self-interest will insure Dana's life but end those of her kin. Encouraged by Dana to give up the enslaved man she loves, Alice succumbs to Rufus's demands and "seduction." Yet he still violently attacks her and threatens her with rape and the selling of her (their) children if she disobeys. Her suicide becomes her "escape" from slavery as well as the abandonment of her children. When Alice dies, Rufus seeks a replacement in their lineage-daughter, Dana. In classic domestic violence-incest tragedy, the father turns to the female child who favors the mother. In the plantation household, under its captivity, "incest" does not apply to the enslaved.

Dana, who countenanced Rufus's brutality, now finds slavery and its ultimate degradation – rape – an unlivable reality, so she turns to mother
herself. In the physical battle that ensues, she kills Rufus and escapes back
into her contemporary world, losing an arm in the dying man's fierce
grip. Butler uses time travel to destabilize Dana's and the readers' modern, post-slavery ("post-racial") self-perceptions. Who is free? Captive?
Sanctified by love?

In *Wild Seed*, the woman Anyanwu is discovered in Africa by Doro,
the immortal, paternal, omnipotent protagonist who begins life as a black
Nubian but prefers to inhabit the bodies of white men. Her longevity and
fertility attract him, and he convinces her to travel to the "new world."
During the colonial era, Doro begins to build a new race with his "wild
seed"; he plans to eventually kill Anyanwu because, he reasons to himself,
wild seed is unpredictable and uncontrollable. As does slavery, Doro consumes black bodies but as hosts for his immortality. As on the plantation,
the bodies devoured most horrifically and consistently are those of black
girls and women with reproductive powers who make their own demands.
Love may exist between Doro and Anyanwu (or Rufus and Alice, and
Rufus and Dana) but it does not negate violence or captivity. Doro's hosts,
over the centuries, include Anyanwu's children. Unlike Rufus, Doro is so
struck by the possible loss of Anyanwu through suicide that he pleads and
negotiates an armistice to prevent it.

In *Mind of My Mind*, telepaths avoid each other's company; sociability
means mental contact and that is overwhelming for them. They find their
children painful to be around because adults cannot block the constant
chaotic, psychic noise coming from youthful minds. The telepaths' PTSD
requires that slave labor, desensitized mutes, maintain family stability to
function in the world of chaos, discord, and violence. Mary fosters slavery
to bring balance to the lives of telepaths and curtail child neglect, abuse,
or murder. (She creates "plantation babies" not destined for slave quarters.) Her diminished virtues allow her to function more like her father,
as a "daddy's girl." Doro, who sought the evolution of a creature such
as Mary, realizes too late that her lethal mind can destroy him. Mary's
maternal sensibilities (daughters do mother their fathers) suffer little emotional vulnerability, although suffering is part of motherhood: Anyanwu
leaves animal form, the only form in which Doro cannot track and attack
her, in order to nurture, just as Dana lets Rufus live longer than necessary in order to rehabilitate him. Mary so lacks conventional nurturing
that she neglects her own young daughter; her husband provides the emotional stability for their child to thrive. Like the other female protagonists,

Mary remains maternal (unlike them she is also an enslaver), creating and destroying life. For all of the black female protagonists, their primary antagonists are familial, dependent men.

"Speech Sounds," the shortest of Octavia Butler's works discussed here, receives the most words for it melds the future into the present moment. Butler describes the story's inspiration as coming from a fight between two men on a dirty, crowded bus that Butler was riding in order to read a draft of *Clay's Ark* to a friend dying from cancer. Butler admits that the story line was likely "inappropriate" but was requested by her friend. Butler witnessed a bloody and brief fight that was inspirational but depressing, leaving her "wondering whether the human species would ever grow up enough to learn to communicate without using fists of one kind or another." According to Octavia Butler: " 'Speech Sounds' was conceived in weariness, depression, and sorrow. I began the story feeling little hope for liking for the human species, but by the time I reached the end of it, my hope had come back. It always seems to do that."

In "Speech Sounds,"[12] Rye's safety in post-apocalypse California is threatened by literacy just as Dana's was in the antebellum South. In the future, the ability to speak, let alone read and write, has largely disappeared. The rage over that loss leads many to brutally persecute the few who can speak or read or both. Rye boards an intercity bus in search of her brother and nephews/nieces who might be living twenty miles away in Pasadena. Rye risks travel. Her male neighbor is a potential stalker and sex enslaver. A "highly specific" pandemic or "illness" had caused her to lose her family and her talents as an intellectual: "Language was always lost or severely impaired. It was never regained. Often there was also paralysis, intellectual impairment, death" (5). For Rye, the illness had "stripped her, killing her children one by one, killing her husband, her sister, her parents." It severed all social ties in its ability to "cut people down." When the driver slams on the brakes and more fights begin as "men fall into screaming passengers," Rye speedily exits. Outside, Rye watches a man with an LAPD uniform soundlessly motioning her away as he clears the bus by tossing in a tear gas canister. He helps gagging passengers, stands down a furious driver, and beckons for Rye to leave with him in his car. Rye hesitates and stands down another man and his companions who threaten her with hand signals, grunts, and gang rape. Reflecting that "Loss of verbal language had spawned a whole new set of obscene gestures," Rye wearily watches her would-be assailant and observes: "People might very well stand by and watch if he tried to rape her. They would also stand and watch her shoot him" (2). After she gives the clear hand signal for him to stop approaching her, he contemptuously walks away, signing. Rye then reluctantly takes a ride from the stranger, Obsidian, who, likely a former policeman, becomes her lover.

Their wordless self-introductions are communicated through signs and sexuality. Rye has met her peer in Obsidian. When she realizes that he can read the map, though, her raging grief momentarily leads to homicidal thoughts. When he signs to ask if she has children, she does not respond; her thoughts disassociate maternal love from captivity, and the narrative she weaves to convince her that ending the maternal was preferable and inevitable because "the children growing up now were to be pitied." They had, in Rye's mind, regressed to animalism: "They would run through the downtown canyons with no real memory of what the buildings had been or even how they had come to be. Today's children gathered books as well as wood to be burned as fuel. They ran through the streets chasing one another and hooting like chimpanzees. They had no future. They were now all they would ever be."

Recounting motherhood through personal and collective grief, Rye dismisses the future. Maternal agency alleviates trauma; political response to violence and captivity in meaningful actions can provide an outlet for suffering. Denying herself hope through agency, Rye tries to convince Obsidian to live with her (he is noncommittal). When a woman flees across the road chased by a man with a knife, Obsidian brakes the car and attempts to save her. The woman also tries to defend herself but is killed when the man stabs her twice. Obsidian shoots him, then, distracted by Rye, he is killed by the injured man. Rye ends the carnage by shooting her lover's murderer with her gun. She is left with three corpses: her lover-protector, the fleeing woman, and the murderer.

When two three-year-olds run from the house where the man and woman had come past Rye to the dead woman whose arm is shaken by the girl in an attempt to wake her, Rye painfully recognizes a dead mother and feels ill. She begins to leave without the children, rationalizing that they "were old enough to scavenge," that she had had enough of grief, and that she "did not need a stranger's children who would grow up to be hairless chimps." Yet she returns for Obsidian's body for burial and then decides to bury the mother as well. That compassion toward a slain captive maternal changes reality. As Rye drags the woman's body toward the car, the children make noises, then the little girl screams "No!" and utters the ultimate toddler command, "Go away!" Her brother protectively shushes her, first with a command: "Don't talk," then with a whisper: "Be quiet." Rye's world collapses.

Executive functioning explodes: Rye wonders if their mother had taught them to talk; if the children were born "after the silence." With three living and three dead, Rye assembles a future that had not existed: "What if children of three or fewer years were safe and able to learn language? What if all they needed were teachers? Teachers and protectors." An intellectual and an educator before, Rye is now a captive maternal. Realizing that the children were not "mindless chimps," she mourns the loss of Obsidian-the-protector, for now "there was something worth protecting." She decides to raise the children spared by the illness, gently carries and places the mother next to Obsidian in the car-hearse, and then carries the children to the front seat. To the crying children, she reveals what was hidden from her male lover, whispering to soften a rusted voice "I'm Valerie Rye.... It's all right for you to talk to me."

Conclusion: Wishing for the Happiness of the Beloved

Butler's writings pose an interesting contrast with Toni Morrison's *Beloved*. Morrison's Pulitzer Prize–winning novel is based on the 1856 tragedy of fugitive slave Margaret Garner, who when trapped in Ohio by bounty hunters working under the 1850 Fugitive Slave Act, attempted to kill her small children and murdered one daughter rather them have them abused in captivity. After her release from prison, Sethe is haunted by an embodied, supernatural being, Beloved, a young female who enters her home. Memories of rape and terror, misery and intimacy, guilt and maternal love, shaming and love follow. The lives of Sethe, her teen daughter Denver, and her lover Paul D, who is seduced by Beloved, are hijacked by the insatiable desires of the sacrificed succubus, who consumes and haunts the captive maternal. It seems that only the black female child (the three-year-old in "Speech Sounds," Mary in *Mind of My Mind*, Alice in *Kindred*, Anyanwu's daughters in *Wild Seed*) has the power to destabilize the captive maternal. Both seek to be free.

Here is where Butler and Morrison differ. Sethe and her family (once Beloved is vanquished) remain within a black community that first censored and then saved her. Its punished her because she acted, regardless of the terrors of sexual-racial captivity, with god-like powers, with the legitimate authority to create and take life. She usurped and rivaled the powers of the enslaver. And it doesn't matter that she did so out of love, so the black community abandons her. Butler's protagonists actually unapologetically exercise such authority. Although they largely refrain from violently euthanizing their progeny, they tend to reserve the right to do so in pursuing an elusive freedom and with the mandate that if the achievement of freedom will be their most notable failure, creativity will be the hallmark of their matrix: intimacy and emotional intelligence, theorizing and political agency.

Hanging our dirty laundry out to dry in cemeteries, where she plants herself as wild seed, Octavia Butler cleanses captivity. Her personal battles with anxiety and depression were shouldered with courage and resilience that allowed a brilliant artistry. Despite her early, unnatural demise, she remains scattered among countless readers, growing mirrors and windows and prying open sliding glass doors.

CHAPTER 15

More than Theater: Cherríe Moraga's
The Hungry Woman *and the Feminist*
Phenomenology of Excess

Lakey

Her name, too, was written there in the dust.
Did you see her? She who wrote without letters
the picture of a disappearing planet?
She knew in advance what it would mean, their arrival.
She saw us, her pueblo, a cactus tuna
bleeding in the heat.
                                    – Cherríe Moraga (2011), "A Color of a Nation"

The Hungry Woman: A Mexican Medea, like much of Cherríe Moraga's
theatrical work, exists along the razor-sharp edge between political critique and aesthetic creation, between ritual ceremony and theatrical
performance, between being and what has been, between daily life and
mythology, and between losing a culture and finding oneself in the process
of cultural creation. It is really no surprise, then, that a set of paradoxes
emerges at the opening lines of *The Hungry Woman* when the actress playing Cihuatateo East (one of the "Divine Women" in Aztec mythology)
begins the play with the line "This is how all stories begin and end" (9),
then briefly tells the pregnancy story of Coatlicue (the Aztec "Mother of
all Gods" – a maternal Earth deity), and then changes character by placing
a red hat on her head, so as to become an aging nurse caretaker who states
a slight reiteration of the play's opening line: "This is how all days begin
and end" (9). From the opening scene on stage, Aztec goddess and nurse
caretaker emerge as one and the same and different simultaneously – as
do the concepts of "story" and "day." At the center of the play's beginning
and ending is a focus on women through the reclaiming of estranged goddess narratives, the retelling of the lost stories of women's lives silenced by
white male history, and a feminist casting of all women actresses (with the
exception of one boy).

Right from the "Prelude," Moraga abandons clearly delineated forms
of signification and uses the physical space of the stage to blur the

meaningful boundaries between actually existing objects, memories, identities, languages, and concepts. This in-betweenness is not just a hybrid of race, sexual identity, gender, and class identity markers. Rather, Moraga's in-betweenness highlights the razor-sharp edge in-between as a site where the active collective language of mythological and historical story in the oral tradition simultaneously parallels and contradicts the lived experience of individual action taking place in the day.

Moraga uses her work to reassess the concept of identity as a site of collective action that can change the day-to-day realities of exploitation and oppression. In doing so, Moraga's work formulates the "in-between" as a place of excess. As a place of excess, Moraga's in-between takes on an element of superabundance. This location of superabundance is one of privilege as it exists within the lived experience of neoliberalism while also exceeding the barriers and boundaries created by neoliberalism's economic, social, linguistic and cultural borders. As such, Moraga's philosophy views theater as *more than* a reflection of the world. *The Hungry Woman* in particular builds on this philosophy of excess in order to create change and push the "world" beyond itself. In this way, Moraga gives credit to Djelal Kadir's conceptual understanding of the concept "world" as a verb: to world.[1] Moraga's in-betweenness becomes an excess that reorganizes, reclaims, and "reworlds" the negative identity claim against the queer Chicana mother writer as "being excessive" and turns it into a positive position of creative privilege. Therefore, I argue that Moraga's in-betweenness is a foundation for a particular brand of feminist critique that focuses on the marginalized experience of the queer Chicana mother's body as a phenomenological excess. How so?

Phenomenology is generally defined as the study of the appearance of things as they arise in conscious experience and what that appearance means to the structures of consciousness. In the twentieth century, phenomenology traditionally focused on a first-person view of conscious experience that places the unmarked[2] white male of the West at the center. Through her writing and theater, Moraga challenges the traditional understanding of phenomenology by highlighting the profound internal and external dissonance experienced by a feminist lesbian Chicana mother whose life does not fit within any cultural, social, or political framework. By starting from the marginalized and dislocated experience of the lesbian Chicana mother, Moraga's literary framework in *The Hungry Woman* highlights the dual characteristics of in-betweenness and excess experienced by a woman living within oppressive structures of patriarchy, racism, and homophobia.

The Hungry Woman pushes back against the concept of excess as some-thing considered wrong or "excessive" and reframes it as more than enough. In *The Hungry Woman*, and most of Moraga's literature, "more than enough" becomes a site of power. In what follows, I argue that Moraga's literature, especially her theater, gives rise to a feminist phenomenology of excess that is grounded in the study of embodied conscious experience of the lesbian Chicana mother. This feminist phenomenology reclaims the experience of "more than enough" as the site of feminist critique and as a location of practical and political action from within the system itself. By using her literary engagement in essays, poems, and theater, Moraga reshapes the canon of literary philosophy by reframing the structures of conscious experience from the forgotten, silenced, and marginalized les-bian Chicana mother as "other." Through a feminist phenomenology of excess on the border in-between, Moraga uses literature as political action and as a tool to gain self-knowledge, awareness, and agency.

Inspired by the legacy of the United Farm Workers' theater, El Teatro Campesino, and the Chicano civil rights movement as a whole, Moraga takes the very real circumstances of her own life and the lives of oppressed Chicana/o and queer peoples and creates a theatrical phenomenology of in-betweenness that fuses all human action and performance with the fundamental unity of all living things as an experience of a life in-between that is always slightly beyond definition and understanding. Hers is the paradoxical phenomenology of social action at the border: a description of the intimate link between individual identity, social protest, and col-lective memory. Moraga's in-betweenness is an embodied process of cul-tural performance that resists "Anglo domination" and "male domination" (Moraga, "Art in America," 159) with the reclamation of "the indigenous origins of theatre" as those of ritual and myth, "whose ultimate goal is to teach and spiritually heal its participants" (Moraga, "Art in America," 159). Primarily informed by the praxis philosophies of social protest theater as a whole, Moraga challenges all aspects of the social order that has come before her and continues in the present by reclaiming the lost or margin-alized mother and queer within the Chicana/o tradition. In doing so, she asserts a phenomenology that arises out of the cutting edge of life – an edge that is simultaneously in between all else and an excess of multilayered meanings, histories, experiences, and languages that cannot be properly absorbed back within the dominant hegemonic narrative system. Moraga's is a process philosophy of consistent in-betweenness that is in constant creation through the performance of story as difference and change, func-tioning and existing within the cyclical return of communal life.

I

Describing herself as *la güera*, "the fair skinned girl," Moraga spent much of her youth "passing" as white and straight. When she narrates her experience of coming out as a lesbian in her twenties, Moraga claims that the lid of silence and shame used to marginalize her sexual identity was lifted when she began to write and read love poems about women. The oral form of her poetic endeavors formed an immediate overlap with the oral histories of indigenous Americans bound to the collective memory told to her by her mother in childhood. By the 1990s Moraga's poetry transformed into theatrical performances inspired by the fragmented Chicana/o ritual practices of her youth as well as the inherited legacy and study of Aztec and Maya myth.

Moraga highlights the importance of writing out of the in-between location of myth and history in the "Forward" to *The Hungry Woman*. "In recent years, I've come to understand myth as a similarly divine(d) gift, an opening into the past, told in character and image, that can provide a kind of road map to our future" (ix). *The Hungry Woman* rewrites the master narrative of the West by crossing the story of Euripides' Medea with the violent mythology of four "fallen" women figures from the indigenous American tradition: La Llorona, Coyolxauhqui, the Hungry Woman, and Coatlicue.[3]

According to conventional mythic retellings, the Hungry Woman is a woman whose body is covered with mouths. She is broken into tiny pieces by the gods to create earth and sky, in hopes of destroying her insatiable desire, only to leave a legacy of open-mouthed hunger in every piece of earth and sky she creates. La Llorona, a common legend in Mexico and Central America, is a frightening woman who drowns her own children as a revenge for sexual betrayal and then haunts the woods and the streets weeping and searching for children to replace the ones she has killed. Coyolxauhqui is the moon goddess and daughter of Coatlicue who ends up dismembered by her brother Huitzilopochli when she tries to murder Coatlicue. Combining these stories with the Euripides Medea myth allows Moraga to blend and highlight the way each myth justifies women's oppression, exile, and/or punishment. Building on the myths by combining them and bringing them back to life as ritual on stage, Moraga enacts the important challenge Chicano drama critic Jorge Huerta finds essential in the resuscitation of "Mexican legendary figures along with Aztec and Mayan gods and concepts" all the while maintaining a queer feminist critique of "both the Mexican and the North American hegemonies" embedded in the indigenous American myths (*Chicano Drama*, 18).

Building out of the parallels between the classical Greek myth of
Medea and various indigenous American myths and then inserting her
own critique of patriarchy, homophobia, and xenophobia, Moraga's *The
Hungry Woman* reclaims and radicalizes the mythic past to dismantle
destructive sociopolitical influences within the Chicano community as a
move toward corrective "healing" of the community as a whole. In doing
so, *The Hungry Woman* offers a mythic and performative reimagining of
the subject position of the resisting and revolutionary lesbian Chicana
mother in exile. The play takes a position generally overlooked or dismissed within the dominant cultural spheres of the United States and
reformulates that subject position within the controversial in-between
spaces of the hegemonic mythic narratives. In what Paula Straile-Costa
argues is Moraga's postmodern use of *bricolage* ("Myth and Ritual in *The
Hungry Woman*," 212), *The Hungry Woman* layers the similarities of the
Greek and Mexican traditional myths and then slices open the meaning
imbedded in that layering through the integration of ritual, dance, dei-
ties, and icons on stage.

This layered signification combined with ritualized movement creates
a socio-symbolic dialectical critique of state and ideological apparatuses.
Linking key historical characters, such as the exiled Medea of Euripides,
with the historical internalized exile of queers, feminists, and Chicanos
in the United States allows Moraga to reclaim the prominent critique of
the Chicano movement against Anglo-American imperialism while also
inserting a critique of the Chicano movement's own sexism and homophobia. Building out of the traditions of El Teatro Campesino and the
values of the Chicano movement as a whole, Moraga continues to create a
phenomenological critique that values self-determination and affirmation
combined with unified political action and a belief in the right to land
and language (Straile-Costa, "Myth and Ritual in *The Hungry Woman*,"
213). As a powerful lesbian revolutionary Chicano mother, Medea embodies the challenge Moraga levels at the Chicano movement when she states
that the movement perpetuates a:

> *Machista* view of women, based on the centuries-old virgin-whore paradigm
> of *la Virgen de Guadalupe* and *Malintzin Tenepal*. Guadalupe represented
> the Mexican idea of *la madre sufrida*, the long-suffering Indian mother,
> and Malinche was *la chingada*, sexually stigmatized by her transgression
> of "sleeping with the enemy," Hernán Cortes. Deemed traitor by Mexican
> tradition, the figure of Malinche was invoked to keep Movimiento women
> silent, sexually passive, and "Indian" in the colonial sense of the word. (*Last
> Generation*, 157)

The history of La Malinche is invoked in *The Hungry Woman* through the overlap with Euripides' Medea character. Euripides' Medea and La Malinche were both "given" in sexual servitude as a gift and expected to use their bodies and languages to mediate between two powerful patriarchal nations. Moraga's Medea reframes these patriarchal narratives by putting them in overlap and highlighting the continuance of these narratives in practical forms both within the colonized relations between the U.S. and the Chicana/o populations and between the Chicano movement and feminist queer revolutionaries dismissed by the movement as a whole.

Typical of most of her work, *The Hungry Woman* allows Moraga to reclaim the passion of El Movimiento (the self-proclaimed name of the Chicano movement in the 1960s and 1970s) and its power to fuse performance art with social protest. In focusing on the goddess stories and the displaced narratives of queer Chicana motherhood in general, Moraga pushes back against El Movimiento's embrace of "Mexican machismo and Aztec warrior bravado" (Moraga, *Last Generation*, 156). In performance, the action on the stage reframes the narrative from the space of a forgotten and silenced revolutionary queer mother whose story is in parallel with the marginalized and oppressed goddesses of traditional myth. Highlighting several interlocking systems of domination while also challenging them by using the position of excess as a foundation for critique, Moraga steers her audience toward the true object of sociopolitical oppression and domination. This object is not the murdered son of Medea, nor is it the collective men who suffer under the sins and rages of the goddesses in Mexican and indigenous American myth. No, the true object of sociopolitical oppression and domination in this play is the queer Chicana mother who lives in a mental hospital/prison on the border in between, but whose position doubles as a site of excess. Medea is more than woman – she is lesbian. She is more than mother – she is goddess. Moraga uses Medea's position in *The Hungry Woman* as the in-between object "other" of sociopolitical oppression to gain a critical perspective on sexism, racism, and homophobia. This critical perspective uses literary narrative to educate the audience as well as expose and act against the powers embedded in white male neoliberal imperialism in the United States.

Moraga's Mexican Medea displaces the mediated subject/object so that layers of forgotten and silenced memories, knowledges, and practices are highlighted in the same location as the more dominant hegemonic social, historical, and mythical systems. Importantly, these layers of forgotten and silenced object forms are not relegated to a secondary status, but in fact, they highlight the significant mythical and historical parallels without allowing for a common neutral ground of absolute mediation. By adding more than "two points of view" (lesbian, feminist, revolutionary, mother, Chicana), Moraga rewrites what Slavoj Žižek refers to as an "irreducible gap" (20) vis-à-vis a layered location between parallels within the mythical and historical as well as the paradoxes that lead to the ineffable spiritual realm on stage. This divine and/or spirit realm in *The Hungry Woman* is signified by the myths themselves, by the ritual performances of song and dance given by the chorus of Cihuatateo (Aztec spirits of warrior women who died in childbirth), by the altar to Coatlicue that opens the play, and by Aztlán itself (the spiritual homeland of the Aztecs). Within this alternative realm, an ineffable real or spiritual realm, Medea as a character exists and *The Hungry Woman* as a performance is said to take place. Returning to El Teatro Campesino's philosophy "Theater of the Sphere," Moraga's *The Hungry Woman* integrates the anti-imperialist struggle in continuity with a spiritual realm that is enacted in the "daily flesh-and-blood particulars of human life" (Broyles-González, *El Teatro Campesino*, 121). It is precisely the place of excess, a place of minimal difference, that Moraga's phenomenology comes alive as a concern not only with political and social realms, but as a concern of the spirit and of the heart.

II

Moraga's Medea is an exiled Chicana revolutionary woman forced from the homeland Aztlán,[4] a post-revolutionary land that Medea fought for as a leader in an ethnic civil war that balkanized half of the United States in a dystopian future. As a character, Medea is simultaneously the "living Coatlicue" (the Aztec "Mother of all Gods"), a refiguration of the Mexican La Llorona myth, the Hungry Woman in Aztec mythology, and a lesbian mother who sacrifices her son. Much like Euripides' Medea, Moraga's Medea lives in exile, but Moraga reconfigures this exile within Aztec myth and iconography and U.S.-Mexican history, highlighting the way indigenous Americans became exiles in their own land after the 1848 Treaty of Guadalupe-Hidalgo.

Moraga's Medea lives with her son Chac-Mool[5] in a "kind of metaphysical border region between Gringolandia (U.S.A.) and Aztlán" (Moraga, *The Hungry Woman*, 6) named Phoenix, Arizona.[6] This in-between region is simultaneously 1) a mental hospital; 2) a border prison; 3) the liminal space between life and death; 4) the liminal space between day and night, namely dusk and dawn; 5) the ambiguous line between mythological story and historical movements and processes of day-to-day life; 6) for Chac-Mool, it is also the space between boyhood and manhood; and 7) for Medea, it is also the space of exile between free expression of a lesbian identity and slavery as a wife caught in a heterosexual marriage forced on her from the outside.

Medea lives in this in-between location because she is banished from Aztlán by the "law" (and her husband Jasón) for loving and having sex with a woman. After serving on the front lines of the winning Chicano revolution, Medea is first relegated (like all women) to a subjugated role as mother and housewife and then thrown into exile for falling in love with her girlfriend, Luna (who is also Chac-Mool's moon-goddess sister Coyolxauhqui). Forced from the home and culture she fought for, she is placed outside of the hegemonic field of power and experiences life from a position in between myth and reality, sanity and insanity, life and death.

As such, Moraga's Medea exists as an excess at all points of significa-tion and ontology. Her links to the myths she embodies helps her refuse the boundaries of a petrified and strictly defined identity. Much like the Phoenix bird in mythological history and the Aztec creation story she rep-resents, Medea and the border she lives within are in a process of constant creation and renewal. Each time Medea reenters the stage she dies and comes alive again. In fact, the play ends with the death of Chac-Mool and the death of Medea. Pushing the boundaries of the concepts of life and living, the final scenes of *The Hungry Woman* leave the audience unsure if either Medea or Chac-Mool were alive or if they were ghostlike memories throughout the prior scenes.

Playing with the ambiguities in between a plethora of binaries (includ-ing life and death), Moraga stretches the boundaries of phenomenology to include an experience of spiritual unseen forces connected to indigenous ritual practices involving communication with the ancestors. This phe-nomenology is a philosophy of perception that experiences and under-stands the boundaries in between myth and history as an excess that allows non-hegemonic features to break through, thereby revealing layers of imagery and meaning that challenge stagnant Manichean forms of rep-resentation. How so?

Moraga combines the myths of Coyolxauhqui, Huitzilopochtli, and Coatlicue to highlight the in-between location of death and destruc-tion in the processes of the traditional Aztec creation story. The story of Coyolxauhqui, Huitzilopochtli, and Coatlicue is a creation myth that essentially explains the movement of the sun, moon, and stars across the sky and that highlights the importance of death to creation and existence in general. In order for the sun (Huitzilopochtli, who is also Chac-Mool or the "Son" in Moraga's play) to exist, he must kill his sister Coyolxauhqui who was attacking Coatlicue along with her 400 brothers, the stars. In the traditional myth, Huitzilopochtli cuts off Coyolxauhqui's head (which then becomes the "face" of the moon) and flings it up in the sky to bring comfort to his mother, the earth deity Coatlicue. In order for the sun, moon, and stars to move into their prospective locations each day and night, a violent removal must take place. That removal leads to a tempo-rary relocation of the celestial bodies in the underworld, the world of the ancestors. The rotation of the sun, moon, and stars requires a daily cycle of regeneration – the death of each in the underworld and the emergence, or birth, into the night sky. Coatlicue (the earth deity) is also reframed as the Mexican Hungry Woman who swallows the sun (the Son) each night and gives birth to light each morning. Thus the dual murder/sacrifice is also reformulated within the play as the natural cycle of birth and death that happens in the rotation of the celestial bodies.

Because Moraga changes the plot line of Euripides' Medea to include an ambiguous dual murder/sacrifice of Medea (Coatlicue) and Chac-Mool (Huitzilopochtli), death becomes the very gift of life and a necessity for existence. This paradox, one that is found in the layers of stories from a mix of traditions in *The Hungry Woman*, shapes Moraga's phenomenology and rewrites the perspectives of those that exist at the border (in between) as a position and perception of excess. Each character means more than a single being or meaning. Medea, Luna, and Chac-Mool in particular hold positions on the border in between nations, cultures, mythologies and worlds. It is the dual emergence of the border as in between and as excess that allows Moraga to use a feminist critique to reframe the tra-ditional unmarked hegemony in twentieth-century phenomenology and to critique the structures of hegemony in white male neoliberal capitalism as well. *The Hungry Woman* rewrites the lost goddesses and heroines of Moraga's Mexican and Western ancestors as lesbian Chicanas whose lives and daily actions push back against structural sexism and homophobia to assert their own power and voice.

III

Chac-Mool's murder/sacrifice scene opens with the figure of Medea dressed in the long white nightgown that is the traditional gown of Coatlicue. As Medea begins to prepare for the ritual sacrifice/murder of Chac-Mool, the "Son," she states, "Coatlicue, this is my holy sacrifice"

(88). The addition of ritualized language and dress, as well as the integration of Mexican religious iconography, emphasizes the traditional Euripides Medea murder into a ritualized murder sacrifice. As a sacrifice, Chac-Mool dies for "the people," thus exchanging the son's death in the Greek myth for a sacrifice in the effort to decolonize the future by killing out the cycle of patriarchy and homophobia imbedded in the nation of Aztlán. Chac-Mool signals the violent sacrifice of what Tanya González refers to as the "restrictive nationalist thinking not only of U.S. ideas about citizenship and national identity, but also of the Chicano movement" ("The (Gothic) Gift of Death," 69). Medea's sacrifice, made out of love for her son and the future of "the people," creates a new nation inspired by the love of the revolutionary lesbian Chicana mother exiled for her queerness and her feminist stand against patriarchy. Medea's sacrifice of Chac-Mool initiates a new concept of nationalism, one indebted to Moraga's own vision of a "Queer Aztlán" – a "Chicano homeland" that would "embrace *all* its people, including its jotería" (Moraga, *Last Generation*, 147). A queer Aztlán would end the historical colonization of the female body and the Chicano people alike and "must be historically and sexually specific" (Moraga, *Last Generation*, 149). In line with Moraga's phenomenological critique as a whole, her nationalist philosophy unravels the multivalent, silenced, and oppressed voices of history and builds on them to create what Lisa Tatonetti refers to as "a radical place of possibility for the future of Chicana/o culture" ("A Kind of Queer Balance," 229).

The opening scene of *The Hungry Woman* begins after Chac-Mool has died and then relives. It ritualizes the sacrificial murder of Chac-Mool at the end of the play after the audience learns that Medea has been exiled for her lesbianism and has been in an ongoing struggle with Jasón over parenting rights to Chac-Mool. As one would suspect, parenting rights and bloodlines are constantly and immediately attached to citizenship and status within the nation of Aztlán. Bloodlines in Aztlán also connect back to property rights and ownership as we learn that Jasón needs Chac-Mool in order to keep and claim his private property. In the scene where Chac-Mool is sacrificed, we learn that Chac-Mool has decided to answer his father's call to return to Aztlán to "become a man."[7] Because Jasón's current wife is barren, Chac-Mool is needed in Aztlán so that Jasón can regain his property and assure his bloodline. As soon as she understands Jasón's true motives, Medea resists the return of Chac-Mool to Aztlán and becomes unwilling to let her boy become like the rest of the men in Aztlán – men who have perpetuated a form of colonization and subjugation against the female body and what Moraga refers to as "the female earth" (*Last Generation*, 150).

The links between land, language, and nation unfold even farther in a dialogue between Medea and Chac-Mool, where Medea equates Chac-Mool with Aztlán and land in general:

> MEDEA (Grabbing him by the shoulders.) You're my land, hijo. Don't you see that? You're my land! (85)

Land, spirit, and blood coalesce into an alternate form of nation and nationhood that simultaneously resists the perpetual assertion of patriarchy and machismo found in Aztlán as whole. This falls in line with Moraga's own vision of a queer Aztlán where "la Chicana Indígena stands at the center, and heterosexism and homophobia are no longer the cultural order of the day" (*Last Generation*, 150). Resisting the repetition of the colonized Chicana queer body by Aztlán, Medea equates Chac-Mool's desire to return to Aztlán and take part in the initiation of the passage from boyhood to manhood with Aztlán's capacity to teach Chac-Mool to "despise a mother's love, a woman's touch" (Moraga, *The Hungry Woman*, 74). In turn, Chac-Mool's sacrifice is the only way to create the new nation founded in the queer Chicana Indígena. Therefore, Medea takes responsibility for the murder of Chac-Mool, but also recognizes the act of murder as an act of love in the foundation of a new nation – a nation that cannot and will not allow ongoing violence and oppression of women and queers.

Medea's actions resist and disrupt the traditional patriarchal laws of Chicano nationalism through an act of sacrificial[8] love. The sacrificial act combines life and death in a paradoxical space and relocates the sacrifice as a gift of decolonization (González, "The (Gothic) Gift of Death," 70–4). The death of the son becomes the death of patriarchal domination and helps create a cultural nationalism that resonates with Moraga's overall call for a nationalism grounded in the experience and critique of the feminist lesbian Chicana mother. This Chicana nationalism would refuse "to recognize the 'capricious' political boundaries imposed by the US government" (Moraga, "Art in America," 157). This refusal takes place within an alternative understanding of nation focused on "people bound together by spirit, land, language, history, and blood" (Moraga, "Art in America," 157) and not the nation-state. This new nation resists the dominant patterns of patriarchal and colonial law found in Jasón's Aztlán. By removing his claims to "blood" and "land," Medea reverses the position of power reclaiming the space in between as a fertile ground on which to build a new nation – a queer

Aztlán that arises out of a mother's sacrifice of her son for the better of this world and *el pueblo* as a whole.

IV

In her *A Xicana Codex of Changing Consciousness: Writings 2000–2010*, Moraga states: "I write to remember. I make rite (ceremony) to remember. It is my right to remember" (81). The repetition of "remember" in this passage, and the fact that each line is set on its own within the formatting of the page, marks this passage as a manifesto integrating the act of remembering with the acts of ritual, writing, and the integration of Western concepts of human rights. *The Hungry Woman*'s "Epilogue" integrates this radical space of remembering in order to highlight the role of language as a practical, metaphysical, political, and geographical borderland occupied by oppositional influences that cannot be integrated and erased.

After Chac-Mool's murder-sacrifice in the previous scene, the "Epilogue" opens with the ritualized movement of the Cihuatateo on stage in accompaniment with the music of the flauta and tambor. Luna, Medea's lesbian lover, enters the room and informs Medea that she was "stopped at the border" after Medea states: "You've come back. I thought you'd never come back" (*The Hungry Woman*, 93). After a brief conversation, Luna hands Medea a clay model of the Cihuatateo. Medea asks in response: "Is that how I died, Luna? Giving birth to myself?" (96). Luna responds that she does not know, embraces Medea, and exits. The Cihuatateo begin chanting and Chac-Mool enters the stage. Medea asks: "Are you a ghost?" (97). Chac-Mool answers: "No" (97). After some dialogue where Chac-Mool explains to Medea that she is in an insane asylum, "a prison" (98), he takes her to the window and asks her to look out at the moon.

> CHAC-MOOL: Come here, Mom. ¿Ves la luna?
> [*CHAC-MOOL grabs his mother's hand, takes her to the small window.*]
> MEDEA: La Luna. That was her name.
> CHAC-MOOL: Mom.
> MEDEA: Mom. The sun is too bright.
> CHAC-MOOL: No, mira. Do you see the moon? There to the left, just above those hills. (*She cranes her neck to see*).

Immediately after this conversation takes place, Chac-Mool declares that he is taking Medea home, and gives her a small paper cup with powdered herbs to drink. Although the scene does not include Medea's death, her impending death is linked to the rebirth of Chac-Mool, the memory of Luna, and the ongoing mix of languages used throughout the play.

In this final scene, Moraga highlights the significant overlap between the character name "Luna" and the vision of the moon outside the window. The visual image of the moon, the character Luna, and the Aztec goddess Coyolxauhqui are all invoked in the language of the stage, which includes spoken and performed linguistic messages fused together, creating an excess of meaning. When Chac-Mool gives the (poisoned?) liquid to Medea, he gathers her into his arms, and she falls asleep in a *pietà* image reminiscent of the work of Renaissance sculptor Michelangelo Buonarroti. Whereas Euripides' Medea returns to Athens under the protection of its king, Moraga's "Epilogue" tells the hybrid tale of new nation and language that goes beyond the intersections and assimilations of various linguistic and cultural systems. This is apparent in Moraga's use of the *pietà* image, as with most of Moraga's metaphorical and allegorical overlaps; this image is reminiscent of the original position of the classic Chac-Mool figurines but includes an addition of another human being to signify both Aztec and Renaissance imagery.

In the statement "the sun is too bright" we are reminded that night, the sleep of one half of the Earth, is necessary for life continually to exist. Like death and birth, dark and light continue on daily cycles, clinging to each other for existence. As the scene closes and the light fades, only the face of the shimmering moon remains outlining the Cihuatateo (symbolic of warrior women and the four directions) as they dance silently in the fading light. Thus the play ends by highlighting the perception and experience of the lesbian Chicana mother as on the border in between and in excess. *The Hungry Woman* uses this feminist phenomenology of excess to kill off the destructive recreation of the unmarked hegemonic male in patriarchy. In turn, the dual death/sacrifice founds the emergence of the revolutionary lesbian Chicana mother as political actor and the potential foundational myth in the literal appearance of a queer Aztlán.

WORKS CITED

Accomando, Christina. "'All its people, including its jotería': Rewriting Nationalisms in Cherríe Moraga's Queer Aztlán." *Humboldt Journal of Social Relations* 31(1/2) (2008): 111–24.

Anzaldúa, Gloria. *Borderlands/La Frontera: The New Mestiza*. San Francisco, CA: Aunt Lote Books, 1999.

Broyles-González, Yolanda. *El Teatro Campesino: Theater in the Chicano Movement*. Austin: University of Texas Press, 2006.

González, Tanya. "The (Gothic) Gift of Death in Cherríe Moraga's *The Hungry Woman: A Mexican Medea*." *Chicana/Latina Studies* 7(1) (Fall 2007).

Huerta, Jorge. *Chicano Drama: Performance, Society and Myth*. Cambridge: Cambridge University Press, 2000.

Kadir, Djelal. "To World, to Globalize-Comparative Literature's Crossroads." *Comparative Critical Studies* 41(1) (2004): 1–9.

Miller, Mary and Marco Samayoa. "Where Maize May Grow: Jade, Chacmools, and the Maize God." *Anthropology and Aesthetics* 33(1) (1998): 54–72.

Moraga, Cherríe. "Art in America: Con Acento." *Frontiers: A Journal of Women Studies* 12(3) (1992): 154–60.

The Hungry Woman: A Mexican Medea/Heart of the Earth: A Popul Vuh Story. New York: West End Press, 2001.

The Last Generation. Boston, MA: South End Press, 1993.

Loving in the War Years: lo que nunca pasó por sus labios. 2nd ed. Cambridge, MA: South End Press, 2000.

Straile-Costa, Paula. "Myth and Ritual in *The Hungry Woman: A Mexican Medea*: Cherríe Moraga's Xicana-Indígena Interpretation of Euripides' *Medea*." In *Unbinding Medea: Interdisciplinary Approaches to a Classical Myth from Antiquity to the 21st Century*, edited by Heike Bartel and Anne Simon, 208–23. London: LEGENDA, 2010.

Tatonetti, Lisa. "'A Kind of Queer Balance': Cherríe Moraga's Aztlán." *MELUS* 29(2) (Summer 2004): 227–47.

Yarbro-Bejarano, Yvonne. *The Wounded Heart: Writing on Cherríe Moraga*. Austin: University of Texas Press, 2001.

Žižek, Slavoj. *The Parallax View*. Cambridge, MA: MIT Press, 2006.

CHAPTER 16

Nawal el Saadawi: Writer and Revolutionary

miriam cooke

"We live in one world under patriarchal capitalism. I am opposed to anything that divides us. The differences between people and cultures that literature erases, theory generalizes and abstracts."

This is how Egyptian writer Nawal El Saadawi articulated her personal philosophy and life choices during a September 2014 meeting with Chinese women writers at Beijing Normal University. Whereas theory specializes and distances the object of study, El Saadawi argued, the imaginary brings the object close in order to deal with the particular individual in her daily struggles, joys, and challenges. "I write what I lived in my village Kafr Tahla," El Saadawi elaborated. "When with a sincere intent a writer dives deep into their reality the story will become universal."[1] Theory loses the particularity that is at the heart of the universal. Diving deep into her reality means returning again and again to her birthplace by the Nile, even while traveling the globe.

Like Henri Bergson's binary epistemology that distinguishes between intuition and analysis, between grasping the motion of an object from within as opposed to from without, between the absolute and the relative, El Saadawi contrasts the creative impulse with the theoretical endeavor. Description, history, and analysis, Bergson writes:

[L]eave me in the relative. Only by coinciding with the person itself would I possess the absolute ... an absolute can only be given in an intuition, while all the rest has to do with analysis. We call intuition here the sympathy by which one is transported into the interior of an object in order to coincide with what there is unique and consequently inexpressible in it. Analysis, on the contrary, is the operation which reduces the object to elements already known.... There is at least one reality which we all seize from within, by intuition and not by simple analysis. It is our own person in its flowing through time.... In so far as abstract ideas can render service to analysis, that is, to a scientific study of the object in its relations with all others, to that extent are they incapable of replacing intuition. (*Introduction to Metaphysics*, 4, 6–7, 9, 17, 18)

214

While Bergson's intuition – that transports us into the interior of an object in order to coincide with what there is unique and consequently inexpressible in it – is not synonymous with creativity, it is suggestive of the pure apprehension seized in El Saadawi's understanding of creativity. For El Saadawi, creativity brings body, mind, and spirit together: "When you are creative, when you are writing," she once said, "you don't feel limited because your imagination can transcend anything (Simpson, "She Came," 2005).

In what follows, I explore El Saadawi's life and writings to show that although she marks a separation between theory and creativity, they are in fact interconnected in all that she does. Two sides of the same coin, theorizing lived experience is inseparable from the realm of the imaginary because each feeds and enriches the other. Many of her literary works were written in tandem with a scholarly study informed by a medical or religious or geopolitical research project in which she was engaged. These literary projects emerge directly out of her work as a medical doctor or a self-taught scholar of religions, especially Abrahamic religions, or a human rights advocate. Medicine, fiction, and activism intertwine in all that she does.

From Medicine to Literature

El Saadawi was born in 1931 in Kafr Tahla, a poor village on the banks of the Nile. Like all village girls, she was considered nubile before puberty and when she was eleven, suitors began to knock at the door. The young Nawal knew that if she was to escape tradition and the fate of her cousin Fatima who married at fourteen and spent the rest of her life in Kafr Tahla devoted to family and fields, she had to leave the village. In 1943, the girl got on a train headed for the capital where she lodged with an aunt. Twelve years later in 1955, she graduated from Cairo University's medical school and went on to become the director of public health and ultimately a world-famous writer and human rights activist.

Although she did leave the village, Kafr Tahla stayed with her as a source of inspiration and a moral compass. It appears in harrowing novels like *God Dies by the Nile* (1974) where peasant women are relentlessly policed for violations of stringent codes of village honor, they are raped, and their genitals are cut. To give birth, they leave the field briefly, deliver themselves, and return to their furrow, baby strapped to the back. Invitations pour in from the world's capitals, from remote towns, from international organizations, and from local women's cooperatives, and the village girl

hops on the next plane, hoping that her deeply ethical and richly cosmopolitan voice will touch someone and make a difference.

Theorizing data from medical, social, or political research often accompanied a creative project. One of her first novels, *Memoirs of a Woman
Doctor* (*Mudhakkirat tabiba*), came out in 1958 while she was practicing
medicine near Kafr Tahla. The product of three years of psychiatric work,
this early attempt at crafting fiction evokes the impoverished state of her
women patients. Presenting her clinical experience in literary form allowed
El Saadawi to tell a particular story that universalized the conditions in
which rural Egyptian women lived, subjected to harsh gender codes and
the devastating outcome of decades of British colonial rule. During the
following decade, while she was still practicing medicine, she published
only one novel. *Searching* (in Arabic *al-Ghaib* or *The Absent One*) appeared
in 1968, and it told the story of Fuada, a chemist whiling her life away in
the Ministry of Biochemistry. Mirroring her disillusionment with her profession at the Ministry of Health, the novel presents a caste of unattractive
male officials and the women who have to cope with them. At that time,
fiction had functioned cathartically; it was an avocation.

The turning point came in 1972 when El Saadawi published *Women and
Sex*, her analysis and condemnation of the injustices Egyptian women suffer, notably excision.[2] This scholarly exposition of the failure of the state to
provide medical services to its most needy citizens caused a scandal, and
she was dismissed from her position as editor in chief of *Health* magazine
and the director of health education. The official end of her medical career
launched her into the world of literature and political activism.

Even before her dismissal in 1972, El Saadawi had entertained serious
doubts about her medical career. In conversation, she often repeated that
her writings healed more people, especially women, than her clinical work
ever could. With one novel she could reach thousands of girls and women
whose bodies and minds she would have had to treat individually and
over extended periods and even then not known if they were better for the
treatment. With a novel, the cure was quicker, more effective, and more
widespread.

Woman at Point Zero (*Imra'a 'inda nuqtat sifr*, 1975) proved her point.
The novel was an immediate success. The night before her execution for
murder, a prostitute called Firdaus, or Paradise, tells a psychiatrist of her
seriatim-sexual exploitation at the hands of those she had trusted, especially men in her family. Like so many women around the world whom
sexual abuse drives to murder, Firdaus kills her pimp. At a time when
incest was not generally acknowledged, the novel indicted all men, not

only Firdaus' male relatives, who feel entitled to abuse girl relatives. Like Betty Friedan's "sickness without a name," the revelation of the trauma of incest named a disease so many girls had suffered without understanding it. Like *Memoirs of a Woman Doctor*, this novel was intertwined with medical research she had been conducting at Qanatir Women's Prison in 1974. She had interviewed more than twenty women in the prison's mental clinic, including a woman called Firdaus, and she published the data in *Women and Neurosis in Egypt* (*Al-mar'a wa al-sira' al-nafsi*) in 1976.

The composing of these two books exemplifies the ways El Saadawi's approaches to writing reflect the distinction that Bergson made in psychology between analysis and intuition. Psychology, Bergson wrote:

> proceeds by analysis. It resolves the self, first given to it in the form of a simple intuition, into sensations, feelings, images, etc. which it studies separately. It therefore substitutes for the self a series of elements which are the psychological facts.... Although they place states side by side with states, multiply their contacts, explore their intervening spaces the self always escapes them, so that in the end they see nothing more in it than an empty phantom.... [T]o the detached psychological states, to those shadows of the self the totality of which was, for the empiricists, the equivalent of the person, rationalism, to reconstitute the personality, adds something still more unreal, the vacuum in which these shadows move.... Analysis operates on immobility, while intuition is located in mobility or, what amounts to the same thing, in duration. (*Introduction to Metaphysics*, 22, 23, 29, 31–2, 43)

Analysis works with numerous, separate facts and elements; intuition grasps the inexpressible self – the subject of creative writing – that escapes the empiricists. Bergson insisted on the primacy of intuition because from it "one can pass on to analysis, but not from analysis to intuition" (44). It is worth noting that El Saadawi wrote the novel before completing the psychological study, having passed from the intuition characteristic of the creation of literary figures to analysis of several women's narratives of abuse and violence. The psychological study is virtually unknown in contrast with its literary counterpart.

The difference between these two texts appears in the passionate portrayal of a single individual whose traumas stay with the reader long after closing the book, as opposed to the cold enumeration of symptoms. Firdaus is the product of El Saadawi's ability to place herself but also the reader "directly, by an effort of intuition, in the concrete flowing of duration," to cite Bergson's vivid articulation of the creative process (Bergson, *Introduction to Metaphysics*, 56). This duration is the sense of continuity inherent in individual existence that cannot be analyzed but only intuited, and from that intuition comes analysis.

Concise and raw, the novel *Woman at Point Zero* hit a nerve, and with its translation into English in 1983, El Saadawi was launched as an international feminist writer. The messages from around the world after its translation into more than thirty languages and the fact that the novel has become required reading in women's studies courses more than justified her decision to exchange her scalpel for a pen.

Islam

El Saadawi's literary prominence gave her a public voice that she used to decry injustice in Egypt and to attack the Islamists' draconian policing of women's appearance and behavior in public spaces. During the 1980s, not only Egypt but also other Muslim-majority countries witnessed the emergence of political Islam. Ayatollah Khomeini's 1979 Islamic Revolution in Iran presaged the Islamists' growing influence. Ironically, like the Islamists she critiqued, El Saadawi opposed President Anwar Sadat and his policies at home and abroad, notably the 1978 Camp David Accords with Israel. In 1981, the Sadat regime imprisoned El Saadawi. A year later, the Muslim Brothers' long-term opposition to Sadat culminated in his assassination.

After Husni Mubarak assumed power, El Saadawi was released. In her 1985 *Memoirs from the Women's Prison* (*Mudhakkirat fi sijn al-nisa*), she described the emotional rollercoaster of prison swinging frantically between grief and joy, "pain and pleasure, the greatest beauty and the most intense ugliness ... In prison I found my heart opened to love – how I don't know." Love fought loathing in the cell she shared with Islamist women sternly covered even though they were with women only. The Islamists might have been the enemy of her enemy Sadat, but that did not make them her friends. She turned her voice and pen to their iniquities.

Soon after her release, while writing her prison memoir, she founded the Arab Women's Solidarity Association (AWSA), the first independent feminist organization in Egypt that soon developed a parallel international association. El Saadawi had two mottos for AWSA: the veil shrouds the mind; women's bodies are not shameful until they are veiled. She called for joint action against the growing intolerance of men, especially those oppressing women in the name of Islam. She invited Arab women from all twenty-two Arab countries to share their stories and strategies and thus empowered them to contest political parties that used Islam as a front for their grab for power at home and in the nation. In 1991, El Saadawi led AWSA International's protest against the Gulf War (Stephan, "Arab Women's Solidarity Association International"). Mubarak's men closed AWSA along with its magazine, *Nun*.

Even before mobilizing international action against the president and also his enemies the Islamists, analyzing their power and danger in newspaper articles and in her speeches at home and abroad, El Saadawi was writing a novel that lyrically linked her twin struggles. *The Fall of the Imam* (*Suqut al-imam*, 1987) deals with the hypocrisy of faux Muslims who seem to be opposing secular regimes but are in fact in cahoots with them. The novel indicts Islamic and secular male authorities who feel entitled to rape, exploit, and punish women for crimes they have committed. The heroine Bint Allah is the illegitimate daughter of a religious leader who had raped her mother and now wants to kill this emblem of his sin. She is called Bint Allah, meaning in Arabic Daughter of Allah, a concept deemed heretical, yet the only possible name for a girl in a country where mothers cannot give their offspring their names. The circular narrative keeps returning to Bint Allah running from her father and his agents. Almost liturgical in its formulaic repetitions, the novel takes readers through an increasing crescendo of fear and loathing.

El Saadawi distilled the cruelty and hypocrisy of religious leaders in her creation of the imam even while she was fighting those same leaders in her Association and in newspaper articles. Never afraid of controversy, she put herself in Bint Allah's mind and heart and body, turning around in terror as the imam's men chased her in life and in her dreams. Intuitively, she had begun her campaign against the erasure of the mother's name that she would later pursue in the law courts. *The Fall of the Imam* infuriated the Islamists who recognized themselves in this fictional story. They put her on their death list. Far from being cowed into silence, she was provoked into publishing an even more trenchantly critical novel entitled *The Innocence of the Devil* (1992). Her only concession to her nervous publisher was not to use the title that she later insisted on for the English translation but to name it *Gannat wa Iblis* (*Gannat and the Devil*). The action takes place inside a psychiatric hospital – emblem of Egypt in thrall to fanatics. A modern fable, the novel revolves around a woman patient called Gannat, like Firdaus meaning Paradise. In the interaction among the patients (two of the patients imagine themselves to be God and Satan), nurses, and guards, we read about the dangers of Islamic extremism for women.

This novel promoted El Saadawi to number one on the Islamists' death list. Some self-appointed judges had staged a mock heresy trial that they published in late 1992. *Nawal El Saadawi in the Dock* was quickly and cheaply distributed in major Egyptian cities. Mimicking Ayatollah Khomeini's 1989 fatwa against Salman Rushdie for heretical passages in his 1988 *Satanic Verses*, their open call to punish a writer for what they called heresy endangered her life. Disingenuously claiming to "protect" her, the government sent guards to her apartment, where they remained around the clock. Always connecting the dots between oppressors and their common agendas, however divergent they might seem, she distrusted the arrangement. A mere ten years earlier, such guards had held her captive in Qanatir Women's Prison; it was time to leave. In January 1993, she moved with her husband, Sherif Hetata, to Duke University.

Autobiography

It was the first time she had taught in a university and it was during her four years in Durham, North Carolina, that El Saadawi theorized the connections between dissidence, women, and creativity in the classroom and also in her literary autobiography. Other attempts at writing her life had turned into novels as she realized that she was exposing herself and those close to her to a scrutiny she was not yet prepared to endure (202). However, in this exile, *Daughter of Isis* (*Awraqi Hayati* or *My Papers My Life*) never veered from the autobiographical pact.

She tells the coming-of-age story of a feminist who already as a child knew that she should not marry and that God was unfair to mothers because he did not allow them to pass their names on to their children – written as though the memory had once been a reality, the name of the mother recurs in this campaign to honor mothers. Little Nawal realized that God is the God of men and that He approves of female genital mutilation; why otherwise would women invoke Him while they cut and bury the clitoris (11, 26–7)? Her God, who is also her grandmother's God of justice, comes to her once in a vision (135) when she is a child, but she loses Him. Religious men undermine her spiritual life; they "betrayed" the Qur'an; they made her hate religion (216). Cutting through the intervening years, she touched the child she thought she had lost: "anger had never stopped accumulating in me since the day I was born … I do not know how the child in me remained alive" (163, 206). Somehow, and probably through writing, the child rebelling in the sixty-five-year-old woman had survived to prevent her from compromise in what became a lifelong demand for justice.

In contrast with her academic and fictional writing, the narrator in *Daughter of Isis* is surprisingly vulnerable. When she had her first menses she was afraid that people would know that her body was in a state of shame; years later, in the Duke University library, she wanted to hide her aging body. She narrates her genital cutting at her mother's hands and the shock of betrayal by those she loved. She laments social disapproval of expressions of affection that inhibit mothers from openly expressing love for their children even if this maternal love burns "like a flame but held back" (152). Long after her mother dies, her longing for the tenderness of her touch aches on the page. Throughout the autobiography and usually after describing a tender moment, the memory of her mother's hand on her child's face returns. In such a world of repressed love, women become cruel to each other: "It was the cruelty that had grown in them through suppression, the steam held back under pressure until their bodies were filled with it to bursting point. It was a black cruelty under a smooth skin from which the hair had been ripped off to leave it with the smoothness of a snake" (195). Vivid visual imagery turns repressed emotions into dangerous animals.

Contradictions reveal the ambivalence in the text and of course in her life, indeed in all of our lives. She loved school and then she hated it (217); it represented freedom and a future (164) but also a torment. At Nabawiya Musa Secondary School in Abbasiya, she could not stand the school's headmistress and namesake Nabawiya Musa, who had pioneered Egyptian feminism and women's education.

> For me she was never a pioneer or a model ... (she) was like German headmistresses under Hitler, or French headmistresses in schools run by nuns. And she hated the girls. When our eyes met I could read the hate in her look, read hate for the self she carried around in black. School under her had become for me like a funeral where everything was the color of mourning. (161)

The child's hatred did not diminish in the memory of the sixty-five-year-old who might have been expected to recognize the courage and daring of this disappointed woman.

As for the medical profession, she cannot come to terms with her feelings: "The word doctor had a magical ring in my ears. It seemed to rescue me from the stares of the men, carry me up to the heavens, where I soared like a winged bird ... I hated the doctors, especially the medical inspector" (100; see 172–3). The idea is magical; the reality – especially the need to deal with cancer – quite other (204). She mocks medical students flirting over the cadavers they were dissecting. She criticizes doctors who cannot recognize the links between sickness, poverty, and politics (291–2). It is through the writing of this literary text that *both* writer and reader can better understand why El Saadawi left the medical profession.

These contradictory emotions reflect the particular reality of her life, but also of ours everywhere. Love of our parents may mix with hatred and frustration. Her father who excludes her from God's sacred circle was also the nationalist who had participated in the 1919 revolution. He reassures her when her Arabic teacher denounces her (215–16) and insists, against his wife's remonstrance, that Nawal and her sisters be educated. Then when she succeeds he wants her to leave to help her mother at home. Her father is not the model for the dreadful fathers in her fiction but rather a conflicted person trying to work out how to mesh his hopes for his daughter with his anxieties about social expectations. He was, we learn toward the end of the autobiography, "a very gentle father" (207).

El Saadawi does not write of this feminist awakening as a deliberate process that can be followed because it is not. She weaves stories into the stream of days, *ayyam*, Arabic for days but also battles[3]: "Writing became a weapon with which to fight the system.... The written word for me became an act of rebellion against injustice exercised in the name of religion, or morals, or love" (292). Creativity in life and writing mirrored each other in the struggle to seize the rights due her as a woman. The autobiography ends as it began with the intensity and passion of the dreaming child who has her life ahead of her and who relishes the challenge of writing her dreams into stories. This literary form reflected and developed her feminist thinking:

> autobiography is more real, more true than fiction, more creative, and more steeped in art ... My pen has been a scalpel which cuts through the outer skin, pushes the muscles, probes for the roots of things. Autobiography has lifted me above the daily grind to see my life emerge under a different light.... As I write, I experience moments of thrill, of deep pleasure never experienced since I was a child. (293–4)

For more than twenty years after her dismissal from the Ministry of Public Health, she continued to represent her literary career in medical terms. The scalpel shapes the strokes of her pen to probe for the roots of things and to create and meet the person she thought she was and, perhaps, should be.

Controversy and Provocation

In 1997, during the last weeks of her sojourn at Duke University, El Saadawi watched a puppet show written and performed by some students. It engaged her as a puppet character with Thomas Merton, Simone Weil, and Mahatma Gandhi in a debate about the role of God in human lives. At a crucial moment from beneath the stage boomed God's voice telling them that He was sick of their quarrels and that He was resigning. To everyone's amazement, El Saadawi was thunderstruck. She had never before heard God's voice, she exclaimed. During the following four days and nights she wrote her play *God Resigns at the Summit Meeting* (*Allah yastaqil fi al-qimma*) that summons prophets and women for a meeting with God. When Satan offers to resign none of the prophets is willing to replace him. Instead, God resigns. Theater allowed her to stage her angry refusal of religious pretexts to deprive women of their rights, rights that these very religions – Islam, Christianity, Judaism – guarantee. Although she said that she would not, could not publish the play in Arabic, she did in 2008. She smuggled it into a bundle of her complete works that her publisher Madbuli had agreed to put out. *God Resigns at the Summit Meeting* created pandemonium. The Islamic university and supreme court of al-Azhar accused her of apostasy and prosecutors called for the destruction of all her books and initiated a lawsuit demanding the revocation of her Egyptian nationality. In 2008, she defeated the case.

This court case was not the first that the state and religious institutions had mounted against her. In 2001, she gave an interview in which she called the kissing of the black stone of the Kaaba in Mecca a pagan act. Islamic scholars were up in arms against this woman who had blasphemed one of Islam's most sacred rituals during the Hajj, or pilgrimage to Mecca. They appointed an Islamist lawyer who demanded that as an apostate she be divorced from her husband, Dr. Sherif Hetata. She won the case.

In 2007, she was again accused of apostasy, this time with her daughter Mona Helmy, a poet and writer, for their demands to honor and legalize the right to carry the name of the mother so that illegitimate children like Bint Allah could be named. Not only did they win the case in 2008, but they were also instrumental in the promulgation of a new law giving children born outside marriage the right to use their mothers' names. In that same year, FGM or female genital mutilation was banned after El Saadawi's fifty years of campaigning against it in fiction and nonfiction forms.

The Revolution of 2011

In late December 2010, under the aegis of the revived AWSA, El Saadawi convened a conference entitled *Women and the 21st Century – Feminist Alternatives*. Women from twenty-five Muslim-majority countries gathered in Cairo to discuss solutions to the religious violence plaguing their societies. Although the conference took place a few days before the people rose up against President Mubarak, there was no intimation among the conferees that the kind of popular, pro-peace, democratic uprising that they were demanding would break out on January 25, 2011.

Within eighteen days, the people had toppled Mubarak from a throne he had prepared for his son. Many filmed and photographed the mass demonstrations that took place all over the country but notably in the iconic Tahrir Square. El Saadawi published two books about the revolution: her 2013 memoir, *Arab Revolutions* (*al-thawrat al-`arabiya*), and a 2014 novel, *Indeed It Is Blood* (*Innahu al-dam*). Whereas the memoir celebrates the first heady days of Tahrir, the novel explores without romanticism the impoverished lives of a few of the participants.

Reflecting on El Saadawi's experiences during her country's revolution, *Arab Revolutions* tracks the interaction of fear, anger, and strength. She situates Tahrir in a long line of family activism going back to 1919 when her father demonstrated against the English. She recalls the 1946 girls' demonstration against the English that she had led. In 2011, she is again "that schoolgirl walking in the demonstration and shouting: Down with the king! Down with the English! As though time did not exist" (97–9). Protesting injustice and corruption was a way of life for her but also, she insists, for the Egyptian people. Tahrir was merely another, if more exciting link in a chain of revolutionary events that made all of her struggles worthwhile: "I can scarcely believe that this is the same Egypt that caused me so much sadness and hardship.... Tahrir became my *watan* for which I have been searching since childhood" (112–13). In detail, she records meetings in her Shubra Gardens apartment with young men and women dreaming of a new world where justice would reign. Every morning, one or two men would pick her up – sometimes on a motorbike – and take her to the Square. At night, late, she would return exhausted but elated to collapse into bed. She ridicules the thugs who rode into the Square on camel and horseback to disperse the crowds. Empowered by childhood memories of courage, anger, and fearlessness, she fights them with words and her child's anger that pushes the adult to break the wall of fear.

Blood, the novel she was writing at the same time as the memoir, tackles the revolution from a very different angle. Weaving the tapestry of social relationships out of which the revolution emerged, the narrative begins in Tahrir Square with shouts of "Down with the regime," then enters the Mother Tent where the leaders camp out for days, and then unpeels the lives of a few of its occupants. It ends back in the Square with the hypocrites unmasked (at least to the reader) and their victims lionized.

Unlike the memoir, the novel is less about the revolution and more about the revolutionaries and their commitment to changing the world. Fuada and Saadiya dominate. For different reasons, they had spent time in prison together, Fuada as a political prisoner, and Saadiya as a common criminal called "The Murderer." She killed her husband for stealing her money and letting their baby son die while she was working in the fields (144). Both women gave birth to daughters on the cell's cold, hard floor (145). Equality inside, however, did not persist beyond the prison walls. Fuada, the brilliant journalist, rejoined her journalist husband, Shakir, in their bourgeois apartment and their lackluster newspaper. When she was fired for incendiary political writing, her colleagues and even her boss tried in vain to persuade her to moderate her rhetoric. El Saadawi undercuts this apparently principled behavior in her description of Fuada's condescending relationship with her former cellmate – repeating on several occasions when Saadiya was distraught: "don't worry, we're family" (143, 204). Fuada uses the memory of prison to connect with Saadiya because her political pretensions depend on being close to someone from this class. Saadiya, on the other hand, lives in a hovel in Cairo's infamous City of the Dead and makes a meager living cleaning Fuada's apartment. The dream that keeps her going through the humiliation of serving her cellmate is to earn enough money to send sixteen-year-old Hanadi to college whence she might hope to overcome her status as daughter of a servant (111).

Shakir is the villain of the novel and El Saadawi's most elaborate theorizing of the empty rhetoric and utter depravity of armchair leftists and pseudo-feminists. Shakir resents his wife for her international reputation and refusal to moderate her political stance that exposes him to danger (39). After patronizingly telling Saadiya's daughter Hanadi to make time for the revolution, "This regime cannot fall without everyone participating in the demonstrations," he rapes her, secure in the knowledge that his secret is safe with his servant's daughter (207–16). He plagiarizes passages from an unreviewed book by a feminist colleague at the newspaper where he and his wife work. His book comes out to great fanfare and no one, not even the author, denounces him (256–7). When his psychiatrist realizes that he is a closet Islamist, Shakir lashes out at the sensuousness of women and neglect of their prescribed duties under Islam. When confronted by the contradiction between his spoken and written words, he remains cool: "Yeah, real life is quite other than words in books" (261). The denouement that the reader has been led to expect, that Shakir will admit or be forced to admit his crimes or mistakes, never happens. The plagiarized book, the rape, and his secret affiliation with the Islamists remain hidden. He has committed these crimes with impunity. El Saadawi has not written a moralizing melodrama but rather portrayed the different personalities who participated in the revolution.

Hanadi will not find justice but she does find strength through her participation. Despite her post-abortion hemorrhage, she stays for days in the Mother Tent in the Square (263). Fuada pays her and her mother a tentative, voyeuristic visit bearing food and fruits – she has done her bit for the revolution. Having learned who raped her daughter, Saadiya refuses the gifts and resigns although her situation has become so desperate that she cannot afford even the meager rent of her room among the graves. She imagines a confrontation with Shakir. However, when she meets him, she says nothing (203, 220–3).

This novel introduces us to the bourgeois pretenders but also to the real revolutionaries who pay a high price, a price that is symbolized in blood. After leading "the largest demonstration against the corrupt regime that had made her life a misery," Saadiya disappeared (274). In a state between dreaming and waking, Hanadi imagines her mother bleeding on the tarmac and the narrative flashes back to prison where, in like manner, Saadiya had bled on the concrete floor after giving birth. This blood, Hanadi proclaims, will nourish the revolution. The police kill the charismatic student leader Jalal Asad by slashing his leg and leaving him to bleed to death. They use tear gas, water hoses, and live ammunition to attack another revolutionary, a young collector and seller of forbidden books that he hid underneath the tent: "Muhammad lost his left eye to a skilled sniper, but he survived and the books survived and he sold them to whoever wanted them" (256). It will take more than gouging out eyes to deter real revolutionaries.

Blood is a dark novel that keeps circling back to prison with its smells, sounds, and eerie resemblance to life outside. It spares none of the opportunists like the morgue doctors who take bribes for autopsies, and the nurses who sell unclaimed cadavers to medical students, and at the end of the day they share the spoils (12). Then there are the Islamists who prowl the Square looking for opportunities to harass secular demonstrators.

What are we to make of the radical contrast between the memoir of the revolution and its novel? Is El Saadawi presenting a chronological assessment of the fate of the revolution? Did she meet people at a later stage of Tahrir who shook her faith in the revolution? Or should we read the two texts together without trying to resolve their apparent contradictions? Is this not how real revolutions evolve with their spectacular highs and desperate lows? El Saadawi wrote, "The revolutions are all aborted including

Occupy Wall Street. But creativity is never aborted that is why we write. God wrote his books for the same reason."[4] Underlying such pessimism of the will, however, is the optimism of the mind: the revolution is ongoing, even if underground; it will return.

Conclusion

Literary form has played an important role in El Saadawi's feminist trajectory. Circular narratives, repetitions, and oneiric landscapes through which women wander in search of safety from predatory men reappear in many of her stories. She sometimes creates spontaneous and passionate texts responding to a need to write and communicate immediately what she is examining in the clinic or in a scripture or in the streets. She wrote *Woman at Point Zero* in a week and *God Resigns at the Summit Meeting* in four days and nights. When writing her prison memoirs, she expressed openly the anguish, the torment of giving birth to the book:

> I've freed myself completely to write it, letting everything else go for its sake. It's intractable, like unattainable love. It wants me, my entire being, mind and body, and if it can't have that it will not give itself to me at all. It wants all or nothing – it's exactly like me.... It wants no competition for my heart and mind – not that of a husband, nor a son or daughter, nor preoccupation of any sort, not even on behalf of the women's cause.

This relationship with creative writing exemplifies Bergson's effort of intuition that experiences and renders the concrete flowing of duration within the individual, in this case the individual prisoner: "Whoever has worked successfully at literary composition well knows that when the subject has been studied at great length, all the documents gathered together, all notes taken, something more is necessary to get down to the work of composition itself" (Bergson, *Introduction to Metaphysics*, 81). Composition requires the intuition that opens up the heart of the subject in a way that analysis cannot.

El Saadawi has also crafted slow, careful texts that tease out a problem that must be explicated and resolved. Taking up the major themes that have characterized her writing and her life, *The Novel* (*Al-riwaya*, 2005) rehearses the ways women cope with sexual violence, marital infidelity, the hypocrisy of religion, and the corruption of national and international politics that inevitably harm women the most. Unlike the novels or autobiographical works, *The Novel* is an experimental study of the intertwinement of writing in the creation of a feminist self: "Her life became her first novel" (1). We might add that all of her novels have become her life.

Connecting the dots between sex, class, gender and politics informs her life. She has never veered from a postcolonial feminist multiple critique that remains vigilant toward her many different readers and their sensitivities and responds to their objections (cooke, *Women Claim Islam*, 107–38). Keenly conscious of the critique of feminism as an arm of Western imperialism, she always links her criticism of homegrown misogyny with imperial ambitions in the region. She has not wavered from her central message: the battles against colonialism, class prejudice, and patriarchy both secular and religious are so intertwined that if one is emphasized over the others the struggle will fail.

Intolerant of those who give up, El Saadawi declared shortly before her eightieth birthday, "I am becoming more radical with age. I have noticed that writers, when they are old, become milder. But for me it is the opposite. Age makes me more angry" (Khalilee, "Nawal El Saadawi: Egypt's Radical Feminist").

WORKS CITED

Bergson, Henri. *Introduction to Metaphysics*. Trans. T. E. Holme. New York: Philosophical Library, 2003.

cooke, miriam. *Women Claim Islam: Creating Islamic Feminism through Literature*. New York: Routledge, 2001.

El Saadawi, Nawal. *Nawal El Saadawi in the Dock*. Cairo: Dar al-Rawda lil-Nashr wa al-Tawzi, 1992.

   Arab Revolutions. Beirut: Sharikat al-Matbuat lil-Tawzi wa al-Nashr, 2013.

   Daughter of Isis. Trans. Sherif Hetata. London: Zed Press, 1999.

   The Fall of the Imam. Trans. Sherif Getatata. London: Methuen, 1988.

   God Resigns at the Summit Meeting. Cairo: Madbouli, 2006.

   The Hidden Face of Eve: Women in the Arab World. Trans. Sherif Hetata. London: Zed Press, 1980.

   Indeed It Is Blood. Beirut: Sharikat al-Matbuat lil-Tawzi wa al-Nashr, 2014.

   The Innocence of the Devil. Sherif Hetata. London: Methuen, 1994.

   Memoirs of a Woman Doctor. Trans. Catherine Cobham. San Francisco, CA: City Lights, 1989.

   Memoirs of the Women's Prison. Trans. Marilyn Booth. Toronto: Women's Press, 1994.

   The Novel. Trans. Omnia Amin and Rick London. Northampton, MA: Interlink, 2009.

   Searching. Trans. Shirley Eber. London: Zed Press, 1988.

Woman at Point Zero. Trans. Sherif Hetata. London: Zed Press, 1983.

Khalilee, Homa. "Nawal El Saadawi: Egypt's Radical Feminist." *The Guardian* (April 15, 2010): http://www.theguardian.com/lifeandstyle/2010/apr/15/nawal-el-saadawi-egyptian-feminist. Accessed December 6, 2014.

Simpson, April. "She Came, She Spoke Her Mind." *Newsmith* (2005): http://www.smith.edu/newssmith/winter2005/saadawi.php. Accessed December 21, 2014.

Stephan, Rita. "Arab Women's Solidarity Association International." *Encyclopedia of the Modern Middle East and North Africa* (2004): http://www.encyclopedia.com/doc/1G2-3424600300.html. Accessed May 23, 2015.

CHAPTER 17

"The Woman Who Said 'No'": Colonialism, Islam, and Feminist Resistance in the Works of Assia Djebar[1]

Jane Hiddleston

As a number of critics have argued, there has been a regrettable tendency among European and American feminists to graft homegrown models of feminine subjectivity and insubordination onto women of different cultures grappling with diverse (if overlapping) patriarchal systems across the globe. Chandra Mohanty has famously denounced the abstractions of European and American feminisms, and demonstrated that "cross-cultural feminist work must be attentive to the micropolitics of context, subjectivity and system, as well as to the macropolitics of global economic and political systems and processes."[2] In addition, Marnia Lazreg has shown how even the most emancipatory feminist theories can themselves be inflected with misguided stereotypes, as Algerian and, more broadly, Arab women continue to be associated with an Orientalist imagery that emphasizes both sexuality and victimhood, and there is little proper understanding of real women's agency and values.[3] Certainly, the reductive implications of overarching categories such as those of "Third World women" or "Arab women" have now been laid bare, a move that calls for a better understanding of other cultural forms of feminist resistance as alternatives to those imposed by European literature and thought.

The work of francophone Algerian writer Assia Djebar offers an extensive reflection on women's double oppression by both colonialism and Islam in Algeria, and although much has been written on her own project of resistance, less attention has been paid to her use of figures of feminist revolt from within the Islamic world. Djebar herself self-consciously explores her own double heritage as an Algerian girl who had the unusual privilege of attending the primary school where her father taught, then the French boarding school in Blida, followed by the Ecole normale supérieure at Sèvres, and her work is littered with references to her European reading material as well as to Arab and Islamic cultural history. Accordingly, critics have explored her interaction with major French feminist thinkers alongside Arab scholars and activists in a celebration of her brand of international, dialogic feminism. Priscilla Ringrose's book *Assia Djebar: In Dialogue with Feminisms* is a detailed study of the parallels between Djebar's conceptions of feminine subjectivity, relationality, and writing and those of Hélène Cixous, Luce Irigaray, Julia Kristeva, and Fatima Mernissi, and Rita Faulkner's highly astute article on psychoanalysis and anamnesis in Djebar draws on both Irigaray and Egyptian feminist Nawal El Saadawi to sketch a transnational feminism that bridges Arab and French models.[4]

There are, however, two formidable female figures in Djebar's work who stand out, and whose role in her conception of women's resistance will be further elucidated here in order to signal how her feminist thinking emerges also from her Islamic cultural heritage. The first is Fatima, the daughter of the Prophet Mohammed, and the focus of the one of the central scenes in Djebar's novel exploring women's activity in the early days of Islam, *Loin de Médine* (*Far from Madina*). Fatima is a devoted daughter, and yet she is also "the woman who said 'no,'" first when she resists her husband, Ali's, desire to take another wife, and second when she steadfastly claims her rights to her father's inheritance after his death, when the first Caliph Abou Bekr and his officials try to deprive her of her due. The scene of Fatima's refusal in *Loin de Médine* is a crucial moment of Islamic feminist resistance, yet she is also significant in Djebar's thinking more broadly, as her relationships both with her father and with other women, as well as her use of language, are reflected in Djebar's analyses of the family and of women's self-affirmation elsewhere. Indeed, in a reflection on rivalry between women and fatherly love, Djebar finishes by implicitly comparing herself to Fatima in her most recent and most candid autobiographical work, *Nulle part dans la maison de mon père* (*Nowhere in My Father's House*). Djebar's title refers to the dispossession that colonialism caused in Algeria, to the Algerian girl's loss of her heritage, and yet because Fatima too does not inherit, Djebar's narrator suggests, "I could almost hear her quietly sigh, 'nowhere, alas, nowhere in my father's house.'"[5]

Alongside Fatima, the storyteller Scheherazade (or Shahrazad, as she is known in the Arab world) appears intermittently if fleetingly in Djebar's writing, and shapes her thinking on the relationship between resistance, intellect, and narrative. In the frame tale of the *Thousand and One Nights*, Scheherazade spins tales each night to prevent the bloodthirsty King Schahriar from continuing to kill the girls and women he serially deflowers, not only in order to distract or entertain him, but to provoke him to alter his thinking through her stories of injustice toward women alongside female empowerment. Both Fatima and Scheherazade, like Djebar herself, construct their revolt through the skillful manipulation of language, and their presence in Djebar's work fuels her conception of resistance through literature. Literature for all these women is a space where official discourses can be challenged, where orthodoxies can be undermined, and where new perspectives can be offered to unsettle the assumptions harbored by those in positions of authority. Poetry and storytelling create alternative forms of language and trigger the perception of different modes of seeing via the imagination. At the same time, however, Fatima and Scheherazade are provocative in that they generate reflection on difficulties in relationships within families and between women as they struggle to maintain a feminist solidarity. A reading of Djebar through her evocations of Fatima and Scheherazade uncovers her commitment to a feminism forged within Islamic or Arab cultures, in particular through literature, but it also raises broader questions concerning the interpersonal tensions that complicate the process of feminist self-affirmation.

The Beloved Daughter

More than one critic has noted the parallel between Djebar and Fatima. As Clarisse Zimra notes, Fatima is Assia Djebar's real name, and she goes on to suggest, "without making too much of the coincidence, one cannot help noticing a shared stubbornness between the writer herself and her chosen character."[6] And picking up on Djebar's own reference to Fatima in *Nulle part dans la maison de mon père*, Ernspeter Ruhe notes that the narrator does not undertake this confessional work alone, but "is accompanied by one of her shadows," namely, Fatima.[7] Fatima herself is a key figure in Islam; she is the Prophet's most beloved daughter, a model of piety, and, according to Moroccan sociologist Fatima Mernissi, Islam's "most edifying model of womanhood."[8] According to Christopher Clohessy's study of her, she emerges in particular in later sources as an ideal woman, and even comes to function as a sort of figurehead during the 1979 Islamic Revolution in Iran, in that she embodies both feminine modesty and commitment to her faith and country.[9] Djebar's exploration of Fatima in *Loin de Médine*, however, opens with some scattered biographical details but notes nevertheless the lack of reference to her in the early chronicles of Islam. Representing fidelity to the Prophet and to Islam through her rapid conversion, she has been conceived, according to Djebar, as a spiritual figure whose devotion to her father was so intense as to perplex the chroniclers, yet Djebar's own depiction of her foregrounds her significance as a strong and resourceful woman representing feminist self-affirmation within Islam. Like Djebar herself, she speaks out against inequality and uses her eloquence in the service of women's rights, to provide a model for successive generations of dispossessed women: "Fatima, thus deprived of her rights, is the first in an endless procession of daughters, whose *de facto* dispossession, often applied by brothers, uncles, sons even, will be an attempt to stay the course of the intolerable feminist revolution of Islam in this seventh century of the Christian era!"[10] She is "the beloved daughter," and yet she is also the woman who instigates a feminist resistance to the paternal law.

Fatima says "no" twice in Djebar's narrative. The first is her response to Ali's demand for another wife, in which Mohammed supports her in a gesture of tender fatherly protectiveness, despite his own polygamy, and despite the fact that Islamic law permits men to take up to four wives. Djebar focuses here on the strength of Mohammed's affection for her, manifested by his momentary turning away from the role of Prophet in support of his flesh and blood, and the scene is significant in that it demonstrates the father's unwieldy contestation of the wider patriarchal system on behalf of the daughter he loves. Fatima's second and most significant "no" is uttered alone, and takes the form of her refusal to accept Abou Bekr's conviction that women do not receive inheritance rights, together with an affirmation that Islam allows girls to inherit, not the prophecy itself, but material property. Once again, the refusal demonstrates a wider importance, in that Fatima is far less concerned with her comfort and possessions than with her rights, and with other Muslim women's rights as daughters despite their oppression by male relatives. In both cases, moreover, the father is himself at odds with patriarchy, and it is this curious relationship between paternal intimacy and patriarchal Islamic law that goes on to trouble Djebar's narrator in her own reflections on women's freedom in *Nulle part dans la maison de mon père*. Her feminist thinking maintains and indeed explores this complex role of the father inaugurated at the moment of Fatima's revolt.

Djebar's earlier autobiographical work, *L'Amour, la fantasia* (*Fantasia: An Algerian Cavalcade*), opens with a scene that sets up the paradoxical position of the father in the young girl's nascent revolt. Although Fatima's extraordinary devotion to her father is transmuted now into a perhaps more troubled relationship, the separation in Fatima's story between the father and the law is clearly further developed and also problematized here. Djebar's evocation at the beginning of *L'Amour, la fantasia* of the young girl "hand in hand with her father" as he walks her to school in a gesture of defiance against the assumption that girls should stay at home, mirrors at first the Prophet's defense of Fatima and of women's equality.[11] Djebar's father then appears intermittently in both *L'Amour, la fantasia* and *Nulle part dans la maison de mon père* as the emancipatory figure who allowed her an education, and who granted her access to the French language and to self-expression. Nevertheless, if Mohammed's dual role as father and Prophet puts him in conflict with himself ("the father in him, which till then stirred his heart with kindliness and hope, addresses the messenger in himself, to express aloud a mere mortal's spiritual confusion"), Djebar's father in her autobiographical narratives also uneasily represents both support and authority.[12] The opening scene of *L'Amour, la fantasia* may portray the father taking his daughter to school, but it also depicts his rage when he finds that, having learned to read and write, she has entered into correspondence with a boy. This conflict is developed at much greater length in *Nulle part dans la maison de mon père*, when the father who gave her freedom through education is enraged to see her baring her legs when riding her bicycle. On one hand the defender of his daughter's rights, the father is now on the other hand the man who enforces the law, the voice of patriarchy. Much later, after a dispute with her boyfriend Tarik (the sender of the missives referred to in *L'Amour*), Djebar's narrator is haunted by the refrain "if my father finds out ... I will kill myself ... kill myself!" and the father now represents a patriarchal authority that she both fears and desires to please.[13] Her self-affirmation against the restriction on her freedom as a woman requires, like that of Fatima, a strained combination of filial devotion and a broader defiance against the father's law.

In addition, Djebar's narrative of Fatima's refusal in *Loin de Médine* emphasizes her eloquence and poetry, as well as her ability to attend both to the intricacy of language and to the resulting ambiguity in the wording of the law. Fatima is able, for example, to arouse the sympathy of the officials who listen to her, and, mimicking the Prophet's own lyricism, "she becomes, in the verses which slowly flow from her, the poetic expression of the remorse that they should feel."[14] Her argument, moreover, rests on her ability to interpret on multiple levels. If Abou Bekr and the others only read Mohammed's sayings literally, interpreting "that which is a gift cannot be inherited" as a practical statement against her inheritance, Fatima reads symbolically the spiritual principle that the role of Prophet is not to be passed on.[15] Indeed, as Zimra suggests, Fatima's battle with Abou Bekr is "steeped in semantics," turning on conflicting understandings of Mohammed's "don."[16] This attentiveness to linguistic nuance is precisely at the center of the broader Islamic concept of *ijtihad*, which Djebar explains in the French version of her text relates to an intellectual effort, related to *djihad,* an internal struggle. Fatima's ability to use and read language in all its complexity, then, also reinforces the notion that Islamic thought is an ongoing, irresolute endeavor. At the same time, Fatima's "no" is addressed to Abou Bekr not so much in his role as her father's friend, but in his role as Mohammed's successor because she believes that her husband, Ali, should have been the next rightful Caliph. This dispute heralds the division between Sunni and Shia Muslims, with Shi'ites following Fatima and Ali, but what is significant for my current purposes is that Fatima's affirmation and interrogation of Abou Bekr represents the difficulty of interpretation: "Fatima represents doubt, their doubts. As long as she is alive, she, the sole heir by blood lineage and personality of Muhammad the man, she embodies the constantly open question about the legality of the succession!"[17]

Fatima's "no" is, then, an example of feminist resistance founded on linguistic mastery, on persuasive self-expression at the same time as attentive reading. Once again, Djebar too uses poetic language to articulate her refusal of patriarchal authority and her commitment to self-expression in a context where women have been silenced. Not only is Djebar's writing, like Fatima's refusal, an articulate assertion of her rights as a woman, but it too gains force through its attention to language and its power to mislead. Both Djebar and Fatima speak up for themselves, but they are also alert to linguistic ambiguity, and Djebar indeed repeatedly expresses her mistrust of excessive clarity. Colonial and Islamic violence against women has taken place in part through the appropriation of their voices, their determination according to rules and value systems not created by them. An autobiography in French, moreover, is for Djebar too violent a self-disclosure; it is, she suggests in *L'Amour, la fantasia,* "to lend oneself to the vivisector's scalpel," destructive because in revealing, it distorts, reduces, even negates the subtlety of thought and experience.[18] Djebar and Fatima express their resistance to oppression through linguistic self-affirmation, then, but both know that what their language brings is not clarity but questioning, "the doubt" that warns against the sorts of orthodoxies that have marginalized women through history.

Later in Djebar's *Loin de Médine,* Fatima returns in a further exploration of the problems afflicting the process of feminist self-affirmation. Fatima's intense affection for her father is now shown to introduce conflict into her relationship with Aisha, his young wife and said to be one of his favorites, as their respective feelings of grief after his death, together with the question of succession, generate rivalry between them. The self-assertion of each woman at this point works against the other, and this competition between women as they seek to stand up to patriarchal oppression will again trouble Djebar's reflections on feminist resistance as they develop throughout her work. Djebar shows how, after Mohammed's death, "power has swung symbolically between wife and daughter"[19] and this antagonism leads to six months of silence between them. As Mernissi writes, this conflict is developed much later, long after Fatima's death, when Aisha leads armed troops against the Caliph Ali at the Battle of the Camel, but in Djebar's text the focus is on the solitude of both women as their conflicting positions force them to grieve separately.[20] Just as Fatima uttered her eloquent "no" on behalf of Islamic women, Aisha too represents women's linguistic power, as she becomes the first of the "rawiyates," female transmitters of the Prophet's words, "the very source of the living word. Of every word a woman can utter, moreover on the essential matters."[21] For both women, as for Djebar, mastery of language signifies agency, influence skillfully executed through words. They operate, nevertheless, in a political situation that pits them against one another.

Djebar uses Fatima and Aisha to explore women's creative use of language, their self-affirmation not so much through argument as through poetry, through their attentiveness to allusion and suggestion. Clarisse Zimra argues that the text "reclaims Woman's verb":[22] Fatima articulates the "no" of generations of oppressed Muslim women, and as a "rawiyate," Aisha represents the centrality of a woman's narrative in the history of Islam. Fatima's rivalry with Aisha, however, is reflected later in several of Djebar's depictions of feminine relations and serves for her as a focal point indicating the difficulty of assuming a feminism founded on solidarity between women. For Djebar, women's resistance is founded on self-expression, but this individualism leaves relations between women, as well as with the father, highly problematic. Djebar's female characters, and in particular the narrator of *Nulle part dans la maison de mon père*, are determined to challenge their oppression, and yet their interpersonal relationships as a result become extremely complex. Indeed, the narrator's relationships with other women are far from straightforward. The French girl Mag is for a period her "sister in literature," as they avidly share reading material, but when they meet again after the War of Independence their interaction is strained. Later, her relationship with her beloved Tarik is temporarily shattered by the presence of another girl, Mounira, who seems to present herself as a competitor for Tarik's affections.

The narrator's dismay at Mounira's intervention in her relationship with Tarik leads to the culminating disaster of the narrative: her failed suicide attempt, when she throws herself under a tram. The moment is

again paradigmatic, in that it inaugurates a lifelong desire to flee, reen-
acted in varying forms by multiple female characters across Djebar's corpus. The scene is key to Djebar's feminist thinking, however, because it
reveals the potential antagonism between women as they find themselves
condemned to compete in their shared desire to escape. Like Fatima and
Aisha, Djebar's narrator and Mounira are seeking fulfilment in a world
where decisions are made for them, where conventions are shaped and
governed by men, and where their resistance seems to require opposition
to other women. Mounira too suffers from the restrictions of patriarchal
law, as, although precocious in her interactions with the other girls, she
comes to school "wrapped up from head to toe in her white veil," and
the narrator wonders if she is perhaps a victim of her father's "compulsive
severity."[23] The conflict between Fatima and Aisha, as well as that between
the narrator and Mounira, leads Djebar's narrator to wonder: "Does not
every community of women destined to sequestration find itself condemned from the inside by divisions ineluctably sharpened by a rivalry
between prisoners who resemble one another?"[24] Djebar's reflections on
Fatima, and her reworking of Fatima's story in her own autobiographical work, show, then, both her commitment to speaking out for women,
and her understanding of the tensions in that process. Crossing the father
she loves, as well as the other women whose cause she also champions,
Djebar's narrator sketches a feminist resistance based on self-assertion and
questioning, yet still doubtful about its implications and form.

The Tireless Storyteller[25]

If Djebar uses Fatima to prefigure a feminism based on linguistic mastery, although still plagued by the interpersonal tensions it creates, then
Scheherazade provides a model of feminism in which these features are
even further intensified. In the frame tale of the *Thousand and One Nights*,
Scheherazade is the compelling storyteller, who volunteers to spend the
night with the bloodthirsty King Schahriar in a bid to end his serial murder of young women. Horrified by his own and his brother's wives' bra-
zen infidelities, Schahriar vows to exact his revenge by taking a wife each
night only to kill her the following morning, and on hearing news of this
brutality, the brave Scheherazade, daughter of the grand vizier, voluntarily
decides to give herself to the king in the belief that she can end the violence. Importantly, then, she is in no way another victim, placed passively
in the hands of her assassin, but a willing agent determined to use her
intelligence to save other women from the king's horrific injustice. She

may be "a perfect beauty," then, but above all she is sharp-witted and eru-
dite: "[she] had courage, wit, and penetration infinitely above her sex."[26]
Scheherazade successfully saves herself, as well as the king's other potential victims, by asking for her sister Dinarzade to be present in the bed-
chamber in order to wake her each day before dawn; she then captivates
Schahriar with her storytelling, so that again and again he is compelled to
keep her alive another day to hear the narrative's continuation.

As Suzanne Gauch demonstrates, Scheherazade (like Fatima) stands up
to oppression not only for herself but on behalf of all women placed in the
position of victim, and, in recounting tales of male violence and female
resourcefulness, she manages to change the king's very vision of femininity.[27] Critics have noted the multiple misreadings of Scheherazade's role in
the West, as Somaya Simi Sabry has argued that in the European translations her intellectual abilities are reduced to a footnote in favor of an
emphasis on her beauty and seductiveness.[28] Fatima Mernissi, moreover,
comments further on the exoticized rehashings of the *Thousand and One
Nights* (the very addition of "Entertainments" to the title trivializes the stories), and, even more, notes that Edgar Allan Poe's "Thousand and Second
Tale" ends with Scheherazade being killed, as if she knew too much.[29] But
she is a highly significant figure for Arab feminism, and, as I shall demonstrate, for Djebar in particular, precisely because of her intelligence and
her ability to attain power, like Fatima, Aisha, and Djebar herself, through
words. As Fedwa Malti-Douglas argues, moreover, her storytelling is a
pedagogical tool; Scheherazade teaches the king not to submit immediately to sexual desire but to keep his mind alive through the continual
return to the narrative each night.[30] The structure of the work, whereby
stories are interrupted and interwoven, requires an openness to deferral,
to reflection. And even more, as Marina Warner has shown, the dynamic,
intercultural form of the *Nights* as a whole, created and recreated out of
diverse, often unidentified sources from different cultures and epochs,
enacts a resistance to orthodoxy, "to lift the shadows of rage and despair,
bigotry and prejudice, to invite reflection, to give the princes and sultans
of this world pause."[31]

While Fatima stands up against injustice and inequality, Scheherazade
resists overt brutality against women, together with the heinous coupling
of violence with sexual desire. And, to return to Djebar, *L'Amour, la fantasia* is a narrative that too denounces the cooptation of women's bodies
as spoils of war. Broadly, it is not difficult to read Djebar the writer as a
reinvented Scheherazade, challenging injustice by means of her storytelling and her life-writing. Indeed, as Nawar Al-Hassan Golley argues, Arab

women autobiographers can themselves be seen as modern Scheherazades who, rather than fighting for survival, even make their lives through writing.[32] An exploration of the intertext of the *Nights* for a reading of *L'Amour*, however, is revealing not only because Djebar's persona sets out to tell her own story through the lens of the experiences of other oppressed women, but also because from the outset her narrative revolts against the positioning of women as sexual victims. In the initial evocation of the colonial conquest of Algiers, for example, the city is figured as a woman, "like a figure sprawling on a carpet of muted greens" awaiting her husband on the wedding night, but the imagery of spilt blood also seems to associate the invasion with rape.[33] This is, moreover, not merely a convenient metaphor, but represents a disturbing association of colonial power with sexual possession that recurs several times through the narrative. The soldiers' letters home, for example, after the subjugation of the city, betray the fantasy of a "tamed Algeria," as, perhaps like King Schahriar, their power is enhanced through their conquest of a woman.[34] A later scene, in which two girls, Fatma and Mériem, entertain French soldiers only to be subsequently killed by them, confirms this protest against the implication of power struggles with sexual violence.

Many of the feminist commentaries on Scheherazade cited so far, however, tend to emphasize the storyteller's success in teaching King Schahriar of his errors. Yet Gauch notes that despite minor differences between various versions of the ending of the *Nights*, most of those produced in Europe suggest that when Schahriar indeed promises to renounce the law he imposed upon himself, Scheherazade assumes the role of queen and is no longer the storyteller. Order is restored, then, but this remains nonetheless the old patriarchal order. In Djebar's narrative, the questionable success of the storyteller's project of resistance becomes far more prominent, as, although she has uncovered a history of brutality against women, the narrator doubts her ability to liberate the women in whose names she writes. Djebar's narrator, like Scheherazade, exposes a series of horrific episodes of violence against women, and reveals women's cruel mistreatment as their abuse is referenced with casual disdain by male tyrants, in this case the French colonial officials. The soldiers' pride and grandiloquence, for example, is punctured by Djebar's attention to the image of a woman's foot severed from her body so that her anklet can be stolen, a cursory detail recorded only briefly in Bosquet's account of his triumph. Yet Djebar's narrator is aware that her version also fails to capture the voices and experiences of these abused and oppressed women. She may, like Scheherazade, set out to alter perceptions of what is just and unjust in the treatment of women, but she doubts whether her narrative too can really overturn old hierarchies.

Moreover, just as Fatima and Aisha's rivalry represented an obstacle to any feminist solidarity, Scheherazade's relationship with her sister is, in Djebar's reworking of it, a further instance of tension between women in revolt. In the *Nights*, Dinarzade is Scheherazade's watchful companion, staying awake in order to rouse her sister in time to restart her story and deflect the king's murderous impulse for another day. In the novel *Ombre sultane* (*A Sister to Scheherazade*), Djebar draws on Scheherazade and Dinarzade in her depiction of the relationship between two co-wives, Isma and Hajila, as Isma watches over her replacement in her interactions with their abusive husband. Recalling the frame tale of the *Nights*, Djebar on one level seems to want to celebrate this feminine complicity, this assurance provided by the woman's double: "Dinarzade, the sister, will be keeping watch near at hand; she will be close by while they embrace; she will look on at their carnal feast, or at least give ear to it. And the sultan's bride will be reprieved for one day more, then for a second; to be sure, the tales she spins help save her, but first and foremost it is because her sister has kept watch and woken her in time."[35] However, in *Ombre sultane*, Dinarzade's role as guardian is recast to uncover the possible tensions between sisters as they struggle against their mistreatment by men. Isma may be watching over Hajila, but it is she who deliberately paired the other woman with a violent man in order to liberate herself from his attentions. She goes on to narrate Hajila's story, tracing the halting steps of her resistance as she starts to leave the house, veiled, in order to walk in the streets alone, and at the end of the narrative, provides her with the key that assures her escape. And yet in retaining control over the narrative, Isma emphasizes her own position of power, charting Hajila's development using the second-person pronoun almost as if it is she who dictates her actions. Her shadowy presence is that of a *voyeuse*, as she enjoys the freedom that Hajila lacks.

Isma, then, is perhaps not so much Dinarzade, the watchful and caring sister, but the spinner of tales herself. Djebar deliberately blurs the positions of the two characters from the outset: one is figured as the shadow for the other, but it is not clear which is the queen and which is the observer: "Which of the two is the shadow who will become the sultan's bride? Which one is to be the bride at dawn, only to dissolve into a shadow before noon?"[36] Isma asserts her primacy over Hajila by taking control of the story, *she* is the Scheherazade who narrates to assert her freedom, and this is at the expense of the other woman – indeed,

Dinarzade too does not speak. Moreover, Anjali Prabhu goes even further in her reading of the novel, arguing that to assert herself, Isma requires Hajila's weakness against which to define herself in opposition. Through a close analysis of style, Prabhu shows that Isma describes Hajila in order to exclude her, and the latter's lack of sensuality, for example, is highlighted as counter to Isma's own discovery of pleasure in her new relationship. Asserting oneself through narrative, then, as Scheherazade and Isma do, requires at the same time the fixing of the other.[37] If Fatima and Aisha found that in standing up for themselves they opposed the other, here, even worse, Isma's liberation requires Hajila's further subjugation.

Prabhu's reading of *Ombre sultane* is provocative, even tendentious, in its evocation of the potential oppression of one Algerian woman by another. Yet Djebar's text certainly seems ambiguous in its presentation of the relationship between Scheherazade and Dinarzade, or Isma and Hajila, as if she wants to imagine a shared resistance between women against patriarchy, while also remaining disconcertingly aware of their inevitable position as rivals in that system. And if the role of Scheherazade as women's liberator, by means of her storytelling, is intermittently thrown into question in Djebar's work, then Dinarzade's task of listening is similarly more complicated than feminist readers may want. As we have seen, Isma does not adhere to her role as watchful keeper, and more broadly, the very process of listening to other women is frequently presented as problematic by Djebar's narrating personae. Lise Gauvin has discussed Djebar's own dual enactment of both Scheherazade and Dinarzade's roles, designating her as "a novelist who is at once storyteller and listener, wife and sister."[38] Yet Gauvin's elegant evocation of her doubling as storyteller and listener does not attend to the difficulties obstructing both roles. In the collection of short stories, *Femmes d'Alger dans leur appartement* (*Women of Algiers in their Apartment*), for example, Djebar prefaces her depiction of generations of Algerian women's suffering with a confession of anxiety concerning her distance from them.[39] The character Sarah in the story "Femmes d'Alger dans leur appartement," moreover, listens to old tape recordings of *hawfi* women's songs in an effort to recapture and transcribe their lyrics for a documentary, but the nostalgic lamentations she discovers take the form merely of allusive fragments. And reflecting on all her work in the series of essays *Ces voix qui m'assiègent*, Djebar concedes that the voices to which she sets out to attend are for the most part lost, silenced, irretrievable: "*the sound of lost words*."[40]

Existing reflections on Djebar's relationship with feminism have tended to foreground French models, which, although also emphasizing

the significance of an alternative feminine language, largely depend
on a European psychoanalytic cultural tradition. With Fatima and
Scheherazade, Djebar explores a feminism, or more specifically a vision
of feminist creativity, derived from Islamic culture. Djebar's literary project continues the work of Fatima and Scheherazade in its reclaiming of
women's equality, in its denunciation of women's mistreatment and bru-
talization, and in its affirmation that creative language itself can challenge
patriarchal structures of thinking. Through Fatima and Scheherazade,
she shows how eloquence and storytelling can be deployed to achieve
the practical liberation of women from oppression, and literature itself
emerges as a site of questioning, an invitation to the reader or listener to
think differently. Literature, however, is itself not a locus for the establish-
ment of an alternative ideology, as both Djebar and her female characters
do not use their eloquence in the service of a new orthodoxy, even a feminist one. Rather, it allows Djebar to bring to light Algerian women's experiences of oppression by both colonialism and Islamic patriarchy without
claiming to use those experiences in the service of a preconceived agenda.
Like Fatima, Djebar asserts herself through her use of language, and like
Scheherazade, she tells tales of other women's mistreatment in order to
call for justice. But she is at the same time acutely aware of women's differences, of their potential alienation from one another, and of the risk she
runs in attempting to understand the diversity of their history. Moreover,
she examines, through Fatima and Scheherazade, the tensions individual
women's self-assertion cause in their negotiations with others – with their
fathers, in the case of Fatima, and in the case of both, with their sisters,
with other female family members, and other suffering women. Djebar's
feminist thinking is accompanied always by this uncertainty, by the doubt
incarnated by Fatima, and by the shadow of the sultan queen. Her contribution to feminism is at once this multifaceted exploration of Islamic
feminist rebellion through literature, and an anxious revelation of the tensions that feminist self-affirmation might bring in its wake.

Notes

1 Introduction

1 For an extended analysis of the intersections between Habermas and feminism as well as Adorno and feminism, see, for example, my discussion in *Feminist Theory in Pursuit of the Public*.

2 For an analysis of the influence of Bakhtin and Arendt within feminist theory, see my chapter "Feminism, Gender, and the Literary Commons" in *The Values of Literary Studies: Critical Institutions, Scholarly Agendas*.

2 "Original Spirit": Literary Translations and Translational Literature in the Works of Mary Wollstonecraft

1 See Susan Bassnett, "Introduction," in *Translation Studies* (London and New York: Routledge, 2014), 1–15.

2 See Sherry Simon, *Gender in Translation: Cultural Identity and the Politics of Transmission* (London and New York: Routledge, 1996), 8–11.

3 See ibid., 43–8; Julie Candler Hayes, *Translation, Subjectivity & Culture in France and England, 1600–1800* (Stanford, CA: Stanford University Press, 2009), 141–56.

4 Mary Wollstonecraft, *The Works of Mary Wollstonecraft*, ed. Janet Todd and Marilyn Butler (London: Pickering & Chatto, 1989), vol. 2, 5.

5 Barbara Godard, "Theorizing Feminist Discourse/Translation," in *Translation, History & Culture*, edited by Susan Bassnett and André Lefevere (London and New York: Cassell, 1990), 87–96 (94).

6 Josephine Grieder, *Translations of French Sentimental Prose Fiction in Late Eighteenth-Century England: The History of a Literary Vogue* (Durham, NC: Duke University Press, 1975), 40.

7 William Godwin, *Memoirs of the Author of A Vindication of the Rights of Woman* in *A Short Residence in Sweden and Memoirs of the Author of "The Rights of Woman,"* edited by Richard Holmes (London: Penguin, 1987), 226.

8 Wollstonecraft, *Works*, vol. 3, 5.

9 Wollstonecraft, *Works*, vol. 2, 5; ibid., 215.

10 Edward Young, *Conjectures on Original Composition* (1759) (Leeds: The Scholar Press, 1966), 10.

11 See Alexander Fraser Tytler, *Essay on the Principles of Translation* (1791), ed. Jeffrey F. Huntsman (Amsterdam: John Benjamins B.V., 1978), passim.

12 Wollstonecraft, *Works*, vol. 2, 6.

13 See Mary Wollstonecraft, *Rettung der Rechte des Weibes*, ed. Christian Gotthilf Salzmann, trans. by Georg Friedrich Christian Weissenborn, 2 vols. (Schnepfenthal: Verlag der Erziehungsanhalt, 1793), esp. vol. i, 69; vol. ii, 214.

14 Wollstonecraft, *Works*, vol. 2, 5.

15 Ibid.

16 Ibid.

17 Alessa Johns, *Bluestocking Feminism and British-German Cultural Transfer, 1750–1837* (Ann Arbor: University of Michigan Press, 2014), 68.

18 Cf. Christian Gotthilf Salzmann, *Moralisches Elementarbuch* (1783) (Dortmund: Harenberg, 1980), 154–6 and Wollstonecraft, *Works*, vol. 2, 87–8.

19 See Barbara Taylor, *Mary Wollstonecraft and the Feminist Imagination* (Cambridge: Cambridge University Press, 2003), 95–132; Johns, *Bluestocking Feminism*, 71–2.

20 Wollstonecraft, *Works*, vol. 4, 359.

21 Salzmann, *Elementarbuch*, 214–15. My translation.

22 Wollstonecraft, *Works*, vol. 4, 113.

23 Ibid., 390.

24 Ibid., 113.

25 Johns, *Bluestocking Feminism*, 72.

26 Ibid., 66.

27 Ibid.

28 Stéphanie-Félicité de Genlis, *Adèle et Théodore, ou Lettres sur l'éducation*, 2nd ed. (Paris: Lambert, 1782) vol. 1, 445.

29 Stéphanie-Félicité de Genlis, *Adelaide and Theodore, or Letters on Education* (1783), ed. Gillian Dow, trans. by Thomas Holcroft (London: Pickering & Chatto, 2007), vol. 1, 160–1.

30 Wollstonecraft, *Works*, vol. 5, 174.

31 Wollstonecraft, *Works*, vol. 4, 422.

32 Wollstonecraft, *Works*, vol. 1, 57.

33 Wollstonecraft, *Works*, vol. 4, 361.

34 Ibid., 389.

35 Ibid., 449–50.

36 Ibid., 388.

37 Wollstonecraft, *Works*, vol. 2, 74.

38 Salzmann, *Elementarbuch*, 246. My translation.

39 Wollstonecraft, *Works*, vol. 6, 111.

40 Wollstonecraft, *Works*, vol. 2, 128.

41 Johns, *Bluestocking Feminism*, 74.

42 Wollstonecraft, *Works*, vol. 4, 472.

43 Ibid., 374–6.

44 Wollstonecraft, *Works*, vol. 2, 28.
45 Wollstonecraft, *Works*, vol. 1, 90.
46 Ibid.
47 Ibid., 123.
48 Ibid.

3 *Jane Eyre, Incidents in the Life of a Slave Girl,* and the Varieties of Nineteenth-century Feminism

1 Others read this pivot as two strands in the novel, or two different ways of reading it; Azim echoes this split in her review of feminist criticism of *Jane Eyre*.
2 See Meyer on Brontë's ambivalence toward race-based slavery, at times identifying with the oppressed yet at others embracing imperial attitudes.
3 See Yellin, Introduction, xvi, for her wide reading and Gates, Preface and Introduction, xvi–xviii, for evidence of a contemporary formerly enslaved woman writer who knew and alluded to *Jane Eyre*.

4 Progressive Portraits: Literature in Feminisms of Charlotte Perkins Gilman and Olive Schreiner

1 See Evelyn Verster, *Olive Emilie Albertina Schreiner (1855–1920): A Bibliography* (Cape Town: University of Cape Town Libraries, 1972); and Gary Scharnhorst, *Charlotte Perkins Gilman: A Bibliography* (Boston, MA: Twayne, 1985).
2 See Charlotte Perkins Gilman [hereafter CPG], *Women and Economics: A Study of Economic Relations between Men and Women as a Factor in Social Evolution* [hereafter *W & E*] (Boston, MA: Small Maynard & Co., 1898); and Olive Schreiner [hereafter OS], *Woman and Labour* [hereafter *W & L*] (London: Unwin, 1911). For instance, see Barbara Scott Winkler, "Victorian Daughters: The Lives and Feminism of Charlotte Perkins Gilman and Olive Schreiner," *Michigan Occasional Paper* XIII (Winter 1979).
3 See my *The Feminism of Charlotte Perkins Gilman: Sexualities, Histories, Progressivism* [hereafter Allen, *FCPG*](Chicago: University of Chicago Press, 2009), 8 and n. 366–7; Mary Jo Deegan, "Introduction," in *With Her in Ourland* (Westport, CT: Praeger, 1997), 2, 41, and 46–67; and Haley Salinas, "A Sociological Analysis of Charlotte Perkins Gilman's *Herland* and *With Her in Ourland,*" *Discourse of Sociological Practice* 6 (Fall 2004): 127–35.
4 For extending "portraiture" to political discourses like feminism, see Walter Benjamin, "The Work of Art in the Age of Its Technological Reproducibility," in *Walter Benjamin: Selected Writings Volume 3, 1935–1938* (Cambridge, MA: Belknap Press of Harvard University Press, 2002); Richard Brilliant, *Portraiture* (Cambridge, MA: Harvard University Press, 1991); and Harry Backlund, "Portrait," in *Chicago School of Media Theory: Theorizing Media since 2003* (Chicago: 2010).
5 See Rosaleen Love, "Darwinism and Feminism: The 'Woman Question' in the Life and Work of Olive Schreiner and Charlotte Perkins Gilman," *Australasian Studies in History and Philosophy of Science* 2 (1983): 113–31.

6 OS, *Undine* [completed 1876] (London: Benn, 1929); *The Story of an African Farm* (London: Hutchinson, 1883); and *From Man to Man; or Perhaps Only* (London: Unwin, 1927).

7 See OS, *Trooper Peter Halket of Mashonaland* (London: Unwin, 1897); *Dreams* (London: Unwin, 1890); *Dream Life and Real Life. A little African Story* (London: Unwin, 1893); and *Stories, Dreams and Allegories* (London: Unwin, 1923).

8 See OS and Cronwright-Schreiner, *The Political Situation* (London: Unwin, 1896); OS, *Thoughts on South Africa* (London: Unwin, 1923); *An English South African's View of the Situation* (London: Hodder and Stoughton, 1899); and *Closer Union* (London: Fifield, 1909).

9 Allen, *FCPG*, 8.

10 Ibid., 293–4.

11 See Carole Pateman, *The Sexual Contract* (Stanford, CA: Stanford University Press, 1988).

12 See CPG, *W & E*, 7, 23–38, m 37–9, 54–6, 58–9, 71, 78–81, 125, 141–2, 144–5, 167, 225–37; OS, *W & L*, 97–110; and CPG, *The Man Made World* (New York: Charlton), 175–9.

13 Gubar calls Schreiner's "sex parasitism" feminist misogyny, although Stanley finds this criticism ahistorical and "a loud example of the phenomenon it describes." See Susan Gubar, "Feminist Misogyny: Mary Wollstonecraft and the Paradox of 'It Takes One to Know One,'" *Feminist Studies* 20 (Fall 1994): 453–73; and Liz Stanley, *Imperialism, Labour and the New Woman: Olive Schreiner's Social Theory* [hereafter *ILNW*] (Durham, NC: Sociology Press, 2002), 176.

14 See Barbara A. White, *The Beecher Sisters* (New Haven, CT: Yale University Press, 2008).

15 Allen, *FCPG*, 14, 16–17, and 360; Stanley, *ILNW*, 19–27.

16 See Margaret Hobbs, "The Perils of 'Unbridled Masculinity': Pacifist Elements in the Feminist and Social Thought of Charlotte Perkins Gilman," in *Women and Peace: Theoretical Historical and Practical Perspectives*, edited by Ruth Pierson (Kent: Croom Helm, 1987), 149–69.

17 See Allen, *FCPG*, 311–12 and 337–49.

18 Ibid., 137–47. See also Aileen Kraditor, *The Ideas of the Woman Suffrage Movement, 1850–1920* (New York: Columbia University Press, 1965), 50, 102, and 120; and Ann J. Lane, *To Herland and Beyond: A Life of Charlotte Perkins Gilman* (New York: Meridien, 1991), 184. And see OS, "Letter on Woman Suffrage (May 1908), in *The Letters of Olive Schreiner, 1876–1920*, edited by Samuel E. Cronwright-Schreiner (London: Fisher Unwin, 1924) [Appendix G.] Ref. 214.

19 See Helen Bradford, "Olive Schreiner's Hidden Agony: Fact, Fiction, and Teenage Abortion," *Journal of South African Studies* 21 (December 1995): 623–41.

20 T. S. Emslie, "Introduction," in *Karoo Moon: Olive Schreiner*, edited by T. S. Emslie (Cape Town: Stonewall Books, 2004), x.

21 Bradford, "Olive Schreiner's Hidden Agony," 633; and Stanley, *ILWN*, 59.

22 See Mei-Fang Chang, "Narrative Decomposition for Utopian (Re-) Composition: The New (Wo)Man in Olive Schreiner's *From Man to Man*," *Research in African Literatures* 44 (Spring 2013): 107.

23 See Stanley, *ILNW*, 95–8; and Chang, "Narrative Decomposition," 106–7 and 119–21.

24 See OS to Karl Pearson, July 19, 1885, 840/4/1/21–26, University College London Library, Special Collections; Judith A. Allen, "Mid-Victorian Prostitution, the Contagious Diseases Acts (1864–1869) and the Early Repeal Campaign," in *London Low Life: Street Culture, Social Reform and the Victorian Underworld*, edited by Judith A. Allen, Peter Bailey, and Ruth Livesey (Malborough: Adam Matthew Digital, 2012), 1–6; and Deborah Gorham, "'The Maiden Tribute to Modern Babylon' Re-examined: Child Prostitution and the Idea of Childhood in Late-Victorian England," *Victorian Studies* 21 (Spring 1978): 353–79.

25 OS to Editor, *Daily News*, December 28, 1885, HRC/Olive Schreiner Letters/ OS-Daily News/1 Harry Ransom Center, University of Texas, Austin; and Judith R. Walkowitz, "Going Public: Shopping, Street Harassment and Streetwalking in Late Victorian London," *Representations* 62 (Spring 1998): 1–30.

26 See OS to Havelock Ellis, November 11, 1888, in *Olive Schreiner Letters*, 142; and OS to Havelock Ellis, November 2, 1888, in *Olive Schreiner Letters: Volume I 1871–1899*, edited by Richard Rive (Oxford: Oxford University Press, 1987), 142.

27 See Carolyn Burdett, "DOCUMENT: A Difficult Vindication: Olive Schreiner's Wollstonecraft Introduction," and OS, "Introduction to the Life of Mary Wollstonecraft and The Rights of Woman [fragment]," *History Workshop Journal* 37 (1994): 177–88 and 189–93. See also Laura Chrisman, "Allegory, Feminist Thought and the *Dreams* of Olive Schreiner," *Prose Studies: History, Theory, Criticism* 13 (May 1990): 135.

28 Allen, *FCPG*, 39; and see Helen Lefkowitz Horowitz, *Wild Unrest: Charlotte Perkins Gilman and the Making of "The Yellow Wall-Paper"* (New York: Oxford University Press, 2012).

29 Allen, *FCPG*, 48–50.

30 Ibid., 139.

31 Ibid., 69.

32 See Stanley, *ILNW*, 29–30.

33 Joyce Avrech Berkman, "Schreiner, Olive Emilie Albertina (1855–1920), Author and Social Theorist," *Oxford Dictionary of National Biography* [hereafter *ODNB*] Oxford University Press, 2004; online edn., May 2006 [http:// www.oxforddnb.com/view/article/35972, accessed November 30, 2014].

34 OS, "The Woman Question," *Cosmopolitan* 28 (November and December, 1899): 45–54 and 182–92; Allen, *FCPG*, 163; and Nancy Cott, *The Grounding of Modern Feminism* (New Haven, CT: Yale University Press, 1987), 20 and 49.

35 These were: CPG, *Concerning Children* (1900), *The Home, Its Work & Influence* (1902), *Human Work* (1904), and *The Man-Made World or Our Androcentric Culture* (1911), and finally *His Religion and Hers: The Faith of Our Fathers and the Work of Our Mothers* (1923).

36 The uncollected *Forerunner* nonfiction treatises were: "Humanness," "Our Brains and What Ails Them," "Growth & Combat," "The Dress of Women," "Studies in Social Pathology," with "The Man Made World" the only one extracted and published in Gilman's lifetime.

37 All these serialized novels, as well as one unpublished are now published. She also published *Suffrage Songs and Verses* (1910), essays, poems, and short stories. See Denise D. Knight, *Charlotte Perkins Gilman: A Study of the Short Fiction* (New York: Twayne, 1997), 58.

38 See CPG, *W & E*, 167; and Allen, *FCPG*, 142 and 141–3. See OS to John Hodgson, 1914/15?, HRC/Olive Schreiner Letters/OS-John Hodgson/32; and OS to Havelock Ellis, November 17, 1915, HRC/CAT/OS/5a-ii, Harry Ransom Center, University of Texas, Austin.

39 OS to Karl Pearson, June 16, 1886, Karl Pearson 840/4/2/81–87, University College London Library, Special Collections.

40 OS to Adela Villiers Smith nee Villiers, July 1912 in *The Letters of Olive Schreiner, 1876–1920*, 309–1.

41 See Edward Carpenter, *My Days and Dreams: Being Autobiographical Notes* (New York: Charles Scribner's Sons, 1916), 229.

42 Joyce Avrech Berkman, "Schreiner, Olive," *ODNB* [accessed November 30, 2014].

43 See Louise Green, "Olive Schreiner and the Labour of Writing," *English Academy Review: Southern African Journal of English Studies* 29 (Supplement 1, 2012): 166; and Cherry Clayton, *Olive Schreiner* (Boston, MA: Twayne, 1997), 11, 19–20, 22, and 31–7.

44 Schreiner, *From Man to Man* [collected in *Olive Schreiner: Karoo Moon*, ed. T. S. Emslie], 589.

45 See Anne McClintock, *Imperial Leather: Race, Gender, and Sexuality in the Colonial Contest* (New York: Palgrave, 1995), 287–8.

46 Schreiner, "Three Dreams in a Desert," in *Dreams* (London: Unwin, 1899) 68–70.

47 See CPG, "When We Fly," *Harper's Weekly* 35 (November 9, 1909): 1650 and 1664.

48 See Allen, *FCPG*, 262.

49 See Denise D. Knight, ed., *The Later Poetry of Charlotte Perkins Gilman* (Newark: University of Delaware Press, 1997), 177; and Jill Rudd and Val Gough, "Introduction," in *Charlotte Perkins Gilman: Optimist Reformer*, edited by Jill Rudd and Val Gough (Iowa City: University of Iowa Press, 1999), ix–xix.

50 Gilman, *What Diantha Did* (Auckland: Floating Press, 2010), 46, 95–103.

51 Ibid., 129.

52 CPG, *The Crux*, 230–5.

53 See for instance, CPG, "The Vintage," *Forerunner* 7 (October 1916): 253–7 and "His Mother," *Forerunner* 5 (July 1914): 169–72.

54 CPG, "Cleaning up Elita," *Forerunner* 7 (January 1916): 1–4.

55 CPG, "Turned," *Forerunner* 2 (September 1911): 227–32.

56 CPG, "Mag-Marjorie," *Forerunner* 3 (1912): 318, 320, and 325.

57 See Denise D. Knight and Jennifer S. Tuttle, eds., *The Selected Letters of Charlotte Perkins Gilman* (Tuscaloosa: University of Alabama Press, 2009), 91.

58 See Olive Schreiner, "The Woman Question," *Cosmopolitan* 28 (November 1899): 45–54 and (December 1899): 182–92.

59 CPG to George Houghton Gilman [hereafter GHG], November 3, 1899, in *Journey from Within: The Love Letters of Charlotte Perkins Gilman, 1897–1900*, edited by Mary A. Hill (Lewisburg, PA: Bucknell University Press, 1995), 308.

60 CPG to GHG, November 5, 1899, in Hill, *Journey from Within*, 309.

61 CPG to GHG, January 9, 1900 in Hill, *Journey from Within*, 338.

62 Stanley, *ILNW*, 81–8.

63 See Kimberly Hamlin, *From Eve to Evolution: Darwin, Science, and Women's Rights in Gilded Age America* (Chicago: University of Chicago Press, 2014). For examples, see Eliza Burt Gamble, *The Evolution of Woman* (London: G.P. Putnam's Sons, 1893); Antoinette Brown Blackwell, *The Sexes throughout Nature* (New York: G. P. Putnam's Sons, 1895); Mona Caird, *The Morality of Marriage* (London: George Redway, 1897); Cicely Hamilton, *Marriage as a Trade* (New York: Moffat, Yard and Company, 1909) and Evelyn Sharp, *Rebel Women* (London: A. C. Fifield, 1910). For discussion of their critique by anti-feminists, see Allen, *FCGP*, 191–202.

64 Historians plot the fall of the Progressive movement in its wake: see Michael McGerr, *"A Fierce Discontent": The Rise and Fall of the Progressive Movement in America 1870–1920* (New York: Simon & Schuster, 2010), 281–302. And see Stanley, *ILNW*, 92–5, 36–7, and 40–2.

65 See Liz Stanley and Andrea Salter, "'Her Letters Cut are Generally Nothing of Interest': The Heterotopic Persona of Olive Schreiner and the Alterity-Persona of Cronwright-Schreiner," *English in Africa* 36 (October 2009): 7–30.

66 Unknown to CPG, n. d. [1921?], CPG Papers, Arthur and Elizabeth Schlesinger Library on the History of Women in America [SL], 177/149/1/33.

67 Samuel D. Schmalhausen to CPG, June 19,1930; CPG to Schmalhausen, June 23, 1930, CPGP, SL 177/122.

68 CPG, "Parasitism and Civilized Vice," in *Woman's Coming of Age*, edited by S. D. Schmalhausen (New York: Liveright, 1931), 110–26.

69 CPG to Katharine Beecher Chamberlain, April 1, 1932, in *The Selected Letters of Charlotte Perkins Gilman*, 191.

70 OS to Edward Carpenter, October 26, 1905, Edward Carpenter Archive, 359/90, Sheffield Archives & Local Studies, Sheffield; and Simon Lewis, "Reading Olive Schreiner Reading W. E. B. Du Bois," *Research in African Literatures* 45 (Summer 2014): 155.

71 See, for instance, Gertrude Atherton, "Literary Developments in California," *Cosmopolitan* (January 10, 1891): 272; Helen Campbell, "Charlotte Perkins

Stetson: A Sketch," *Time and the Hour*, April 16, 1898; "The Ideal Home," *New York Times*, December 2, 1903, 983; and "Mrs. Charlotte Perkins Gilman," *Current Literature* 36 (May 1904): 511.
72 Stanley, *ILNW*, 95.

5 Feminist Poetics: First-Wave Feminism, Theory, and Modernist Women Poets

1 Stott pinpoints 1906 as the first journalistic use of the term *feminist* in America, derived from the French *feministe* in use by the 1890s and crossing the channel to England in the 1890s (14).
2 Stein's experimental insistence on multiplicity of meaning in *Tender Buttons* is often read as a coded expression of lesbian desire.
3 It should be noted, of course, that the use of vivid imagery, narrative, and graphic details often provided women like Sanger or Gilman with fuel for their arguments. In Loy's poem, the imagery is a foregrounded method of critique, rather than used secondarily to illustrate a discursive argument.
4 Loy wrote across genres, although during her lifetime her primary publications were poetry. Thematically, similar issues of gender cross from poetry into autobiography, essays, and short fiction. However, the poetry's experiments with language and form are most pronounced in relation to gender ideologies. The *Manifesto* shares this textual quality and indicates her interest in the visual (usually poetic) page as a space of meaning making.
5 See Orleck for a full history of industrial feminism.
6 This rationale necessarily is partial in many ways, particularly in regard to the range of poets publishing; the focus on social progress through accessible forms of communication; and other socio-literary dynamics of African American print culture and community.
7 In Patton and Honey, *Double-Take*, 109. Unless indicated otherwise, all future quotes in this chapter are taken from this collection.

6 Woolf and Women's Work: Literary Invention in an Obscure Hat Factory

1 Alex Zwerdling, *Virginia Woolf and the Real World* (Berkeley: University of California Press, 1986), 220.
2 Janis Paul, *The Victorian Heritage of Virginia Woolf: The External World in Her Novels* (Norman, OK: Pilgrim Books, 1987), 79.
3 As cited in Susan Squier, *Virginia Woolf and London: The Sexual Politics of the City* (Chapel Hill and London: University of North Carolina Press, 1985), 72.
4 Katherine Mansfield, "Review, *Athenaeum*, 21 November 1919," in *Virginia Woolf: The Critical Heritage*, edited by Robin Majumdar and Allen McLaurin (London and New York: Routledge, 1975), 82.
5 Ann-Marie Priest, "Between Being and Nothingness: The 'Astonishing Precipice' of Virginia Woolf's *Night and Day*," *Journal of Modern Literature* 26(2) (Winter 2003): 80.

6 Suzanne Raitt, "Virginia Woolf's Early Novels: Finding a Voice," in *The Cambridge Companion to Virginia Woolf*, edited by Susan Sellers (Cambridge: Cambridge University Press, 2010), 29.

7 As cited in Ronald McCail, "A Family Matter: *Night and Day* and Old Kensington," *The Review of English Studies* 38(149) (February 1987): 27.

8 Naomi Black, *Virginia Woolf as Feminist* (Ithaca, NY and London: Cornell University Press, 2004), 27.

9 Michael Tratner, *Modernism and Mass Politics: Joyce, Woolf, Eliot, Yeats* (Stanford, CA: Stanford University Press, 1995), 55.

10 Kate Flint, "Virginia Woolf and the General Strike," *Essays in Criticism* 36(4) (October 1986): 323.

11 Fuhito Endo, "Radical Violence Inside Out: Woolf, Klein, and Interwar Politics," *Twentieth Century Literature* 52(2) (Summer 2006): 176.

12 Jane Marcus, *Virginia Woolf and the Languages of Patriarchy* (Bloomington and Indianapolis: Indiana University Press, 1987), 11.

13 Alison Light, *Mrs. Woolf and the Servants: An Intimate History of Domestic Life in Bloomsbury* (New York: Bloomsbury, 2008), xviii, 145–7.

14 Light, *Mrs. Woolf and the Servants*, 37.

15 Ibid., 250.

16 Theodor Adorno, *History and Freedom, Lectures 1964–1965*. Ed. Rolf Tiedmann. Trans. Rodney Livingstone (Cambridge: Polity, 2006).

17 See, for example, Marcus, *Virginia Woolf and the Languages of Patriarchy*, 28; and Paul, *The Victorian Heritage of Virginia Woolf*, 81. Also, Avrom Fleishman, *Virginia Woolf: A Critical Reading* (Baltimore, MD and London: Johns Hopkins University Press, 1975), 24.

18 Ibid.

19 Squier, *Virginia Woolf and London*, 85.

20 Eileen Sypher, *Wisps of Violence: Producing Public and Private Politics in the Turn-of-the-Century British Novel* (London and New York: Verso, 1993), 145.

21 Virginia Woolf, *Night and Day* (New York: Barnes & Noble Classics, 2005), 389.

22 Ibid., 310.

23 Ibid., 341.

24 There has been considerable critical interest speculating on Woolf's commitment to feminism as well as on feminism's adoption of Woolf. See, for example, Zwerdling, "Woolf's Feminism in Historical Perspective," 210–42; Laura Marcus, "Woolf's Feminism and Feminism's Woolf," in *The Cambridge Companion to Virginia Woolf*, 142–79; Sowon S. Park, "Suffrage and Virginia Woolf: 'The Mass behind the Single Voice,'" *The Review of English Studies*, New Series 56(223) (February 2005): 119–34; Beth Rigel Daughterty, "Feminist Approaches," in *Palgrave Advances in Virginia Woolf Studies*, edited by Anna Snaith (New York: Palgrave, 2007); Toril Moi, *Sexual/Textual Politics: Feminist Literary Theory* (London and New York: Routledge, 1985.

25 Ibid., 146.

26 Virginia Woolf, "Character in Fiction," in *Selected Essays*, edited by David Bradshaw (Oxford: Oxford University Press, 2008), 38.

27 Ibid., 45.
28 Ibid., 42.
29 Ibid., 45.
30 Ibid., 47.
31 Ibid., 42.
32 *Night and Day*, 67.
33 "Character in Fiction," 42.
34 *Night and Day*, 70.
35 Virginia Woolf, *To the Lighthouse*, edited by David Bradshaw (Oxford: Oxford University Press, 2008), 70.
36 Virginia Woolf, "Professions for Women," in *Selected Essays*, edited by David Bradshaw (Oxford: Oxford University Press, 2008), 142.
37 *Night and Day*, 32.
38 Ibid., 6.
39 Ibid., 85.
40 Ibid., 99.
41 Ibid., 90.
42 Ibid., 101.
43 Ibid., 124.
44 Ibid., 237.
45 Ibid., 37–8.
46 Ibid., 417.
47 Ibid., 429–30.
48 Paul, *The Victorian Heritage of Virginia Woolf*, 86.
49 *Night and Day*, 172.
50 Ibid., 171.
51 Ibid., 172.
52 Priest, "Between Being and Nothingness," 66.
53 Erich Auerbach, *Mimesis: The Representation of Reality in Western Literature*, trans. Willard Trask (Princeton, NJ: Princeton University Press, 1953), 540.
54 Ibid., 541.
55 *Night and Day*, 146–7.
56 Ibid., 223.
57 Ibid., 224.
58 Ibid.
59 Ibid., 225.
60 Ibid.
61 Ibid., 231.
62 Ibid., 180.
63 Ibid., 174.
64 Ibid., 230.
65 Ibid., 27.
66 Ibid., 26.
67 Ibid., 86.
68 Ibid., 195.

69 Ibid., 112.

70 Ibid., 116.

71 Ibid., 440.

72 Black, *Virginia Woolf as Feminist*, 39. During Woolf's period of participation in the Guild, the issues of concern were wages, housing, public health, public economy, education, pensions, and pacifism because these touch "the purse-bearer and the home-maker in her daily work" (ibid., 41). The beliefs attributable to the English cooperative movement were "the utopian goal of the creation of the 'Co-operative Commonwealth, a New Jerusalem where 'production for use' would be the guiding principle. There, public life would be democratically controlled by the users – by the workers in their capacity as consumers. Community ownership of production would be an essential element of the Co-operative Commonwealth, but the key would be a system of self-government that would eliminate individualism, class conflict, and orientation of profit characteristic of capitalism" (Naomi Black, *Social Feminism* [Ithaca, NY and London: Cornell University Press, 1989], 111). It could be argued that Woolf's challenge to conventional subjectivity followed along some of these lines, where the subject itself was open to the influx of random encounters along the path of modern life: in a sense, the subject might be seen as inherently cooperative.

73 Virginia Woolf, "Memories of a Working Women's Guild," *Selected Essays*, edited by David Bradshaw (Oxford: Oxford University Press, 2008), 152.

74 Ibid., 156.

75 Ibid., 157.

76 Ibid., 158.

77 Virginia Woolf, *A Room of One's Own* (New York and London: Harcourt Brace Jovanovich, 1929, 1957), 37–8.

78 Virginia Woolf, *Jacob's Room, the Waves* (New York: Harcourt, Brace & World, 1923), 173.

79 Ibid., 176.

80 Ibid.

81 For more on this question and its relation to theory, see my *Gender Work: Feminism after Neoliberalism* (New York: Palgrave, 2013).

7 Walking in a Man's World: Myth, Literature, and the Interpretation of Simone de Beauvoir's *The Second Sex*

1 Margaret A. Simons opened this debate in 1983 when she published her groundbreaking essay, "Silencing Simone: Guess What's Missing from *The Second Sex*." See also Moi, "While We Wait," and Glazer, "Lost in Translation."

2 Both Simons and Moi cite this inaccurate translation of Heidegger's *Dasein*, which the French philosophical tradition has translated from German as "la réalité humaine." In English, we use Heidegger's original term. Unaware of the philosophical connotations of "la réalité humaine," Parshley

unwittingly removed Beauvoir's explicit references to Heidegger from his English translation.

3 There was some confusion about this grammatical point in the critical debate of Borde/Malovany-Chevallier. In her original review, Moi argued that the new translation was not grammatically valid, a position that she later revised when pushed about it in the ensuing comments to say that the translation was not grammatically necessary. On the other hand, Daigle argued that the Parshley translation did not make grammatical sense but made more overall sense given Beauvoir's philosophical stance in the volume that follows ("The Impact of the New Translation of *The Second Sex*"). Daigle, whose conversance with French otherwise shows through in her nuanced evaluations of the new translation, claims that Beauvoir would have had to write "on ne naît pas <u>une</u> femme, on le devient" for Parshley's translation to be grammatically correct (339). Given the examples of the French nutrition site and the nineteenth-century sculpture that I have cited, this argument does not seem to hold water.

4 For more detailed information on this debate beyond Moi ("The Adulteress Wife. Rev. of *The Second Sex*") and Daigle ("The Impact of the New Translation of *The Second Sex*"), see Bauer (Rev. of *The Second Sex*), Sommers ("Not Lost in Translation"), and Rodier and Parker (Rev of *The Second Sex*).

5 For example, in Eugene Kaelin's large work entitled *An Existentialist Aesthetic: The Theories of Sartre and Merleau-Ponty*, Beauvoir's name is glaringly absent, and Kaelin dismisses Beauvoir because she "blindly accept[s] the tenets of [Sartre's] rising school of thought" (20).

6 I have explained this concept of literature as an appeal in more detail in Scheu, "The Viability of the Philosophical Novel."

7 The connection, in fact, between Beauvoir's aesthetic theory and Heideggerian *mitsein* or "being-with" needs fleshing out, but the lengthy explanation required will not fit within the confines of this chapter. On Beauvoir and Heidegger, see Gothlin, "Reading Simone de Beauvoir with Martin Heidegger," Bauer, "Beauvoir's Heideggerian Ontology," and Scheu, "Living-with."

8 This is my translation for "Les données de la biologie." Borde/Malovany-Chevallier translate this as "The Data of Biology." Again, there is a valence in French that this translation misses, for "donnée" is not just "data," but also something that is given, that is taken for granted or generally accepted.

9 Translation modified. Borde/Malovany-Chevallier translate "sarabande" literally, as "saraband," and yet, in French, "sarabande" literally means a courtly dance AND figuratively means a whirl or a commotion. The English does not seem to have this second, figurative meaning. Furthermore, they make active verbs – "seizes," "castrates," etc. – into present participles, thereby losing the force of Beauvoir's voice. Other minor adjustments come when Beauvoir's passage sounds awkward in the translation.

10 See, for example, Hekman, *Gender and Knowledge*, 73–9 and Lloyd, *The Man of Reason*, 96–102.

11 For wonderful analyses of this concept in Beauvoir's work, see Heinämaa, "Simone de Beauvoir's Phenomenology of Sexual Difference," and "The Body as Instrument and as Expression."

8 Decapitation Impossible: The Hundred Heads of Julia Kristeva

1 All translations from the original are mine.

2 According to the ancient Greek myth, Athena sprang out of Zeus' head fully armed.

3 See "The *Vital* Legacy of the Novel and Julia Kristeva's Fictional Revolt."

4 Women 100 [A Hundred/Without] Heads.

5 All translations from the original are mine.

6 In *Visions capitales* Kristeva writes: "Murder is prohibited, says the God of the Bible, but this moral law can become a possibility on the condition that we recognize that the cut is structural" (97); "Is decapitation the emblem of a social and historical division? Or perhaps the brutal confession of our internal fragmentations …? The self-perception of a fundamental imbalance …?" (114).

7 For a fascinating analysis of the distinct challenges, predicaments, and deadlocks of Eastern European intellectuals during and just before the collapse of communism, see Miglena Nikolchina's *Lost Unicorns of the Velvet Revolutions* (2013).

8 Kristeva discusses Georges Bataille and his "Acephale" in *Visions capitales* (150–2).

9 At the end of the novel Olga, one of the central female characters, publishes a book for children entitled *Les Samouraïs*. Joëlle Cabarus, the psychoanalyst whose narrative voice and perspective dominates the novel, writes: "all literature is perhaps for children.… After all, perhaps there is no point in writing other than to recreate the game of life and death for the use of the kids that we forget we are" (458–9). All translations from the original are mine.

10 As we are informed, the "Samurai excelled in the art of war, as well as in poetry, calligraphy and the ritual of tea" (book cover).

11 In her interview with Éliane Boucquey, Kristeva emphasizes the need to reconceptualize "Women" as a "plural of singulars." See "Une(s) femme(s)," 128. All translations from the original are mine.

12 See, for example, Atack, "The Silence of the Mandarins."

13 "[C]et 'oeuvre au noir'" in the original. See *Visions capitales*, 114.

14 "Through the structure of reference, through the opposition between the committed literature of Dubreuilh and the revolutionary literature which Sinteuil argues for, and through the opposition between power and subversion of power, existentialism is shown to be an inadequate understanding of subjectivity, identity and consciousness.… *Les Samouraïs* can therefore be read as the fulfillment of a powerful wish to take the place of the hegemonic intellectuals, quite literally rendering them speechless," Atack argues ("The Silence of the Mandarins," 248).

15　See, for example, *Les Samouraïs*, 144, 177–82.

16　For example, *The Old Man and the Wolves* (138–9, 152), *Possessions* (3, 4, 9).

17　See *Thérèse* (65–6, 612).

18　The character of Martin, associated with Scherner's circle, is also significant in this respect.

19　See Kristeva's depiction of the characters of Alba and Vespasian in *The Old Man and the Wolves*. See also Stephanie's reaction to Pauline's lack of shame: "But I'm ashamed for Pauline: I often do feel embarrassed on behalf of people incapable of feeling shame themselves. I feel the humiliation they can't feel; their typically human impenetrability affects me like a kind of arrogance, deals me a mortal blow" (*Possessions*, 208).

20　In a 1991 interview Kristeva tells Vassiliki Kolocotroni: "In considering fiction, the writing of novels, one might think that it is a totally different thing, but for me there are links, there are bridges; it is more a question of putting something into practice. I am concerned with the same subjects – foreignness, violence, death – but without treating them in a metalinguistic fashion. I have the ambition of looking from within" (Guberman, *Julia Kristeva: Interviews*, 222).

21　This is the title of section 2, part III of the novel.

22　In *Irony's Edge* Linda Hutcheon cites Georges Palante, who argues: "Woman is primarily a physiology and a sensibility, not a brain. Irony, a cerebral attitude in that it affirms the primacy of intelligence over sentiment, is suspect and antipathetic to her" (epigraph; my translation).

23　It "is not necessary to think of a Sophist as singular, whereas an ironist is always singular," Kierkegaard writes (147).

24　According to Sylvia, St. Thérèse's uniqueness lies in her "disillusioned detachment" and "mild irony" (*Thérèse mon amour*, 520).

25　Discussing the distinct ironic perspective she adopts in *Les Samouraïs*, Kristeva tells Bélorgey: "The characters' self-irony and the narrator's ironic view of such characters as Olga, Hervé, Bréhal, Scherner, and Lauzun create a corrosive force, but also a deliberate form of sympathy and affection" (Guberman, *Julia Kristeva: Interviews*, 250).

26　Kierkegaard writes: "In one sense the ironist is certainly prophetic, because he is continually pointing to something impending, but what it is he does not know" (*Concept of Irony*, 261).

27　I am paraphrasing Roy Martinez here in his discussion of Kierkegaard's irony. Irony, he writes, "refuses to surrender to the mere given; faith transforms given actuality into a promise" (18).

9　Shattering the Gender Walls: Monique Wittig's Contribution to Literature

1　Crowder specifies that this materialist position is "explicable without recourse to deterministic thinking if we comprehend that men dominate women in order to appropriate women's labor and that women develop survival strategies under conditions of extreme physical and psychological violence" (66).

2 The full title is *Feminist Issues: A Journal of Feminist Social and Political Theory.* Monique Wittig was its advisory editor.

3 Sarraute adds: "They happen in an instant, and apprehending them in the rush of human interactions demands painstaking attention." http://www.theparisreview.org/interviews/2341/the-art-of-fiction-no-115-nathalie-sarraute. Accessed December 5, 2014.

4 *Le Robert & Collins*, 188.

5 French materialist feminists like anthropologist Nicole-Claude Mathieu and sociologist Colette Guillaumin, as well as Wittig, employ the word "mark" with this understanding in their writings. The binding of little Chinese girls' feet that lasted for most of the past millennium, the branding of slaves with the initials of their owners on plantations, or the yellow star that Jews were obliged to wear in Nazi Germany are examples of the marking of social groups.

6 From here on all emphases are mine and the quotes are from the original edition (Minuit, 1964). The English version is taken from the 1966 edition (Simon & Schuster), except for its translation of the "on" by "you." Although "one" might sound awkward, its meaning is closer to the indeterminate in gender and number French pronoun. The English translations of Wittig fictions have all been problematic.

7 Valerie comes from the Latin word *valere*: to have value.

8 These elements are evocative of the opoponax's "real" and fictive significations.

9 Understood as a perspective, not an identity. See Crowder, "Universalizing Materialist Lesbianism."

10   Hélène Cixous: Writing for Her Life

1 Hélène Cixous, "Un effet d'épine rose," in *Le Rire de la Méduse, et autres ironies* (Paris: Galilée, 2010), 29; my translation.

2 On this early American reception of Cixous, see Kamuf, "To Give Place: Semi-approaches to Hélène Cixous," *Yale French Studies* 86 (1995): 69–89.

3 For a passage where *vol* and *voler* force the English translators to decide the undecidable, see "The Laugh of the Medusa," trans. Keith Cohen and Paula Cohen, *Signs*, 1, 4 (Summer 1976): 887.

4 Hélène Cixous, *Le Prénom de Dieu* (Paris: Éditions Bernard Grasset, 1967); *The Exile of James Joyce*, trans. Sally A. J. Purcell (New York: David Lewis, 1972).

5 Jacques Derrida, *Voice and Phenomenon*, trans. Leonard Lawlor (Evanston, IL: Northwestern University Press, 2011); *Of Grammatology*, trans. Gayatri Chakravorty Spivak (Baltimore, MD: Johns Hopkins University Press, 1974); "Plato's Pharmacy," in *Dissemination*, trans. Barbara Johnson (Chicago: University of Chicago Press, 1983).

6 Hélène Cixous and Cathérine Clément, *The Newly Born Woman*, trans. Betsy Wing (Minneapolis: University of Minnesota Press, 1986), 64; translation modified.

7 "All Derrida's work traversing-detecting the history of philosophy is devoted to bringing this to light. In Plato, Hegel, and Nietzsche, the same operation continues: repression, repudiation, distancing of woman; a murder that is mixed up with history as the manifestation and representation of masculine power" (*Newly Born Woman*, 130, n 1). With one of the very few revisions for the 2010 reedition, Cixous underscores this alliance in the text as well. To the sentence "Now it has become rather urgent to question this solidarity between logocentrism and phallocentrism" ("Laugh," 65), she has added "With a liberating push from Jacques Derrida, now it has become ... " (*Le Rire de la Méduse*, 75).

8 For her most sustained analysis of Derrida's writing practice, see Cixous, *Portrait of Jacques Derrida as a Young Jewish Saint*, trans. Beverley Bie Brahic (New York: Columbia University Press, 2004).

9 In his very fine preface to *Le Rire de la Méduse, et autres ironies*, Frédéric Regard suggests that one understand the essay's manifesto function as that of "a text turned toward an objective external reality in which it seeks to make an offensive concretely palpable" (*Le Rire de la Méduse*, 12).

10 In a long dialog-in-writing with Frédéric-Yves Jeannet about her work, Cixous comments on the mention of "novel" in her early texts: "what is on the cover is deceptive. What does it matter what the publisher wants to put there, wanted to put there, on the covers, at the time I let it go because I didn't know myself what I should say to replace it. These were still such traditional questions, I was completely indifferent to them. The word 'novel' is a fiction." Hélène Cixous and Frédéric-Yves Jeannet, *Rencontre terrestre* (Paris: Éditions Galilée, 2005), 21.

11 Mairéad Hanrahan has recently forged the term *semi-fiction* to designate Cixous's writing: see Hanrahan, *The Semi-Fictions of Hélène Cixous: Thinking at the Borders of Fiction* (Edinburgh: Edinburgh University Press, 2014).

12 Hélène Cixous, *Dream I Tell You*, trans. Beverley Bie Brahic (Edinburgh: Edinburgh University Press, 2006).

13 Hélène Cixous, *Hyperdream*, trans. Beverley Bie Brahic (London: Polity Press, 2009).

14 Hélène Cixous, *Philippines*, trans. Laurent Milesi (London: Polity Press, 2011).

15 Hélène Cixous, *So Close*, trans. Peggy Kamuf (London: Polity Press, 2009), 99.

16 In *Dream I Tell You*, Cixous characterizes this act of transcription as taking dictation from the dream: "Docile I say not a word the dream dictates I obey eyes closed. I have learned this docility. The dream commands. I do. I have no thoughts no responses" (1).

17 Cixous considers her father's death and, in general, the experience of having lost everything the "condition on which beginning to write becomes necessary – (and) – possible" ("Coming to Writing," in *"Coming to Writing" and Other Essays*, ed. Deborah Jenson, trans. Deborah Jenson et al.

[Cambridge, MA: Harvard University Press, 1992], 38). See also "The School of the Dead," in Cixous, *Three Steps on the Ladder to Writing*, trans. Susan Sellers and Sarah Cornell (New York: Columbia University Press, 1994), passim.

18 Hélène Cixous, *Or, Les Lettres de mon père* (Paris: Éditions des femmes, 1997).

19 See Mairéad Hanrahan, "The Place of the Mother: Hélène Cixous's *Osnabrück*," *Paragraph* 27(1) (2004): 6–20.

20 But the title also lets one hear *homme mère*, that is, man-mother. Cixous previously forged this name in writing of Derrida's essay about his dying mother, "Circumfession": "He is *homme* plus *mère*. He is *homme mère*, thus blind" ("Contes de la différence sexuelle," in *Lectures de la différence sexuelle*, edited by Mara Negrón [Paris: Éditions des femmes, 1994], 37; my translation).

21 *Rencontre terrestre*, 56, from an exchange dated June 2001. But she could have made the same assertion at any time.

22 Jacques Derrida, *H.C. for Life*, trans. Laurent Milesi and Stefan Herbrechter (Stanford, CA: Stanford University Press, 2006).

23 Hélène Cixous, *Osnabrück*, excerpt trans. Peggy Kamuf, in *The Portable Cixous*, edited by Marta Segarra (New York: Columbia University Press, 2010), 78.

24 Hélène Cixous, "Sorties," in Cixous and Catherine Clément, *The Newly Born Woman*, trans. Betsy Wing (Minneapolis: University of Minnesota Press, 1986), 78.

25 "But in truth, there are, coming from my life, but very few elements concerning my *own* [propre] person, don't you find? Almost the whole stage is occupied by characters, those near to me, crowds of beings that in fact make me but are not me. My *own* life remains unknown" (*Rencontre terrestre*, 123; my translation).

26 *Hamlet* II, 2, 550–1 in the Folger Edition. Hamlet is recommending the players to Polonius: "Do you hear, let them be well used,/ for they are the abstract and brief chronicles of the/ time."

27 From the "Prière d'insérer," a loose folio that French publishers sometimes issue with their books when asking booksellers "kindly to insert" it into the printed volume. Its four pages are unnumbered and it bears the title "To My Readers."

28 Hélène Cixous, *Chapitre Los* (Paris: Éditions Galilée, 2013), 13; my translation.

29 The writer, who is never identified as such in *Chapitre Los*, would appear to be Carlos Fuentes, who died May 15, 2012.

11 Subversive Creatures from behind the Iron Curtain: Irmtraud Morgner's *The Life and Adventures of Trobadora Beatrice as Chronicled by Her Minstrel Laura*

1 On GDR fiction of the 1970s, see Emmerich, *Kleine Literaturgeschichte der DDR*, 239–395. Kaufmann emphasizes that GDR feminism was voiced in fiction (*Aussichtsreiche Randfiguren*, 50).

2 Linklater, *"Und immer zügelloser wird die Lust,"* 89; Lange, *Ausgewählte Reden und Aufsätze*, 232–57.

3 Morgner (1933–90) studied literature in Leipzig (1952–6), and worked for a literary magazine (1956–8) and as a freelance writer (since 1958) until her death from cancer. *The Life and Adventures of Trobadora Beatrice as Chronicled by Her Minstrel Laura* (1974) became a best seller in both East and West Germany. Since 2000, it has been available in English translation, to which I refer with the abbreviated title *Trobadora Beatrice*, or TB, throughout this chapter.

4 On the link between Morgner's fantastic world and the GDR of the 1970s, see Wildner, *Experimentum Mundi*, 13; and Dahlke, "Leben und Abenteuer der Trobadora Beatriz," 288–9.

5 Von der Emde, Nordmann, Lewis, Marven, and Herminghouse emphasize the subversive potential of Morgner's aesthetics.

6 On Laura and Beatrice, see Marven, "The Trobadora's Legacy," 56; Rytz, "Pandora auf dem Brocken," 252; and Soproni, "Raum und Identität in Irmtraud Morgners," 150–2.

7 The intermezzi build on fragments Morgner could salvage from *Rumba auf einen Herbst* (*Rumba for an Autumn*), which was censored in the wake of the Eleventh Plenum of the Central Committee of the ruling Socialist Unity Party (SED) in 1965. See Westgate, *Strategies under Surveillance*, 76–86; Linklater, *"Und immer zügelloser wird die Lust,"* 73; Kaufmann, "'Der Hölle die Zunge rausstrecken…,'" 1517; Landa, "Feminismus und Systemkritik im mittelalterlichen Kostüm," 201, 208; and Dahlke, "Leben und Abenteuer der Trobadora Beatriz," 292.

8 See West German scholars Hilzinger and Gerhardt, East German critic Damm, and Morgner (interview with Huffzky). By the mid-1980s, Morgner no longer rejected feminism (Lemmens, "Frauenstaat. Interview mit Irmtraud Morgner," 55).

9 Martin, Bammer, Nordmann.

10 Herminghouse, "Die Frau und das Phantastische in der neueren DDR-Literatur," 248.

11 Marven, "The Trobadora's Legacy," 55. See Linklater, Rytz, Martens, Wildner, Lewis, Herminghouse, and von der Emde.

12 Dahlke, "Leben und Abenteuer der Trobadora Beatriz," 279–81; Kaufmann, *Aussichtsreiche Randfiguren*, 52.

13 See Wölfel, *Rede-Welten*, 116; Detken, "Weibliche Geschichte und Erinnern," 139–40; and von der Emde, *Entering History*, 156–61.

14 Westgate, *Strategies under Surveillance*, 176–90.

15 See, for example, Laura's "Enclosure for the Express Letter to Rome, poste restante" (TB, 274–5).

16 On the prevalence of Bloch's principle of hope in most GDR literature in the 1970s see Emmerich, *Kleine Literaturgeschichte der DDR*, 276. See Wildner "'Odysseys and the Silent Siren'" for an analysis of the Salman trilogy based on Bloch.

17 On Melusine as political figure subverting the myth, see Detken, "Weibliche Geschichte und Erinnern," 133–7.

12   Christa Wolf: Literature as an Aesthetics of Resistance

1 Because Wolf's aesthetics were developed under socialism, I will restrict my discussion to texts written before the fall of the Wall. My readings of Wolf's oeuvre are based on my study, *Christa Wolf's Utopian Vision: From Marxism to Feminism.* Unless indicated otherwise I will use extant published English translations; dates refer to German publication and will differ from translated versions.

2 As she did in *No Place on Earth* (1979) and *Cassandra* (1983).

3 As she did in "Selbstversuch" ("Self-Experiment," 1973) and "Neue Lebensansichten eines Katers" ("New Memoirs of a Tomcat," 1974).

4 A nonlinear, self-reflexive, self-interrupting writing style became the hallmark of Wolf's writing beginning in 1965 with her short story "An Afternoon in June."

5 As articulated, for example, in her early essay collection *The Reader and the Writer* (1972).

6 See her essay "Touching" and *Conditions of a Narrative.*

7 Wolf mentions the following texts in the fourth *Cassandra* lecture: *The First Sex; Mothers and Amazons; Goddesses; Patriarchy; Amazons, Warrior Women, and He-Women; Women–the Mad Sex?; Women in Art; God-Symbols, Love-Magic, Satanic Cult; Male Fantasies; Female Utopias–Male Casualties; Women and Power; The Sex Which Is Not One; The Secret of the Oracle; Utopian Past; Outsiders; Cultural-Historical Traces of Repressed Womanhood; Mother Right; Origin of the Family, Private Property and the State; Woman's Wild Harvest; The White Goddess; Woman as Image; A Room of One's Own; Womanhood and Letters* (*CON,* 273).

8 As formulated in both *The Groundwork of the Metaphysics of Morals* and *The Critique of Practical Reason.*

9 Wolf had a narrow, skewed understanding of Western feminism – likely derived from the media – that viewed feminists as man-haters who sought to replace male domination with female domination. Her historically grounded analyses of patriarchal gender relations emphatically rejected feminist separatism.

10 "Subjektive Authentizität: Ein Gespräch mit Hans Kaufmann" (*GW* 4, 409).

11 As articulated by Sandra Harding, Nancy Hartsock, and Hilary Rose, among others.

12 In calling her male transsexual "Anders," which means "different" in German, Wolf is playing with, and inverting, Simone de Beauvoir's definition of woman as the Other.

13 As outlined in his *Principle of Hope.*

14 For an excellent discussion of Wolf and feminist standpoint epistemologies, see Rossbacher, *Illusions of Progress,* especially 52–94.

15 From 1946–58 the United States conducted a series of twenty-three H-bomb tests on the Bikini atoll.

16 Hagelstein is based on an actual historical figure and the events Wolf describes are authentic.

13 Naked Came the Female Extraterrestrial Stranger: Applying Linda M. Scott's *Fresh Lipstick* to Sue Lange's *The Textile Planet*

1 Marla, in accordance with fashion blogger Leandra Medine's tongue-in-cheek take on dressing while female, becomes a "man repeller." Medine defines this term as "she who outfits herself in a sartorially offensive mode that may result in repelling members of the opposite sex. Such garments include but are not limited to harem pants, boyfriend jeans, overalls, shoulder pads, full length jumpsuits, jewelry that resembles violent weaponry and clogs" (Medine http://www.manrepeller.com/2010/04/what-is-man-repeller.html).

2 The section title for this section refers to Robert A. Heinlein's novel *Stranger in a Strange Land.*

3 See Marleen S. Barr, *Feminist Fabulation: Space/Postmodern Fiction* (Iowa City: University of Iowa Press, 1992).

4 Scott Hillard provides examples of how science fiction portrays fashion: "Spray-on clothing is one of the more popular futurist fantasies. In *Galactic Pot-Healer*, Philip K. Dick talks about foam sprayed directly onto the body that would quickly dry and form disposable clothing. In *Return from the Stars*, Stanislaw Lem talks about a hotel stocked with cans upon cans of sprayable socks, suits, bathrobes, and dresses allowing women to wear unique dresses every day. Jack Vance mentioned a green pulp that would spray on wet and dry into velvet in his novel *Abercrombie Station*. It makes you wonder: If so many science fiction writers were convinced this was the future, why don't we have it?" (Hillard, "10 Weirdest Inventions").

14 Captive Maternal Love: Octavia Butler and Sci-Fi Family Values

1 Octavia Butler coauthored works with novelists Sam Delaney and Walter Mosley. Her work has drawn comparisons to those of Toni Morrison and resonates with the writings of other prominent black women SF authors: Tananarive Due, Andrea Hairston, Nalo Hopkinson, N. K. Jemisin, Nnedi Okorafor, and Nisi Shawl.

2 Rudine Sims Bishop, "Mirrors, Windows, and Sliding Glass Doors," *Perspectives: Choosing and Using Books for the Classroom* 6(3) (Summer 1990).

3 See Joy James, "The Black Matrix: Maroon Philosophy at Democracy's Borders," *The Black Scholar* 43(4) (Winter 2013).

4 The phrase "'plantation' domesticity" is a reference to "plantation babies," a phrase former Black Panther Party member Afeni Shakur (mother of

Tupac Shakur) used in her memoir; Shakur references pregnancies and babies brought up in repressive conditions of racism and poverty. See *Afeni Shakur: Evolution of a Revolutionary*, with Jasmine Guy, New York: Atria Books, 2005.

5 See Cheryl Harris, "Whiteness as Property," *Harvard Law Review* 106 (June 1993).

6 Extensively discussed elsewhere, the 1999 Wachowski film, which immortalized Neo, Morpheus, and Trinity, features both a black male lead, Lawrence Fishburne as Morpheus, and a human versus machine war of liberation that erases the black female protagonist.

7 Halle Berry's *X-Men* character, Storm-Ororo Munroe, Kenyan and African American, is considered a minor player.

8 See Vincent Woodward's *The Delectable Negro: Human Consumption and Homoeroticism under US Slavery* (New York: New York University Press).

9 In "Gambling against History: Queer Kinship and Cruel Optimism in Octavia Butler's *Kindred*" (Rebecca J. Holden and Nisi Shawl, eds., *Strange Mattings: Science Fiction, Feminism, African American Voices, and Octavia Butler* (Aqueduct Press, 2013), Susan Knabe and Wendy Gay Pearson argue that, similar to how LGBTQ politics are reduced to sexuality, black politics are reduced to sex and sexuality; both groups (which overlap) embody sexualities queered and criminalized respectively by sodomy and miscegenation laws.

10 Juliet Lapidos, "Chauvinist Pigs in Space," *Salon* (March 5, 2009), examines Battlestar Galactica's antifeminism.

11 Bassett turned down the 2000 *Monster's Ball* role of the hypersexual, abusive black mother whose black husband is executed (by the white prison warden she will live with) and whose (pre)teen son is killed in an automobile accident. Halle Berry received an Oscar for that role.

12 http://boblyman.net/englt392/texts/speech_sounds.pdf.

15 More than Theater: Cherríe Moraga's *The Hungry Woman* and the Feminist Phenomenology of Excess

1 In the essay entitled "To World, to Globalize – Comparative Literature's Crossroads," Kadir argues: "[I]t might be apposite to the discussion of world literature and globalization to take the word 'world' as a verb, and to read globalization not as a boundless sweep but as a bounding circumscription. *To world* and *to globalize*, then, would have to be parsed in light of their subject agencies and their object predicates" (2).

2 By "unmarked" I simply refer to language theory that locates the unmarked as what is human. In much of the United States, "human" generally means "white, middle-class male." In order to get someone to see something different when the word *human* or *person* is used, you must begin "marking" them. He is marked with an "s" to become she. Man is marked with "wo" to

become woman. Cherríe Moraga is marked with the identity claims of lesbian Chicana mother woman. Each of these markers pushes her further away from the center, and therefore further away from the hegemonic concept of person-hood or humanity in the mainstream United States.

3 In the text "Looking for the Insatiable Woman," Moraga speaks about the figure of Medea as the combined myth of the Mexican La Llorona, the pre-Columbian myth of dismemberment and creation of the moon deity Coyolxauhqui, the Aztec myth of the Hungry Woman, and of course, the Greek myth of Medea. "*And at last, upon encountering this myth – this pre-capitalist, pre-catholic mito – my jornada began to make sense. This is the original Llorona y tiene mucha hambre. I realized that she has been the subject of my work all along, from my earliest writing, my earliest feminism. She is the story that has never been told truly, the story of that hungry Mexican woman who is called puta/bruja/jota/loca because she refuses to forget that her half-life is not a natural-born fact*" (143).

4 Aztlán is the legendary pre-Columbian mythical homeland of the Aztecs said to be located in northwestern Mexico or the southwestern United States (right along the areas claimed by the 1848 Treaty of Guadalupe-Hidalgo). It was reclaimed by the Chicano movement of the 1960s and 1970s as a mythical vision of a future Chicano community and culture – a utopian vision of the world after the Chicano revolution called for by the movement.

5 *Chac-mool* is a term used to describe a pre-Columbian Mesoamerican sculpture associated with sacrificial stones and thrones. They are reclining figures some-times associated with fallen warriors and are often considered intermediaries between the spirit and physical realms (Miller and Samayoa, "Where Maize May Grow," 54–72).

6 Phoenix takes its name from the mythical bird that perpetually dies in flames and is born again.

7 The actor playing Chac-Mool is the only actor on stage of the male sex. Effectively reversing the prohibition of women on stage during many of the historical performances of Medea, Moraga even makes Jasón double as Cihuatateo South. In doing so she also demonstrates the performative nature of gender, as Judith Butler argued in *Gender Trouble*.

8 Tanya González notes that in Euripides' Medea story a woman makes a sacri-fice but it is not recognized as such because sacrifice is acknowledged only in the realm of men and/or patriarchy. Because Medea's actions are the actions of a woman, they are not interpreted as answering a higher call. González argues that Moraga's Medea undoes the "ideology behind the 'monstrous' story of sacrifice and vengeance and hunger" in the patriarchal versions not only of the Medea myth, but in the myths of the Hungry Woman, La Llorona, and Coyolxauhqui. In Moraga's *The Hungry Woman*, González argues, "death is sac-rifice" through a Coatlicue state. Coatlicue, we are reminded, is the goddess that "swallows the sun every evening and gives birth to light every morning" (González, "The (Gothic) Gift of Death," 65–6).

16   Nawal el Saadawi: Writer and Revolutionary

1 "A Conversation with Nawal El Saadawi." Beijing Normal University, September 23, 2014.

2 She elaborated on female genital mutilation in her 1980 *The Hidden Face of Eve* that for the first time tells from her personal experience how excision is practiced and what are its long-term implications.

3 Her admiration for Taha Husayn and his autobiography *Al-Ayyam* is unbounded. It may have inspired her to write about her childhood. The almost tactile quality to his writing also distinguishes his description of a blind child's world.

4 In a June 19, 2014, e-mail to the author.

17   "The Woman Who Said 'No'": Colonialism, Islam, and Feminist Resistance in the Works of Assia Djebar

1 Assia Djebar, *Far from Madina: Daughters of Ishmael*, trans. Dorothy S. Blair (London: Quartet Books, 1994).

2 Chandra Talpade Mohanty, *Feminism without Borders: Decolonizing Theory, Practising Solidarity* (Durham, NC: Duke University Press, 2003), 223.

3 See Marnia Lazreg's study of Algerian women in *The Eloquence of Silence: Algerian Women in Question* (London: Routledge, 1994).

4 See Priscilla Ringrose, *Assia Djebar: In Dialogue with Feminisms* (Amsterdam: Rodopi, 2006); Rita A. Faulkner, "Psychoanalysis and Anamnesis in the National Allegory of Nawal El Saadawi and Assia Djebar." *Esprit Créateur* 48(4) (2008): 69–80.

5 Assia Djebar, *Nulle part dans la maison de mon père* (Paris: Fayard, 2007), 207. My translation.

6 Clarisse Zimra, "When the Past Answers Our Present: Assia Djebar Talks about *Loin de Médine*." *Callaloo* 16(1) (1993): 116–31 (p. 117).

7 Ernspeter Ruhe, "Enjambements et envols, Assia Djebar échographe," in *Assia Djebar: Littérature et transmission,* edited by Wolfgang Asholt, Mireille Calle-Gruber, and Dominique Combe (Paris: Presses Sorbonne nouvelle, 2010), 37–53 (p. 41). My translation.

8 Fatima Mernissi, *Women and Islam: An Historical and Theological Inquiry* (Oxford: Blackwell, 1991), 108.

9 Christopher Clohessy, *Fatima, Daughter of Mohammed* (Piscataway, NJ: Gorgias Press, 2009).

10 Djebar, *Far from Madina*, 79.

11 Assia Djebar, *Fantasia: An Algerian Cavalcade*. Trans. Dorothy S. Blair (London and New York: Quartet, 1994), 3.

12 Djebar, *Far from Madina*, 64.

13 Djebar, *Nulle part dans la maison de mon père*, 370. My translation.

14 Djebar, *Far from Madina*, 80.

15 Ibid., 74.

16 Zimra, "When the Past Answers Our Present," 120.

17 Djebar, *Far from Madina*, 74.

18 Djebar, *Fantasia*, 156.

19 Djebar, *Far from Madina*, 263.

20 Mernissi also discusses the political complexity of Aisha's role at the time of the battle. See Mernissi, *Women and Islam*, 53–8.

21 Djebar, *Far from Madina*, 260.

22 Clarisse Zimra, "Not so Far from Madina: Assia Djebar Charts Islam's Insupportable Feminist Revolution." *World Literature Today* (1996): 823–34 (p. 832).

23 Djebar, *Nulle part dans la maison de mon père*, 209–10.

24 Ibid., 207.

25 In the French, Djebar refers to Scheherazade as "l'intarissable conteuse." The English translation, however, changes the structure of the sentence to refer to the storyteller's "unfailing inspiration," which does not quite produce the same effect. "The tireless storyteller" is therefore my translation. See Assia Djebar, *Ombre sultane* (Paris: Lattès, 1987), 103; *A Sister to Scheherazade*, Trans. Dorothy S. Blair (London and New York: Quartet, 1987), 95.

26 *Arabian Nights' Entertainments*, ed. Robert L. Mack (Oxford: Oxford University Press, 2009), 10.

27 See Suzanne Gauch, *Liberating Shahrazad: Feminism, Postcolonialism and Islam* (Minneapolis: University of Minnesota Press, 2007), x.

28 Somaya Sami Sabry, *Arab-American Women's Writing and Performance: Orientalism, Race, and the Idea of the Arabian Nights* (London: I. B. Tauris, 2011).

29 Fatima Mernissi, *Scheherazade Goes West: Different Cultures, Different Harems* (New York: Washington Square Press, 2001).

30 Malti-Douglas argues that the stories show that "it is through fiction that the proper uses of desire can be learned." See Fedwa Malti-Douglas, *Woman's Body, Woman's Word: Gender and Discourse in Arabo-Islamic Writing* (Princeton, NJ: Princeton University Press, 1991), 25.

31 Marina Warner, *Stranger Magic: Charmed States and the Arabian Nights* (London: Chatto and Windus, 2011), 436.

32 See Nawar Al-Hassan Golley, *Reading Arab Women's Autobiographies: Shahrazad Tells Her Story* (Austin: University of Texas Press, 2003).

33 Djebar, *Fantasia*, 6.

34 Ibid., 57.

35 Djebar, *A Sister to Scheherazade*, 95.

36 Ibid., 1.

37 Anjali Prabhu, "Sisterhood and Rivalry in-between the Shadow and the Sultana: A Problematic of Representation in *Ombre sultane*." *Research in African Literatures* 33(3) (2002): 69–96.

38 Lise Gauvin, "Les femmes-récits ou les déléguées à la parole," in *Assia Djebar: Littérature et transmission*, edited by Wolfgang Asholt, Mireille

Calle-Gruber, and Dominique Combe (Paris: Presses Sorbonne nouvelle, 2010), 55–66 (p. 55). My translation.

39 Assia Djebar, *Women of Algiers in their Apartment*. Trans. Marjolin de Jager (Charlottesville, VA:, 1992), 1.

40 Assia Djebar, *Ces voix qui m'assiègent... en marge de ma francophonie* (Paris: Albin Michel, 1999), 77. My translation.

Index